Use of Visual Displays in Research and Testing: Coding, Interpreting, and Reporting Data

D1714786

A Volume in:
Current Perspectives on Cognition, Learning and Instruction

Series Editors
Gregory Schraw
Matthew T. McCrudden

Current Perspectives on Cognition, Learning and Instruction

Series Editors

Gregory Schraw
University of Nevada—Las Vegas

Matthew T. McCrudden
Victoria University of Wellington

Use of Visual Displays in Research and Testing: Coding, Interpreting, and Reporting Data

Edited by

Matthew T. McCrudden
Gregory Schraw
Chad W. Buckendahl

INFORMATION AGE PUBLISHING, INC.
Charlotte, NC • www.infoagepub.com

Library of Congress Cataloging-in-Publication Data

The CIP data for this book can be found on the Library of Congress website (loc.gov).

Paperback: 978-1-68123-101-3
Hardcover: 978-1-68123-102-0
eBook: 978-1-68123-103-7

CONTENTS

SECTION III

VISUAL DISPLAYS IN QUANTITATIVE, QUALITATIVE, AND MIXED METHODS RESEARCH

SECTION IV

VISUAL DISPLAYS TO REPORT TESTING AND ASSESSMENT DATA

SECTION I

INTRODUCTION

CHAPTER 1

VISUAL DISPLAYS IN RESEARCH AND TESTING

Theoretical and Practical Considerations

Matthew T. McCrudden, Gregory Schraw, and Chad W. Buckendahl

ABSTRACT

We provide a rationale for this volume; namely, that including visual displays in research and testing can enhance comprehension and processing efficiency. We state four goals for the volume: (a) advance the field with respect to the use of visual displays in research and testing, (b) identify general design principles that can help researchers use visual displays to more effectively conduct and communicate their research, (c) present reviews of representative research, and (d) identify how well-designed visual displays can improve the communication of research and testing. A summary of each chapter is provided and linked to these goals. The chapters are organized into three sections. Section I includes three chapters that collectively addresses theoretical frameworks and universal design principles for visual displays. Section II includes four chapters that examine the use of visual displays in quantita-

Use of Visual Displays in Research and Testing: Coding, Interpreting, and Reporting Data,
pages 3–13.
Copyright © 2015 by Information Age Publishing

tive, qualitative, and mixed methods research. Section III includes three chapters that focus on using visual displays to report testing and assessment data.

VISUAL DISPLAYS IN RESEARCH AND TESTING: THEORETICAL AND PRACTICAL CONSIDERATIONS

This volume addresses the use of visual displays in research and testing. Specifically, we aimed to address the use of visual displays in coding, interpreting, and reporting of data. We define visual displays as graphic representations of information that are communicated to learners (Schraw, McCrudden, & Robinson, 2013). Visual displays can be presented in isolation or in combination with other types of media (e.g., written or spoken text, video presentation) to make a multimedia instructional message. The main reasons to include visual displays in research and testing are to increase surface, deeper, and transfer learning; and to increase processing efficiency (i.e., the rate at which individuals comprehend; Hoffman & Schraw, 2010) and learning by giving learners a conceptual scaffold for understanding information (e.g., Eitel, Scheiter, Schüler, Nyström, & Holmqvist, 2013; Mayer, 2005; McCrudden, Magliano, & Schraw, 2011; Robinson & Kiewra, 1995). For instance, in McCrudden et al. (2011), participants who studied a visual display before reading about cause-effect relations demonstrated better memory for the causal sequence than participants who read the text, despite the fact that participants in both groups studied the information for an equivalent amount of time.

Increased processing efficiency is important because it can facilitate comprehension without increasing processing effort. Individuals have finite resources (i.e., cognitive resources and time) to devote to comprehension of multimedia messages. High-quality visual displays can promote optimal use of these finite resources in three main ways. One way is by decreasing cognitive load (i.e., information processing demands; Larkin & Simon, 1987; Vekiri, 2002). A display may convey a complex system or idea more effectively than a text; hence the adage, "A picture is worth a thousand words." For instance, a diagram of the heart can impose lower processing demands than a text description of the heart because it provides both an external representation to reduce load and an integrated model of the heart's components. A second way is by increasing processing capacity, which occurs because processing load is distributed between verbal and visual processing channels (Mayer, 2013). For instance, when processing a multimedia message that consists of text and a display, words are processed through the verbal channel, whereas the diagram is processed through the visual channel. By accessing both channels, overall processing capacity is increased because the load is distributed. A third way is by making important information salient (Hegarty, Canham, & Fabrikant, 2010). Visual displays are salient, or stand out, in physical contrast to written text and helps individuals select important information. For instance, a display has different visual features and uses different conventions than written text, which increases the likelihood that the displays direct individuals to important information, which can lead to further processing of its contents.

GOALS

We undertook this volume to address four goals. One goal is to advance the field with respect to the use of visual displays in research and testing. Visual displays have several information-processing benefits for users. Typically, users are tacitly assumed to be consumers of research. In this volume, we explicitly targeted both producers and consumers of research. That is, we sought to advance the field with respect to how producers of research use visual displays to not only focus on how to communicate research findings to consumers, but also how researchers can use visual displays to code, analyze, and interpret their data. Thus, we aimed to promote the explicit use of visual displays in both the creation and communication of knowledge.

A second goal is to identify general design principles that can help researchers use visual displays to more effectively conduct and communicate their research. Although visual displays can promote comprehension and learning, some displays achieve these aims more effectively than others. There are several principles for researchers to consider when they aim to develop effective visual displays, including matching the strengths of a particular display to the ideas the display is meant to convey (Smith, Best, Stubbs, Archibald, & Roberson-Ray, 2002); reducing extraneous processing (Lane & Sandor, 2009; Sweller, 1999); and promoting accuracy (Tufte, 2001), visual guidance (Hegarty et al., 2010; Lane & Sandor, 2009), and structural coherence (Latour, 1990; Tufte, 2001).

Matching refers to using displays that are optimally suited to conveying certain types of ideas or relations between ideas (Smith et al., 2002). For instance, a matrix is well suited for comparing and contrasting ideas (Robinson & Schraw, 1994), whereas a sequence is well suited for conveying causal and temporal relations (McCrudden, McCormick, & McTigue, 2011). Extraneous processing refers to designs that minimize processing activities that do not contribute to comprehension (Mayer, 2013). For instance, including unimportant or decorative information in a display can obscure important key ideas. Accuracy refers to designs that convey their intended meaning and facilitate similar interpretations across users (Smith et al., 2002). That is, designs should be intuitive for a given audience, and the design of the display should lead individuals to converge on similar understandings. Visual guidance refers to designs that highlight important and relevant information and make it easier to integrate this information (Lane & Sandor, 2009). For instance, a display that spatially integrates related pieces of information reduces an unnecessary visual search compared to a display in which related ideas are spatially separated. A graph could include a scatterplot of the actual data and the least-squares regression line. Information such as the values of correlations in inferential information could be included as text that is embedded in the graph. Doing so can help the reader integrate the information conveying in the graph and text. Structural coherence refers to design properties that make clear the individual components in a visual display, the relations among those components, and a description of the process that is being modeled (Tufte, 2001).

Related to design principles, Gutierrez, Schraw, and Stefik (this volume) identify some considerations that individuals should consider when developing a visual display: (a) What type of information will be presented—text, graphics, or both, (b) What is the design format—static, dynamic, or a combination, (c) What is the complexity of the information, and would a narrative be more appropriate, and (d) Who is the audience (e.g., technical expertise)? Similarly, Lane (this volume) identifies three design principles for graphs: They should be easy to perceive, reduce the cognitive demands placed on the reader, and informative.

A third goal of this volume is to present reviews of representative research. Schraw and Gutierrez (this volume) discuss a content analysis that identifies the use of 14 general types of visual displays and score them for interpretive complexity. Their review focused on articles published in the *Journal of Educational Psychology*, which consists primarily of quantitative research, over a 5-year time frame. Plano Clark and Sanders (this volume) did a content analysis that identifies the use of joint displays in mixed methods research. Their review focused on articles published in the *Journal of Mixed Methods Research* over a 7-year time frame. These chapters provide an overview of the use of visual displays in research articles.

The fourth goal is to identify how well-designed visual displays can improve the communication of research and testing. Specifically, we wanted to identify best practices in the use of visual displays in quantitative, qualitative, and mixed methods research and testing. We recruited experts in each of these areas to identify some best practices. In their respective areas, the authors describe how visual displays are beneficial, explain why they are beneficial, include numerous illustrative examples of visual displays, and provide general guidelines for the use of visual displays. Thus, the authors of the chapters in this volume identify best practices and provide examples to model the use of visual displays to encourage their use and to explicitly inform readers of the principles and ideas to consider when developing visual displays for research and testing.

SUMMARY OF CHAPTERS

Our aim with this volume was to provide researchers with a framework that helps them use visual displays to organize and interpret data and to communicate their findings in a comprehensible way within different research methods (e.g., quantitative, mixed) and testing traditions that improves the presentation, understanding, and use of findings. Further, we aimed to include contributions from leading scholars in testing and quantitative, qualitative, and mixed methods research. The volume's focal question was What are the best principles and practices for the use of visual displays in the research and testing process, which broadly includes the analysis, organization, interpretation, and communication of data? The 10 following chapters enabled us to address this question. Section I includes three chapters that collectively address theoretical frameworks and universal design principles for visual displays. Section II includes four chapters that examine the use of visual displays in quantitative, qualitative, and mixed methods research. Section III includes three chapters that focus on using visual displays to report testing and assessment data.

Section I

Section I includes focuses on theoretical frameworks and universal design principles for visual displays. In Chapter 2, Gutierrez, Schraw, and Stefik provide a comprehensive description of design principles for the development of effective visual displays. Visual displays are commonly used in a variety of settings such as articles, books, and multimedia presentations. Clearly, visual displays can promote comprehension. But some visual displays are more effective than others. Why? What are the best ways to design a visual display and what basic principles should be taken into consideration when designing a visual display? The authors systematically address these questions. They begin by providing a historical perspective for the design of visual displays that includes the theoretical frameworks used to justify the use of particular design principles, which foreshadows their subsequent review of empirical evidence and is interpreted in light of these theoretical perspectives. They compare and contrast these theories so that design principles can be understood through different lenses and evaluate the merits of each theory. Next, they review evidence on the use of displays in educational contexts and identify human factors that influence comprehension and interpretation of visual displays, including metacognition, working memory, attention span, and processing efficiency (via cognitive load). Then they identify three research-based themes that inform principles of visual design display and development. These themes are parsimony of the visual display (i.e., convey meaningful ideas with as few elements as possible), relevance to the task and viewer (i.e., abstain from including superfluous information or the display lose its relevance), and universal minimum standards (i.e., follow general conventions for communicating ideas). Then they provide a comprehensive description of best practices. Finally, they discuss implications of our review for research, theory, and learning.

In Chapter 3, Lane focuses on a particular type of visual display in quantitative research: graphs. He discusses three general principles to be considered when a person develops graphs for scientific publications. First, graphs should be easy to perceive. Important or relevant information should be salient so that the reader can readily identify the information. Second, graphs should reduce the cognitive demands placed on the reader. Comprehension may be more effortful or may suffer if the reader engages in extraneous processing, or processing that does not promote or lead to comprehension (Mayer, 2013). For instance, integrating displays with text reduces extraneous processing because the reader does not have to search the main text to understand the data represented in the display. Third, graphs should be informative. Lane provides multiple examples to illustrate each of these principles, both what is effective and features to avoid because they reduce effectiveness. Further, he includes a detailed summary of specific design principles (e.g., related items should be group perceptually) that emanate from the general principles. This chapter is an easy-to-use, concrete, theoretically driven, and comprehensive overview of a principle-based approach to effectively communicate quantitative data in graphs.

In Chapter 4, Schraw and Gutierrez conducted a content analysis of the prevalence of visual displays in report research. Despite the prevalence of visual displays in the reporting of research, there is limited information about the variety, complexity, and cognitive processing demands of visual displays. So while the presence of visual displays is generally beneficial for enhancing comprehension of research results, less is known about the frequency and variety of visual displays that are used to report research findings. To shed light on this topic, the authors conducted a content analysis of research articles appearing in the *Journal of Educational Psychology* between 2010 and 2014. They identified the types of displays used, created a data-driven typology to categorize each type of display, developed scoring criteria that pertained to the information in the display, and constructed a scoring rubric to evaluate the interpretive complexity of each display. They identified the number of articles that included displays, the number of displays per article, the frequency of different types of displays, the level and frequency of interpretive complexity for each type of display, and relations among article length, amount of information, and interpretive complexity. The authors indicate that the ability to interpret displays is related to experience in using displays and expertise.

Section II

Section II focuses on the use of visual displays in quantitative, qualitative, and mixed methods research. In Chapter 5, Pastor and Finney discuss the use of visual displays in planning and presenting quantitative research. In particular, they highlight the benefits of using path diagrams to represent a family of statistical models known as structural equation models (SEMs). Path diagrams depict theoretical relationships among variables. They indicate that path diagrams can express a theory visually and communicate the statistical models (e.g., estimated parameters) that are used to test the theory. They note that path diagrams are used quite frequently in articles in which researchers use SEM, SEM textbooks, and in software programs. Nonetheless, despite that fact that many introductory or commonly used statistical procedures (e.g., *t*-test, ANOVA, multiple regression, MANOVA) are subsumed under SEM and that path diagrams can represent them visually, path diagrams are used much less frequently in quantitative research and in the teaching of quantitative methods. Aside from the benefits of using visual displays in general, using visual displays for SEM procedures in particular is useful because they can explicate the number and nature of the models that are being examined, help individuals create a mental representation of the structural components of the theory, and facilitate comparisons between different models. The authors describe the advantages of using visual display in planning a quantitative research study (e.g., theoretically driven research questions), in communicating quantitative research (e.g., promote comprehension without overwhelming the reader), and in teaching quantitative methods (e.g., highlight commonalities among techniques subsumed under the same larger conceptual framework). They provide numerous examples in which visual displays can be used in quantitative research and guidance on how to use SEM software to generate displays in both research and teaching. This chapter makes three important contributions to quantitative analysis by describing how visual displays promote theory-driven research and communicating that research to consumers, providing strategies for using displays in the research and teaching, and identifying a rationale for why displays should be used more frequently given their beneficial properties.

In Chapter 6, Guetterman, Creswell, and Kuckartz describe how visual displays can be used in mixed methods research. The defining feature of mixed methods research is integration of quantitative and qualitative findings in complementary ways. That is, quantitative and qualitative data are integrated such a way that conclusions can be drawn from both datasets that extend beyond each dataset in isolation. However, achieving integration can be challenging as there is no single way to integrate datasets, particularly given the variability in mixed methods designs. To address this challenge, these authors advocate the use of joint displays. A mixed methods joint display is used to represent the interpretation of quantitative and qualitative data analysis or results in a single visual display (Creswell, 2015). The authors provide a rationale for the use of joint displays and why they are useful. They briefly review mixed methods data analysis from a historical perspective, which suggests that the use of joint displays is a logical next step in development of mixed methods research. Next, they describe how to create joint displays. They provide guidance on how to use software to generate displays to inform the data analysis and interpretation, as well as the communication of data and results to readers. Then they provide explicit links between six common mixed methods designs and joint displays. They use general display frameworks and concrete examples to demonstrate a variety of ways in which data from mixed methods studies can be integrated. This chapter provides a much needed solution to the challenge of how researchers can use visual displays to analyze data and communicate their findings and interpretations to readers.

In Chapter 7, Plano Clark and Sanders examine the use of visual displays in mixed methods research. Similar to Guetterman et al. (this volume), they focus on the use of joint displays, which are used to integrate quantitative and qualitative data in mixed methods research. Although joint displays can help researchers identify patterns within their data and communicate their findings, there is limited information available on how to use joint displays to effectively communicate mixed methods research. The authors did a systematic examination of the use of joint displays for articles published from 2007 to 2014 in the *Journal of Mixed Methods Research*, a premier peer-reviewed journal for empirical and methodological work in mixed methods research. They focused on the different ways in which joint displays are used and their key features. For their analysis, they identified four major categories of joint displays. The first category was conceptual, which conveyed the justifications for the use of mixed methods design. The second category was research process, which was the most prevalent and summarized the methods and procedures in the study's research process. The third category was connection/development, which was the use of a joint display to depict how results from one phase of a mixed methods study was connected to or informed a subsequent phase of the study. The last category was integrated results, which involved the explicit combination of quantitative and qualitative results. They provide templates, examples, and recommendations to help researchers design and use joint displays to communicate findings to readers. The chapter provides an excellent guide for individuals who conduct mixed methods research because it provides a nice overview of various ways to use joint displays and encourages researchers to be mindful of what they should consider when communicating their designs and findings to readers.

In Chapter 8, Feucht, Marchand, and Olafson describe how visual displays can be used in the learning and teaching of research, with an emphasis on qualitative research. Specifically, they focus on the use of student-constructed concept maps as a tool to develop and assess students' understanding of research methods and design. Concept maps are visual displays that represent concepts and the relationships between these concepts. They can be used to present information to students, as mean for students to present their knowledge, and to assess what students know (Nesbit & Adesope, 2013). They briefly compare the processes (e.g., scoring data, generating codes) and products (e.g., conclusions, themes, models) of qualitative analyses. They distinguish among three levels of qualitative analysis, including the text, table, and graphic level, then focus in particular on the graphic level. Next, they describe a five-step process to scaffold the use of concept maps in instruction using a socioconstructivist perspective. They provide two classroom-based examples of how concept maps can promote learning and enable assessment of learning. In the first example, graduate students created concept maps in preparation for a qualitative research proposal. In the second example, graduate students used concept maps in the mixed-evaluation research studies as part of a group project. In both examples, the concept maps are used as tools to assess gaps in students' understanding, provide an impetus for discussion, and overall understanding of the research cycle. The authors provide clear and usable instructions for the using concept maps in learning and assessment. Their examples illustrate how visual displays can be used in learning and assessment in a practical, pedagogically sound, and theoretically grounded way.

Section III

Section III includes focuses on using visual displays to report testing and assessment data. In Chapter 9, Zvoch and Stevens focus on the use of visual displays to communicate longitudinal data analyses (e.g., growth-modeling research). There has been an increase in the use and technical complexity of longitudinal data analyses. A high level of expertise is required to understand these data. However, many stakeholders for whom these data are relevant are unfamiliar with the technical complexities of these types of data. A challenge for researchers is how to communicate these data in a way that is useful and comprehensible to these stakeholders. One effective way to translate these data is through the use of visual displays. Displays enable researchers to summarize very sophisticated data and patterns visually and make this information accessible to stakeholders. The authors provide a brief historical overview and articulate the crucial importance of achievement growth as a basis for school accountability. They indicated that achievement growth enables researchers, policymakers, and school leaders to make more informed decisions about how to assess and meet the needs of all students, and in particular, students with disabilities. However, for these data to be useful, stakeholders need to understand the patterns that they reveal. Using a large dataset of actual data, the authors provide numerous examples of the types of research questions that can be address using longitudinal analyses and demonstrate how these data can represented effectively in a visual display. The authors do an excellent job of connecting sophisticated data to real-world challenges that can be addressed by those data and demonstrate how those data can be represented in visual displays to communicate the findings to key stakeholders.

In Chapter 10, Foley describes how visual displays can be used to increase comprehension of assessment results. Uncertainty (i.e., error) is ubiquitous in educational and psychological testing. The degree of uncertainty affects the score precision and reliability. A higher degree of uncertainty reduces reliability, whereas a lower degree of uncertainty increases reliability. Independent of uncertainty is the consumer's comprehension of a test score, and it is problematic when there is a discrepancy between the degree of error associated with a test score and the consumer's interpretation of that test score (e.g., increased risk of misinterpretation or overinterpretation of test results). Foley describes how visual displays can be used to improve comprehension of test results by integrating measures of uncertainty (e.g., confidence bands, error bars) that are used with assessments (e.g., student score reports, state reports comparing demographic groups) into visual displays. He begins by identifying how sources of error affect the uncertainty of assessment results. Next he provides numerous examples of ways in which visual displays can be used to communicate this uncertainty such that test users/consumers are more likely to gain an accurate understanding of the degree of uncertainty associated with a particular assessment. Then he describes various options that are available to effectively communicate assessment results and explains why they are effective. He concludes by providing recommendations for ways in which assessment developers can use visual displays to more effectively communicate uncertainty to test users/consumers. One is to integrate indicators of uncertainty (e.g., error bands) directly into or near the visual displays. A second is to include users/consumers in the construction of the visual displays. Third, when possible, tailor or customize visual displays to users by providing information that is understandable and relevant to the particular user. Lastly, assessment developers should share with each other (e.g., via publications, conference presentations) more- and less-effective ways that assessments can be communicated to stakeholders.

In Chapter 11, Zenisky discusses the role of visual displays in results reporting, or the reporting of data about knowledge and skills to intended users. She begins by providing an overview of results reporting, which involves data pertaining to individuals or groups. This distinction is critically important because the nature of the data that a researcher includes in a research report, and the inferences that can be drawn from the data, differ based on whether the report pertains to an individual or groups. Further, other factors, such as the purpose of the assessment, need to be considered in results reporting. Thus, results reporting entails collating different types of data to provide an overall picture that is more comprehensive than individual pieces of information. One effective means for integrating multiple pieces of information in a coherent picture is through visual displays. The author provides numerous examples and visual displays to illustrate various ways to do results reporting that take into account different types of data elements and target groups. In particular, a very timely element in the chapter is an emphasis on the visualization practices in the two emerging areas of online communications and growth modeling. For instance, with respect to online communications, individual stakeholders can interact with a dataset in a way that enables them to construct a tailor-made visual display based on their goals for understanding the data. Drawing upon evidence from the psychometric reporting literature, the author provides a clear and useful set of recommendations on the use of visual displays to communicate assessment data to various stakeholders.

In sum, we believe that this collection of chapters can advance the field with respect to the use of visual displays in research and testing by providing researchers with a framework for using visual displays in a way the helps them organize, interpret, and communicate their findings in a comprehensible way within different research and testing traditions.

REFERENCES

Creswell, J. W. (2015). *A concise introduction to mixed methods research.* Thousand Oaks, CA: Sage.

Eitel, A., Scheiter, K., Schüler, A., Nyström, M., & Holmqvist, K. (2013). How a picture facilitates the process of learning from text: Evidence for scaffolding. *Learning and Instruction, 28,* 48–63.

Hegarty, M., Canham, M. S., & Fabrikant, S. I. (2010). Thinking about the weather: How display salience and knowledge affect performance in a graphic inference task. *Journal of Experimental Psychology: Learning, Memory, and Cognition, 36,* 37–53.

Hoffman, B., & Schraw, G. (2010). Conceptions of efficiency: Applications in learning and problem solving. *Educational Psychologist, 45,* 1–14.

Lane, D. M., & Sandor, A. (2009). Designing better graphs by including distributional information and integrating words, numbers, and images. *Psychological Methods, 14,* 239–257.

Larkin, J. H., & Simon, H. A. (1987). Why a diagram is (sometimes) worth 10,000 words. *Cognitive Science, 11,* 65–100.

Latour, B. (1990). Drawing things together. In M. Lynch & S. Woolgar (Eds.), *Representation in scientific practice* (pp. 19–68). Cambridge, MA: MIT Press.

Mayer, R. E. (Ed.). (2005). *The Cambridge handbook of multimedia learning.* New York, NY: Cambridge University Press.

Mayer, R. E. (2013). Fostering learning with visual displays. In G. Schraw, M. T. McCrudden, & D. Robinson (Eds.), *Learning through visual displays* (pp. 47–73). Greenwich, CT: Information Age.

McCrudden, M. T., Magliano, J., & Schraw, G. (2011). The effects of diagrams on online reading processes and memory. *Discourse Processes, 48,* 69–92.

McCrudden, M. T., McCormick, M., & McTigue, E. (2011). Do the spatial features of an adjunct display that readers complete while reading affect their understanding of a complex system? *International Journal of Science and Mathematics Education, 9*(1), 163–185.

Nesbit, J. C., & Adesope, O. O. (2013). Animated and static concept maps. In G. Schraw, M. McCrudden, & D. Robinson (Eds.), *Learning through visual displays* (pp. 303–328). Greenwich, CT: Information Age.

Robinson, D. H., & Kiewra, K. A. (1995). Visual argument: Graphic organizers are superior to outlines in improving learning from text. *Journal of Educational Psychology, 87,* 455–467.

Robinson, D. H., & Schraw, G. (1994). Computational efficiency through visual argument: Do graphic organizers communicate relations in text too effectively? *Contemporary Educational Psychology, 19*(4), 399–415.

Schraw, G., McCrudden, M. T., & Robinson, D. (2013). Visual displays and learning: Theoretical and practical considerations. In G. Schraw, M. T. McCrudden, & D. Robinson (Eds.), *Learning through visual displays* (pp. 3–17). Greenwich, CT: Information Age.

Smith, L. D., Best, L. A., Stubbs, D. A., Archibald, A. B., & Roberson-Ray, R. (2002). Constructing knowledge. The role of graphs and tables in hard and soft psychology. *American Psychologist, 57,* 749–761.

Sweller, J. (1999). *Instructional design in technical areas.* Camberwell, Australia: ACER.

Tufte, E. R. (2001). *The visual display of quantitative information* (2nd ed.). Cheshire, CT: Graphics Press.

Vekiri, I. (2002). What is the value of graphical displays in learning? *Educational Psychology Review, 14,* 261–312.

SECTION II
THEORETICAL FRAMEWORKS AND DESIGN PRINCIPLES

CHAPTER 2

DESIGN PRINCIPLES FOR VISUAL DISPLAYS

Past, Present, and Future

Antonio P. Gutierrez, Gregory Schraw, and Andreas Stefik

ABSTRACT

This chapter considers a variety of design principles for effective visual displays. Though displays are common in textbooks and professional research articles, very few researchers have proposed design principles that foster the best possible presentation for the understanding of displays. Our main goals were to provide a historical description for the design of visual displays and to identify evidence-based best practices to consider when designing visual displays. To do so, we surveyed four theoretical frameworks that have been used to conduct research on visual displays. We also identified three common themes across these models based on design parsimony, the relevance of information, and the use of universal design principles. We next identified three critical human factors (i.e., metacognition, working-memory capacity, and the cognitive load of information) identified in the literature as especially important for understanding visual displays. These factors are discussed in

Use of Visual Displays in Research and Testing: Coding, Interpreting, and Reporting Data,
pages 17–46.

the context of historically important design frameworks developed between 1980 and the present. We next summarize research-based visual display design principles from a variety of theoretical frameworks and disciplines, providing a comprehensive description of best practices. Finally, we discuss implications of our review for research, theory, and learning.

Keywords: visual display; design principles; visual display guidelines; learning from visual displays; visual design display research-based practices.

This chapter considers a variety of design principles for effective visual displays. Though displays are common in textbooks and professional research articles, few researchers have proposed design principles that foster the alignment between the presentation and the intended interpretation and use of displays. Our main goal was to provide a historical description for the design of visual displays for the purpose of identifying key evidence-based design principles for their use. To do so, we surveyed four theoretical frameworks that have been used to conduct research on visual displays. We also identified three common themes across these models based on design parsimony, the relevance of information, and the use of universal design principles. We next identified three critical human factors (i.e., metacognition, working-memory capacity, and the cognitive load of information) identified in the literature as especially important for understanding visual displays. These factors are discussed in the context of historically important design frameworks developed between 1980 and the present.

The remainder of this chapter is divided into six sections. The first provides a discussion of definitions of visual displays over the last 30 years. Section two compares four different theoretical frameworks that have been used to understand the effects of visual displays on information processing and learning. Section three considers the individual and collective contribution of these models to our understanding of the effectiveness of visual displays. The fourth section reviews how human factors influence the processing of visual displays. Section five examines the development of salient design principles over the last 30 years. Section six considers implications for future research and design practice.

DEFINTIONS AND HISTORICAL BACKGROUND

Definitions of Visual Displays

Visual displays help learners to understand conceptual information more clearly and frequently serve as valuable supplements when reading technical information. In the most general sense, visual displays (VDs) can be defined as any organized arrangement of information that allows viewers to effectively and efficiently extract meaningful understanding about the information and then quickly link it to prior knowledge, if such prior knowledge exists. In this sense, VDs include text, static graphics and images, and more recently, dynamic VDs that enable the user to actually manipulate the VD and hence maximize learning and comprehension from it. Researchers, most notably learning scientists and cognitive psychologists, have offered a variety of definitions that share some degree of variability. For example, Hinze et al. (2013) define VDs as any external visual representation that permits the user to take abstract symbols and transform them to concrete anchors of information through features such as color, size, shape, and proximity. Ferguson (1992) describes VDs as external representations, such as diagrams, graphs, maps, and architectural schematics, that are (and have been) used by scientists and other technical experts to communicate scientific and technical information to others. Yet other researchers have been either more vague by describing VDs as representations external to the individual from which they must extract meaning, or more highly specific, such as those who conduct research on dynamic visual representations. Schwartz (1995), for instance, argues that VDs are simply representations and that representational understanding is crucial to human learning. For the purpose of our discussion of VD design principles that follows, we define VDs as any external representation, including but not limited to text, graphics, images, equations, conceptual frameworks, tables, and complex hybrids that combine several types, which permits consumers of information to extract meaning, comprehend, and interpret the information conveyed in them.

Background and Summary of Previous Research

From the perspective of the VD user rather than the designer, visual literacy is the ability to read and write visual materials (Yeh & Cheng, 2010, p. 251). Discussions of visual literacy and VDs are neither recent nor have the debates always been scientific in nature. The first philosophical debates regarding visual literacy began circa 369 BC with Plato. In his epistemological essays in *Theatetus* (in Allen, 1965), Plato writes,

> I would have you imagine, then, that there exists in the mind of a man a block of wax . . . When we wish to remember anything which we have seen, or heard, or thought in our own minds, we hold the wax to the perception and thoughts, and in that material receive the impression of them as from the seal of a ring; and . . . we remember and know what is imprinted as long as the image lasts; but when the image is effaced or cannot be taken, then we forget and do not know.

William Playfair (1786), in his *The Commercial and Political Atlas*, posited that graphics are effective only insofar as the designer can effectively exploit the human information-processing system, although he never empirically examined any of his claims. Since Playfair, several other pioneers during the 19th century have attempted to design VDs ranging from population densities and migrations in maps to the shifts in national wealth and purchasing power (i.e., inflation). Nevertheless, even though these pioneers had a general understanding of VDs and their design, they too did not empirically investigate their hypotheses regarding VD design and comprehension. It was not until the beginning of the 20th century that theory and research on VDs took off. In his theory of social development, Lev Vygotsky (1962) argued that diagrams permit learners to structure and restructure their ideas by making them personally meaningful and concrete. Therefore, even in the early 20th century, researchers like Vygotsky began to theorize about the influence of VDs on individuals' ability to learn from a task. More recently, contemporary researchers have focused on the importance of the features of VDs. For instance, researchers since the 1980s have debated the features of VDs that either facilitate or hinder individuals' ability to effectively, efficiently, and accurately interpret information contained in VDs.

Visual literacy skills are essential for the interpretation and design of VDs. Visual literacy permits VD designers to gain a better understanding of the processes necessary to create displays that convey meaning succinctly, accurately, and effectively. Visual literacy skills enable designers to understand how the consumer will interpret the VD, and thus strive to anticipate potential difficulties in consumer comprehension. Designers can subsequently use sound design principles to mitigate, compensate, or circumvent these problems. For instance, visual literacy allows designers to better grasp the human information-processing and perceptual system, such as the process by which consumers engage with the VD, encode the information contained within it, manipulate it in working memory, and link this information to *relevant, correct* prior knowledge stored in long-term memory. Thus, designers can use research-based best practices while developing VDs to accurately and meaningfully convey even the most complex information by not only better creating the actual VD but by remaining ever mindful of the shortcomings of the human information and perceptual system (e.g., limited attention span and working-memory capacity; see Kosslyn, 1985). With respect to consumers, visual literacy allows them to more meaningfully engage well-developed VDs and maximize cognitive and dispositional characteristics employed during comprehension. A VD that is designed using research-based best practices facilitates consumers' effective, accurate, and efficient processing of the information contained in the VD via their information and perceptual processing systems and use deeper, meaningful comprehension strategies to better interpret and understand the VDs. Well-developed VDs may entice consumers to *want* to engage with the VD, increase situational awareness and interest in the task, and thus improve VD comprehension. In sum, effective visual literacy skills are relevant and important to both VD designers and consumers.

THEORETICAL FRAMEWORKS IN VISUAL DISPLAY RESEARCH

Across most empirical investigations of the influence of VD features on comprehension and VD design principles, four theoretical frameworks are consistently adopted by researchers: (a) Marr's (1982) *Three Levels of Information Processing* model, adapted by Kosslyn (1985); (b) the *Two-Stage Graph Comprehension Process* model (Kosslyn, 1989; Pinker 1991; Shah & Hoeffner, 2002); (c) Lowe and Bouchiex's (2008) *Animation Processing Model*; and (d) Mayer's (2009) *Cogni-*

tive Theory of Multimedia Learning. It is important to note that although there are several variations of these four frameworks (e.g., Ainsworth, Bibby, & Wood, 2002; Kriz & Hegarty, 2007; Mayer & Wittrock, 1996), we focus on theories (a) through (d) for two reasons. The first is because these four encapsulate the remaining others relatively well. The second is because an exhaustive discussion of the theories behind VD comprehension is beyond the scope of this chapter. These four frameworks are more fully discussed separately in the sections that follow.

Three Levels of Information Processing Model

Figure 1 presents Marr's (1982) model, *Three Levels of Information Processing* (TLIP). The TLIP model essentially partitions information processing of visual data into three primary phases. Marr and his colleagues (Kosslyn, 1985; Marr, 1982) argued that the flawed nature of the human information-processing system has profound implications for the way individuals interpret visual information. If designers of visual data either intentionally or inadvertently violate the principles discussed in the following sections at any or a combination of these phases, individuals may either only partially understand the information being conveyed or they may entirely misinterpret it. In the perceptual image phase, the visual system is especially sensitive to more general features of VDs such as (a) discrimination of lines and other markers of dimensions, (b) global position of said lines and markers, and (c) relations of lines and markers. The information gleaned from VDs is converted into individual perceptual units which are then transferred to and manipulated in Phase 2, short-term memory. These perceptual units are held briefly in short-term memory (also referred in the literature as working memory) and manipulated based on the demands of the task associated with the VD. Once transferred to short-term memory, the perceptual units can be manipulated and reorganized in a variety of ways to facilitate encoding and to better prepare this information to be connected to the next phase. In order for the perceptual units extracted from the VD to make sense and be appropriately interpreted, the perceptual units, now reorganized and manipulated in short-term memory, must be linked to prior knowledge (e.g., schemata, mental maps, prior experiences, etc.), which can only be achieved by accessing information from long-term memory storage. The following section briefly discusses the potential pitfalls of each phase and highlights the need to consider the limitations of the human visual information-processing system when designing VDs.

Kosslyn (1985) and Marr (1982) were among the first to acknowledge the factors that influence human perception of visual data and proposed the TLIP model to conceptually posit how the limitations in the human visual information-processing influence comprehension and interpretation of VDs. Kosslyn asserted that if the global features of VDs (e.g., lines and other markers) are too dim, imperceptible, or small, the perceptual units would not be appropriately—and more importantly, accurately—perceived by the visual system. He argued that, with respect to the first phase, it is not uncommon for humans' visual perceptions to be

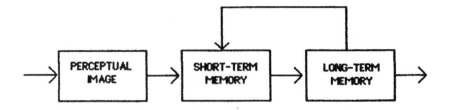

FIGURE 1. Marr's (1982) Three Levels of Information Processing model, adapted by Kosslyn (1985).

systematically distorted and thus create problems for the accurate interpretation of perceptual units extracted from VDs. Hence, from the outset, the potential for errors in the interpretation and comprehension of VDs is present—this before taking into account other within-person characteristics that influence comprehension and interpretation of information (e.g., cognitive factors and quality of the VDs themselves, among others). Assuming the information from Phase 1 is not significantly distorted so as to create problems in the more accurate interpretation of perceptual units, the rather limited short-term memory capacity of individuals (Bertin, 1983; Kosslyn, 1985; Wainer, 1996) creates undesirable outcomes for the accurate manipulation of the perceptual units transferred from Phase 1 (e.g., difficulties in properly encoding information due to overtaxing short-term memory capacity such as by unnecessarily increasing cognitive load; Kosslyn, 1985; Tufte, 1983). Finally, in Phase 3, individuals must access relevant prior knowledge about the concepts being conveyed by the VDs in order to accurately and more fully comprehend and interpret its meaning. Kosslyn stated that the success of this final phase is heavily reliant on individuals' ability to access to actual "relevant" information from long-term memory, which may sometimes fail (Anderson & Bower, 1973; Lindsay & Norman, 1977), as individuals draw incorrect inferences regarding the VDs because they link the VDs to incorrect, irrelevant prior knowledge. This therefore increases the likelihood of misinterpretation of the VDs. Regarding this last point, Kosslyn declares, "Part of this comprehension process involves drawing inferences about the [visual] input, some of which can result in a display [whether intentionally or inadvertently] presenting 'lies' about the data" (1982, p. 502).

Two-Stage Graph Comprehension Process Model

The *Two-Stage Graph Comprehension Process* (TSGCP; Figure 2) model first developed by Kosslyn (1989) and later refined by Pinker (1991) and Shah and Hoeffner (2002), posits that individuals' interpretation of VDs is fundamentally a two-stage process. In the first stage, bottom-up processing, the interpreter uses

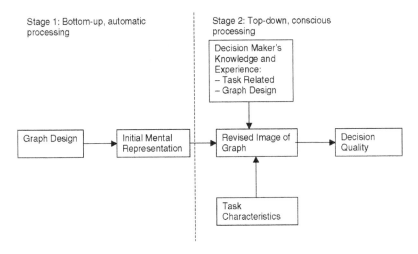

FIGURE 2. Two-Stage Graph Comprehension Model. Adapted from Raschke and Steinbart (2008).

mainly lower-order automatized strategies to encode and internalize the elements and features of VDs. It is in this bottom-up processing stage that individuals develop an overall schematic, or gist, of the general meaning of the information conveyed in the VD. In Stage 2, top-down processing, individuals consciously and deliberately link relevant, correct prior knowledge to the information contained in the VD. The top-down processing stage is characterized by deeper processing strategies (e.g., analysis, synthesis, inferential processing) that require higher-order thinking skills. Thus, the TSGCP model specifies that VD comprehension and interpretation is based on both features inherent in the VDs and individual differences in cognitive processing and prior knowledge that vary by interpreter.

Figure 3 presents Lowe and Boucheix's (2008) *Animation Processing Model* (APM). Like Marr's (1982) model, later adapted by Kosslyn (1985), the APM focuses on the central role of human perceptual processes in the meaningful learning from VDs. The early phases of the APM describe the meaningful extraction of information from the referent VD by uncovering the relations between what the VD is attempting to convey, what the individual is actually perceiving, and the task. Fundamentally, Lowe and Boucheix argue the following about their VD model, "The effectiveness with which this information is extracted therefore makes an important contribution to the ultimate quality of the mental model that is built and the learner's capacity to perform referent-related tasks." (2008, p. 651).

Phase 1 of the APM involves the partitioning of the flow of information from the learner's visual processing system and the VD; this process is iterative, ongoing, and dynamic. Like the perceptual units of the TLIP model, the APM considers "individual event units" as the fundamental unit of information conveyed

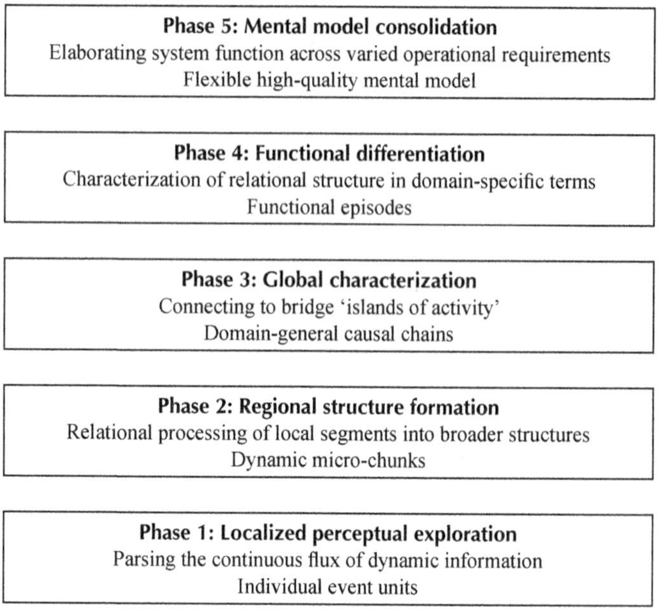

Phase 5: Mental model consolidation
Elaborating system function across varied operational requirements
Flexible high-quality mental model

Phase 4: Functional differentiation
Characterization of relational structure in domain-specific terms
Functional episodes

Phase 3: Global characterization
Connecting to bridge 'islands of activity'
Domain-general causal chains

Phase 2: Regional structure formation
Relational processing of local segments into broader structures
Dynamic micro-chunks

Phase 1: Localized perceptual exploration
Parsing the continuous flux of dynamic information
Individual event units

FIGURE 3. Lowe and Boucheix's (2008) Animation Processing Model.

by the VD; these individual event units constitute mutually exclusive pieces of information and their relevant actions at the local level. Next, learners are able to combine individual event units into larger pieces of information, known as micro-chunks, by internalizing and meaningfully integrating localized individual events units of the VD. Lowe and Boucheix (2011) state that the individual event units are integrated into local segments or connected regional structures, which is also a dynamic and deliberate process, in Phase 2 of the APM. They admit that learners in Phase 2 face particularly difficult challenges because the quality of their integration of localized event units to larger regional segments is predicated heavily on prior knowledge. In other words, their success at Phase 2 is mediated primarily by domain expertise (c.f. Kriz & Hegarty, 2007) regarding the referent information contained within the VD. It is during the transition from Phases 2 to 3 that interpretation of the VD transitions from domain-specific knowledge, favoring experts, to domain-general causal reasoning in which learners integrate regional structures in Phase 2 to larger processes of activity. It is during Phase 3 processing that information regarding VDs is transformed from more localized units (individual event units in Phase 1 and regional information structures in Phase 2) to more global elements (i.e., global characterization) that are then merged to a coherent, holistic interpretation in Phases 4 and 5. In Phase 4, functional differentiation, learners characterize the relations among these more global elements in domain-specific terms. Finally, in Phase 5, mental model consolidation, learners focus on a holistic, global interpretation of information in the VDs through the elaboration of system functions across varied processing requirements; Lowe and Boucheix (2011) refer to this processing as learners' development of a high quality, flexible representation of the VD (i.e., a mental model).

An often-used example of this process is how a piano produces sound. In Phase 1, individuals see a display of the piano sound-producing mechanism and view each piece as an individual unit. In Phase 2, individuals connect what they know about pianos to the display and begin to relate the individual pieces together. In Phase 3, individuals link the subsystems of the display of the sound-producing mechanism to a holistic, global representation and mentally see how all the parts function together to make the hammer strike the strings to produce the piano's sound. It is noteworthy to mention that the APM hitherto only carries empirical support for Phases 1–3. The theoretical claims found in Phases 4 and 5 have yet to be scientifically vetted.

Cognitive Theory of Multimedia Learning

Mayer's (2009) *Cognitive Theory of Multimedia Learning* (CTML; Figure 4) model specifies that in order for learners to develop a coherent and meaningful mental model of the information conveyed by the VD, relevant information needs to be linked from the information contained in working memory to the correct prior knowledge in long-term memory. These theoretical claims are not unlike those proposed by TLIP and the APM. However, unlike these two frameworks for the comprehension and interpretation of VDs, the CTML model explicitly distinguishes between verbal and visual information. The CTML posits that it is in working memory in which verbal and visual information regarding visual cues are organized, structured, and manipulated to facilitate the integration of both aspects of the human information-processing system with pertinent prior knowledge accessible via long-term memory.

According to the CTML, information presented via audio or verbal form is organized in working memory through the auditory-verbal processing system—the top portion of Figure 4—whereas the information presented as visual is organized through the visual-pictorial system—the bottom portion of Figure 4. The CTML presupposes that both aforementioned modalities for processing information in working memory have rather limited capacity, and thus, like the TLIP and APM, it accounts for errors in the human information-processing system when interpreting information contained within a VD. As such, the CTML takes into consideration the moderating effect of cognitive load on learners' ability to comprehend and interpret information from VDs.

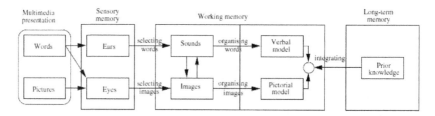

FIGURE 4. The Cognitive Theory of Multimedia Learning. Figure adapted from Mayer (2009).

Research on Visual Displays Among the Visually Impaired

While visual displays are likely the most studied, due to their generalizability across a wide range of the population, the concept of universal design, essentially the idea that a technology or user interface should be usable by all, including those with disabilities, is important to consider for underrepresented groups. For example, given that blind or visually impaired users might need auditory or tactile interfaces to understand materials, some literature exists on how to support these people.

While it may be reasonable to assume that replacing visual displays with tactile displays for individuals with visual impairments would be an effective means for adapting instructional materials, this is a misconception. More specifically, of the approximately 1.3 million people who are legally blind in the United States, only approximately 10% know braille (NFB, 2009). The impact is similar for children, with only 10% learning Braille. While obviously dire, the reasons for this vary, one obvious fact being that that typical electronic braille displays are expensive. For example, at the time of this writing, the HumanWare Brailliant B 80 refreshable braille display costs up to $7,000 (a top-end device). Although other assistive technology exists for the visually impaired (e.g., Voice Over, JAWS, 3-D printers, and tactile maps), braille remains the mainstream state-of-the-practice in assisting the visually impaired to interpret VDs (NFB, 2009). At present, however, no descriptive data are available on the usage of these other technologies. Further, even if tactile displays were adopted for text, understanding more complex graphics, like bar charts or figures, can be challenging. While advances have been made in translating visual content to tactile forms, significant technical challenges remain toward making such technologies mainstream (e.g., see Ladner et al., 2005). Additionally, while the literature on the use of auditory technologies is outside the scope of this article (for a review, see e.g., Stefik, Hundhausen, & Patterson, 2011), the reader can likely understand that there remain significant challenges to translating highly visual content to either tactile or auditory representations.

Summary

It is important to synthesize the previous brief discussion of the four theoretical frameworks on VDs in order to gain greater insight on VD development and design principles. This section compares the four models as well as discusses the relative merits and needs of each. By virtue of having temporal precedence, the TLIP is the simplest of the three models. Yet the model's simplicity is a strength rather than a weakness. Both Marr (1982) and later Kosslyn (1985) were able to develop a detailed yet cogent set of VD design principles based on the TLIP that are more exhaustive than any other attempt to date. The greatest contribution of the TLIP, in terms of better understanding how individuals interpret VDs, is in beginning with the premise that all information processed by the human information-processing system is inherently flawed (i.e., not necessarily veridical), the magnitude of which varies by context and individual. The TSGCP is unique in that it explicitly differentiates between the two stages of processing information from a VD, bottom-up and top down, and thus it partitions comprehension and interpretation of VDs into features of VDs themselves and idiosyncratic cognitive processing factors of individuals. However, the TSGCP is not as germane to the topic of VD design as other models, especially the TLIP. The AMP takes the simplicity of the TLIP and elaborates on many of the principles embedded in it. Among the contributions of the AMP is the elaboration of how individuals take information from the VD, encode it in working memory, manipulate and organize it accordingly, and use relevant prior knowledge in long-term memory to make appropriate inferences regarding the message the VD is attempting to convey. Thus, information processing in the AMP goes from localized domain-specific knowledge to more global domain-general structures that allow for more generalized inferences to the formation of high quality mental models that are used to holistically evaluate the VD. However, little to no empirical evidence exists supporting theoretical claims made in Phases 4 and 5 of the AMP, making it difficult to judge its overall utility and limiting its explanatory power as it pertains to evidence-based VD design principles.

Of all fours models, the CTML is the most complex insofar as it makes explicit and clear many processes that were implicit in the former three models. As an extension of the TLIP, its contribution is that it is more encompassing than either the TLIP, TSGCP, or AMP in that it accounts for information about VDs that could be transmitted through verbal/audio rather than purely visual formats. Given the relative merits and needs of each, all models, albeit to varying degrees, take into account limitations in the human information-processing system and caution VD designers to consider these when designing VDs. The recommended evidence-based practices for VD development predicated on these models will be treated in detail in subsequent sections of the chapter. Research regarding the features and design characteristics of VDs that either facilitate or hinder interpretation and comprehension have three main foci: (a) best practices for VD design principles, focused primarily on features inherent in the VDs themselves (e.g., Gillan, Wickens, Hollands, & Carswell, 1998; Jin, 2013; Kosslyn, 1985; Lane & Sándor, 2009; Naftaliev & Yerushalmy, 2013); (b) research investigating the circumstances under which individuals best learn from and comprehend VDs (e.g., Canham & Hegarty, 2010; Lowe & Bouchiex, 2011; Post, van Gog, Paas, & Zwaan, 2013; Schüler, Scheiter, Rummer, & Gerjets, 2012); and (c) within-person characteristics that influence learners' comprehension and interpretation of VDs (e.g., Ainsworth & Loizou, 2003; Florax & Ploetzner, 2010; Hinze et al., 2013; Kriz & Hegarty, 2007). We will discuss this research more thoroughly in the sections that follow.

THE CONTRIBUTION OF THEORETICAL MODELS

Explanatory Power of Models in Understanding Visual Displays

The models discussed in the previous section contribute to our understanding of VDs in three important ways. One is that they allow both VD designers and consumers to gain a deeper, more holistic understanding of the human information-processing and perceptual system. From the designers' perspective, this results in producing VDs that are mindful and respectful of the strengths and shortcomings of this system and thus increase interpretability and comprehension and minimize errors. On the part of the VD consumer, the models highlight the necessity to be attentive to the VDs and the information they attempt convey, properly encode the information and manipulate it in working memory, and connect that information to correct, relevant prior knowledge in long-term memory, thereby constructing a more complete, higher quality mental model. Therefore, the models provide both VD designers and consumers a deeper appreciation for how humans process, perceive, and interpret information and how these processes are affected by choice of media in which to convey information. Second, these models make salient that VD design, interpretation, and comprehension involves more than cognitive (and metacognitive factors such as conditional knowledge and comprehension) skills and processes. In order to fully understand VDs, one needs to take into account dispositional/motivational characteristics as well, such as interest, goals, and utility-value beliefs. However, the role that motivational characteristics play in the interpretation of VDs is an understudied area that warrants additional empirical inquiry. Third, the models highlight the need to consider the method in which the VDs are to be rendered. As the VD is en route from designer to consumer (out in the proverbial ether, if you will), neither the designer nor the consumer will have control over how the VD will be rendered and ultimately presented. Even with today's modern rendering capabilities, afforded by ever-greater computing power, the VD may be rendered in inappropriate formats or relatively poor quality (e.g., due to higher costs for rendering higher quality displays). Hence, by anticipating that the VD may be poorly rendered, designers can take steps from the outset to mitigate, if not completely eliminate, this problem.

Gaps in Explaining Aspects of Human-Information and Perceptual Processing

Although the models, taken together, provide a comprehensive and fuller understanding of the how humans perceive, process, interpret, and comprehend VDs, the models are not without gaps. Lowe and Boucheix's (2008) AMP appears to be the only one to directly address higher-order thinking processes and skills in Phase 4, but especially Phase 5, in which metacomprehension and metarepresentation are necessary and essential. Ironically, to the authors' own admission, this is the part of their model that lacks very much needed empirical evidence. Boucheix, Lowe, Putri, and Groff (2013) add additional evidence of the model for Phases 1–3, yet even here they expressly caution the reader that Phases 4 and 5 were not addressed in their empirical investigation. Phase 3 of their model comes closest to discussing the role of higher-order thinking processes, even though this is not explicitly described by the authors. Therefore, the models do not clearly or effectively disentangle cognitive and metacognitive—including metacomprehension and metarepresentation skills—processes. Moreover, the models do not cogently articulate the role of higher-order thinking processes in perceiving, processing, interpreting, and comprehending VDs.

Common Cross-Model Assumptions of Visual Display Design Principles

Even though the models vary in some respects, they do share three common, general themes. All models recommend (although the emphasis varies) that VDs be designed with simplicity and parsimony in mind. This directly supports Tufte's (1983) warning to avoid what he termed "chart junk," or irrelevant, superfluous information that contributes little, if at all, to the main idea(s) conveyed by the VD. The take-home lesson here is not to add unnecessary elements to the VDs for the mere purpose of making them appear aesthetically pleasing. Chart junk, beyond not offering the VD any additional explanatory power, has the unintended consequence of increasing cognitive load, overly taxing attention and working memory, and worst of all, has the potential to disrupt the retrieval of correct, relevant prior knowledge essential to interpretation and comprehension of the VD (i.e., resulting in an incomplete, poor-quality mental model). Research on the seductive details effect (e.g., Garner, Gillingham, & White, 1989; Lehman, Schraw, McCrudden, & Hartley, 2007), which is informative regarding the previous statement, has found that individuals tend to focus on irrelevant, superficial information that conveys no meaning regarding the main task, to the exclusion of the relevant, important information. Including chart junk could have this very detrimental effect.

A second common theme, strongly related to the first, is the need to include only relevant, important information in VDs (Gillan et al., 1998; Hegarty, 2004; Naftaliev & Yerushalmy, 2013). In other words, design the VD such that only information that is truly relevant and important to the designers' main idea(s) is included. Moreover, in cases where the information to be displayed is complex—either because of the sheer amount of information presented, a combination of features and media, or all of these characteristics—the VD will necessarily be complex. For instance, some VDs could be deemed "complex hybrids" because they combine text with diagrams, pictures, or other graphics; or those that combine static and dynamic VD elements. When using these complex hybrids, the models concur that designers should pay particular attention to make most salient the more important, relevant features, particularly when the most relevant, important features are more esoteric to the consumer.

A third common theme is the use of universal conventions for conveying meaning in VDs. This is especially true for VDs that do not use text but instead rely on symbols and other more abstract features of VDs. This third theme has become increasingly more critical, as the exchange and availability of information has shifted from a very localized to a global scale, thanks, in no small part, to the Internet. The reasons for this are twofold. The first is that the use of these universal symbolic conventions circumvents any differences in how consumers may interpret (or conversely, misinterpret) information in VDs because of linguistic nuances found in idiomatic expressions that either do not translate well or at all. The second is that universal conventions also circumvent any cultural idiosyncrasies that may create difficulties in interpreting and comprehending VDs.

RESEARCH ON HUMAN FACTORS INFLUENCING THE INTERPRETATION OF VISUAL DISPLAYS

The following section describes the most important human factors that influence the interpretation of VDs. These include metacognition, working memory, attention span, and issues related to the cognitive load of visual displays that facilitate or disrupt efficient processing and accurate interpretation of display information. The need for designers to more carefully consider the guidelines that have thus far been presented (and those that will be offered in the next section) hopefully will become more apparent in this section. Research on VDs used in classroom and learning settings have highlighted the role of metacognition and metacomprehension in the interpretation of VDs. For instance, Hinze et al. (2013) found that metacognitive conditional knowledge—the when, where, and why individuals apply strategies given task demands—influences how individuals interpret and meaningfully extract information from VDs. Paik and Schraw (2013) concluded that both directive (i.e., a VD element that draws individuals' attention to a particular portion of the display) and representational (features that convey content of the display) animations impeded metacomprehension by creating a false sense of understanding the information contained in displays (i.e., an illusion of knowing), but that this effect was moderated by expertise. Other studies have supported similar findings (Ainsworth & Loizou, 2003; Hinze et al., 2013; Kriz & Hegarty, 2007; Mason, Lowe, & Tornatora, 2013), in which experts more efficiently and effectively interpret information contained in VDs than novices, primarily because they focus more on the deep meaning of the VDs whereas novices easily misinterpret VDs because they tend to direct attention to the more irrelevant, surface features of the displays (Gegenfurtner & Seppänen, 2013; Hegarty, 2004; Kriz & Hegarty, 2007). From a VD design perspective, this is problematic because, as Wainer and colleagues (Gillan et al., 1998; Lane & Sándor, 2009; Raschke & Steinbart, 2008; Wainer, 1996) have reported, some of the VDs that are used to convey information make salient irrelevant information in the display, making it easier to misinterpret information. This problem is exacerbated by the intentions of the designers themselves. Tractinsky and Meyer (1999) demonstrated that VD designers may have vested interests in how they display their information. Thus, readers may be faced with VDs that, either intentionally or inadvertently, create unwarranted favorable or unfavorable interpretations of the information in the display (Rascke & Steinbart, 2008).

Raschke and Steinbart (2008) proposed an interesting and innovative approach to dealing with the human factors that affect accurate interpretation of VDs. Rather than focus their investigation on improving the VDs themselves or admonishing designers, they designed a training aimed at enhancing accurate interpretation of VDs and minimizing misinterpretation or the tendency to be misled by poorly designed VDs. However, they discovered that training individuals on how to more accurately and meaningfully interpret VDs by requiring them to justify the inferences and decisions drawn from them was effective only for experts but not for novices; nevertheless, the effect size was low, Cohen's $d = .12$. This finding is particularly alarming given that those who could stand most to benefit from such interventions are novices because they are the most prone to making inferential errors when interpreting VDs. The only design principles were, when displaying trends, (a) the visual magnitude of a trend should accurately reflect the actual quantitative change in the data and (b) properly label and align the VD in a way in which readers (at least in the Western world) have been taught to interpret such data—the VD should portray time as moving chronologically from left to right on the horizontal axis (p. 25).

Other research studies on VD comprehension have focused on other human factors in decision making. These include working-memory capacity (e.g., Astle, Kamawar, Vendetti, & Podjarmy, 2013; Schüler et al., 2012; Wright, Jansen, & Wyatt, 1998), attention span (e.g., Florax & Ploetzner, 2010; Lowe & Boucheix, 2011; Wright et al., 1998), cognitive load (e.g., Eitel, Scheiter, Schüler, & Nyström, 2013; Lane & Sándor, 2009; Post et al., 2013), motivation and disposition (e.g., engagement, interest, and utility value; Boucheix et al., 2013; Raschke & Steinbart, 2008), and shortcomings on the human perceptual system (Kosslyn, 1985; Wainer, 1996). For instance, Cromley, Snyder-Hogan, and Luciw-Dubas (2010) found that students who used diagrams engaged in more meaningful strategy use and deeper cognitive processing while learning science concepts than those who used only text, who tended to rely on more superficial strategy use. Canham and Hegarty (2010) concluded that prior knowledge affects both how individuals select what aspects of complex VDs to attend to and how they interpret and draw inferences from them. Their research supports the information reduction hypothesis (see Haider and Frensch, 1996, 1999), in which including as much relevant information about the main points of the VD, facilitates readers' attention to the more salient important features. In their take-home lesson, they state, "We have highlighted the importance of selection of task-relevant information as a critical step in graphics comprehension, and shown how both knowledge and good display design can facilitate this process." (2010, p. 163).

Additional research has shown that self-generated drawings of VDs have beneficial effects. Mason et al. (2013), for example, found that when students were given an opportunity to re-create, and thus reinterpret VDs, richer and more accurate drawings were predictive of increased comprehension. Moreover, they posited that self-generated drawings facilitate deeper processing because it encourages individuals to purposefully slow information processing, allowing for more careful, thoughtful examination of all elements in the VDs; this in turn allowed for a more accurate mental model. Other strategies have also been found to improve VD interpretation. Post and associates (2013) showed that language choice, linguistic ability, and culture influence how individuals perceive, process, and interpret VDs. This is especially true for individuals whose culture, language, and methods of expression differ from those of the VD designer. Thus, designers should consider readers' culture and linguistic ability when developing VDs, especially those that include large amounts of text. This is even more pressing when the information embedded in the VDs is heavily culturally or linguistically nuanced and complex. Finally, research on working-memory capacity and attention span has found that individuals' rather limited working-memory capacity and attention span should be considered when designing VDs (Florax & Ploetzner, 2010, Kosslyn, 1989).

Summary

In this section, we reviewed some of the human factors that contribute to the interpretation and comprehension of VDs. The consensus of the research literature we have presented is that, from a cognitive/information-processing perspective, the limited working memory and attention of individuals, coupled with shortcomings in human perceptual processing (i.e., visual-spatial ability and the phonological loop) already place individuals at a disadvantage, even before they approach the task of interpreting and comprehending VDs. From a perceived relevance perspective, the research converges on the conclusion that poorly designed and constructed VDs may lead individuals to either partially engage with the information in the VDs or completely ignore it altogether, in either case leading to inaccurate interpretation or the drawing of incorrect inferences. It appears that individuals may either strive toward maximizing cognitive efficiency as they set about interpreting VDs or they adopt a more minimalist approach and are cognitively lazy toward the task. Moreover, we have presented some guidelines for the design of VDs, taking into account human-cognitive and dispositional character-istics. These are summarized here as follows: (a) develop effort-intensive inter-ventions that force the consumer of VDs to self-explain why they have interpreted or drawn the inferences they have about the VDs; (b) when displaying trends, the visual magnitude of a trend should accurately reflect the actual quantitative change in the data, and the VD should portray time as moving chronologically from left to right on the horizontal axis (Raschke & Steinbart, 2008); (c) use diagrams to supplement text to increase the likelihood of individuals engaging in deeper, meaningful processing (Cromley et al., 2010); (d) design VDs as simply and parsimoniously as possible so that the expert-to-novice effect in VD interpre-tation is mitigated (Canham & Hegarty, 2010); (e) take into consideration linguis-tic and cultural differences in consumers of VDs by using simpler descriptions that are free of technical language whenever possible; and (f) designers should not intentionally mislead readers by attempting to make their meaning, expressed in VDs, more favorable.

VISUAL DISPLAY DESIGN AND DEVELOPMENT PRINCIPLES

Thus far we have covered a variety of factors that influence how individu-als engage with and interpret VDs. This leads us to a better understanding of research-based practices for the design of VDs. Common themes among these principles and guidelines are parsimony of the VD, relevance to the task and to the consumer, and universal minimum standards all VDs must meet to be meaningful. With respect to the first point, VD designers need to understand that the VD must convey as much meaningful information with as few elements as possible. This is related to the second point. If the VD includes too much superfluous information, individuals may fall prey to the seductive detail effect, and hence, the information in the VD will lose relevance to the task and the consumer. Finally, an adequate VD must contain a universal set of standards that dates back to the work of Marr (1982) and Kosslyn (1985). Without these basic elements, the VD will be infe-rior. Moreover, it is important to reiterate the role of visual literacy for both VD designer and consumer. Without a basic degree of visual literacy, VD designers would not be able to develop meaningful VDs and consumers would be incapable of interpreting the VD, no matter how sophisticated it may be.

Recommendations on Features of Visual Displays

Recommendations on the features inherent in the format or medium of VDs and guiding universal design principles have been varied. However, the general consensus is that VD designers do not give sufficient thought to their audience or to the optimum features in VDs that would maximize the interpreters' ability to grasp the meaning found in the VD. For instance, Kosslyn and colleagues (Bertin, 1983; Jarvenpaa & Dickson, 1988; Kosslyn, 1985, 1994; Tufte, 1983) state that effective VDs are those that enable individuals to efficiently and accurately extract information and make decisions about the meaning of the information being conveyed. Interestingly, even when the data presented in VDs is accurate and relevant to the message, the VD itself may be designed in such a way as to increase misinterpretations, which can subsequently lead interpreters to reach the wrong conclusions or inferences about the data (Beattie & Jones, 2002; Tufte, 1983). For example, when using a VD to show growth trajectories of populations on a map, using color shaded gradations, such as from green to red, to indicate growth may lead people to miss this crucial point as different colors do not intuitively convey "increase" in quantity. Along this vein, research has shown that designers of VDs must take into account the limits of the information-processing system to effectively develop VDs with their audience in mind (Kosslyn, 1985; Lowe & Boucheix, 2008, 2011; Mayer, 2009). To highlight this point, Kosslyn (1985) remarked, "Graphics are intended to be read by human beings, who have information processing systems with specific properties. Thus effective graph design requires an understanding of human visual information processing." (p. 499). Beyond these limitations, however, certain features and elements in, and formats of, VDs are more effective at conveying the intended meaning, whereas others are less effective and even hinder comprehension. For example, Tuttle and Kershaw (1998) argue that graphics are superior to tables when decisions about data involve integrating elements from larger volumes of information. Other research, on the other hand, has found that graphs and images, even when they are dynamic as opposed to static, do not add benefit to VD comprehension (e.g., Dillon & Jobst, 2005; Sung & Mayer, 2012).

In a review of five books related to the comprehension of VDs and the information-processing system in the early 1980s, Kosslyn (1985) makes broad statements regarding VDs and offers five universal design principles for VDs, including (a) actions that maximize individuals' ability to perceive VD elements; (b) principles to compensate for working-memory difficulties; (c) guidelines to increase the likelihood that the VD information held in working memory will connect to the relevant, appropriate prior knowledge from long-term memory; (d) guidelines for formats and purposes; and (e) guidelines for particular data and which features best display them. Kosslyn's synthesis continues to be a seminal piece insofar as it is still widely accepted and cited in the literature. Table 1 contains the principles described by Kosslyn and a brief description of each.

In his comprehensive list of principles and guidelines, Kosslyn (1985) provides a number of concrete, specific pieces of information related to each of the principles. The most relevant considerations for Principle 1 of Table 1 are sufficient discriminability, visual properties, information-processing priorities, and perceptual distortions. With respect to specific Guideline 1.1.1, absolute thresholds of perceptibility are essential; in other words, individuals must be able to clearly see and distinguish various features of the VD. This is especially critical when the designer intends to use a range of features, such as colors, symbols, shapes, and markers in a single VD. If these elements are not properly distinguishable, the

TABLE 1. Kosslyn's Five Visual Display (VD) Design Principles From a Synthesis of Five Books

General Design Principle	Local Design Principle	Specific Guideline
1. Getting Information Into the System	1.1 Adequate Discriminability	1.1.1 Elements of the VD must be perceptible and distinguishable from one another
	1.2 Visual Properties	1.2.1 Varying these elements can be used to convey different type of information, within limits
	1.3 Processing Priorities	1.3.1 Some elements of the VD are more noticeable than others
	1.4 Perceptual Distortion	1.4.1 Limitations to the human information processing system may result in systematic distortion of the VD
2. Working Memory Constraints	2.1 Perceptual Grouping	2.1.1 The way humans organize information, known as a perceptual unit, determines the amount of information that can be organized and manipulated in working memory; information organized into the incorrect units will not be interpreted
	2.2 Memory Capacity Limitations	2.2.1 Approximately four perceptual units can be organized and manipulated in working memory at any given time
3. Long-Term Memory Processing	3.1 Ambiguity in Labels and Designs	3.1.1 Ambiguous patterns are created when humans access irrelevant, incorrect prior knowledge; poor labels, titles, and element positioning contribute to this problem
	3.2 Inferences	3.2.1 VDs can be designed such that it may lead some to access irrelevant, incorrect inferences, resulting in a deceptive display (whether intentionally or inadvertently on the part of the designer)
4. Formats and Purposes	4.1 Communication, Analysis, and Storage	4.1.1 VDs can be used for three fundamental purposes; a given format may be more optimum for conveying particular information
	4.2 Type of Question	4.2.1 The essence of the interpretation of information in the VD is determined by the question(s) the designer expects the interpreter to answer from the data; to this end, different types of VDs are more appropriate to certain questions because they make certain kinds of information more readily accessible
5. Data and Formats	—	Different VDs are better suited to conveying different types of information

interpreter will miss the information at best, or completely misinterpret at worst. Kosslyn also cautions VD designers to account for differences in the rendering process of VDs, as this is often ignored by designers. For instance, VDs are often rescaled in the production/publication process, leaving the VD in at times poorer quality than the designer anticipated. This in turn can lead to failure to perceive relevant data or outright misinterpretation of information.

Color should never be used to convey information on a continuum (Local Design Principle 1.2) because it is better suited to information on nominal or ordinal measurement scales. Rather than using color to convey greater magnitudes of something (because color is not psychologically inherently ordered on a continuum; Kosslyn, 1985, p. 503), designers should use, for example, smaller or larger shapes (e.g., dots, squares, triangles, etc.). In terms of processing priorities (Local Design Principle 1.3), Kosslyn (1985) argues that VDs should be designed such that the more important information in the display is the most salient with respect to features because the visual system is especially discriminatory when it comes to line weights, positioning and size, shading, colors, and such. This last point was vehemently argued by Tufte (1983) in decrying the unfettered use of "chart junk," features or elements of displays that do not strengthen its meaning or utility of one's ability to interpret them. Finally, designers should be aware that humans are not particularly skilled at determining volume, which is exacerbated by poor VD design or rendering (for a discussion, see Teghtsoonian, 1965). To obviate distortion of information presented in VDs, designers should be mindful that perception is not linearly related to the physical dimensions of VDs (e.g., Dodwell, 1975; Frisby, 1980). Individuals also tend to systematically "delude" themselves into what they saw (but did not actually see) or the actual dimensions of what they saw in a VD, most typically by underestimating the area. Therefore, to avoid these illusions in perception, designers should consistently overrepresent the physical dimensions, especially when presenting information related to size and volume (Bertin, 1983; Kosslyn, 1985; Marr, 1982; Tufte, 1983).

This next set of guidelines is particularly relevant for VDs designed to present quantitative data and information. Wainer (1996) and others (Gillan et al., 1998; Lane & Sándor, 2009) asserted that VDs developed for quantitative data reporting are unique to other forms of VDs, and thus, should have their own design principles associated with them. The most compelling argument in proposing design guidelines specific to VDs conveying quantitative data is that readers interpreting VDs with such data can easily misinterpret the information. Unlike VDs discussed thus far, in which making mistakes in interpretation affects the understanding of the specific context in which they are embedded, VDs with quantitative data may lead to erroneous inferences and conclusions with respect to the entire topic being examined in the information. For instance, Wainer (1996) argued that designers of VDs presenting quantitative data should pay particular attention to the way error (e.g., measurement error, standard errors of estimating statistics, standardized residual scatterplots, variance, and standard deviations) is interpreted by the reader. According to Wainer,

> Whenever we discuss information we must also discuss its accuracy. Effective display of data must: (1) remind us that the data being displayed do contain some uncertainty, and then; (2) characterize the size of that uncertainty as it pertains to the inferences we have in mind, and in doing so; (3) help keep us from drawing incorrect conclusions through the lack of full appreciation of the precision of our knowledge. (p. 101).

Table 2 summarizes the design guidelines of Wainer (1996) and associates.

Gillan et al. (1998) offer a succinct decision tree pertaining to VD design (see Figure 5). Although it may oversimplify the VD design process, the decision tree provides a good starting point for designers wishing to create displays that are meaningful and interpretable not only for themselves but for the consumer as well.

TABLE 2. Design Principles Specific to Visual Displays of Quantitative Data

Source		Guideline	Aspect Addressed
Wainer (1996)	1.	When displaying many error statistics across cases, providing readers with the maximum value of the standard error provides a conservative value of the overall error terms and significantly decreases the likelihood of concluding that error across cases is vastly different, when in fact it is not. This value is easily obtained by taking the upper bound of the standard error and multiplying by.	Error
	2.	Control for Type I error-rate inflation when comparing many observations, readers can avoid making erroneous inferences by multiplying the value we are comparing against by the total number of comparisons, thus providing a conservative estimate of the new region of rejection and what lays beyond (see Bonferroni, 1936), regardless of whether we have a test statistic and its associated p-value.	
	3.	It is poor practice to include every possible standard error in larger datasets because it creates unnecessary cognitive load and detracts from the primary data structure.	
	4.	Designers should give additional, more thorough consideration as to the actual use of the data, as this may greatly simplify how the VD is designed and presented.	
	5.	These guidelines provide a protection against the technically naïve user by explicitly including confidence bounds of multiple comparisons.	
	6.	Making the physical size, and thus, the visual impact, of data points proportional to their error via error bars may not always be appropriate because it clutters the VD and it makes salient to the reader the most poorly estimated data.	
	7.	If data increase, the VD should likewise become larger or go higher; in other words, more should in fact indicate more.	

(continued)

TABLE 2.   Continued

Source	Guideline	Aspect Addressed

Gillan et al. (1998)	1. VD designers should understand the tasks in which readers engage when they look at the displays.
	  a. The choice of VD type depends on the readers' experience, knowledge, and expectations.
	  b. The choice of VD depends on the readers' informational needs.
	  c. The choice of VD depends on the characteristics of the variables in the investigation, particularly the independent variable.
		Accuracy of Information

2. VDs should accommodate the readers' sensory capabilities and limitations (see, also Kosslyn, 1985; Wickens, 1992); designers have no control over the conditions under which the VD will be rendered, and hence quality control should be a primary consideration.
    a. Readers will need to detect all indicators, verbal labels, and quantitative labels.
    b. Readers will likely be required to discriminate among different indicators, symbols, and key definitions.

3. The VD should consider readers' perceptual tasks of VD comprehension and meaning-making.
    a. Make the most important theme of the VD available to the reader at the global level; in other words, do not make readers search for the main theme of the VD.
    b. Make the most important features prominent and salient.
    c. Do not clutter the VD and include all VDs of the same theme in one consolidated VD; however, use spatial proximity for displays the reader may search for sequentially.
    d. Make the VD as simple and uncomplicated as logistically possible, given the information contained in the VD—readers will abandon the VD if they cannot easily determine the relations of various VD elements.
    e. In conjunction with the previous point, minimize the number of perceptual operations required by the reader.
    f. Use axes and tick marks liberally, but only when truly necessary to segment information (axes) or facilitate the estimation of specific values (tick marks).
    g. Stevens' Law (Stevens, 1975) should be considered to understand the relation between physical amount of the VD and perceived amount.
    h. Use 3-dimensional graphs sparingly; humans have been shown to grossly misinterpret volume (e.g., Kosslyn, 1985).
    i. Use similar patterns, shapes, and symbols to indicate data that are related and dissimilar ones for data that are unrelated.

4. Readers' cognitive tasks when interpreting VDs involve integrating text and visual information, maintaining the information accurately in working memory, and linking this to the relevant prior knowledge stored in long-term memory.

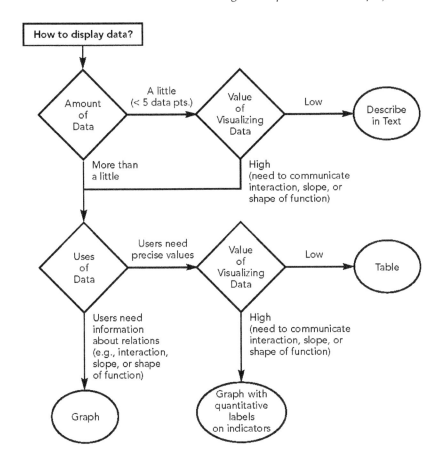

FIGURE 5. Steps VD designers should consider when developing VDs. Adapted from Gillan, Wickens, Hollands, and Carswell (1998).

Jin (2013) provides a comprehensive review of VD guidelines as they pertain to dynamic and interactive digital text. Her guidelines provide a more contemporary approach to VD design than previous research. Table 3 presents recommendations from her exhaustive review of the interactive digital text literature.

In her experimental investigation on the application of these VD design guidelines, Jin (2013) concluded that the VD design guidelines facilitated learners' engagement with the task, comprehension of information conveyed in the text, and improved retention of important, relevant information about the topic. These findings are congruent with similar studies investigating the role of VD design on text comprehension (e.g., Kieras, 1985; Lorch & Lorch, 1996; Lorch, Lorch, & Inman, 1993; Sung & Mayer, 2012; Surber & Schroeder, 2007).

TABLE 3. Visual Design Guidelines for the Use of Dynamic and Interactive Digital Text (Jin, 2013)

Global Design Principles	Local Design Principles	Specific Guidelines
1. Aiding in the comprehension of text structure	1.1 Visualize the relationships between the paragraphs and pages 1.1.1 Present the related paragraphs in a single page 1.1.2 Locate the pages that are 1.2 Visualize hierarchical structure between pages and present the selected page in the overall hierarchical structure context 1.2.1 Present the hierarchical structure of the total pages using the hyperbolic tree technique and enlarge the selected page in the overall hierarchical structure context interconnected in meaning closer to each other or present them in an identical background color so that they can be detected as a same group visually	Use space to separate the paragraphs, subsections, and chapters from one another (Hartley, 1985) Place closely related elements together (Lohr, 2003) Use color to help users understand what does and does not go together (Leavitt & Shneiderman, 2006) Use longer, scrolling pages when users are reading for comprehension (Leavitt & Shneiderman, 2006) Visualize the relationships between the pages (Jonassen & Wang, 1993; Sung, 2009) Use a multiwindow browser to organize pages hierarchically (Kandogan & Shneiderman, 1997) Visualize information with a focus-context technique that allow the viewer to inspect the specific part in detail without losing global context (Lamping & Rao, 1996) Use tree diagram, treemap, and corn tree to visualize the hierarchical information structure (Jerding & Stasko, 1998)
2. Draw attention to important, salient features of the display	2.1 Visualize the meaning of the keywords or key phrases with motion: Present the title or key phrases dynamically in an image so that their meanings can be visually prominent 2.1.1 Present the title or key phrases dynamically in an image so that their meanings can be visually prominent 2.2 Present keywords or key phrases in order: Present keywords or key phrases by each page in consecutive order using a time-based presentation technique 2.2.1 Present keywords or key phrases by each page in consecutive order using a time-based presentation technique	Convey tone of voice, emotion, and personality through moving characters (Ford, Forlizzi, & Ishizaki, 1997) Direct or manipulate explicitly the attention of the viewer through a time-based presentation of the text (Lee et al., 2002) Summarize the learning materials or lectures to enhance comprehension and recall of content (King, 1992; Wittrock & Alesandrini, 1990) Design summary pages at the end of e-learning lessons (Alessi & Trollip, 2001)

Summary

In this section we covered a wide array of VD universal design principles and guidelines. These principles and guidelines are intended to address the VDs themselves rather than human individual differences (e.g., perception, cognitive processing, and disposition) that influence how individuals interpret VDs. The take-home lessons from this section for designers to consider are (a) what type of information are you presenting—text, graphics, or both? (b) In what format will the VDs be presented—statically, dynamically, or a combination? (c) What is the complexity of the information? If the information is too complex to display, perhaps narrative would be more appropriate? (d) Who will be your audience? What is the technical expertise of your audience? and (e) although your display may have adhered to the sound principles and guidelines of a good VD, in which medium will the VD be presented (i.e., the way in which the VD is rendered and passed along to the reader may degrade its quality for reasons beyond the designers' control)? If designers give more careful thought to these questions, raised by the research we previously covered, development of good VDs will be facilitated.

IMPLICATIONS FOR THEORY, RESEARCH, AND PRACTICE

Implications for Theory

We surveyed the research literature in this chapter to identify design principles for constructing VDs. The research literature we covered throughout included discussions of the influence of expertise and prior knowledge on VD interpretation. Thus, our review has bearing on theoretical discussions of novice to experts and may even hint at how VD interpretation progresses from novice to expert judgment. Our brief investigation also led us to cognitive/information-processing theories regarding how human beings encode, process, manipulate, store, and retrieve key information relevant to adequately interpreting VDs. For instance, if readers are incapable of appropriately encoding VD information, maintain and manipulate it in working memory, link this information only to relevant background knowledge stored in long-term memory, misinterpretations and erroneous inferences may result. Moreover, individuals' higher-order thinking skills (e.g., metacognitive conditional knowledge and comprehension monitoring, among others) influence the manner in which they interpret information provided in VDs. Therefore, understanding VD design principles may also contribute to a greater understanding of cognitive and information-processing theories. Finally, some of the research presented examined dispositional characteristics and how they potentially influence VD interpretation. Utility-value beliefs, for example, may contribute not only to how individuals engage VDs but also how and why they persist in the task of comprehending VDs. Thus, motivational theories may shed light on why certain features of VDs lead people to engage/disengage, persist/abandon VD comprehension.

Implications for Research

Despite the fact that much work has been done on optimum VD design principles, the relation between human factors and VD design, and the interpretation of complex information, many unanswered questions remain. For instance, no empirical investigation to date has endeavored to synthesize all of the empirical findings on optimum (as opposed to poor) VD design principles. At the moment, much of the literature on VDs, including best practices regarding design, although related, remain largely disjointed. Because most of the research we surveyed was quantitative in nature, we believe that a fruitful avenue for future inquiry should be a meta-analysis of all quantitative research on VD design considerations. However, perhaps it is much too early to attempt such a synthesis of the literature, given that many of the design principles offered by researchers such as Kosslyn, Bertin, Tufte, Wainer, and Gillan remain, as of now, empirically uninvestigated. It may seem more appropriate to first provide additional empirical examinations of VD design principles before a meta-analysis of the research is undertaken. Additionally, we believe that the avenue opened by Rascke and Steinbart (2008), regarding interventions targeted at interpreters rather than designers, holds many possibilities for VD design and interpretation. It is the only empirical investigation to date, to our knowledge, which addresses interventions in VD interpretation. We encourage researchers to pick up the mantle and engage in examinations investigating how these interventions may improve VD interpretation while others examine how specific design principles enhance or hinder VD interpretation. Although addressing two aspects of VDs, these strands of research ultimately converge on the same outcome, namely, improving interpretation and comprehension of VDs.

Implications for Design Practice

We believe the research we have discussed in this chapter, especially the discussion on VD design principles and human factors influencing individuals' interpretation of VDs, also bear on practitioners, particularly educators and designers. With respect to educators, gaining a better understanding of optimum, research-based principles for VD design may facilitate their teaching individuals how to more accurately and correctly interpret VDs. This is particularly important in early childhood, an age in which research has shown that children can be taught the necessary inhibitory control to better comprehend VDs (Astle et al., 2013). From the side of the designers, additional empirically based information on best practices for designing VDs will enable them to more easily anticipate problems in interpretation and improve the design right from the outset because, once published and out of their hands, designers have very little, if any, control over how their VDs are rendered.

Summary of Gaps in Visual Display Design Ripe for Future Research

In the preceding sections of the implications, we have presented what we think is the current state of the evidence on each section, and we have provided some areas where gaps remain. In summary, we believe the major problem with VD design principles in the past is that they do not make tangible scientific predictions about user interfaces in practice, making them insufficiently falsifiable. For example, in *Cognitive Dimensions of Notations* (Green, 1989), while the principles sound viable on paper, in practice, they do not inform programming-language designers what words to use or VD authors what kind of graph will best represent a particular kind of data for a given population. Scholars who support the cognitive dimensions of notations framework paint with a broad brush, thus succeeding in providing guidance, but failing in the specific kinds of reliable predictions they can make in practice; in other words, little of what they provide with respect to theoretical claims has been empirically investigated. Therefore, these theories provide broad guidance, but modern work should focus on theories that allow for actual predictions of specific design decisions on human behavior, as this would ultimately be more useful, and falsifiable, than a purely "scientific" theory of visual displays.

REFERENCES

Ainsworth, S., Bibby, P., & Wood, D. (2002). Examining the effects of different multiple representational systems in learning primary mathematics. *Journal of the Learning Sciences, 11*, 25–61.

Ainsworth, S., & Loizou, A. T. (2003). The effects of self-explaining when learning with text or diagrams. *Cognitive Sciences, 27*, 669–681. doi:10.1016/s0364-0213(03)00033-8

Allen, R. E. (1965). *Studies in Plato's Metaphysics.* London: Routledge.

Anderson, J. R., & Bower, G. H. (1973). *Human associative memory.* Hillsdale, NJ: Erlbaum.

Astle, A., Kamawar, D., Vendetti, C., & Podjarmy, G. (2013). When this means that: The role of working memory and inhibitory control in children's understanding of representations. *Journal of Experimental Child Psychology, 116*, 169–185. doi:10.1016/j.jecp.2013.05.003

Beattie, V., & Jones, M. J. (2002). Measurement distortion of graphs in corporate reports: An experimental study. *Accounting, Auditing, & Accountability Journal, 15*, 546, 564. doi:10.1108/09513570210440595

Bertin, J. (1983). *Semiology of graphs.* Madison: University of Wisconsin Press.

Boucheix, J., Lowe, R. K., Putri, D. K., & Groff, J. (2013). Cueing animations: Dynamic signaling aids information extraction and comprehension. *Learning and Instruction, 25*, 71–84. doi:10.1016/j.learninstruc.2012.11.005

Canham, M., & Hegarty, M. (2010). Effects of knowledge and display design on comprehension of complex graphics. *Learning and Instruction, 20*, 155–166. doi:10.1016/j.learninstruc.2009.02.014

Cromley, J. G., Snyder-Hogan, L., & Luciw-Dubas, U. A. (2010). Cognitive activities in complex science text and diagrams. *Contemporary Educational Psychology, 35,* 59–74. doi:10.1016/j.cedpsych.2009.10.002

Dillon, A., & Jobst, J. (2005). Multimedia learning with hypermedia. In R. E. Mayer (Ed.), *The Cambridge handbook of multimedia learning* (pp. 569–588). Cambridge, MA: Cambridge University Press.

Dodwell, P. C. (1975). Pattern and object perception. In E. C. Carterette & M. P. Friedman (Eds.), *Handbook of perception* (pp. 267–300). New York, NY: Academic.

Eitel, A., Scheiter, K., Schüler, A., & Nyström, M. (2013). How a picture facilitates the process of learning from text: Evidence for scaffolding. *Learning and Instruction, 28,* 48–63. doi:10.1016/j.learninstruc.2013.05.002

Ferguson, E. S. (1992). *Engineering and the mind's eye.* Cambridge, MA: MIT Press.

Florax, M., & Ploetzner, R. (2010). What contributes to the split-attention effect? The role of text segmentation, picture labeling, and spatial proximity. *Learning and Instruction, 20,* 216–224. doi:10.1016/j.learninstruc.2009.02.021

Frisby, J. P. (1980). *Seeing: Illusion, brain, and mind.* Oxford, UK: Oxford University Press.

Garner, R., Gillingham, M. G., & White, C. S. (1989). Effects of 'seductive details' on macroprocessing and microprocessing in adults and children. *Cognition and Instruction, 6,* 41–57.

Gegenfurtner, A., & Seppänen, M. (2013). Transfer of expertise: An eye-tracking and think aloud study using dynamic medical visualizations. *Computers & Education, 63,* 393–403. doi:10.1016/j.compedu.2012.12.021

Gillan, D. J., Wickens, C. D., Hollands, J. G., & Carswell, C. M. (1998). Guidelines for presenting quantitative data in HFES publications. *Human Factors, 40,* 28–41.

Green, T. R. G. (1989). Cognitive dimensions of notations. In A. Sutcliffe & L. Macaulay (Eds.), *People and computers* (pp 443–460). Cambridge, UK: Cambridge University Press.

Haider, H., & Frensch, P. A. (1996). The role of information reduction in skill acquisition. *Cognitive Psychology, 30,* 304–337.

Haider, H., & Frensch, P. A. (1999). Eye movement during skill acquisition: More evidence for the information-reduction hypothesis. *Journal of Experimental Psychology: Learning, Memory, and Cognition, 25,* 172–190.

Hegarty, M. (2004). Dynamic visualizations and learning: Getting to the difficult questions. *Learning and Instruction, 14,* 343–351. doi:10.1016/j.learninstruc.2004.06.007

Hinze, S. R., Rapp, D. N., Williamson, V. M., Schultz, M. J., Deslongchamps, G., & Williamson, K. C. (2013). Beyond ball-and-stick: Students' processing of novel STEM visualizations. *Learning and Instruction, 26,* 12–21. doi:10.1016/j.learninstruc.2012.12.002

Jarvenpaa, S. L., & Dickson, G. W. (1988). Graphics and managerial decision making: Research-based guidelines. *Communications of the ACM, 31,* 764–774. doi:10.1145/62959.62971

Jin, S. (2013). Visual design guidelines for improving learning from dynamic and interactive digital text. *Computers & Education, 63,* 248–258. doi: 10.1016/j.compedu.2012.12.010

Kieras, D. (1985). Thematic processes in the comprehension of technical prose. In B. K. Brilton & B. Black (Eds.), Understanding expository text (pp. 97–118). Hillsdale, NJ: Erlbaum.

Kosslyn, S. M. (1985). Graphics and human information processing: A review of five books. *Journal of the American Statistical Association, 80*, 499–513.

Kosslyn, S. M. (1989). Understanding charts and graphs. *Applied Cognitive Psychology, 3*, 185–226.

Kosslyn, S. M. (1994). *Image and brain: The resolution of the imagery debate*. Cambridge, MA: MIT Press.

Kriz, S., & Hegarty, M. (2007). Top-down and bottom-up influences on learning from animations. *International Journal of Human-Computer Studies, 65*, 911–930.

Lane, D. M., & Sándor, A. (2009). Designing better graphs by including distributional information and integrating words, numbers, and images. *Psychological Methods, 14*, 239–257. doi:10.1037/a0016620

Ladner, R. E., Ivory, M. Y., Rao, R., Burgstahler, S., Comden, D., Hahn, S., . . . Groce, D. (2005). Automating tactile graphics translation. In proceedings of the 7th international ACM SIGACCESS conference on Computers and Accessibility (pp. 150–157). Retrieved from http://doi.acm.org/10.1145/1090785.1090814

Lehman, S., Schraw, G., McCrudden, M. T., & Hartley, K. (2007). Processing and recall of seductive details in scientific text. *Contemporary Educational Psychology, 32*, 569–587. doi:10.1016/j.cedpsych.2006.07.002

Lindsay, P. H., & Norman, D. A. (1977). *Human information processing*. New York, NY: Academic.

Lorch, R. F., & Lorch, E. P. (1996). Effects of headings on text recall and summarization. *Contemporary Educational Psychology, 21*, 261–278. doi:10.1006/ceps.1996.0022

Lorch, R. F., Lorch, E. P., & Inman, W. E. (1993). Effects of signaling topic structure on text recall. *Journal of Educational Psychology, 85*, 281–290.

Lowe, R. K., & Boucheix, J. (2008). Learning from animated diagrams: How are mental models built? In G. Stapleton, J. Howse, & J. Lee (Eds.), *Theory and applications of diagrams* (pp. 266–281). Berlin, Germany: Springer.

Lowe, R. K., & Boucheix, J. (2011). Cueing complex animations: Does direction of attention foster learning processes. *Learning and Instruction, 21*, 650–663. doi:10.1016/j.learninstruc.2011.02.002

Mason, L., Lowe, R., & Tornatora, M. C. (2013). Self-generated drawings for supporting comprehension of a complex animation. *Contemporary Educational Psychology, 38*, 211–224. doi:10.1016/j.cedpsych.2013.04.001

Marr, D. (1982). *Vision*. San Francisco, CA: Freeman.

Mayer, R. E. (2009). *Multimedia learning* (2nd ed.). New York, NY: Cambridge University Press.

Mayer, R. E., & Wittrock, M. C. (1996). Problem-solving transfer. In D. C. Berliner & R. C. Calfee (Eds.), *Handbook of educational psychology* (pp. 47–62). New York, NY: Macmillan.

Naftaliev, E., & Yerushalmy, M. (2013). Guiding explorations: Design principles and functions of interactive diagrams. *Computers in the Schools, 30*, 61–75. doi:10.1080/07380569.2013.769084

National Federation for the Blind, Jernigan Institute (NFB). (2009, March 26). The braille literacy crisis in America: Facing the truth, reversing the trend, empowering the blind. *NFB*. Retrieved from https://nfb.org/images/nfb/documents/pdf/braille_literacy_report_web.pdf

Paik, E. S., & Schraw, G. (2013). Learning with animation and illusions of understanding. *Journal of Educational Psychology, 105*, 278–289. doi:10.1037/a0030281

Pinker, S. (1991). Rules of language. *Science, 253*, 530–535.

Playfair, W. (1786). *The commercial and political atlas.* London, UK: Corry.

Post, L. S., van Gog, T., Paas, F., & Zwaan, R. A. (2013). Effects of simultaneously observing and making gestures while studying grammar animations on cognitive load and learning. *Computers in Human Behavior, 29*, 1450–1455. doi:10.1016.j.chb.2013.01.005

Raschke, R. L., & Steinbart, P. J. (2008). Mitigating the effects of misleading graphs on decisions by educating users about the principles of graph design. *Journal of Information Systems, 22*, 23–52.

Schüler, A., Scheiter, K., Rummer, R., & Gerjets, P. (2012). Explaining the modality effect in multimedia learning: Is it due to a lack of temporal contiguity with written texts and pictures. *Learning and Instruction, 22*, 92–102. doi:10.1016/j.learninstruc.2011.08.001

Schwartz, D. L. (1995). The emergence of abstract representations in dyad problem solving. *The Journal of the Learning Sciences, 4*, 321–354.

Shah, P., & Hoeffner, J. (2002). Review of graph comprehension research: Implications for instruction. *Educational Psychology Review, 14*, 47–69. doi:1040-726X/02/0300-0047/0

Stefik, A., Hundhausen, C., & Patterson, R. (2011). An empirical investigation into the design of auditory cues to enhance computer program comprehension. *International Journal of Human Computational Studies, 69*, 820–838. Retrieved from http://dx.doi.org/10.1016/j.ijhcs.2011.07.002

Sung, E., & Mayer, R. E. (2012). Five facets of social presence in online distance education. *Computers in Human Behavior, 28*, 1738–1747. doi:10.1016/j.chb.2012.04.014

Surber, J. R., & Schroeder, M. (2007). Effect of prior domain knowledge and headings on processing of informative text. *Contemporary Educational Psychology, 32*, 485–498. doi:10.1016/j.cedpsych.2006.08.002

Teghtsoonian, J. (1965). The judgment of size. *American Journal of Psychology, 78*, 392–402.

Tractinsky, N., & Meyer, J. (1999). Chartjunk or goldgraph? Effects of presentation objectives on content desirability on information presentation. *MIS Quarterly, 23*, 397–420. doi:10.2307/249469

Tufte, E. R. (1983). *The visual display of quantitative information.* Cheshire, CT: Graphics.

Tuttle, B. M., & Kershaw, R. (1998). Information presentation and judgment strategy from a cognitive fit perspective. *Journal of Information Systems, 12*, 1–17.

Vygotsky, L. (1962). *Thought and language.* Cambridge, MA: MIT Press.

Wainer, H. (1996). Depicting error. *The American Statistician, 50*, 101–111.

Wright, P., Jansen, C., & Wyatt, J. C. (1998). How to limit clinical errors in interpretation of data. *The Lancet, 352*, 1539–1542.

Yeh, H., & Cheng, Y. (2010). The influence of the instruction of visual design principles on improving pre-service teachers' visual literacy. *Computers & Education, 54*, 244–252.

Tufte, E. R. (2001). *The visual display of quantitative information* (2nd ed.). Cheshire, CT: Graphics Press.

Vekiri, I. (2002). What is the value of graphical displays in learning? *Educational Psychology Review, 14*, 261–312.

CHAPTER 3

GUIDELINES FOR MAKING GRAPHS EASY TO PERCEIVE, EASY TO UNDERSTAND, AND INFORMATION RICH

David M. Lane

ABSTRACT

Graphs play a critical role in communicating discoveries. In this chapter, the design of graphs for use in scientific publications is discussed in terms of principles for making graphs (a) easy to perceive, (b) understandable by reducing cognitive demand, and (c) informative. Naturally, these goals can be in conflict, so the graph designer must make the appropriate trade-offs. Often the quality of published graphs suffers because designers rely too much on the defaults used by statistical graphing software. Among the recommendations presented here that are at odds with standard practice are (a) direct labels of graphic elements should be used instead of legends, (b) figures should include both graphics and text, (c) box plots should be used instead of bar charts of means.

Use of Visual Displays in Research and Testing: Coding, Interpreting, and Reporting Data,
pages 47–81.

Graphs play a critical role in discovering relationships and patterns as well as in communicating discoveries. This chapter discusses only the latter role of graphs and focuses on how to design graphs for publication in scientific journals. As a result, none of the developments in interactive and dynamic graphics is covered. However, there are many design issues to discuss even for static graphs.

Many articles, chapters, and entire books have been written about designing graphs so, clearly, this chapter cannot provide comprehensive coverage. I focus on three related topics: making graphs easy to perceive, making graphs understandable by reducing cognitive demands, and making graphs informative. Some of the guidelines for making graphs easy to perceive might appear obvious and therefore even insulting to some readers. However, violations of even seemingly obvious guidelines are frequent in published graphics. My suspicion is that many researchers accept the default graphs that their data-analysis software creates even though these graphs are far from optimal.

Graphics software is often responsible for increasing cognitive demands on the observer. For example, graphics software almost always uses legends to indicate experimental conditions rather than directly labeling them, a method that places more cognitive demands on the observer than would directly labeling the condition. Because of graphics software, legends are much more frequent now than they were years ago when graphs were drawn with pen and ink. Another technology that is responsible for increasing cognitive demands is the printing press. Before its invention, graphics and text were integrated in the great works of scientists such as Da Vinci and Galileo. Even though this has not been a technological necessity for many years, graphs and their supporting information remain spatially separated, sometimes even on different pages. The flipping back and forth between sources of information makes interpreting a graph more difficult than necessary.

Most graphs in psychology journals are minimally informative, displaying means but no information about the shapes of the distributions. This is unfortunate since leaving out distributional information likely hinders scientific evaluation. I explore various ways of providing distributional information. In some contexts it is an easy thing to do; in others it can be quite difficult.

Making Graphs Easy to Perceive

Some principles for making graphs easy to perceive are rather obvious whereas others are less so. However, it is not difficult to find graphs published in leading journals that violate even the most obvious principles.

Contrast.

It is important to make sure that the contrast between elements and the background is very large. For example, lines and labels should contrast greatly with the background. This does not necessarily mean that the background has to be white. However, the fairly dark grey background used as the default in older versions of Microsoft Excel reduces the contrast too much. Also, pictures should not be used as backgrounds (Gillan & Sorensen, 2009).

Grid lines.

Generally speaking, graphs are used when exact numeric values are less important than the trends. Therefore, the use of grid lines is often superfluous. However, they can be useful in some circumstances. For instance, as pointed out by Few (2004), gridlines can facilitate the perception of differences in the heights of nonadjacent bars. In situations in which grid lines are necessary, the grid lines should be light so as not to detract from the content of the graph.

Avoiding Clutter.

A cluttered display distracts the reader from the message of the graph. One source of clutter is a poorly positioned element. For example, a legend placed too close to a graphical element can contribute to the clutter. Similarly, Y-axis labels and associated ticks that are too close together can give a display a cluttered look.

For graphs of percentages, clutter can be reduced by indicating that percentages are being graphed through the use of the axis label rather than with each value on the axis. Clutter can also be reduced by rounding off the values. I recently saw a graph in which the values were all whole numbers (0, 2, . . . , 10) but were presented with two decimal places (0.00, 2.00, . . . , 10.00). These decimal places added to the clutter, yet provided no information.

Displays look more organized if they have strong alignments. For example, a legend could be aligned with a graphical element so that the left edges of the legend and the element are the same distance from the left margin, contributing less to clutter than a legend unconnected to any other element.

Finally, as pointed out by Schwabish (2014), filling the bars in bar charts with patterns gives a graph a more cluttered look than filling the bars with different shades of grey. A possible exception to this is when there are too many groups to distinguish easily by their shades of grey.

Principles of grouping.

Frequently, two or more graphic elements are logically related and should be seen as a perceptual group. A few examples are (a) the various elements in a legend, (b) an axis label and the axis, (c) the label of a line on a line graph and the associated line, and (d) points on a scatterplot from the same condition. Both (a) and (b) can be accomplished by the Gestalt principle of proximity: items close together are perceptually grouped. For (c), good continuation and proximity can help group the labels with the lines if the labels are placed at the ends of the lines. For (d), it is sometimes possible to use the principle of similarity to make the points from different conditions form separate perceptual groups. For example, points from the groups could be different shapes such as circles and squares or could be of different colors. This will not be successful if there is too much over-lap because proximity will overpower similarity in this context.

Discriminability and readability of elements.

Although it is common sense to make graphics elements discriminable and readable, there are several considerations that are often ignored. First, one should keep in mind that a graph as originally created may be reduced when published. As a result, elements that appear sufficiently readable or discriminable when created may be less so when published. Second, the vision of many readers, especially older readers, may be less than perfect and these readers may have difficulty reading small text. Although font sizes differ for different fonts, one should consider using a 14-point font when possible and rarely use a font smaller than 12-points.

Fonts can be either "serif" or "sans serif." Serif fonts have decorative "finishes" on the ends of letters, whereas sans serif fonts are plainer and "cleaner" looking. The conventional wisdom is that serif fonts are better for long passages whereas sans serif fonts are better for guide signs on roads, trains, and subways (Moret-Tatay & Perea, 2011). However, practically significant differences between serif and sans serif fonts have not been convincingly shown and therefore either type of font would work well for labels in a graph as long as it is of sufficient size. That said, my subjectively based recommendation is to use sans serif fonts in graphs.

Representing quantitative dimensions.

The most common way to represent values on a quantitative dimension is with the positions of graphic elements such as lines, bars, and points. As shown by Cleveland and McGill (1985), comparisons between values are best achieved when they are made between positions of elements on a common scale. For example, the vertical positions on the tops of bars in bar charts, lines in line graphs, and points in scatterplots all convey quantitative information in this way.

Comparisons between positions along identical but nonaligned elements are fairly accurate but not as accurate as between positions on a common scale. Consider the graphing of fictitious data that consists of the frequencies of different types of errors in four monkeys so as to compare the proportions of error types separately for each monkey. Figure 1 shows the proportions of each type of error using grouped bar charts for which all bars are aligned with a common starting point, whereas Figure 2 uses stacked bar charts in which not all elements are aligned. As these figures show, it is easier to make comparisons with the grouped bar charts. For example, it is easier to compare the proportions of response shift errors made by Monkeys 2 and 4 in Figure 1 than in Figure 2. Notice that gridlines are used in Figure 1 but not in Figure 2. As stated previously, grid lines can make comparisons easier for nonadjacent elements, and this is the case in Figure 1. It would not have been helpful to have gridlines in Figure 2 since the elements being compared do not have a common starting point.

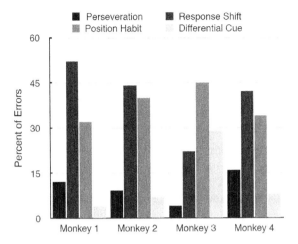

FIGURE 1. Grouped vertical bar charts showing different types of errors as a function of the subject.

This is not to say that stacked bar charts should never be used. For one thing, they make the ratio of parts to the whole easier to see than do grouped bar charts. Further, they are better suited than grouped bar charts for showing totals. Therefore, the researcher should consider the differences between aligned and non-aligned elements when conveying results to the reader.

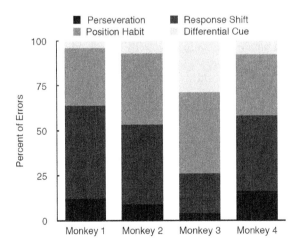

FIGURE 2. Stacked vertical bar charts showing different types of errors as a function of subject.

Area can also be used to represent quantitative values. For example, in pie charts, the areas of the slices represent proportions of the whole. Individuals are relatively inaccurate when making comparisons of areas (Cleveland & McGill, 1985) and therefore pie charts should only be used when fine distinctions between values are not required. It is also important to consider that the psychological perception of areas is not linearly related to actual area. According to Stevens (1957), increasing an area by a factor of k will increase the perception of area by a factor of k^7. Therefore, if one area is twice as large as another area, it will only be perceived as $2^{.7} = 1.62$ times as large. Although there is debate about the accuracy of Stevens' claim, the point that the relationship between perceived quantity and area is not linear should be considered. Recognizing that the relationship is not linear, McGill, Tukey, and Larsen (1978) suggested making the width of box plots proportional to the square root of the value to be represented.

Care should be taken not to represent a quantity by one dimension of a rectangle since it will appear that the quantity is represented by the area. This can exaggerate perceived differences among values, making them much larger than the actual differences. The degree which differences are exaggerated in this manner has been called the "lie factor" (Tufte, 1983). Although graphs that mislead in this way are much more common in the mass media than in statistical graphics, the problem can crop up even in scientific graphs.

Color (hue) by itself should not be used to represent quantitative information because, despite the fact that color is determined by the wavelength, a quantitative and continuous variable, human observers do not perceive the wavelengths of light as varying on a single continuous scale. Instead, observers see different colors as being qualitatively different (Borland & Taylor, 2007; Few, 2004; Kossyln, 2006; Moreland, 2009). Although an observer may be cognitively aware of the mapping of wavelengths to color and able to comprehend the dimension, more effort is required in order to interpret the graph, and patterns are harder to detect than if the dimension could be directly perceived. Therefore, Few's advice (2008, p. 7) to represent a quantitative dimension with "a single hue (or a small set of closely related hues) and vary intensity from pale colors for low values to increasingly darker and brighter colors for high values" is well founded.

Despite the drawbacks of using hue alone to represent a quantitative dimension, hue can be used effectively to distinguish positive from negative values, with saturation and/or brightness used to represent the absolute value. For example, the lowest negative value could be represented by a dark red color with less negative values represented by lighter shades of red. Low positive values could be represented by light shades of green, with increasing values represented by darker shades of green.

Making Graphs Understandable by Reducing Cognitive Demands

The higher the cognitive demands a graph makes on an observer, the longer it takes the observer to comprehend and interpret the graph. Although some graphs, by their very nature, require a fair amount of effort to interpret accurately, good design can reduce cognitive demands. Among the ways to reduce cognitive demands are (a) designing the graph to direct the observer's attention to the key data, (b) facilitating comparisons by organizing the graph so that the to-be-compared values are in close proximity, (c) labeling graphical elements directly rather than using legends, (d) integrating graphics and text so that the observer does not have to search the main text in order to understand the data, and (e) making the labels of graphic elements consistent.

Making the primary message salient.

Typically, there are just one or two key messages that a graph is designed to communicate. Since the presence of extraneous information can hinder performance (Canham & Hegarty, 2010), it is important for the graph to represent the data relevant to these messages in a way that automatically captures the observer's attention. As a simple example, suppose a researcher is interested in the slope of the linear relationship between Quantitative and Verbal SAT scores and chose to use a scatterplot to illustrate the relationship. Figure 3 contains a graph that emphasizes the regression line and therefore makes the relationship clear. On the other hand, suppose the purpose of the graph were to illustrate that one subject scored much higher on Quantitative SAT than would have been predicted from their Verbal SAT score. Figure 4 shows the same data as Figure 3, but is modified so that (a), the score in question, is displayed more prominently than the other

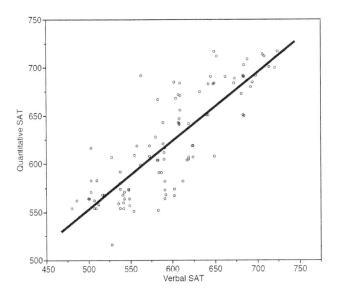

FIGURE 3. Scatter plot emphasizing the regrssion line.

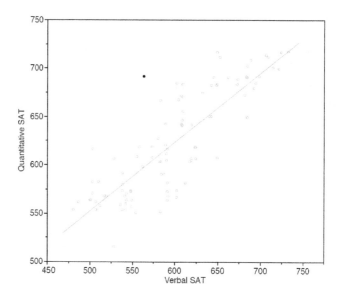

FIGURE 4.   Scatter plot emphasizing the outlier.

points, and (b), the salience of the regression line, is decreased. These changes make the relevant data stand out and capture the observer's attention.

Figure 5 contains an interaction plot showing the means of three groups over five trials. This figure is designed to convey the key finding that Group L's performance did not increase after Trial 3, in contrast to the other two groups, whose performance increased monotonically across all trials. Notice that the contrast between Group L and the other groups is made to stand out by using black to represent Group L's data and grey to represent the data for the other groups. Due to the Gestalt grouping principle of similarity, the visual difference between Group G and the other groups leads the observer to perceive two perceptual groups (one for Group G and one for the other groups) rather than three (one for each group). As noted by Kossyln (2006), the complexity of a line graph is determined by the number of groups rather than the number of lines.

In both of these examples, the graphs could have been interpreted even without the emphasis on the key findings. However, emphasizing these findings can make them immediately obvious and lessen the cognitive demands on the observer.

Legends.

Graphs are easier to interpret if the graphic elements (such as lines) are labeled directly rather than indirectly through the use of legends. If Figure 5 contained legends rather than direct labels, then more effort would be required to associate the lines with the respective groups. The labels in Figure 5 are placed at the ends of the lines, following Kossyln's (2006) recommendation. Placing the labels at

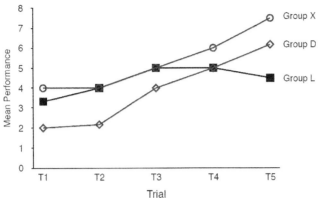

the end of the lines groups the lines and their respective labels using the Gestalt grouping principles of good continuation and proximity. If the lines are not sufficiently separated at their ends, then there would not be space to separate the labels. When this is the case, alternatives such as putting labels next to the associated lines at other portions of the graph should be considered. Arrows pointing to the associated lines are sometimes helpful.

When bar charts are used to display data for a large number of groups, there may not be enough room for direct labeling if a vertical chart is used. In this case, a horizontal bar chart with each row representing a different category should be used.

If it is necessary to include a legend on a graph, care should be taken that the legend is not so salient that it competes for attention with the graph itself. For example, it is rare that a legend should be given a border, and in cases in which a border is used, the border should be light and inconspicuous.

Consistency.

Graphs are easier to comprehend if there is a consistent mapping of visual and semantic elements. Consider how to label the lines in a plot of the interaction in a Gender (2) x Treatment (2) factorial design. A consistent mapping is shown in Table 1 in which the male means are all shown by squares and female means are all shown by circles. Similarly consistent, drug means are shown by filled shapes and placebo means are shown by unfilled shapes. A graph that is consistent requires less effort to process.

Graphs should also be consistent in the scaling of the dependent variables so that, for example, if better performance is represented by a higher score on one variable, it should also be represented by a higher score on another variable. An example of inconsistent scaling would be if one measure were the number of items correctly recalled on a recall test and the other measure were the percentage of incorrect responses on a spelling test. The scaling would be consistent if the

TABLE 1. A Consistent Mapping of Conditions to Symbols

Gender	Treatment	Symbol
Male	Drug	■
Male	Placebo	□
Female	Drug	●
Female	Placebo	○

percentage correct rather than the percentage incorrect on the spelling test were used.

In addition to being internally consistent, the graphs within an article or presentation should be consistent with each other. For example, if fill patterns are used to indicate conditions in a bar chart, the same mapping of conditions to patterns should be used in all graphs.

Graphs should be consistent with the inferential statistics presented in the main body of the paper. For example, if the inferential statistics involve differences among means, then means should be shown in the graph. Box plots that display means are preferable to those that do not because they maintain this kind of consistency. A graphical portrayal of variability should be consistent with the error term used in the inferential statistics. As a simple example, if a correlated t-test is performed, the variability shown in the graph should be the variability of the difference scores since that is the variability used in the t-test.

If a grey scale is used to differentiate the bars in a bar graph for an ordered variable such as trial number, then the darkness of the fill bars should be increased corresponding to the value of the ordered variable. Thus, making the darkness for trials increase from light to dark over trials would be a consistent ordering. If the variable is a categorical variable, then the bars should be ordered from smallest to largest with the darkness of the bars increasing.

It is also important to make a graph consistent with conventions. For example, higher values should be represented by higher vertical positions on the Y-axis. Although this may seem too obvious to mention, I just saw a graph in a scientific publication in which the Y-axis represented response time with longer times at the bottom of the axis. Presumably, this was done to be consistent with the convention that higher values represent better performance and the scaling of accuracy for which lower values are better. However, I believe that the convention of putting higher values higher on a graph is more strongly ingrained and should be the overriding factor in choosing the direction of the scale. As noted previously, is important that the scales of the two dependent variables (response time and accuracy) have consistent directions, but this could have been accomplished by graphing error rates instead of rates of correct responses.

Facilitating comparisons.

A graph should be designed to facilitate the most important comparisons. Normally this is done by making the representations of the to-be-compared data next to each other. For example, suppose the purpose of an experiment were to compare the effectiveness of two types of training in terms of the proportion who failed to complete the training. In order to improve the generalizability of the findings, the experiment included both male and female subjects. Figure 6 shows a bar chart of the results. Since the main research question is the difference between training conditions, the bars comparing the results for the two conditions are adjacent separately for each gender. This makes it easy to see that the proportion failing was slightly higher for passive training than for active training for both genders. If the main research interest were gender differences, then the hierarchical arrangement would be changed so that the bars for the genders would be adjacent for each training type.

When comparisons between non-adjacent as well as adjacent bars are important, grid lines can be used to facilitate the comparisons. As noted before and shown in Figure 2, grid lines should be light and unobtrusive.

As noted earlier, Cleveland and McGill (1985) found that comparisons are best between positions of elements on a common scale. In practice, this means it is easier to compare values represented by standard bar charts than by stacked bar charts.

Integrating text and graphics.

It is rare for a graph in a scientific journal to contain all the information required to interpret the results properly. Instead, readers are expected to consult the main text to find additional information necessary for understanding and interpreting the results. This additional information could consist of such things as

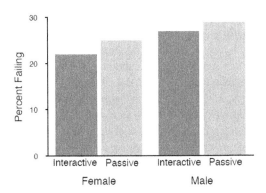

FIGURE 6.   Bar chart making it easy to see the difference between the interactive and passive conditions.

significance tests, confidence intervals, and measures of effect size. Rather than require a reader to consult external text that might even be on another page, a figure could contain the additional information by including text as well as graphics. Indeed, centuries ago, Leonardo da Vinci and Galileo both integrated images, diagrams, and text in their works (Tufte, 2006, p. 83; Wainer, 1997, p. 144). Following Gutenberg's invention of movable type, however, images and text are often separated to expedite the printing process. However, because low-cost high-quality laser printers have been available for over 25 years, this practice of separating figures and text is no longer necessary.

Many experts in the design of statistical graphs have argued that graphs and text should be integrated. For example, Wainer (1997, p. 144) stated that, if possible, figures and text should be integrated to form a single perceptual unit; Few (2004, p. 124) stated that rather than separate text and graphics, they should be blended together; Tufte (2006, p. 83) stated that displays of evidence should bring together verbal, visual, and quantitative information; and Schwabish (2014) stated that integrating text and graphics helps readers understand the content.

The artificial separation of text and graphics violates principles that educational researchers have found that lead to good comprehension and memory. First, it violates the spatial contiguity principle (Mayer, 2005), which states that graphics and explanatory text should be presented in close proximity. Similarly, it violates the split attention principle (Ayres & Sweller, 2005), which states that materials should be integrated physically and temporally so that readers do not have to integrate them mentally. Both Mayer (2005) and Ayres and Sweller (2005) provide summaries of the strong evidence that learning is facilitated by integrating text and graphics.

Although not standard practice, graphs and text are occasionally integrated to some extent. In one recent example, figures with scatterplots also contained textual representations of p and r^2 (Polta et al. (2013).

Figure 7 is an example of integrating text within a graph. The fictitious data are from a Groups (3) x Trials (5) design in which trials is a within-subjects factor. The sources of variation and the probability value of each is shown in the upper left-hand portion of the figure. Notice that the text is positioned so that it does not detract from the perception of the graph and that the text is of lighter weight than the elements of the graph. Although it is conventional to report the F statistic and degrees of freedom in addition to the probability values, this was not done here because it is desirable to keep the space occupied by the text to a minimum. This additional information should be reported in the main body of the article.

Often, detailed statistical information is necessary to fully understand the results. In these cases, it can be valuable to embed a full table within a graph. Figure 8 shows the results of a study of the effect of different types of smiles on the leniency given to an offender. The bottom portion of the figure contains box plots and the upper portion contains a table with inferential statistics important for interpreting the box plots.

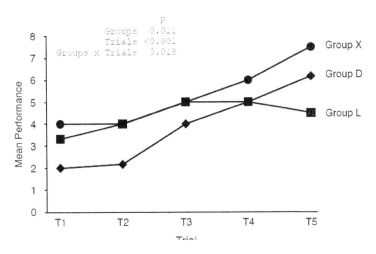

FIGURE 7. An example of integrating text within a graph.

Both Figures 7 and 8 place fewer cognitive demands on the reader than the standard format that separates inferential statistics from the graph and requires the reader to switch back and forth between the main text and the figure in order to interpret the data.

Information other than inferential statistics can also usefully supplement graphs. For example, information about an outlier or influential observation, an event explaining a sudden change in a time series, and a label pointing to an interesting part of the graph are some of the possible contexts in which the use of text in graphs could be valuable.

Making Graphs Informative

More than a quarter century ago, Tufte (1983, p. 92) famously said, "Above all else, show the data." Unfortunately, most graphs in psychology journals show very little data. Wilkinson and the Task Force on Statistical Inference (1999) criticized graphs in psychology for focusing on central tendency to the exclusion of other aspects of the distribution and stated, "Whether from a negative motivation to conceal irregularities or from a positive belief that less is more, omitting shape information from graphics often hinders scientific evaluation." (p. 601).

More recently, Sándor and Lane (2007) surveyed graphs in two leading psychology journals and found that only 10% of them contained distributional information other than measures of central tendency. Even a casual analysis of current journals shows that not much has changed since then. Of the 12 articles in a recent issue of the *Journal of Experimental Psychology: Learning, Memory, and Cognition* (May 2014), every article contained at least one graph showing differences

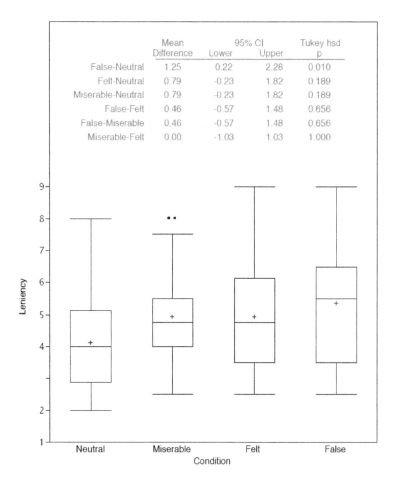

FIGURE 8.   A second example of integrating text within a figure.

between experimental conditions, and none of these graphs showed distributional information other than central tendency. On a positive note, two articles included scatterplots to present the relationships between variables. It is important to note that this issue of a journal was the only one for which I tallied the types of graphs, and therefore these results are not a result of "cherry picking."

Avoid the ubiquitous information-light bar chart of means.

Bar charts have a long history, first used by Joseph Priestly in 1765 who plotted the life spans of famous people and by William Playfair in 1786 who plotted Scottish imports and exports (Wainer, 2005). More recently, bar charts of means have become very popular, with these bar charts comprising more than half of the graphs appearing in the two psychology journals surveyed by Sándor and Lane (2007). The first use of bar charts of means is unclear.

It is important to distinguish bar charts of quantities such as (a) ages of people, (b) monetary values of goods imported each year, (c) percentages, and (d) frequencies from bar charts of means. In the former case, all available values are plotted and no information is obscured. In the latter case, one summary statistic is used to represent all values, thus leaving out information about the shape of the distribution.

Wilkinson et al.'s (1999) argument that omitting information about the shape of a distribution hinders scientific evaluation implies that a bar chart of means is an ineffective way to communicate scientific results. Consistent with this assertion are the views of a growing number of researchers who have argued that bar charts of means should be replaced by other graph types, notably box plots (Krzywinski & Altman, 2014; Lane & Sándor, 2009; Loughin, 2004; Streit & Gehlenborg, 2014).

A typical example of a bar chart is shown in Figure 9. This bar chart is based on data from a demonstration exercise in a statistics class in which times to name a series of colors were recorded for 31 female and 16 male students. This bar chart shows clearly that the mean time for the females was lower than the mean time for the males. However, as is the case with bar charts of means, this graph does not present information about the shapes of the distributions, the possible presence of outliers, or the relative sample sizes.

Figure 10 adds 95% confidence intervals to Figure 9, indicating the uncertainty in the estimation of the population means. These intervals are of limited value, however, because the most important uncertainty is typically the uncertainty about the difference(s) between means and not the uncertainty about the means themselves (Loftus & Masson, 1994). It is too much to expect even a highly sophisticated reader to be able to infer the uncertainty about the difference between means from the uncertainty about individual means. This task is quite difficult even in the simplest case of equal sample sizes and homogeneous variances because even then the reader would have to (a) recall that the standard error of the difference between means is 1.41 times larger than the standard error of the mean, (b) be able to estimate how much lower the relevant value of t would be due to the increased degrees of freedom, and (c) combine this information mentally into a usable form. Unequal sample sizes, multiple tests, and/or unequal variances make this task many times more difficult. Finally, the relationship between error bars and significance tests is poorly understood by the majority of even *authors* of psychology, behavioral neuroscience, and medical journal articles (Belia, Fidler, Williams, & Cumming, 2005). For example, a common misconception is that a difference between means is not significant if the confidence intervals overlap. This is false, as can be seen in the present example in which the difference between means is significant with a probability value of 0.017 even though the 95% confidence intervals overlap.

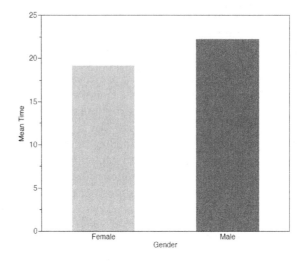

FIGURE 9.   A typical bar chart.

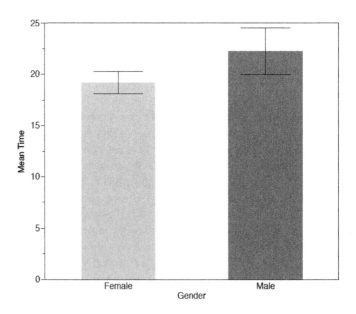

FIGURE 10.   A bar chart with error bars showing 95% confidence intervals.

Wendorf (2012) suggested a method for adjusting the lengths of errors bars so that significance is indicated by whether the error bars overlap. Multiple tests that occur with designs with more than two conditions are taken into consideration by basing adjustments on the Tukey's *HSD* test (Tukey, 1991). The bar chart in Figure 11 uses this error bar method on the same data as the graph in Figure 8. The only nonoverlapping error bars are the neutral and false smile conditions, indicating that only this difference is significant.

Wendorf's (2012) method of creating error bars is a big advance, with his error bars being more informative than error bars based on standard errors of individual means. However, there are still considerations that make it less than a general solution. One is that it is difficult to apply his method to designs with unequal sample sizes and/or unequal variances. These problems are tractable in two-condition designs for which error bars could be based on the Tukey-Kramer test when there are unequal sample sizes or on the Welch test in conjunction with the Bonferroni correction when there are unequal variances (Hayter, 1984). However, there are no clear ways to handle these problems when there are more than two conditions. A second consideration is that a graph that focuses the reader's attention on whether or not differences are significant is likely to encourage readers to interpret the significance tests as all-or-nothing rejections of the null hypothesis, a

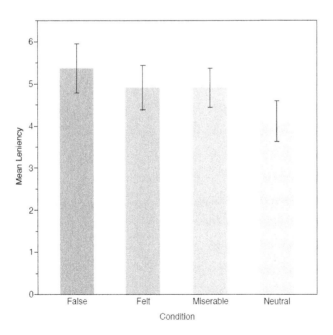

FIGURE 11. A bar chart with modified error bars useful for comparing conditions.

practice that has been frequently and severely criticized (Gelman & Stern, 2006; Loftus, 1993; Tukey, 1991; Wilkinson et al., 1999).

Figures with bar charts that indicate significant differences with asterisks have the same problem. Figure 12 shows bar charts made from fictitious data consisting of 20 subjects from each of four groups. The asterisk indicates that the difference between Condition A and Condition D is significant at the 0.05 level (the unseen p is 0.036). What is not evident from this figure is that the probability value for the difference between Conditions A and C is 0.055, providing a strong hint of a real difference. Interestingly, it is not easy to determine from Figure 12 that the mean for Condition D of 57.10 is higher than the mean of Condition C of 56.57.

A more fundamental problem with using error bars to communicate inferential statistics is that inferential statistics often do not lend themselves naturally to graphical displays. For example, a small numerical difference in probability values such as the difference between 0.01 and 0.02 represents a large difference in the strength of evidence against the null hypothesis. Moreover, as evident from Figure 12, an important difference in probability values is barely perceptible. This further supports the view that values and confidence intervals are types of information that are more effectively shown in text integrated within a figure than represented graphically (Lane & Sándor, 2009).

In summary, the bar chart, a graph type ubiquitous in psychology journals, is deficient in many respects. Most importantly, bar charts do not reveal anything

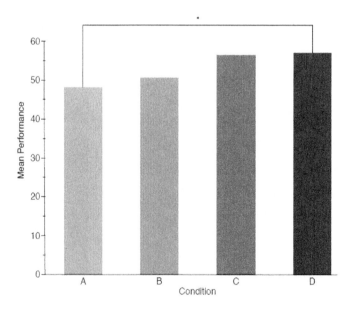

FIGURE 12.   A bar chart indicating a significant difference with an asterisk.

about distributions other than their means. Second, error bars in bar charts do little to aid in the interpretation of the data since, although they represent the uncertainty about individual means clearly, they make it very difficult to assess the uncertainty about differences between means. Similarly, the standard type of error bars does not indicate significant differences in an understandable way. Although the modified error bars suggested by Wendorf (2012) allow readers to determine which conditions are significantly different from each other, these error bars focus on "reject/do not reject" information and therefore are *less* useful than simple textual presentations of the probability values.

Use box plots instead of bar charts.

Box plots described by Tukey (1977) take up about the same amount of space as bar charts but display considerably more information. There are many variations on box plots (for a review, see McGill, Tukey, & Larsen, 1978). Following the principle that the graphs should correspond to the inferential statistics in the main text, a variation of box plots showing means should be used when the inferential statistics in the text pertain to means.

The information conveyed by box plots but not from bar charts can be seen by comparing Figures 12 and 13, which were constructed from the same fictitious data. Both figures show the differences among means clearly. However, Figure 13 also shows that (a) there is an outside value and a far-out value in Condition A and two outside values in Condition D, (b) there is considerably less variability in Condition D than in Conditions B or C, (c) the medians of Conditions A and B differ more than their means, whereas (d) the means of Conditions B and C difference more than their medians. Figure 13 also provides some indications of effect sizes in terms of the overlap between distributions. For example, this figure shows that the median of Condition A is approximately equal to the 25th percentile of Condition B; the lowest value in Condition D is (a) about equal to the 25th percentile of Condition C, (b) higher than the 25th percentile of Condition B, and (c) about equal to the median of Condition B.

A natural concern with box plots is that the distributional information they include is distracting. This concern is legitimate and could lead some researchers to eschew box plots in favor of bar charts. However, in situations such as this, it is normally a better solution to improve the design rather than reduce the information presented. In a classic example of this, Tufte (2006, pp. 116–121) redesigned a scatterplot originally created by Sagan (1977) showing the relationship between animals' body weights and brain weights. In his graph, Sagan included a text label for each point in the graph. This design was criticized by Cleveland (1994), who argued that the labels were distracting and should not have been included. In his redesign, Tufte (2006) replaced the points with small pictographs of animals, thus allowing the species information to be preserved without cluttering the graph as a whole.

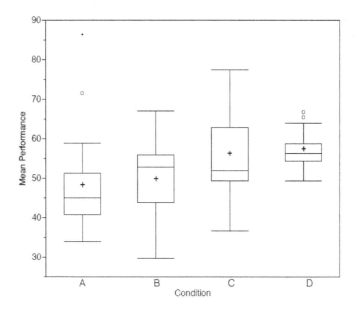

FIGURE 13. Box plots showing distributions of the four conditions.

Figure 14 is a redrawing of Figure 13 designed to emphasize the differences among means and deemphasize the distributional information. In this figure, the differences among means are made salient while retaining the distributional information for interested readers. Alternative versions could emphasize differences among interquartile ranges, as in Figure 15, among medians or even the outside and far-out values.

On some occasions, a researcher may wish to provide more distributional information than is contained in box plots. If there are only two conditions, then a back-to-back stem-and-leaf display, as shown in Figure 16, is a good choice. With three or more conditions, a variation of box plots that contains all the points should be considered (see Figure 17 for an example).

Displaying data with variables controlled.

Many inferential methods involve controlling for extraneous variables. For example, in within-subjects designs, differences among subjects are controlled by including "subjects" as a variable in the analysis. Similarly, in analysis of covariance (ANCOVA), the effect of the covariate is controlled. When a variable is controlled in the inferential statistics, it is important that the variable also be controlled in the distributional information displayed in graphs. Failure to control for these variables in graphs creates a disconnect between the graphs and inferential statistics. In fact, it is common for the disconnect to be so great that readers who

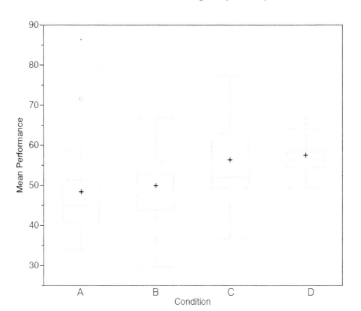

FIGURE 14.   Box plots emphasizing means.

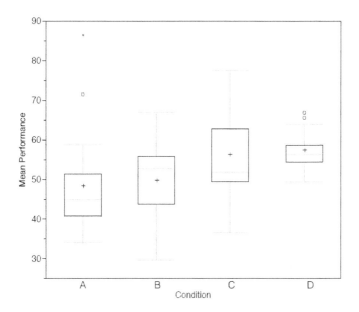

FIGURE 15.   Box plots emphasizing interquartile ranges

Mean = 19.2   Mean = 22.2
Median = 19.0   Median = 22.5

```
              3 0
            9 2
              2 677
           44 2 445
           32 2 23
     11000000 2 01
     999888888 1 99
      7777766 1 77
           54 1 5
```

FIGURE 16.   Back-to-back stem and leaf displays. The means are shown in bold.

view a graph that does not control for the extraneous variable have trouble understanding how a highly significant effect can be significant at all.

Within-subjects designs.

Subjects typically differ greatly from each other and therefore controlling for differences among subjects by using a within-subjects design can increase the power of statistical tests. Graphs of data from within-subjects designs that dis-

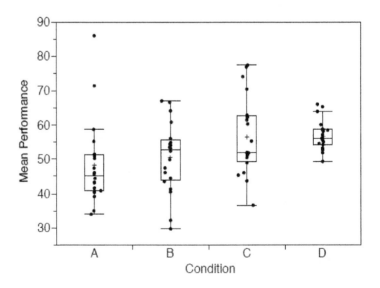

FIGURE 17.   A variation of box plots showing all the points Points are "jiggered" horizontally to prevent overlap.

play distributional data without controlling for between-subject differences make the unexplained (error) variance appear much higher than it is. This is illustrated with fictitious data from a within-subjects design. The covariance matrix in Table 2 shows that both the condition variances (diagonal elements) and covariances between pairs of conditions (off-diagonal elements) are approximately equal. Figures 18 and 19 contain box plots of the three conditions, the former using the raw data and the latter controlling for differences between subjects. The Y-axis scaling is the same for both figures so as to facilitate the comparison between them. Naturally, if only Figure 19 were to be shown, its excess white space would be eliminated.

The means in Figures 18 and 19 are identical, but the variability about the mean is much greater in Figure 18 than Figure 19: the standard deviations for the three treatments are 7.42, 7.75, and 7.58 for the data in Figure 18 but only 3.32, 3.70, and 3.82 for the data in Figure 19. Moreover, the overlap in the distributions is greater in Figure 18 than Figure 19. For example, in Figure 19, the 25th percentile for Treatment 3 is higher than the median of Treatment 1, whereas the reverse is true for Figure 18.

The adjusted box plots were computed with the following two steps: (a) The mean score across the three treatments was computed for each subject and subtracted from the subject's scores in each of the treatments and (b) the mean of all scores was added to every score. These steps remove the effect of subjects from all data.

Knowledge of some of the details of within-subjects ANOVA is necessary in order to understand when the adjusted box plots shown in Figure 19 are appropriate and when they are not. The pattern of variances and covariances for these data approximates what is called "compound symmetry," which occurs when the variances are equal and the covariances are equal. Compound symmetry is a sufficient but not necessary condition for the assumption of sphericity made by within-subjects ANOVA and ensures that the variances of all pairs of differences among treatments are equal. For the example data which do not deviate greatly from compound symmetry, the variances of differences between Treatment 1 and Treatment 2, Treatment 1 and Treatment 3, and Treatment 2 and Treatment 3 are 35.0, 37.5, and 45.5, respectively.

When the variances of differences are approximately the same, as they are here, then adjusted box plots are analogous to box plots in between-subject de-

TABLE 2. Covariance Matrix With Similar Covariances

	T1	T2	T3
T1	55.0	40.0	37.5
T2	40.0	60.0	36.0
T3	37.5	36.0	57.5

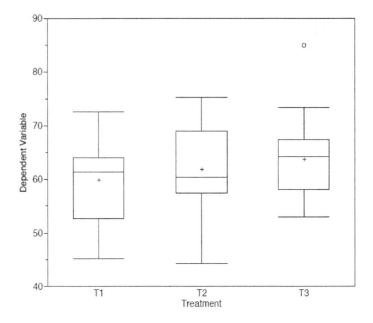

FIGURE 18.   Box plots of the raw data.

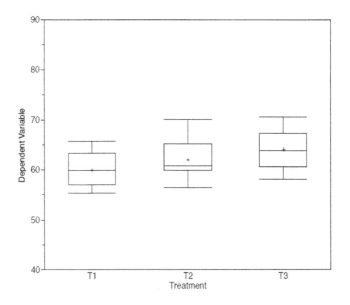

FIGURE 19. Box plots controlling for between-subjects differences.

signs and are readily interpretable. However, when there are large violations of the sphericity assumption, adjusted box plots do not display the fact that some differences between conditions have greater uncertainty than others. When this is the case (as it typically is), it is better to create a box plot of difference scores for each pairwise comparison between conditions.

Table 3 shows the covariance matrix for a different fictitious dataset. Although the variances are about the same, the covariances are very different. This causes the variances of the differences to vary greatly as well, with the variances of differences between Treatment 1 and Treatment 2, Treatment 1 and Treatment 3, and Treatment 2 and Treatment 3 being 21, 60, and 66, respectively.

Figure 20 shows box plots of the three sets of difference scores among three conditions. This graph more accurately represents the variability and is consistent with the inferential statistics that would normally be based on these difference scores. Notice that the variability differs greatly depending on the difference scores involved. This explains the apparent paradox that the mean difference between Treatment 3 and Treatment 1 is larger than the mean difference between Treatment 2 and Treatment 1, even though the probability value is higher for the former comparison than for the latter. Notice that unlike other box plots presented in this chapter, these box plots contain confidence intervals. Confidence intervals are informative in this graph because the comparisons among conditions are implicit in the difference-score variables. Moreover, if the confidence intervals do not include zero, then the difference is significant at the 0.05 level. It is important to present the individual means as well as differences between means, so it would be worthwhile to display them in addition to the difference scores. This is one of the rare cases in which a bar chart of means with error bars would be a good graph to include. Ironically, the fact that a bar chart hides distributional information is an advantage here since the distributions of raw scores do not reflect the distributions or difference scores and consequently are poorly aligned with the inferential statistics. Note, however, that it would be *extremely* misleading to put error bars around the raw-score means.

The approach of displaying box plots for all pairwise combinations of conditions becomes unwieldy as the number of conditions increases. Perhaps the best that can be done is to limit the number of pairwise comparisons displayed to the most important.

TABLE 3. Covariance Matrix With Different Covariances

	T1	T2	T3
T1	33.0	24.0	6.0
T2	24.0	36.0	4.5
T3	6.0	4.5	39.0

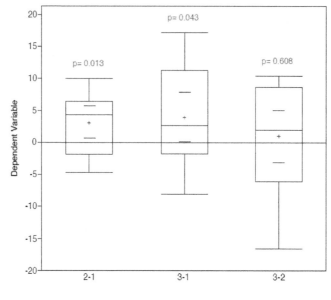

Treatment Differences

FIGURE 20.   Box plots difference scores. The short lines within the boxes are the limits of the 95% confidence intervals.

Designs with both between-subject and within-subject variables have added complexity. A reasonable approach is to create graphs as constructed for within-subjects designs for each level of a between-subjects variable. The ordering of the box plots should depend on the effects that are to be emphasized. In complex designs, a subset of these graphs would have to suffice.

Loftus and Masson (1994) presented a method for constructing and displaying confidence intervals in within-subjects designs that controls for differences between subjects. In essence, they recommend using the pooled error term from the ANOVA to compute the interval. This is a big advance over confidence intervals based on between-subjects variance typical at that time. However, one drawback to their method is that their confidence intervals are all on individual means and their assertion that "confidence in patterns of means (of which the difference between two means is a basic unit) can be judged based on the confidence intervals plotted around the individual sample means" (Loftus & Mason, 1994; p. 5) may be too optimistic in practice, if not in theory (Belia et al., 2005). Additionally, Loftus and Masson (1994) recognized that the pooled error term may be very different from the appropriate error term for any specific comparison as it is for the data shown in Figure 20. Loftus and Masson discussed several possible approaches to this problem. None, however, is simple and straightforward enough to contradict the view that confidence intervals are usually better represented textually than graphically.

Analysis of covariance (ANCOVA).

Just as within-subjects ANOVA controls for the variance due to differences among subjects, ANCOVA controls for variance due to extraneous variable(s). Also, as in within-subjects designs, variance due to these extraneous variable(s) should be removed from graphs.

Figure 21 shows box plots of the performance of two groups on a spreadsheet task. Performance is shown controlling for a measure of cognitive ability used as a covariate. This box plot was constructed by first saving the residuals from the ANCOVA. Since the means of both groups on the residuals are zero, the group means have to be added to the original scores before creating the graph. This is done by adding the adjusted means (sometimes called "least squares means" or "estimated marginal means") for each group to every score in the group. These data are then used for the box plots. This procedure ensures that the covariate is controlled for with respect to the differences between means and the differences among subjects within the groups.

Multiple regression.

In simple regression, a scatterplot showing the regression line is an excellent way to portray the relationship between two variables. The situation is a bit more complex in multiple regression since the regression coefficients represent partial slopes, meaning they are the slope of the relationship between the part of a predictor variable that is independent of all other predictor variables with Y. Therefore, to portray the relations between a predictor variable and Y that corresponds to the multiple regression equation, the part of the predictor that is independent of the other predictor variables should be on the X-axis.

Consider a study evaluating the prediction of College GPA on the basis of High School GPA and SAT. The regression equation is College GPA' = (0.541)(High School GPA) + (0.0008)(SAT) + 0.540.

The graph in Figure 22 is misleading since the variable on the X-axis does not have High School GPA controlled. Figure 23 is a better way to display the relationship since in Figure 23 the variable on the X-axis, SAT.HSGPA, controls for High School GPA. It was created by predicting SAT from HSGPA and saving the residuals. Notice how much weaker the relationship is in Figure 23 than it is in Figure 22.

Displaying trends.

Line graphs are excellent for displaying trends and should be used when the X-axis is an ordered variable. In fact, the propensity of observers to interpret line graphs as trends is so strong that some interpret a line graph with a qualitative independent variable as showing a trend. For example, Zacks and Tversky (1999)

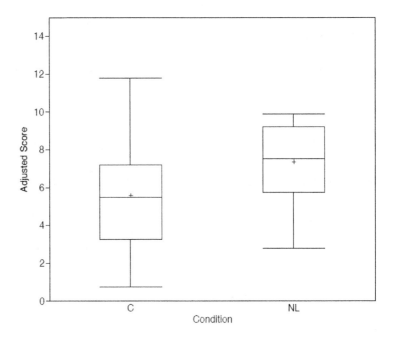

FIGURE 21. Box plots with the effects of the covariates removed.

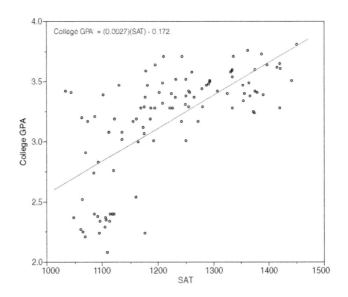

FIGURE 22. The regrssion of college GPA on SAT.

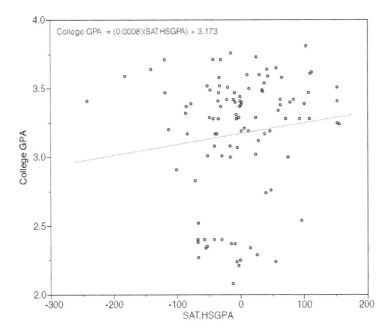

FIGURE 23. The regrssion of college GPA on the part of SAT that is independent of high school GPA.

found that several observers interpreted a line graph with the values "male" and "female" on the X-axis and height on the Y-axis as showing that the more male a person is, the taller he or she is.

When the variable on the X-axis is a within-subjects variable, care must be taken to ensure that a graph of the distribution controls for differences among subjects. This can be done by plotting contrasts among the levels of the within-subjects variable.

As an example, Figure 24 is a good way to display data from an experiment concerned primarily with whether the learning curve is steeper for some groups than others. The box plots in Figure 24 were created by computing the linear component of trend for each subject using the formula: Linear Component = (-2) (T1) - T2 + T3 + (2)(T4) and then creating box plots of these linear components for the three groups.

Alternatively, box plots of pairwise differences might be a better choice, depending on the context. For example, if the dosage of a drug were on the X-axis, then the variability of the differences between adjacent doses would be particularly relevant to determining whether there is evidence for an increased effect with an increase to the next level of the dose.

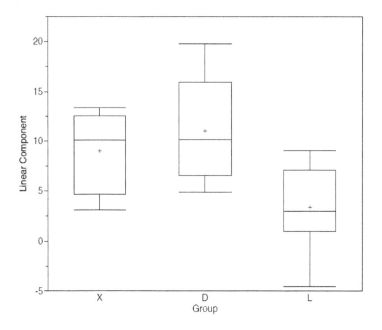

FIGURE 24. Box plots of the linear component of trend.

It is challenging to show trends and distributional data at the same time since, with two or more lines, any additional information would be very distracting. Therefore, it is normally better to make separate graphs, a line graph such as the one in Figure 7, and box plots of a contrast such as those in Figure 24. These two graphs could be combined in one figure or placed in separate figures.

Graphs such as the line graph in Figure 7 should not include error bars based on between-subjects variance. As with bar charts, these error bars can overestimate the variability and uncertainty about the effects and be inconsistent with the inferential statistics. Moreover, the distraction from error bars in line graphs is much worse than in bar charts because the error bars can overlap and cause considerable clutter that interferes with the perception of the trends, although this can be ameliorated somewhat by offsetting the points. Unfortunately, line graphs such as this occur very frequently in psychology journals.

SUMMARY

Table 4 summarizes the principles discussed in this chapter to facilitate the design of graphs that are easy to perceive, make few cognitive demands on the observer, and are highly informative.

As Table 4 shows, there can be trade-offs among these goals. For example, the easiest way to reduce the cognitive demands of a graph is to convey very little information. Naturally, it is the task of the graph designer to take these tradeoffs into account when designing a graph.

The recommendations in Table 4 are followed in the design of scientific graphs to greater and lesser extents. Therefore, it may be valuable to focus on the instances in which the recommendations are most at odds with standard practice. One such recommendation is to label graphical elements directly rather than using legends. Perhaps because of the manner in which statistical software creates graphs, the vast majority of published graphs use legends. Granted, there are times when legends are necessary, but the use of legends when they are not necessary is widespread.

In spite of the fact that there is strong evidence that integrating graphics and text reduces cognitive demand (Ayres & Sweller, 2005; Mayer, 2005) and leading experts in designing graphs recommend integrating graphics and text (Schwabish, 2014; Tufte, 2006; Wainer, 1997), rarely does one see a figure that integrates graphics and text. Presumably, this is due to the tradition of separating graphs and text that dates back to the invention of the printing press.

TABLE 4. Summary of Design Principles

Design Principle	Ease of Perception	Cognitive Demand	Informational value	Comment
Contrast should be high.	Increases the clarity of the foreground information.	Less effort is required to extract information.		It is not necessary to have a black foreground and a white background.
Avoid grid lines.	Reduces clutter.	Less effort required to extract information.		Exception: Use light grid lines to facilitate noncontiguous comparisons.
Reduce clutter.	Makes it easier to perceive the relevant information.	Less effort required to locate and assess relevant information.	Displaying large amounts of information may require some clutter.	Avoid redundant information and use principles of grouping to reduce clutter.
Related items should be perceptually grouped.	Makes perception easier because the number of groups is reduced .	Perceptually grouped information is easier to process.		Legends should be avoid if possible.
Elements should be sufficiently large.	Improves perception of elements.	Less processing is required for easily perceived elements.	Maintaining high readability may limit the amount of information that can be displayed.	The choice between serif and sans serif fonts is less important than the choice of font size. *(continued)*

TABLE 4. Continued

Design Principle	Ease of Perception	Cognitive Demand	Informational value	Comment
Quantitative data are best represented by positions along a common scale.	Applying this principle makes perception of differences easier.	Applying this principle reduces cognitive demand.		It is better to represent differences using grouped rather than stacked bar charts.
Color should not be used to represent a quantitative dimension.	Perception of the dimension is difficult because color is not perceived as an ordered dimension.	Cognitive demand is high.	It is difficult to represent many values accurately with color.	Color is effective for showing the sign of the value when saturation or darkness is used to represent the value itself.
The primary message should be perceptually salient.	Perception is easier.	Cognitive demand is lower.	There can be a trade-off such that including large amounts of information can reduce the salience of the primary message.	Graphs should be used to display the most important information. Additional information can be shown in a table.
Avoid using legends.	Perception is facilitated if labels are grouped with their relevant element.	Perception is reduced if labels are grouped with their relevant element.		If legends cannot be avoided, they should not be so salient that they compete for attention with the graph itself.
Visual and semantic elements should be consistently mapped.		Consistency reduces cognitive demands.		Graphs should be consistent in the scaling of the dependent variables.
Graphs should be consistent with the inferential statistics.		Cognitive demand is high if the graph appears to be inconsistent with the inferential statistics.		The most common inconsistency is to base error bars on between-subjects error and inferential statistics on within-subjects error.
Elements to be compared should be contiguous if possible.	Contiguity facilitates the perception of any difference.	Cognitive demand is lower.		Grid lines can facilitate noncontiguous comparisons.

TABLE 4. Continued

Design Principle	Ease of Perception	Cognitive Demand	Informational value	Comment
Text and graphics should be integrated.	If done judiciously, this should not decrease ease of perception.	Cognitive demand is much lower if the various kinds of information are integrated.	Graphs that include text can be much more informative.	Text should be positioned so it does not interfere with the perception of the graph and should be light so it does not attract too much attention.
Avoid bar charts of means.			Alternatives such as box plots are much more informative.	Although graphs with bar charts of means are standard practice, they are "data poor."
If you do include bar charts of means, error bars should normally not be included.	Ease of perception is increased.	Cognitive demands are lower, especially if the inferential statistics are presented as text.	Although error bars appear to be informative, they are relevant only to individual means rather than differences between means.	Errors bars are informative for difference scores because the mean difference score is usually the statistic of interest.
Show distributional data in addition to measures of central tendency.	The displays may be harder to perceive than displays showing only means.	Cognitive demands are higher.	It is very important to include distributional information.	Box plots, stem and leaf displays, histograms, dot plots, and scatterplots are among the recommended ways to show distributional information.
In designs with variable(s) controlled statistically, displays of distributions should show observations with variables controlled.			The graph will more accurately represent distributional data and therefore be more informative.	In within-subjects ANOVA, the variable controlled is "subjects."
For graphs of trend, it is desirable to have separate line graphs and box plots.	The line graph makes the trends stand out.		The box plots contain distributional data.	The two types of graphs could be included in the same figure.

Finally, despite the strong argument made by Wilkinson et al.'s (1999) that distributional information is critical for the evaluation of scientific data, by far the most common graph is a bar chart of means. These graphs provide very little data and are almost always inferior to box plots. Moreover, these graphs violate the most basic tenet of creating good graphs summed up by Tufte (1983, p. 92): "Above all else, show the data."

REFERENCES

Ayres, P., & Sweller, J. (2005). The split-attention principle in multimedia learning. In R. E. Mayer (Ed.), *The Cambridge handbook of multimedia learning* (pp. 135–146). Cambridge, MA: Cambridge University Press.

Belia, S., Fidler, F., Williams, J., & Cumming, G. (2005). Researchers misunderstand confidence intervals and standard error bars. *Psychological Methods, 10*, 389–396.

Borland, D., & Taylor II, R. M. (2007) Rainbow color map (still) considered harmful. *IEEE Computer Graphics and Applications, 27*, 14–17.

Canham, M., & Hegarty, M. (2010). Effects of knowledge and display design on comprehension of complex graphics. *Learning and instruction, 20*, 155–166.

Cleveland, W. S. (1994). *The elements of graphing data.* Murray Hill, NJ: AT&T Bell Laboratories.

Cleveland, W. S., & McGill, R. (1985). Graphical perception and graphical methods for analyzing scientific data. *Science, 229*, 828–833.

Few, S. (2004). *Show me the numbers: Designing tables and graphs to enlighten* (Vol. 1, No. 1). Oakland, CA: Analytics.

Few, S. (2008). Practical rules for using color in charts. *Visual Business Intelligence Newsletter*, (11).

Gelman, A., & Stern, H. (2006). The difference between "significant" and "not significant" is not itself statistically significant. *American Statistician, 60*, 328–331.

Gillan, D. J., & Sorensen, D. (2009, October). Minimalism and the syntax of graphs: II. Effects of graph backgrounds on visual search. In *Proceedings of the Human Factors and Ergonomics Society annual meeting* (Vol. 53, No. 17, pp. 1096–1100). Sage.

Hayter, A. J. (1984) A proof of the conjecture that the Tukey-Kramer multiple comparison procedure is conservative. *The Annals of Statistics*, 61–75.

Kohr, R. L., & Games, P. A. (1974). Robustness of the analysis of variance, the Welch procedure and a Box procedure to heterogeneous variances. *The Journal of Experimental Education, 43*, 61-69.

Kosslyn, S. M. (2006). *Graph design for the eye and mind.* Oxford, UK: Oxford University Press.

Krzywinski, M., & Altman, N. (2014). Points of significance: Visualizing samples with Loftus, G. R. (1993). A picture is worth 1000 p-values—On the irrelevance of hypothesis-testing in the microcomputer age. *Behavior Research Methods, Instruments & Computers, 25*, 250–256.

Lane, D. M., & Sándor, A. (2009). Designing better graphs by including distributional information and integrating words, numbers, and images. *Psychological Methods, 14*, 239–257.

Loftus, G. R., & Masson, M. E. J. (1994). Using confidence intervals in within-subject designs. *Psychonomic Bulletin & Review, 1*, 476–490.

Loughin, T. M. (2004, April 15) *Sensible graphics for presentations and papers, invited talk, division of biology.* K-State Ecology Research Group, Kansas State University, Manhattan.

Mayer, R. E. (2005). Principles for reducing extraneous processing in multimedia learning: Coherence, signaling, redundancy, spatial contiguity, and temporal contiguity principles. *Cambridge Handbook of Multimedia Learning*, 183–200.

McGill, R., Tukey, J. W., & Larsen, W. A. (1978). Variations of box plots. *The American Statistician, 32*, 12–16.

Moreland, K. (2009). Diverging color maps for scientific visualization. In G. Bebis et al. (Eds.), *Advances in visual computing* (pp. 92–103). Berlin/Heidelberg, Germany: Springer.

Moret-Tatay, C., & Perea, M. (2011). Do serifs provide an advantage in the recognition of written words? *Journal of Cognitive Psychology, 23*, 619–624.

Polta, S. A., Fenzl, T., Jakubcakova, V., Kimura, M., Yassouridis, A., & Wotjak, C. T. (2013). Prognostic and symptomatic aspects of rapid eye movement sleep in a mouse model of posttraumatic stress disorder. *Frontiers in Behavioral Neuroscience, 7.*

Sagan, C. (1977). The dragons of Eden: Speculations on the evolution of human intelligence. New York, NY: Random House.

Sándor, A., & Lane, D. (2007, May) *Graph use in psychology journals.* Poster presented at the annual conference of the Houston Chapter of the Human Factors and Ergonomics Society, Houston, TX.

Schwabish, J. A. (2014). An economist's guide to visualizing data. *The Journal of Economic Perspectives, 28*, 209–233.

Stevens, S. S. (1957). On the psychophysical law. *Psychological Review, 64*, 153–181.

Streit, M., & Gehlenborg, N. (2014). Points of view: Bar charts and box plots. *Nature Methods, 11*, 117–117.

Tufte, E. R. (1983). *The visual display of quantitative information.* Cheshire, CT: Graphics.

Tufte, E. R. (2006). *Beautiful evidence.* Cheshire, CT: Graphics.

Tukey, J. W. (1977). *Exploratory data analysis.* Reading, MA: Addison-Wesley.

Tukey, J. W. (1991). The philosophy of multiple comparisons. *Statistical Science, 6*, 100–116.

Wainer, H. (1997). *Visual revelations.* New York, NY: Springer-Verlag.

Wainer, H. (2005). *Graphic discovery: A trout in the milk and other visual adventures.* Princeton: Princeton University Press.

Wendorf, C. A. (2012). Drawing inferences from multiple intervals in the single-factor design: Derivations, clarifications, extensions, and representations. *Methodology: European Journal of Research Methods for the Behavioral and Social Sciences, 8*, 125.

Wilkinson, L., & the Task Force on Statistical Inference. (1999). Statistical methods in psychology journals. Guidelines and explanations. *American Psychologist, 54*, 594–604.

Zacks, J., & Tversky, B. (1999). Bars and lines: A study of graphic communication. *Memory & Cognition, 27*, 1073–1079.

CHAPTER 4

EXAMINING THE TYPE, FREQUENCY, AND INTERPRETATIVE COMPLEXITY OF VISUAL DISPLAYS APPEARING IN THE *JOURNAL OF EDUCATIONAL PSYCHOLOGY*, 2010–2014

Gregory Schraw and Antonio P. Gutierrez

ABSTRACT

We conducted a content analysis of research articles appearing in the *Journal of Educational Psychology* (JEP) between 2010 and 2014 to identify the type and frequency of different types of visual displays (VDs) used to report research findings. We developed a data-driven typology based on an iterative analysis of research articles in JEP, which enabled us to categorize each type of display into a single visual display category and assess its information processing complexity. We also devel-

Use of Visual Displays in Research and Testing: Coding, Interpreting, and Reporting Data
pages 83–108.

oped scoring rubrics and guidelines based on previous content analyses of textbooks and journals. We posed five research questions, including how many articles were analyzed; how many displays appeared in each article; how frequent was each type of display; what was the distribution of interpretative complexity scores for each type of display; and how were article length, amount of information in displays, and interpretative complexity related? We discussed three main results related to the variety, complexity, and cognitive processing demands of visual displays, and concluded with suggestions for training individuals to use visual displays.

Visual displays (VDs) have been defined generically as graphic representations of information communicated to learners (Schraw, McCrudden, & Robinson, 2013). Previous research suggests that visual displays increase learning in several ways, especially with respect to helping individuals to select the most essential information to study and to identify comparisons between important concepts and to reveal implicit processes such as indirect causal relationships (Dansereau & Simpson, 2009; Schnotz, 2002). Visual displays also may enhance deeper conceptual processing by providing explicit external representations of complex systems that correspond to internal mental models (Abrami et al., 2008; DeSimone, 2007; Mayer, Mathias, & Wetzell, 2002; Richardson & Ball, 2009).

The purpose of this chapter is to develop a typology of visual displays and associated scoring rubrics that can be used to evaluate the type and complexity of displays that appear in research journals. We have three specific goals. One is to summarize and compare existing typologies of visual displays for the reader. A second is to develop a typology that can be used to categorize a variety of visual displays that appear in quantitative research journals. A third is to illustrate an application of this typology using a cross-sectional sample of research articles from the *Journal of Educational Psychology* (JEP) and report descriptive findings about the representation of data and analyses. These goals are important to promoting a better understanding of the information processing demands and instructional strategies that are needed to prepare individuals to become fluent in understanding complex visual information (Glazer, 2011; Mayer, 2013; Richardson & Ball, 2009; Yeh & Cheng, 2010).

This chapter is divided into eight sections. This section provides the purpose and main goals of the chapter. Section two summarizes previous research on visual displays. Section three describes the current study in greater detail, especially the development of the typology and scoring rubrics used in the study, as well as the content analysis process we used to evaluate the research articles. The fourth section describes the methods we used to conduct the study by applying the typology to research articles from JEP, while section five summarizes five research questions and the results of our analyses. Section six discusses the implications of our findings. Section seven considers instructional implications, while section eight makes suggestions for future research.

FINDINGS FROM PREVIOUS RESEARCH

There is surprisingly little research on the design and use of visual displays, given their ubiquity in textbooks, journals, and popular magazines (Schraw et al., 2013). Most of the research that exists has examined different types of note-taking formats (e.g., linear vs. matrix) or text signaling such as highlighting, headings, italics, and bolding (Crooks & Cheon, 2013; Lorch, Lemarié, & Grant, 2011). Other types of displays such as geographical maps, hierarchical structures, and causal diagrams are especially underresearched given their prevalence and importance. Still other kinds of displays such as trend graphs, distribution plots, and statistical charts in general have received virtually no research. This is unfortunate because these types of displays are used frequently in everyday settings (e.g., magazines, digital media), as well as technical manuals and professional journals, and usually require interpretation strategies that are not taught explicitly to students (Catley & Novick, 2008; Yeh & Cheng, 2010).

Recognizing the frequency and complexity of displays in professional journals is essential to understanding how to teach students and other users how to use them effectively. Left to their own interpretative devices, even college students experience trouble understanding and interpreting visual displays (Catley & Novick, 2008; Glazer, 2001; Poliquin & Schraw, 2013; Slough, McTigue, Kim & Jennings, 2010). Research indicates that students of all ages, including college students, experience difficulty using displays. One reason is that half of the graphics included in textbooks are either decorative or unrelated semantically to the text itself (Slough, McTigue, Kim, & Jennings, 2010). Fortunately, even simple instructional interventions that take less than one hour appear to improve learning because it helps students understand both the individual components of visual displays, as well as how to interpret their overall meaning (Mautone & Mayer, 2007; Schwonke, Berthold, & Renkl, 2009).

Instructional studies have reported four generalizable findings. One is that the use of visual displays in contextually supportive learning environments yield consistent gains for both surface and deeper learning (Abrami et al., 2008; DeSimone, 2007; Liben, 2009; McCrudden, Magliano, & Schraw, 2011; Schwonke et al., 2009; Shah & Hoeffner, 2002; van der Meer, 2012). Surface learning might include recall of facts, important concepts, or terminology used in the display or an accompanying text; whereas deeper learning would promote understanding of the integrated conceptual structure of the information, as well as the ability to make inferences through the use of that information to other settings. Although displays appear to improve all types of learning, they may be more helpful for understanding deeper learning compared to surface learning. For example, Poliquin and Schraw (2013) found that students who were trained briefly to interpret multiple-cause, single-effect causal diagrams were better able to reproduce the diagrams and explain the role of direct and indirect effects of causes on the effect.

A second finding is that experts in a domain use visual displays more effectively than novices, due in part to greater prior knowledge (Gegenfurtner & Seppänen, 2013; Schwartz, Verdi, Morris, Lee, & Larson, 2007), even when the latter receive instructional training. Specifically, experts engage in two sophisticated interpretative activities that help them construct a deep understanding of the information. One activity is constructing an integrated mental model to test assumptions about the phenomenon of interest. A second activity is making inferences about what the information in the display means within the broader context of the domain of knowledge they are attempting to model (Roth & Bowen, 2001). These two general skills (i.e., *mental model construction* and *inference generation*) can be mapped to the four more narrowly defined cognitive processes of decoding, translating, interpreting, and evaluating displays (Schönborn & Anderson, 2010).

A third finding is that learners need to be taught how and why to use different types of visual representations. Few studies have reported training students of any age. However, studies that have included some type of training intervention have consistently reported better student understanding than those that did not. This includes a variety of visual displays such as computer note-taking organizers (Crooks & Cheon, 2013), concept maps (Kwon & Cifuentes, 2011; Nesbit & Adesope, 2013), use of text signals and connectives (Cain & Nash, 2011; Lorch et al., 2011), using causal diagrams to understand causal processes described in a text (McCrudden, Schraw, Lehman & Poliquin, 2007; Poliquin & Schraw, 2013), understanding maps (Kastens & Liben, 2007; Rosanno & Morrison, 1996) and tree diagrams (Schwonke et al. 2009). In general, these studies relied on two instructional principles. One was for an instructor to provide an overview of the structure and interpretation of information in the visual display using worked examples (Schwonke et al., 2009). Students who received such instruction performed better than those who did not receive instruction. The second was for students to construct their own interpretation of the display's meaning through self-explanation and small-group collaboration as they attempted to understand it (Kastens & Liben, 2007). Students who self-explained in small groups performed better than those who worked alone; however, self-explanation in either groups or individually substantially decreased representational and interpretative errors (Liben, 2009).

A fourth finding is that some types of displays are more effective than others for communicating specific types of information, although the type of information to be learned and the learning context may determine the effectiveness of different displays. There appear to be three principal constraints on display effectiveness. One is the coherence of the information in the visual display (Smith, Best, Stubbs, Archibald, & Roberson-Nay, 2002; Tufte, 2001). Information is coherent when it is parsimonious, important, well-organized, and displayed in an integrated format that communicates the intended interpretation of the information. The extent to which a visual display is not coherent, individuals fail to understand or even misinterpret information (Carter, 2003; Lane & Sándor, 2009; Shah & Hoeffner, 2002; Smith et al., 2002; Vekiri, 2002). A second constraint is the relevance of the display format to type of communicative argument. For example, causal diagrams are ideally suited to convey causality among a set of variables in a way that matrix notes, data tables, or maps are not. Matching the type of display to the type of intended information is crucial. A third constraint is the relevance of to-be-learned information to the learning task. For example, Hegarty, Canham, and Fabrikant (2010) found that learning-relevant information was remembered better when it was made more visually salient in the display because salient information tends to guide the learners eyes (and mind) to the most essential information. Hegarty et al. referred to this phenomenon as *visual guidance.*

Collectively, these findings suggest that visual displays provide helpful adjunct information to learners that promotes deeper learning and conceptual understanding *provided* that learners possess relevant prior knowledge, are familiar with the type of displays used to augment learning, and are asked to construct an integrated synthesis of the information alone or in small groups. Moreover, the information in displays often yields value-added conceptual information that is not included in the text. When using unfamiliar displays, instruction and practice helps individuals use and understand displays more effectively. Self-explanation and explanation from an expert about interpretative strategies appears to be especially beneficial.

THE PRESENT STUDY

The goal of this study was to develop a data-driven classification typology that could be used to then illustrate how a content analysis of visual displays could be performed. Articles from the 2010–2014 volumes of JEP were selected for use in the study. All of these articles appeared under the same editor. The purpose of the content analysis was to assess the relative frequency of different types of visual displays to better understand the type and complexity of displays that appear in a top-tier research journal. This information is useful from an instructional perspective because it provides a better understanding of the type and complexity of displays in the research literature; thus, consumers of this research can better prepare to interpret different types of displays. In addition, a content analysis of visual displays provides valuable information for graduate programs when training doctoral students to become savvy consumers of research. Although we focused on one research journal, we anticipate that these tools (i.e., a typology of displays and scoring rubrics) can be used or adapted by researchers in other disciplines. Comparing results across journals within a discipline, as well as comparing results between disciplines would provide a more comprehensive picture of different types of displays, their complexity, and how instructional interventions could be designed to ameliorate poor display comprehension skills.

We used JEP in this study as a starting point because it includes high-level research on a wide variety of educational topics, often using very sophisticated statistics. Of course, other research journals in education may differ from JEP in terms of topic coverage and statistical sophistication. We recognize that a comparison of these journals is essential as well. However, we chose to begin our empirical analysis of visual displays in education with a journal that was experimental in nature, yielded 50 articles or more per year, and was likely to include a wide array of visual displays. Ultimately, we expected the content analysis tools developed in our study to generalize closely to a similar content analysis using different journals.

Overview of the Content Analysis Process

We conducted our analysis in four discrete steps. The first was to conduct a preliminary analysis of articles to ascertain what types of displays were included. We noted each display separately and then combined similar displays that served the same general interpretative function (e.g., summarize data, show trends, provide an integrated structure model that links variables in complex ways) into a single category (see Table 1). For example, we combined displays that showed trend lines, regression lines, time series, growth curves or statistical interactions into a single category labeled *trends* because the main purpose was to show change over time in performance or a treatment interaction across one or more groups.

Step two was to create a data-driven typology based on the preliminary analysis that enabled us to categorize each visual display that appeared in the journal. By data-driven, we refer to a typology that was not constructed *a priori* based on a theoretical expectation but rather was based solely on the type of displays that appeared in the journal to serve a specific practical purpose. To do so, the authors randomly sampled 10 articles each that included a variety of VDs. We noted different types of displays and categorized these in to the 14 categories used here. We then selected another sample of 10 different articles per author to determine whether the emerging typology accommodated all of the displays. We also conducted a third round without adding to the 14 categories. We then analyzed all of the articles fused in this study without adding any additional categories. Although our analysis yielded an exhaustive typology in the context of categorizing displays in JEP during the selected time frame, we do not assume it is exhaustive in other contexts, as supported by the brief summary of previous typologies presented below.

Step three was to create scoring criteria that enabled us to denote three aspects of information in the visual display, including the *type of display*, the *amount of information*, and the *interpretative complexity* of the display. We selected these four aspects based on a review of previous content analyses of visual displays in science textbooks. We describe these dimensions in detail in the *constructing the present typology* section below.

Step four was to construct a scoring rubric to assess the interpretative complexity of the visual display. The purpose of this multidimensional rubric was to capture the overall complexity of the display, drawing on previous work in the areas of cognitive load and depth of processing theories. The authors used an iterative process to construct a rubric that was simple, descriptive, could be applied reliably, and broad enough to capture the full range of informational complexity.

TABLE 1. Summary of the Definition, Purpose, and Examples of Different Types of Visual Displays

Type of Display	Display code	Definition	Instructional Purpose	Examples
Data Table	1	Array of numeric values for variables across conditions.	Summarize numeric data.	Descriptive statistics, frequencies, p values.
Text Table	2	Array (e.g., matrix) of text samples used as research materials or measurement products.	Summarize text information or present illustrative examples of text materials.	Appendices of experimental materials; instructions; scoring criteria; instructions. Summary matrix.
Equations and formulas	3	List or explanation of formulas used for computations.	Justification of computations. Replication of analytic procedures.	Appended formulas for HLM analyses. Computational formulas for derived scores.
Theoretical or conceptual model	4	Representation of a process or hypothesized model of relationship among variables.	Show an integrated framework, hypothesis or conceptual model that guides theory and research.	Hypothesized SEM model; logic model.
Structural and causal models	5	Node-link representations that relate variables to one another via weighted paths based on a hypothesized causal relationship.	Show directional or causal relationships between variables.	SEM models; regression-based causal models.
Networks	6	Node-link representations that connect concept nodes to one another via links labeled relationships.	Condense, reorganize, and elaborate on information to create an integrated conceptual understanding.	Concept map, knowledge, spider, and definition maps.
Sequences	7	Relationships among ordered events over time.	Model a system's events over time. Show directional relationships between variables.	Timelines. Flowcharts. Argument and influence maps.
Hierarchies; multilevel models	8	Ordered categorical relationships among concepts or ordered pathways between one event and another.	Classify objects. Show ordered inclusion in a taxonomy. Partition a set of events. Model a chain of ordered events.	Classification trees (vertical or horizontal). Dendrograms. Cladograms. HLMs.
Distributions	9	Show the shape, density, or variability in data.	Understand the statistical properties of distributions. Describe data. Illustrate density functions.	Distributions (e.g., IRT, Rausch). Scatterplots. Wright table. Proportions within categories.

(continues)

TABLE 1. Continued

Type of Display	Display code	Definition	Instructional Purpose	Examples
Trends	10	Show changes and trends in data across time or experimental conditions.	Illustrate changes in performance and trends over time, especially those attributable to an intervention.	Trend lines. Regression lines. Times series. Growth trajectories. Statistical interactions.
Maps and spatial proximity	11	Relationships among objects within a coordinate system, spatial contiguity, similarity, or proximity between two or more objects.	Model physical environments using scaled representations. Show scaled relationship or distance between variables.	Geographical and topological maps. Multidimensional scaling. Cluster analysis.
Graphs, diagrams, plots, charts	12	Frequency and relationship between data in different categories. Show overlap between categories.	Provide descriptive information about dataset across multiple groups or categories.	Bar graph, pie diagram, box & whisker, Venn diagrams; caterpillar and density plots.
Images: picture; screenshot; illustration	13	Static images typically used to show experimental instructions or materials.	Provide examples of what participants viewed during the study.	Photos; screenshots; illustrative work products.
Complex hybrids	14	Any combination of display categories 1 through 13.		Text accompanied by illustrations and formulas. Work products with annotated scoring.

Previous Content Analyses

Our content analysis was guided in part by three previous studies that examined the type of visual displays used in science textbooks. The first study conducted a categorization of ancestral and evolutionary tree diagrams (i.e., cladograms; Catley & Novick, 2008). They surveyed 31 middle and high school science textbooks over the last 20 years. Diagrams first were coded into five mutually exclusive categories that distinguished between the linking systems used in the diagrams. Diagrams were scored to identify the presence or absence of three different branching formats. In addition, diagrams were scored for the presence or absence of seven different properties such as delineation of time, labeling of the root node, and branch thickness. Surprisingly, Catley and Novick (2008) reported that none of the textbooks attempted to explain the diagrams or teach students how to use them.

The second study was conducted by Slough et al. (2010) to compare the type and quality of visual displays in four state of Texas-approved middle school science textbooks. They developed classification criteria based on several analyses from the 1980s and early 1990s. They developed a 13-category typology based on earlier research that is somewhat similar to the typology we describe below in detail. However, there were important differences, such as the drawings, enlargement, and glossary categories that were not applicable to our study. They also rated each display on several dimensions based on contiguity between the graphic and text, clarity of the display caption, and whether the display was linked conceptually to information in the text (i.e., semantic relationship). They found that one third of displays were decorative and not linked substantially to the text. Displays with stronger semantic relationships were judged to be more helpful to users.

The third study was conducted by Gillen, Skryzhevska, Henry, and Green (2010) to compare 17 introductory college textbooks to assess the degree to which they included map interpretation material, important concepts related to map interpretation (e.g., latitude and longitude), and strategies designed to enhance students' map interpretation skills. A content analysis was conducted to assess relevant map concepts. A total of 46 separate concepts were identified that were classified into five broader interpretation categories, including coordinate systems, topographic maps, map projections, symbology, and different types of maps. A comparison was made across the 17 texts using the proportion of texts that covered important concepts and the number of pages devoted to these concepts. Overall, texts differed widely, ranging from coverage of 75% of concepts to 12%. Although all texts included instructional support, texts fell into three categories: (a) texts that covered fewer than 10 topics in less than 10 pages ($n = 3$), (b) texts that covered 20 to 40 topics with an average of 25 pages of instructional support ($n - 12$), and (c) texts that covered 30 or more topics with 30 to 50 pages of instructional support ($n = 2$). Although the three types of text differed in terms of the number of VDs, the authors did not report whether they differed in terms of the number of map interpretation skills.

We also identified one article that compared different types of visual displays in special education and nonspecial education journals. Kubina, Kostewicz, and Datchuk (2010) compared 29 journals to determine the amount of visual displays in special education journals compared to 13 other disciplines in the social (e.g., psychology, sociology) and physical sciences (e.g., chemistry, physics, medicine). The primary outcome variable was the proportion of page space devoted to data displays relative to total page space for each article. Results indicated that the amount of page space devoted to visual displays of data was lower for special education than the other 13 disciplines, and as a rule, one half to one third of journals in the physical sciences. Further, there were few significant differences among journals within the category of special education journals.

Collectively, these studies provided examples of how other researchers created typologies that were used to classify different types of visual displays, the outcome variables they selected as being most important, and guidelines for creating scoring rubrics and assessing the reliability of judges. Our assessment of these studies is that they used too few categories in their typology to distinguish among different types of displays that we wished to quantify. As a result, we began the development of our typology by classifying displays in JEP in a finer-grained manner in order to establish narrow categories in which all displays in the respective categories utilized the same interpretative principles, such as data summary, trends, or hierarchies. Nevertheless, we found the scoring rubrics used in these studies to provide helpful starting points in our analysis, especially in our attempts to assess the amount of information and complexity of displays.

Previous Classification Typologies for Visual Displays

A number of different typologies have been used to classify visual displays. Desnoyers (2011) described a hierarchical taxonomy of displays based on Linnean principles that distinguished three classes of displays based on their information and content. Heer, Bostock, and Ogievetsky (2010) presented a five-category system based on the communicative purpose of displays that are found commonly in science texts. Morse and Lewis (2000) reviewed several different taxonomic approaches used to classify the task demands among different types of displays. Rodriguez and Dimitrova (2011) proposed a four-category system based on the core communicative purpose of the visual displays. Paik and Schraw (2013) developed an eight-category typology based on instructional intervention studies that included text signals, notes, networks, sequences, hierarchies, distributions, maps, and animations.

Several observations are worth noting about these typologies in the larger context of this chapter. One was that classification systems tended to be discipline-specific and focused on displays common within that discipline while excluding displays not common to that discipline; thus, we were unable to locate an agreed-upon system for classifying different types of displays. A second finding was that the existing categorization systems we located have very little in common with one another in terms of organizational scheme such as number of categories or levels of complexity within the system. In the four cases cited above, the organizational frameworks do not resemble one another at all. A third observation was that none of these existing typologies provided an adequate organizational framework for discussing and comparing the visual displays in this chapter because they include structurally different types of displays in a single category or omit important types of displays.

Despite the lack of an agreed-upon typology of visual displays, it is clear that most or all displays possess at least five common features (Eichelberger & Schmid, 2009; Graham, Kennedy, & Benyon, 2000; Morse & Lewis, 2000). One is that displays reduce the amount of information to a more manageable amount, thereby promoting cognitive economy that enables the user to compare and contrast a smaller amount of information (Lane & Sándor, 2009; Kosslyn, 1993). Summary tables, for example, usually attempt to help the viewer make comparisons across four or five dimensions that pertain to the topics being summarized. Second, displays are intended to organize or summarize information in a manner that enables the viewer to readily grasp the intended big conceptual picture (Slough et al., 2010; Tufte, 2001). Third, displays are intended to draw the viewer's attention to the most salient aspect of the information (Hegarty et al., 2008; Mayer, 2005; Vekiri, 2002). Fourth, displays facilitate inference generation by highlighting the significant interrelationships among component variables (Hccr ct al., 2010). Fifth, displays often provide an explicit visual model that can be used as an internalized mental model of events or processes, or used as a retrieval structure in memory to facilitate recall or future learning (Slough et al., 2010). These models may be tentative in nature, as when a student constructs an initial concept map that links related concepts, or they may be stable, as a when a student studies a geographical map of countries in western Europe that may not change for decades.

We suggested above that there is no single unifying conceptual typology in the research literature; nor is there as much empirical research as one would hope for regarding the design and instructional effectiveness of visual displays given their prevalent use. Nevertheless, it is widely believed that displays that possess some or all of the five features summarized in the preceding paragraph promote better understanding with less effort (Lane & Sándor, 2009; Raschke & Stienbart, 2008; Smith et al., 2002; Slough et al., 2010). In particular, several theoretical models described within and beyond this volume suggest that visual displays improve learning due to separate visual and semantic processing channels that increase total cognitive capacity and help to distribute the cognitive load of information across these channels (Kalyuga, 2013; Mayer, 2005; Schnotz, 2002; Vekiri, 2002).

Constructing the Present Typology

We constructed the present typology using the four steps described above (i.e., conduct a preliminary analysis of articles, create a data-driven typology based on a preliminary analysis, create scoring criteria that enabled us to denote three aspects of information in the visual display, and construct a scoring rubric to assess the interpretative complexity of the visual display). We assessed three separate aspects of each display that we categorized. The *type of display* score was based on the 14 discrete categories shown in the final typology in Table 1, which also includes a definition, purpose, and examples of each type of visual display category reported in this study. The *amount of information* score tallied individual units of information in each display to determine how much total information was conveyed. We used four heuristics when counting information units. One was that each unit was counted once as a discrete piece of information. For example, when reporting the statistical significance on p values such as $p < .01^{**}$, we used a score of four to denote the following separate units: p, <, .01, and the double asterisk to denote significance at the .01 level. In the case of structural or hypothesized causal models, we used a simple additive approach to sum the number of variables, pathways, weights, and error terms specified in the model. A second was that each word in a display was counted as a single unit. A third was that visual information that spanned a range of scores was scored as n units that corresponded to the full range. For example, in a scenario in which two trend lines span a range from 0 to 100 using intervals of 10 units, we assigned a score of 10 for each trend line. A fourth was a multiplicative approach in which information units in columns and rows were multiplied to produce a total number of units, such as experimental or quasi-experimental designs in which the number of conditions were multiplied by the number of rows in a data array. We applied these heuristics based on previous content analyses with the main goal of quantifying the number of information units in the display.

Although an additive measure of total informational units is helpful, it was the case that some displays (e.g., multistage structural models) appeared to be more difficult to understand than a simple count of information units would suggest. For this reason, we used a fourth measure we labeled the *interpretative complexity* score to provide a subjective rating of the display's overall complexity. We developed the rubric shown in Table 2 to assess complexity in the most reliable manner. After several iterations, we found the four-point rubric to be the easiest and most useful for scoring. This rubric ranged from low complexity to very high complexity. Complexity varied as a function of informational units with low complexity corresponding to 150 units or less, moderate complexity corresponding to 151–300 units, high complexity corresponding to 301 to 450 units, and high complexity corresponding to 451 units or more. These cutpoints were selected based on the authors' reading of the display; those with less information seemed less complex, whereas those with large amounts of information seemed very com-

TABLE 2. Scoring Rubric for Interpretative Complexity

Level	1: Low Complexity	2: Moderate Complexity	3: High Complexity	4: Very High Complexity
Definition	Easy to understand the main purpose of table with little time or effort. Data in table links explicitly to text.	Requires 1–2 minutes and moderate effort to understand. Information usually can be understood without referring to the main body of text.	Requires several minutes or longer to understand. Usually requires linking information or conclusions in text to visual display to understand completely. Often requires comparisons of trends or outcomes across conditions.	Requires 5 minutes or longer and complete concentration to understand. Requires linking important text themes and conclusions to the visual display. Typically requires complex comparisons of trends or model parameters across several conditions.
Examples	A table of means and standard deviation across several experimental conditions. A simple screenshot graphic such as a bar graph or pie chart.	A large table of correlations (e.g., 20 x 20), or a list of 30 articles with descriptive data used in a meta-analysis.	A very large data array (e.g., 80 articles used in a meta-analysis) or an appendix that requires the reader to integrate text, diagrams, and multiple equations. A structural model with interactions and complex mediated effects. Comparison of multilevel models.	An extremely large data array (e.g., more than 1,000 informational units), complex hierarchical or structural equation models, or complex comparisons of trends over multiple times x experimental conditions).

plex. However, some displays, such as those with stories used as experimental materials, contained a high number of units but very low or moderate complexity. In contrast, some data tables that compared model parameter estimates contained few information units, but were of higher complexity. It is important to note that we constructed our complexity rubric to assess complexity for a *typical reader of JEP who was conversant with the methods and statistical analyses reported in the display*. Untrained readers no doubt would experience far more complexity when trying to interpret these displays.

METHODS

Materials

We used three types of materials to conduct our content analysis. The first was the typology shown in Table 1, which included 14 separate categories of visual displays. As described above, we constructed the typology in an iterative manner during initial practice phases to assure that it would accommodate all of the visual

96 • GREGORY SCHRAW & ANTONIO P. GUTIERREZ

TABLE 3. Summary Scoring Sheet

Number of Pages	Type of Display	Type of Information	Amount of Information	Interpretive Complexity

displays we encountered in JEP. In rare cases when there was uncertainty about how to classify a display, the authors conferred to resolve the uncertainty.

We used the summary scoring sheet shown in Table 3 to record relevant information. Column headings are described in detail above.

We used the information complexity rubric in Table 2 to assess the holistic complexity of each display. We provided definitions of each of the four complexity categories as well as examples of the difficulty of information processing in the display by the experienced JEP reader. This rubric was developed in an iterative fashion during initial practice phases.

Procedures

There were two procedural activities used in the content analysis. The first was training and practice with the scoring materials. We randomly selected 15 articles each that were used to create and refine the scoring rubrics, revise our scoring criteria, and practice using the scoring system. Both authors felt prepared to score the articles after the extended practice phase that took place over a one month period.

We conducted our content analyses over the next three months. Each author scored all articles in either the first and third issue, or second and fourth issue, using the 2010–2014 volumes. All the scoring criteria used in our analysis were objective in nature, with the exception of the information complexity score. The authors met regularly to check and verify the accuracy of these scores through inspection of the visual display and discussion. All differences were settled in discussion such that we reached 100% agreement on the complexity scores.

RESULTS

We posed five research questions, including how many articles were analyzed; how many displays appeared in each article; how frequent was each type of display; what was the distribution of interpretative complexity scores for each type of display; and how were article length, amount of information, and interpretative complexity related?

How Many Articles Were Analyzed?

A total of 258 research articles were reviewed for our analysis. This included all of the articles in the 4-year period. The average article length was 13.63 pages (*SD* = 3.62) in journal pages. The maximum length was 31 pages, including appendices and the minimum was 5 pages. The distribution of article length was approximately normal. All but 15 articles (i.e., 6%) were between 8 and 20 pages. The mode was 14.

How Many Displays Appeared in Each Article?

All articles used at least two displays, while one article used 20 displays, including appendices. A total of 1,918 visual displays appeared in the 258 articles for a mean of 7.43 (*SD* = 3.61) displays per article. A large percentage of articles (93.4% of total) used four displays, which decreased sharply thereafter. Figure 1 shows the relative frequency of visual displays per article, revealing that most articles included 2 to 11 visuals displays with less than 20% of articles using 12 displays or more.

JEP uses four types of display formats, including tables, figures, equations, and appendices. We computed the frequency of each type across the 1,918 total visual displays. There were 1,180 tables (61.5% of total), 553 figures (28.8%), 54 equations (2.8%), and 131 appendices (6.8%). Tables mostly included numeric data and some samples of experimental materials corresponding to display codes 1 and 2 in Table 1. Figures included display codes 4 through 14. Equations included display code 3, while appendices generally included examples of experimental materials such as surveys, rating scales, texts, or scoring rubrics.

As mentioned above, previous content analyses found that a large proportion of displays were decorative in nature. Although we did not rate the decorative nature of displays, we conclude that very few were decorative in nature, perhaps due to strict space limitations in JEP and large amounts of data to report. Of the 1,918 displays included in our analysis, perhaps 20 or fewer displays were characterized as decorative. These displays invariably were pictures or illustrations that included useful but nonessential information.

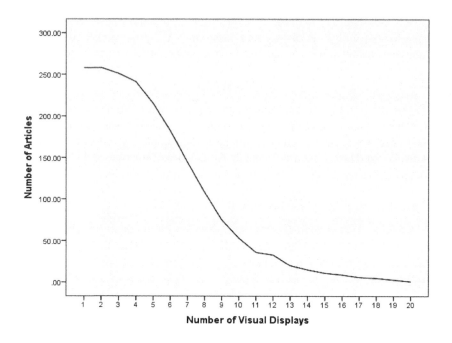

FIGURE 1. Frequency of visual displays per article.

How Frequent Was Each Type of Display?

Table 4 shows the frequency and corresponding percentage of each type of visual display. Data tables (i.e., display code 1 in Table 1) were the most commonly used visual display, accounting for 59% of all displays. The percentage of displays in our typology system was roughly equal to the percentage of tables using the four-category classification system used in JEP. Trend displays accounted for an additional 8%, while text tables accounted for 7.3%. Images (5.5%) and structural models (4.9%) accounted for an additional 10% of all displays. The remaining displays accounted for 15% of displays collectively. Displays using complex hybrids, sequences (e.g., timelines, flowcharts), hierarchies (e.g., dendrograms, classification trees), geographical maps, and networks (e.g., concept maps) were used rarely.

What Was the Distribution of Interpretative Complexity Scores for Each Type of Display?

As mentioned above, the 258 articles yielded 1,918 total visual displays. Table 5 shows the frequencies of low, moderate, high, and very high interpretative complexity scores across the 14 types of visual displays. Approximately 56% of displays were low complexity, while an additional 37% were moderate complexity.

TABLE 4. Frequency and Total Percentage of the 14 Types of Displays

Type of Display	Display Code	Frequency	Percentage of Total Number of Displays
Data Table	1	1,132	59.0%
Text Table	2	140	7.3%
Equations and formulas	3	60	3.1%
Theoretical or conceptual model	4	61	3.2%
Structural and causal models	5	95	4.9%
Networks	6	6	0.3%
Sequences	7	16	0.8%
Hierarchies; multilevel models	8	6	0.3%
Distributions	9	56	2.9%
Trends	10	158	8.0%
Maps and spatial proximity	11	8	0.4%
Graphs, diagrams, plots, charts	12	54	2.8%
Images (picture; screenshot; etc.)	13	106	5.5%
Complex hybrids	14	20	1.0%
Total		1,918	

TABLE 5. Amount of Information and Interpretative Complexity of Displays

Type of Display	Display Code	Interpretative Complexity				Total
		1	2	3	4	
Data Table	1	691	386	49	6	1,132
Text Table	2	98	37	4	1	140
Equations and formulas	3	6	38	15	1	60
Theoretical or conceptual model	4	13	38	10	0	61
Structural and causal models	5	25	51	19	0	95
Networks	6	5	1	0	0	6
Sequences	7	11	5	0	0	16
Hierarchies	8	1	5	0	0	6
Distributions	9	22	29	5	0	56
Trends	10	86	63	8	1	158
Maps and spatial proximity	11	3	1	4	0	8
Graphs, diagrams, plots, charts	12	41	10	1	2	54
Images	13	57	39	9	1	106
Complex hybrids	14	6	10	4	0	20
Total		1,065	713	128	12	1,918
Percentage of total		55.5%	37.1%	6.7%	.6%	

TABLE 6. Bivariate Correlations Between Number of Pages, Total Amount of Information, and Total Complexity Scores

	Number of Pages	Total Amount of Information	Total Interpretative Complexity
Number of Pages	—	.486 ***	.586***
Total Amount of Information		—	.449***
Total Interpretative Complexity			—

Note. N = 258 research articles for each pairwise test. *** denotes statistical significance at the p < .001 level.

Only 7% were of high complexity and less than 1% were of very high complexity. This pattern was true of most of the different types of visual displays with the exception of equations and structural models, which tended to be more complex than the remaining 12 types of visual displays.

How Were Article Length, Amount of Information, and Interpretative Complexity Related?

Most scores in our content analysis were categorical. However, the number of pages per research article and the amount of information score were continuous, while the interpretative complexity score was ordinal. We computed correlations for the number of pages per article, amount of information, and interpretative complexity to determine whether they were positively related. To do so, we calculated a *total information score* that was the sum of information for each visual display that appeared in a research article. We also calculated a *total complexity score* that was the sum of complexity ratings for each visual display in the research article. Both of these summed composite scores were on an interval scale; thus, we tested their significance using Pearson's *r*. As stated above, the mean article length was 13.63 pages, with a standard deviation of 3.62 pages. The mean and standard deviation for the total amount of information scores were 689.86 and 653.28, respectively, while the mean and standard deviation for the total complexity scores were 11.44 and 6.01, respectively. Table 6 shows the bivariate correlations between variables and their statistical significance.

DISCUSSION

Our results yielded three main findings that inform the content of JEP research articles and possible instructional implications. Our first main finding was that the displays were predominantly data or text tables, figures that showed trends, or structural equation models. However, all 14 types of visual displays were used to some extent, and approximately 25% of displays were not tables, trends, or structural models. The finding that visual displays can be sorted into 14 different categories suggested two related conclusions. One conclusion was that readers of JEP must have some degree of visual literacy across the full array of visual displays in Table 1, notwithstanding the finding that 56% of VDs were at the lowest level in our four-level complexity rubric (Yeh & Cheng, 2010). Unfortunately, previous research suggests that students do not possess broad visual literacy (Catley & Novick, 2008; Chittleborough & Treagust, 2008; Glazer, 2011; McTigue & Flowers, 2007) and find it difficult to transfer skills from one type of display to another (Gegenfurtner & Seppänen, 2013). Moreover, given that some of the displays were high or very high complexity, it is unclear whether novice readers would be able to fully understand them.

A second conclusion was that there was a high degree of variability within each type of visual display, suggesting that readers need to have statistical expertise that is both wide and deep. For example, some data tables included only means, standard deviations, and confidence intervals. In contrast, others included standardized and unstandardized regression weights, a variety of model fit parameters for structural models, as well as equations for three-level hierarchical models with nested variables. We found the most complex displays to be those that compared model parameters across multiple models. We found some of these tables quite challenging to understand even within the context of the Results' supporting text explanation. It is unclear whether these tables could be simplified using current design principles (Lane & Sándor, 2009; Smith et al., 2002) to facilitate comprehension. Furthermore, as we discuss below, it is unclear what role visual display training plays in helping readers understand different types of complex displays, as skills do not appear to transfer well across different types of displays, or even using the same displays in different contexts (Gegenfurtner & Seppänen, 2013).

A second main finding was that roughly 90% of visual displays were of low or moderate complexity. This result seems to bode well at face value because most experienced readers should find it relatively easy to locate and understand information within the tables of special interest to them. However, we wish to reiterate that our ratings of complexity assume a moderate degree of expertise interpreting VDs, as well as experience reading JEP-like articles, typical of regular readers or reviewers. Novice readers such as graduate students no doubt experience far more difficulty, while inexperienced readers such as practicing educators and administrators probably find it nearly impossible to fully understand many of the displays. One crucial topic for future research is whether some readers such as lay readers, teachers, and administrators are denied intellectual access to these primary-source articles due to limited training and prior knowledge.

A third main finding was that article length, amount of information, and interpretive complexity were correlated significantly in the .45 to .60 range. This no doubt confirms a gut feeling among readers that longer articles are more complex due to more information and the exponentially increasing complexity of large versus small datasets. One conclusion is that longer articles impose more cognitive demand due to additional information and complexity. Presently, the field has no guidelines for how much complexity in visual displays is acceptable or desirable. Moreover, it is unclear whether several low-complexity displays impose the same cognitive demands as a single high-complexity display. For instance, it may be the case that spatially separated information imposes greater cognitive demands than spatially integrated information, as suggested by the *spatial contiguity hypothesis* (van Merriënboer & Sweller, 2005).

IMPLICATIONS FOR INSTRUCTIONAL PRACTICE

Our findings, along with a review of the literature, raise questions about the role of instruction for improving the usefulness of visual displays. We discuss the beneficial effect of instruction, the acquisition of expertise in display interpretation, the extent to which skills useful for one type of display transfer to other displays, and issues related to optimizing the effectiveness of training. Both individual studies and meta-analyses of the effect on instruction of learning from visual displays reveal that training is beneficial. Students who are trained to use displays learn more at the surface and deeper learning levels (Abrami et al., 2008; Liben, 2009; McCrudden et al., 2011; Rashcke & Steinbart, 2008; Scevak, Moore & Kirby, 1993; Schwonke et al., 2009; Shah & Hoeffner, 2002; van der Meer, 2012). Visual displays seem to have a particularly positive effect on deeper learning such as the construction of an integrated mental model of events and relationships in the to-be-learned material (Mayer et al., 2002; Schwartz et al., 2007).

Less is known about how experts process visual displays. We assume that skilled consumers of research in JEP possess a general type of visual literacy expertise that enables them to read and interpret displays with greater ease and proficiency than others. However, we also assume that experts in different types of statistical data analysis such as multilevel modeling, structural equation modeling, and different types of regression analysis possess a task-specific expertise that enables them to interpret these displays with greater ease and efficiency than well-trained statisticians without deep knowledge of specific statistical modeling procedures. Both from an instructional and research perspective, it is important to conduct studies that reveal how individuals become experts, how much expertise is needed to process complex displays, and whether this expertise appears to transfer to other displays (De Koning, Tabbers, Rikers, & Paas, 2010). Indeed, Gegenfurtner and Seppänen (2013) found that training transferred to "near" cases, which closely resembled the training materials, but did not transfer to "far" examples, which represented novel displays.

Perhaps the most important instructional issue is how to optimize training. Several qualitative analyses have appeared in the literature that examined developing expertise with students and professors (Chittleborough & Treagust 2008; Halverson, Pires, & Abell, 2011; Roth & Bowen, 2001). These studies help us better understand how to train individuals to comprehend visual displays quickly and accurately. As a starting point, we refer the reader to the work of Schönborn and Anderson (2006), who provided 10 instructional guidelines for improving the visual literacy and interpretation of displays. In addition, Schönborn and Anderson (2010) described seven cognitive factors that influence students' ability to learn from visual displays as well as suggestions for designing displays in the most effective manner possible.

Several other issues must be addressed as well. One is related to the amount of training and whether training should be *massed* in a single instructional session or *spaced* across several smaller instructional modules over time. Of the few studies that have used an instructional intervention, most have been brief and massed into a single session. A second issue is whether training should be *stand-alone* or *embedded* within the environment where it will be used. Previous research that focused on improving thinking skills and self-regulation have reported higher gains for the embedded versus stand-alone approaches (Ritchhart & Perkins, 2005). Third, it is important to consider whether training should focus on the individual versus the small, collaborative group. A number of studies indicate that small groups with collaborative discussion and worked examples improve reasoning skills more than when individual students work alone and construct more detailed displays (Kwon & Cifuentes, 2009).

IMPLICATIONS FOR FUTURE RESEARCH

We make four suggestions for future research germane to our content analysis. One is to conduct comparative studies of cognitive and interpretative complexity across different types of visual displays. Although our findings clearly demonstrate that complexity varies within each type of display (see Table 5), this does not preclude substantial differences between different displays. For example, Table 5 shows that trends and structural equation models tend to be at a higher complexity level than data or text tables. We believe that if displays differ in terms of complexity, researchers should examine different instructional strategies to reduce complexity such that less complex displays are used to substitute for more complex displays, more instructional time is provided to adequately train novices to use more complex displays, or additional text information is added to explicitly link information in displays to the main conclusions made in the text. Regarding these studies, we note that previous research has employed a variety of complementary outcome measures to assess different facets of cognitive processing, including study time (McCrudden et al., 2011), eye tracking studies that evaluate attentional intensity (Hegarty et al., 2010), comprehension of information, explicit and inferential information in the to-be-learned materials (Mautone & Mayer, 2007; Lehman et al., 2007; Schwonke et al., 2009), reasoning and problem-solving task (Harrell, 2011), the construction of integrated mental models (Múñez, Orrantia, & Rosales, 2013), and an analysis of inferential errors (Rossano & Morrison, 1996).

A second research suggestion is to explore the extent to which interpretative complexity becomes a cognitive burden on different types of learners because it exceeds the learner's cognitive load capacity (De Koning, Tabbers, Rikers & Paas, 2009; Mayer, 2013; van Merriënboer & Sweller, 2005). We assume that experts many accommodate greater interpretative complexity than novices or emergent experts; however, it is unclear how comprehension is affected when one's cognitive limits are exceeded regardless of one's expertise. Indeed, a variety of studies have examined the constraints imposed on visual display processing due to insufficient prior knowledge (Cook, Wiebe, & Carter, 2007; Schwartz et al., 2007; Schwonke et al., 2009), working memory (Kalyuga, 2013), and spatial ability (Höffler & Leutner, 2007). We suggest that the *total cognitive load* of all of the visual displays used in a text or research article be considered to avoid overload. Related to this point, qualitative studies of how experts compensate for excessive load would provide useful ideas for future instructional studies.

A third suggestion is to compare the type and complexity of displays across different research domains such as motivation, memory processes, and problem solving. Our experience suggests that most researchers work within a specific domain of human learning such as memory processes, or at a still finer grain size such as visual or auditory processing in working memory. We note that some domains of research tend to be experimental (e.g., strategy instruction), whereas others (e.g., motivation) tend to be correlational in nature. It seems reasonable to assume that different domains of research use different statistical approaches and different types of visual displays. Whether these displays also differ in terms of the amount of information and interpretative complexity is unclear. Examining these potential differences via content analyses would be helpful. In addition, if differences exist, thought should be given as to whom, how, and when students working in different domains are given the training they need to master the types of displays they are most likely to encounter.

A fourth suggestion is to expand the current content analysis to consider a variety of different educational research journals. Content analyses of texts and journals are rare in educational research (cf. Slough et al., 2010). We suggest a comparison of both quantitative and qualitative research journals, as well as a comparison between them to determine article length, complexity, and the number and types of visual displays used in these journals. Perhaps most important in these comparisons is identifying dimensions that are common to all journal articles (e.g., data tables) versus unique-to-specific journals. Identifying common properties would help researchers develop a broad instructional intervention that is most likely to provide a core set of essential interpretation skills that transferred across different displays.

IMPLICATIONS FOR PRACTICE

We conclude with two practical suggestions. One is to expand the visual literacy of VDs given that a variety of different displays are common in textbooks and research journals (Yeh & Cheng, 2010). We assume that most readers of research journals have not given a great deal of thought to different displays, their relative strengths and weaknesses, and interpretative complexity. Interpretive complexity is an issue that has not been given sufficient attention with respect to the information readers are intended to learn from the displays. Hence, instructional interventions that focus on teaching individuals to consider type of information and complexity, among other aspects of displays, may be an effective approach to improve design and interpretation of VDs. Along this instructional vein, introducing graduate students early in their educational careers to different displays in the context of research design and statistics classes may promote literacy and the degree to which readers understand the numeric and conceptual implications of VDs.

A second suggestion is to teach the attributes of each type of display in Table 1 directly. Research on teaching VDs has supported two findings. One is that the use of visual displays in contextually supportive learning environments yield gains for both surface (e.g., facts, simple concepts) and deeper (e.g., the integrated conceptual structure of the information, making inferences and interpretations) learning (Abrami et al., 2008; Liben, 2009; McCrudden et al., 2011; Schwonke et al., 2009; Shah & Hoeffner, 2002; van der Meer, 2012). Second, students who receive training performed better than those who did not, using a variety of different displays (Hegarty et al., 2010; Kastens & Liben, 2007; Kwon & Cifuentes, 2009; Mautone & Mayer, 2005; Schwonke et al., 2009). Training may focus on several different aspects of VDs, including component parts (e.g., direct and indirect in causal models), the integrated conceptual structure of the display and what it is intended to convey, or a repertoire of thinking skills (e.g., synthesis, hypothesis testing, making inferences) needed to fully understand displays. Importantly, these three aspects of instructional training appear to complement one another and may create a joint effect on learning that exceeds effects attributable to each.

REFERENCES

Abrami, P. C., Bernard, R. M., Borokhovski, E., Wade, A., Surkes, M. A., Tamim, R., & Zhang, D. (2008). Instructional interventions affecting critical thinking skills and dispositions: A stage 1 meta-analysis. *Review of Educational Research, 78,* 1102–1134.

Cain, K., & Nash, H. M. (2011). The influence of connectives on young readers' processing and comprehension of text. *Journal of Educational Psychology, 103,* 429–441.

Carter, R. (2003). Teaching visual design principles for computer science students. *Computer Science Education, 13,* 67–90.

Catley, K. M., & Novick, L. R. (2008). Seeing the wood for the trees: An analysis of evolutionary diagrams in biology textbooks. *BioScience, 58,* 976–989.

Chittleborough, G., & Treagust, D. (2008). Correct interpretation of chemical diagrams requires transforming from one level of representation to another. *Research in Science Education, 38,* 463–482.

Cook, M., Wiebe, E . N., & Carter, G. (2007). The influence of prior knowledge on viewing and interpreting graphics with macroscopic and molecular representations. *Science Education, 92,* 848–867.

Crooks, S. M., & Cheon, J. (2013). Strategies for note taking on computer-based graphic organizers. In G. Schraw, M. McCrudden, & D. Robinson (Eds.), *Learning through visual displays* (pp. 187–222). Greenwich, CT: Information Age.

Dansereau, D. F., & Simpson, D. D. (2009). A picture is worth a thousand words: The case for graphic representations. *Professional Psychology: Research and Practice, 40,* 104–110.

De Koning, B. B., Tabbers, H. K., Rikers, R. M. J. P., & Paas, F. (2009). Towards a framework for attention cueing in instructional animations: Guidelines for research and design. *Educational Psychology Review, 21*, 113–140.

De Koning, B, B., Tabbers, H. K., Rikers, R. M. J., & Paas, F. (2010). Learning by generating vs. receiving instructional explanations: Two approaches to enhance attention cueing in animations. *Computers & Education, 55*, 681–691.

De Simone, C. (2007). Applications of concept mapping. *College Teaching, 55*, 33–27.

Desnoyers, L. (2011). Toward a taxonomy of visuals in science communication. *Applied Theory, 58*, 119–134.

Eichelberger, H., & Schmid, K. (2009). Guidelines on the aesthetic quality of UML class diagrams. *Information and Software Technology, 51*, 1686–1698.

Gegenfurtner, A., & Seppänen, M. (2013). Transfer of expertise: An eye tracking and think aloud study using dynamic medical visualizations. *Computers & Education, 63*, 393–403.

Gillen, J., Skryzhevska, L., Henry, M. C., & Green, J. (2010). Map interpretation instruction in introductory textbooks: A preliminary investigation. *Journal of Geography, 109*, 181–189.

Glazer, N. (2011). Challenges with graph interpretation: A review of the literature. *Studies in Science Education, 47*, 183–210.

Graham M., Kennedy, J., & Benyon, D. (2000). Towards a methodology for developing visualizations. *International Journal of Human-Computer Studies, 53*, 789–807.

Halverson, K. L., Pires, C. J., & Abell, S. K. (2011). Exploring the complexity of tree thinking expertise in an undergraduate systematics. *Science Education, 95*, 794–823.

Harrell, M. (2011). Argument diagramming and critical thinking in introductory philosophy. *Higher Education Research & Development, 30*, 371–385.

Heer, J., Bostock, M., & Ogievetsky, V. (2010). A tour through the visualization zoo. *Communications of the ACM, 53*, 59–67.

Hegarty, M., Canham, M. S., & Fabrikant, S. I. (2010). Thinking about the weather: How display salience and knowledge affect performance in a graphic inference task. *Journal of Experimental Psychology: Learning, Memory, and Cognition, 36*, 37–53.

Höffler, T. N, & Leutner, D. (2007). Instructional animation versus static pictures: A meta-analysis. *Learning and Instruction , 17*, 722–738.

Kalyuga, S. (2013). Knowledge and working memory effects of learning from visual displays. In G. Schraw, M. McCrudden, & D. Robinson (Eds.), *Learning through visual displays* (pp. 75–96). Greenwich, CT: Information Age.

Kastens, K. A., & Liben, L. S. (2007). Eliciting self-explanations improves children's performance on a field-based map skills task. *Cognition and Instruction, 25*, 45–74.

Kosslyn, S. M. (1993). *Elements of graphic design.* New York, NY: Freeman.

Kubina, R. M., Kostewicz, D. E. & Datchuk, S. M. (2010). Graph and table use in special education: A review and analysis of the communication of data. *Evaluation & Research in Education, 23*, 105–119.

Kwon, S. Y., & Cifuentes, L. (2009). The comparative effect of individually-constructed vs. collaboratively-constructed computer-based concept maps. *Computers & Education, 52*, 365–375.

Lane, D. M., & Sándor, A. (2009). Designing better graphs by including distributional information and integrating words, numbers, and images. *Psychological Methods, 14*, 239–257.

Lehman, S., Schraw, G., McCrudden, M. T., & Hartley, K. (2007). Processing and recall of seductive details in scientific text. *Contemporary Educational Psychology, 32,* 569–587.

Liben, L. S. (2009). The road to understanding maps. *Current Directions in Psychological Science, 18,* 310–315.

Lorch, R., Lemarié, J., & Grant, R. (2011). Signaling hierarchical and sequential organization in expository text. *Scientific Studies of Reading, 15,* 267–284.

Mautone, P. D., & Mayer, R. E. (2007). Cognitive aids for guiding graph comprehension. *Journal of Educational Psychology, 99,* 640–652.

Mayer, R. E. (2005). Principles for reducing extraneous processing in multimedia learning: Coherence, signaling, redundancy, spatial contiguity, and temporal contiguity principles. In R. E. Mayer (Ed.), *The Cambridge handbook of multimedia learning* (pp. 183–212). Cambridge, UK: Cambridge University Press.

Mayer, R. E. (2013). Fostering learning with visual displays. In G. Schraw, M. McCrudden & D. Robinson (Eds.), *Learning through visual displays* (pp. 47–75). Greenwich, CT: Information Age.

Mayer, R. E., Mathias, A., & Wetzell, K. (2002). Fostering understanding of multimedia messages through pre-training: Evidence for a two-stage theory of mental model construction. *Journal of Experimental Psychology: Applied, 8,* 147–15.

McCrudden, M. T., Magliano, J., & Schraw, G. (2011). The effects of diagrams on online reading processes and memory. *Discourse Processes, 48,* 69–92.

McCrudden, M. T., Schraw, G., Lehman, S., & Poliquin, A. (2007). The effect of causal diagrams on text learning. *Contemporary Educational Psychology, 32,* 367–388.

McTigue, E. M., & Flowers, A. C. (2007). Science visual literacy: Learners' perceptions and knowledge of diagrams. *The Reading Teacher, 64,* 578–589.

Morse, E., & Lewis, M. (2000). Evaluating visualizations: Using a taxonomic guide. *International Journal of Human-Computer Studies, 53,* 637–662.

Múñez, D., Orrantia, K., & Rosales, J. (2013). The effect of external representations on compare word problems: Supporting mental model construction. *The Journal of Experimental Education, 81,* 337–355.

Nesbit, J. C., & Adesope, O. O. (2013). Concept maps for learning: Theory, research and design. In G. Schraw, M. McCrudden, & D. Robinson (Eds.), *Learning through visual displays* (pp. 303–328). Greenwich, CT: Information Age.

Paik, E. S., & Schraw, G. (2013). Learning with animation and illusions of understanding. *Journal of Educational Psychology, 105,* 278–289.

Poliquin, A., & Schraw, G. (2013). Strategy training with causal diagrams to improve text learning. In G. Schraw, M. McCrudden, & D. Robinson (Eds.), *Learning through visual displays* (pp. 223–246). Greenwich, CT: Information Age Publishers.

Raschke, R. L., & Steinbart, P. J. (2008). Mitigating the effects of misleading graphs on decisions by educating users about the principles of graph design. *Journal of Information Systems, 22,* 23–52.

Richardson, M., & Ball, L. J. (2009). Internal representations, external representations and ergonomics: Toward a theoretical integration. *Theoretical Issues in Ergonomics Science, 10,* 335–376.

Ritchhart, R., & Perkins, D. N. (2005). Learning to think: The challenges of teaching thinking. In K. J. Holyoak & R. G. Morrison (Eds.), *The Cambridge handbook of thinking and reasoning* (pp. 775–802). Cambridge, UK: Cambridge University Press

Rodriguez, L., & Dimitrova, D. N. (2011). The levels of visual framing. *Journal of Visual Literacy, 30*, 48–65.

Rossano, M. J., & Morrison, T. T. (1996). Learning from maps: General processes and map-structure influences. *Cognition & Instruction, 14*, 109–137.

Roth, W. M., & Bowen, G. M. (2001). Professionals read graphs: A semiotic analysis. *Journal for Research in Mathematics Education, 32*, 159–194.

Scevak, J. J., Moore, P. J., & Kirby, J. R. (1993). Training students to use maps to increase text recall. *Contemporary Educational Psychology, 18*, 401–413.

Schnotz, W. (2002). Commentary: Towards an integrated view of learning from text and IVDs. *Educational Psychology Review, 14*, 101–120.

Schönborn, K. J., & Anderson, T. R. (2006). The importance of visual literacy in the education of biochemists. *Biochemistry and Molecular Biology Education, 34*, 94–102.

Schönborn, K. J., & Anderson, T. R. (2010). Bridging the educational research-teaching practice gap: Foundations for assessing and developing biochemistry students' visual literacy. *Biochemistry and Molecular Biology Education, 38*, 347–354,

Schraw, G., McCrudden, M. T., & Robinson, D. H. (2013). Visual displays and learning: Theoretical and practical considerations. In G. Schraw, M. McCrudden, & D. Robinson (Eds.), *Learning through visual displays* (pp. 3–19). Greenwich, CT: Information Age.

Schwartz, N. L., Verdi, M. P., Morris, T., Lee, T. R., & Larson, N. K. (2007). Navigating web-based environments: Differentiating internal spatial representations from external spatial displays. *Contemporary Educational Psychology, 32*, 551–568.

Schwonke, R., Berthold, K., & Renkl, A. (2009). How multiple external representations are used and how they can be made more useful. *Applied Cognitive Psychology, 23*, 1227–1243.

Shah, P., & Hoeffner, J. (2002). Review of graph comprehension research: Implications for instruction. *Educational Psychology Review, 14*, 47–69.

Slough, S. W., McTigue, E. M., Kim, S., & Jennings, S. M. (2010). Science textbooks use of graphical representation: A descriptive analysis of four sixth grade science texts. *Reading Psychology, 31*, 301–325.

Smith, L. D., Best, L. A., Stubbs, D. A., Archibald, A. B., & Roberson-Ray, R. (2002). Constructing knowledge. The role of graphs and tables in hard and soft psychology. *American Psychologist, 57*, 749–761.

Tufte, E. R. (2001). *The visual display of quantitative information* (2nd ed.). Cheshire, CT: Graphics.

van der Meer, J. (2012): Students' note-taking challenges in the twenty-first century: Considerations for teachers and academic staff developers. *Teaching in Higher Education, 17*, 13–23.

van Merriënboer, J. J. G., & Sweller, J. (2005). Cognitive load theory and complex learning: Recent developments and future directions. *Educational Psychology Review, 17*, 147–177.

Vekiri, I. (2002).What is the value of graphical displays in learning? *Educational Psychology Review, 14*, 261–312.

Yeh, H., & Cheng, Y. (2010). The influence of the instruction of visual design principles on improving pre-service teachers' visual literacy. *Computers & Education, 54*, 244–252.

SECTION III

VISUAL DISPLAYS IN QUANTITATIVE, QUALITATIVE, AND MIXED METHODS RESEARCH

CHAPTER 5

PROMOTING THE USE OF PATH DIAGRAMS IN QUANTITATIVE RESEARCH

Dena A. Pastor and Sara J. Finney

ABSTRACT

Path diagrams, which are visual displays that convey relationships among variables, are used pervasively in teaching and research when the statistical techniques are obvious members of the structural equation modeling (SEM) family. Despite the fact that many traditional statistical procedures (e.g., *t*-test, ANOVA, multiple regression) are subsumed under SEM, their visual depiction via path diagrams is rare. In this chapter, we illustrate the benefits of constructing path diagrams when both planning and presenting research, regardless of the statistical technique employed. Specifically, path diagrams can be created before analyses are conducted to depict competing theoretical models, as well as presented after analyses to convey statistical findings in a holistic manner. We also advocate for the use of path diagrams when teaching statistics. As demonstrated in the chapter, path diagrams are powerful tools for highlighting the similarities and differences among statistical techniques. Their

Use of Visual Displays in Research and Testing: Coding, Interpreting, and Reporting Data, pages 111–144.

early use in statistical training also promotes the more modern model-oriented approach to research (Rodgers, 2010a, 2010b) and eases students' transition to more complicated models. To facilitate the adoption of path diagrams, we discuss their creation in various SEM software programs, which also easily accommodate commonly occurring data issues in applied research (e.g., missing data, nonnormality, measurement error). Given the different estimators and orientation to modeling typically employed in these programs, we briefly describe results obtained when SEM software is used for traditional techniques, along with their corresponding visuals.

Because the format in which information is conveyed (e.g., words, figures, tables) can change how it is perceived (Schraw, McCrudden, & Robinson, 2013), research should guide which formats are used for presenting quantitative research and teaching statistical methods. In a previous chapter, we described how visual displays of results, particularly graphs created to align with the principles of cognitive processing, could enhance understanding of statistical concepts and facilitate more accurate interpretations of results (Pastor & Finney, 2013). That is, our previous chapter focused on the use of visuals after analyses had been conducted. In the present chapter, we turn our attention to a particular visual display known as a path diagram that has utility throughout the research process and when teaching quantitative methods.

Path diagrams are visual displays that concisely convey the theoretical relationships among variables. Hoyle and Panter (1995) describe a path diagram as "an effective means of presenting the full system of relations in a unified and integrated manner and represents a direct translation of theoretical predictions" (p. 159). In addition to providing a visual means by which to express theory, path diagrams illuminate the statistical models (e.g., parameters being estimated, degrees of freedom) used to test the theory. Bollen (1989) credits the creation of path diagrams to Wright (1934), the inventor of path analysis, and to Jöreskog (1973), Keesling (1972), and Wiley (1973) for the use of path diagrams to represent a family of statistical models known as structural equation models (SEMs). Indeed, path diagrams are presented pervasively in articles employing SEM (McDonald & Ho, 2002) and are found in almost every SEM textbook (e.g., Bollen, 1989; Kline, 2011) and software program (e.g., LISREL, Mplus).

Given that many introductory or traditional statistical procedures (e.g., *t*-test, ANOVA, multiple regression, MANOVA) are subsumed under SEM and thus can be represented visually by path diagrams (e.g., Bray & Maxwell, 1985; Dwyer, 1983; Fan, 1997; Graham, 2008; Green & Thompson, 2006, 2012; Hancock, 2010), why aren't these visuals presented more frequently in quantitative research and in the teaching of quantitative methods? That is, path diagrams are rarely provided in introductory or intermediate statistics textbooks (e.g., Aron, Aron, & Coups, 2013; Field, 2013; Tabachnick & Fidell, 2013) or in the software programs (e.g., SAS, SPSS) that are commonly used in statistics courses. Moreover, researchers are not normally encouraged to include path diagrams in their publications unless the statistical model being employed is an obvious member of the

SEM family (e.g., path analysis, models with latent variables). This inconsistency in recommending the presentation of a visual that represents the theory being tested is showcased in texts created to help researchers and reviewers present and evaluate quantitative research. For example, in *The Reviewer's Guide to Quantitative Methods in the Social Sciences,* a text designed for evaluators of research manuscripts, Mueller and Hancock (2010) direct researchers employing SEM to include path diagrams in their articles; however, the same recommendation is not provided for researchers using more traditional procedures, such as ANOVA (Klockars, 2010; Lix & Keselman, 2010), MANOVA (Olejnik, 2010), or multiple regression (Kelley & Maxwell, 2010). Likewise, the APA manual (2010) and derivatives from the manual that focus specifically on reporting results (e.g., Cooper, 2011; Nicol & Pexman, 2010) emphasize the importance of clearly linking the research questions to the analyses; however, the recommendation to use path diagrams for this purpose is limited only to those techniques conventionally considered part of the SEM family.

If visual displays of the statistical model representing the theory are useful, why are these visuals being recommended, and thus employed, for only a subset of quantitative techniques? An answer to this question might be that path diagrams add no value over a verbal description of the models. To counter this argument, we provide a verbal description of a set of hypothetical but theoretically based research questions to illustrate how the addition of visuals clarifies the number and nature of the models being examined:

> Research has indicated that test-taking effort, or the amount of effort examinees expend when completing an exam, is related to test consequences (Wise & DeMars, 2005; Wise & Smith, 2011). More specifically, tests that are low stakes for examinees are associated with lower examinee effort than tests that are high stakes for examinees. However, examinees vary greatly in test-taking effort during low-stakes testing, which begs the question, "What influences the amount of effort an examinee will put forth on a low-stakes test?" Research suggests a gender difference with respect to effort on low-stakes tests, with males expending less effort (e.g., DeMars, Bashkov, & Socha, 2013). Other research emphasizes personality characteristics, such as conscientiousness, with higher conscientiousness resulting in more expended effort (e.g., Barry, Horst, Finney, Brown & Kopp, 2010; Barry & Finney, in press; DeMars et al., 2013). Given that conscientiousness is related to both effort and gender (e.g., Feingold, 1994), we examined whether gender differences in effort are due to some extent to gender differences in conscientiousness. To further clarify the role conscientiousness plays in the relationship between gender and effort, analyses were conducted to explore whether conscientiousness serves as a moderator or a partial or full mediator of this relationship. To control for measurement error in expended effort, a latent variable of effort was modeled using five self-report items representing effort (Thelk, Sundre, Horst, & Finney, 2009).

A reader trying to mentally construct the models that represent the research questions above may have difficulty ascertaining the number of models, as well as their

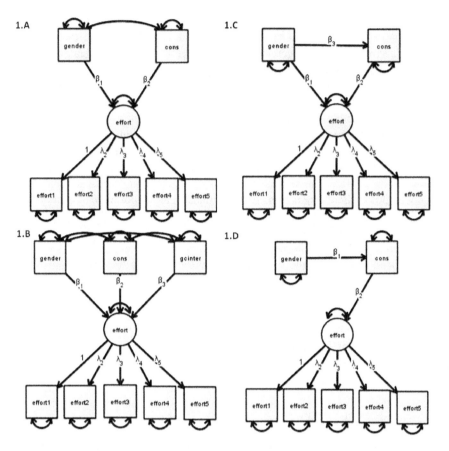

FIGURE 1. Path diagrams for hypothetical research scenario. The four path diagrams align with the research questions. Model 1.A evaluates the unique effect of gender on effort after controlling for conscientiousness. Model 1.B evaluates whether the relationship between gender and effort is moderated by conscientiousness. Model 1.C evaluates whether conscientiousness partially mediates the relationship between gender and effort. Model 1.D evaluates whether conscientiousness fully mediates the relationship between gender and effort. Compared to a verbal description of the research questions, the diagrams clearly illustrate the models being proposed, as well as their similarities and differences. cons = conscientiousness; gcinter = interaction between gender and conscientiousness; effort-effort5 = five Likert items used to measure examinee effort.

similarities and differences. That is, even though the text above is quite typical of a verbal articulation of a set of research questions, the information isn't integrated cohesively. We also suspect that presenting the equations for the measurement and structural components of the models would not prove useful for creating a mental representation of the models. As noted by Boomsma (2000) in an article outlining how to report information from SEM analyses, "a path diagram should be presented rather than the mathematical model equations, which are far more difficult to grasp" (p. 467). That is, oftentimes equations are only understood by those well acquainted with the particular technique, and readers can still be confused by differences in notation.

The path diagrams that could supplement the verbal description are provided in Figure 1. Note how the diagrams visually depict each research question, housing the corresponding parameters in the figure. Moreover, through a simple visual comparison of the diagrams, one can easily note the similarities and differences across models, something that proves difficult with only a verbal description, even if supplemented with equations.

In addition, path diagrams can explicitly depict assumptions. That is, path diagrams often communicate information not contained in a verbal description or obvious from equations (e.g., Figure 1 clearly depicts uncorrelated item errors). In short, although one can consider each model as a composite of several hypotheses, which necessitates specification of present and absent paths (McDonald & Ho, 2002), absent paths are often ignored in the text even though they represent important assumptions. Path diagrams highlight the (often overlooked) assumptions.

This simple example illustrates some of the benefits of path diagrams over the sole use of words. Below, we further detail and demonstrate the advantages of path diagrams when planning and presenting quantitative research, in addition to teaching quantitative methods.

ADVANTAGES OF USING PATH DIAGRAMS IN THE PLANNING OF QUANTITATIVE RESEARCH

With respect to planning research, a commonly cited advantage of the path diagram is the focus on theory instead of the statistical technique. That is, if a theoretically derived path diagram is created during the planning stage, the research questions may be more likely to emanate from theory than from the statistical techniques with which the researcher is most comfortable. In other words, if the theoretical relationships are considered first and the statistical technique second, a situation in which the "tail wags the dog" can be avoided. According to Henson, Hull, and Williams (2010), "the proverbial *tail wags the dog* when the questions researchers ask are determined by their limited knowledge of methods that can be employed to answer those questions" (p. 229). For example, a researcher needs to understand the theory, but not necessarily the specific statistical analysis, to sketch out the path diagrams representing the theoretically based research questions of examinee motivation presented above. Once diagrams are created, a researcher can investigate various techniques that can produce parameter estimates associated with the models and the means by which the models can be compared statistically.

ADVANTAGES OF USING PATH DIAGRAMS IN THE
PRESENTATION OF QUANTITATIVE RESEARCH

With respect to presenting findings, researchers must decide how to effectively communicate results in a way that "permits a reasoned evaluation and understanding of their analysis, yet does not overwhelm or confuse readers" (Hoyle & Panter, 1995, p. 158). Thus, one advantage of using diagrams is that they can promote understanding without overwhelming the reader. As noted in the SEM literature (e.g., Hoyle & Panter, 1995) and in the information processing literature (e.g., Vekiri, 2002), to accomplish this goal, it is advised that parameter estimate values be placed in a path diagram rather than solely in a table or text. Including parameter estimates along with their standard errors in a path diagram clarifies the effects associated with each parameter and also distinguishes parameters that are estimated from those that are fixed to a particular value or absent altogether. By examining the path diagram with the results embedded, researchers and readers can consider the model's parameter estimates comprehensively.

A second advantage is that diagrams can easily communicate the similarities and differences between equivalent models, something that may prove difficult with only a verbal description. Equivalent models are alternative models that yield the same fit to data, thus one cannot use a statistical rationale to choose between models. Determining whether models are equivalent is extremely important to understanding what can and cannot be inferred from the results. Path diagrams are particularly useful in showcasing the parameters or features common across equivalent models (Spirtes, Richardson, Meek, Scheines, & Glymour, 1998). For example, although the degrees of freedom and fit of models 1.A and 1.C in Figure 1 are identical, indicating that these models are equivalent, their path diagrams make it obvious that the two models represent different theoretical perspectives. In short, the presentation of different path diagrams for models with equivalent fit serves to emphasize that the analysis cannot establish directionality (i.e., equivalent model-data fit when the path between gender and conscientiousness is simply a correlation versus a direct path from gender to conscientiousness). That is, the researcher and readers can see that the data are equally consistent with both theories. Importantly, via the diagrams, readers can assess what is common across the two theoretical models (i.e., direct paths to effort from both gender and conscientiousness) and what differs (i.e., the relationship between gender and conscientiousness).

It is important to note that we are not advocating for visuals to replace verbal descriptions or the presentation of equations when planning or presenting results. Instead, aligned with the tenets of information processing, we advocate for the presentation of visuals coupled with a verbal description. Providing a path diagram along with a verbal description of the model (or equations) uses two different channels, the visual and verbal channels, in working memory. By accessing both channels, the burden on any one channel is reduced and the limited resources in working memory are more fully utilized because the learner does not need to hold the model in memory. Moreover, because the information provided visually and verbally is integrated across channels, a deeper understanding of the model is likely. Importantly, diagrams not only deepen understanding of the model for students familiar with the technique, but also allow those less acquainted with the model to understand it better. Given the utility of visuals to reduce cognitive load, organize information into a coherent representation, provide novel information that text cannot communicate, and activate prior knowledge (e.g., Pastor & Finney, 2013), it seems beneficial to not only utilize diagrams for planning and presenting research, but also when teaching quantitative methods.

ADVANTAGES OF USING PATH DIAGRAMS IN THE TEACHING OF QUANTITATIVE METHODS

Two recent reviews indicate that, at best, the typical graduate student completes about four courses in quantitative methods (Aiken, West, & Millsap, 2008; Henson, Hull, & Williams, 2010). Although the options available today for analyzing data are far greater than 30 years ago, training still largely revolves around "traditional" techniques, such as ANOVA or regression. Not only does the training of a typical graduate student focus on traditional techniques, but it is common for the techniques to be taught as distinct, rather than subsumed under the broader general linear modeling (GLM) framework. Furthermore, it is unlikely that students are told that the GLM (and thus all techniques it subsumes) is simply a special case of SEM (e.g., Tanaka, Panter, Winborne, & Huba, 1990).

One advantage of presenting path diagrams to articulate the broader statistical framework when teaching traditional techniques is described by Rutherford (2011), who advocated for the GLM approach when introducing regression, ANOVA, and ANCOVA: "Rather than having to learn about three apparently discrete techniques, it is possible to develop an understanding of a consistent modeling approach that can be applied to different circumstances" (p. 13). By showcasing the logical and mathematical commonalities of techniques subsumed under the larger framework, we emphasize to students that distinctions among techniques are much less important than their commonalities (Dwyer, 1983). That is, just because techniques have different names doesn't mean they are mathematically different (i.e., ANOVA is equivalent to regression and between-subjects MANOVA is equivalent to descriptive discriminant analysis). If the focus of instruction is on what is common across techniques, then the important differences between techniques become more apparent and it becomes much easier to understand when a technique has utility over another. In this chapter, we illustrate how commonalities among several traditional techniques can easily be showcased by highlighting the extreme likeness of their path diagrams. In some cases, the same diagram represents techniques with different names.

A second advantage of using path diagrams when teaching statistics is that it helps learners make connections between introductory and more complicated, yet related, techniques that heavily employ path diagrams (e.g., path analysis, factor models, full SEMs). Unfortunately, it is likely that students first encounter path diagrams when they read research articles that use SEM or in SEM-related coursework. If path diagrams are introduced early in statistical training, then path diagrams for various traditional statistical models could be stored as schemas. Schemas can be thought of as knowledge stored in long-term memory or, as defined by Sweller (2005), "cognitive constructs that allow multiple elements of information to be categorized as a single element" (p. 21). When path diagrams are presented for more advanced techniques, they are likely to activate students' preexisting schemas that are associated with the more traditional methods. The activation of preexisting schemas should not only deepen students' understanding of the advanced technique through the integration of novel information with prior knowledge, but it should also reduce the burden on working memory (van Merriënboer & Sweller, 2010).

A third advantage of presenting path diagrams early in statistics training is that it could facilitate an understanding of and hence adoption of the statistical modeling perspective. Over the past several decades, a modeling revolution has occurred (e.g., Rodgers, 2010a, 2010b). This revolution recognizes the need to specify and compare alternative models to describe our data (e.g., Denis, 2003). That is, with respect to quantitative research, we have moved away from "a set of procedures, applied mechanistically, and moved toward building and evaluating statistical and scientific models" (Rodgers, 2010a, p. 1). In short, this revolution is represented in the following equation: Data = Model + Error (Maxwell & Delaney, 2004). We test competing models and identify the model that best represents our data (results in the least amount of error; Green & Thompson, 2012; Hancock, 2010). Although the modeling perspective is characteristic of advanced techniques such as SEM (Hancock, 2010; Rodgers, 2010a, 2010b), it applies to well-constructed models, no matter how simple or complex (e.g., Green & Thompson, 2012; Maxwell & Delaney, 2004; Tanaka et al., 1990). This perspective is in contrast to a singular focus on null hypothesis significance testing (NHST), which modeling subsumes. As Harlow (2010) notes, "I would go further to state that statistical modeling may be more effective than NHST in allowing and even encouraging researchers to be more motivated to study, analyze and integrate their findings into encompassing and coherent streams of research" (p. 353). Thus, it isn't surprising that there have been calls to reform methodological curriculum to better incorporate a modeling perspective (e.g., Granaas, 2012; Hancock, 2010; Rodgers, 2010a), "rather than limiting teaching to narrow and isolated methodological procedures" (Harlow, 2013, p. 112). Presenting traditional techniques visually via path diagrams during statistics training facilitates an (early) understanding of the modeling perspective, including proposing, examining, and comparing multiple models, as demonstrated below.

In the sections that follow, we illustrate the utility of path diagrams. For this chapter to be self-contained, we begin by showcasing the visual representation of traditional techniques using path diagrams. We then illustrate how visuals of traditional techniques facilitate a model-comparison approach to theory testing. Because our intention is to promote the use of path diagrams, SEM software that generates these visuals is described. Path diagrams are then employed to explain why results obtained from these programs differ from results obtained using more general statistical programs (e.g., SAS). These demonstrations are intended to provide the minimum knowledge necessary to begin using visuals in quantitative research and teaching.

VISUALLY DEPICTING
TRADITIONAL STATISTICAL TECHNIQUES

The path diagrams presented in this section align with the traditional techniques that are typically taught in a first or second statistics course during undergraduate or graduate training. These initial courses typically focus on univariate techniques appropriate for use with a single continuous dependent variable (also called an outcome) and one or more independent variables (also called predictors) that are categorical or continuous in nature. In our illustration, we chose to use between-subjects categorical predictors with only two levels to keep the example simple.

To provide context, variables from a real data example are used. The example data were collected from 6,148 college students at our university who were required to attend a 3-hour testing session where they completed a variety of measures used to assess student learning and development. Because the results from these assessments are used primarily to assess the effectiveness of university programs and hence are low stakes for students, there is concern about the amount of effort students put forth on the exams. For this reason, the Student Opinion Scale (Thelk et al., 2009) was administered at the end of the assessment session to measure test-taking effort. The average of the item responses from this measure (labeled as *effort*) ranges from 1 to 5 and serves as the continuous dependent variable in all models. Characteristics of students thought to be related to effort and used as predictors in the path diagrams are described in Table 1. The data along with SAS and Mplus syntax is available from the first author.

The most simplistic model for the dependent variable *effort* is shown in Figure 2 and is known as the intercept-only model or empty model. In textbooks that label models as separate techniques, this model is often referred to as the one-sample *t*-test. The path diagram for the intercept-only model will be described in detail not only to orient readers to the components of path diagrams (further information about the conventions of path diagrams in SEM can be found in Ho, Stark, & Chernyshenko, 2012), but also because the presentation of a path diagram for this technique is quite uncommon. As is conventional in SEM path diagrams, the variable *effort* is represented with a square in the path diagram because it is an observed (as opposed to latent or unobserved) variable. As the path diagram clearly depicts, this model includes no predictor variables other than the intercept, which is a constant (sometimes referred to as a pseudovariable) that takes on a value of one for all persons. As is conventional in SEM, a triangle with a value of one rep-

TABLE 1. Type, Name, and Description of Predictor Variables

Type	Name	Description
Continuous variables	*cons*	Conscientiousness was measured by the Big Five Inventory (John & Srivastava, 1999). Conscientiousness is considered a personality characteristic characterized by task-directed behavior.
	wav	Work avoidance was measured by the Achievement Goal Questionnaire (Pieper, 2003). Work avoidance is characterized by a desire to complete the least amount of work possible and the valuing of work minimization strategies over learning (Elliot, 1999).
Categorical variables	*gender*	Males and females were represented by values of -.5 and .5 on this variable, respectively.
	jr	Sophomores and juniors were represented by values of -.5 and .5 on this variable, respectively.
Interaction between variables	*gjinter*	The variable gjinter is the product of gender and jr.
	gcinter	The variable gcinter is the product of gender and cons.
	cwinter	The variable cwinter is the product of cons and wav.

Note. The variables *cons* and *wav* were mean centered to avoid issues with nonessential multicollinearity between predictors and their interaction terms (Cohen, Cohen, West & Aiken, 2003, sec. 7.2.4). Contrast coding was used for categorical variables to ease interpretation of their associated parameter estimates and to allow the significance tests for each parameter estimate to align with those obtained for the main effect and interaction terms in a Type III sums of squares approach to ANOVA and ANCOVA. The use of centering and the particular coding scheme adopted for categorical variables affects parameter estimates and their significance tests, but does not affect the R^2 for the model nor whether the model fits significantly better than an intercept-only model. Readers interested in learning more about these topics are suggested to consult Chapters 7 through 9 of Cohen et al. (2003).

resents the inclusion of the intercept in the model (Ho et al., 2012). Because the intercept is predicting *effort*, the path diagram contains a path with an arrow pointing from the intercept to the variable *effort*. The direction of the arrow visually conveys the direction of the regression (the regression of *effort* on the intercept as opposed to the regression of the intercept on *effort*). The coefficient (β_0) listed on this path is the parameter that captures the relationship between the intercept and *effort*, which in this model equals the mean of the dependent variable.

The error, or influences on *effort* not captured by the model, is shown by a circle consisting of *e* and a single-headed arrow from *e* to *effort* (because *e* influences *effort*). A circle is used instead of a square because *e* is latent; that is, the influences on *effort* not captured by the model are considered not observed. The double-headed arrow on *e* represents the error variance (σ_e^2), or the variance that remains in *effort* after controlling for predictor variables in the model. Because there are no predictor variables, σ_e^2 simply equals the total variance of *effort*.

The intercept-only model does more than just describe the mean and variance of the dependent variable. As aforementioned, it is equivalent to the one sample *t*-test and therefore can be used to assess the hypothesis that the population mean

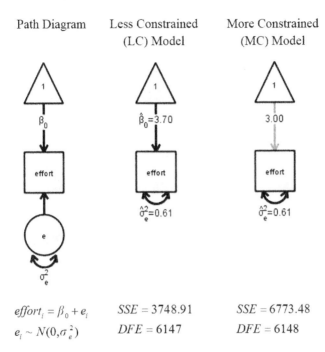

Path Diagram	Less Constrained (LC) Model	More Constrained (MC) Model

$$effort_i = \beta_0 + e_i$$
$$e_i \sim N(0, \sigma_e^2)$$

	$SSE = 3748.91$	$SSE = 6773.48$
	$DFE = 6147$	$DFE = 6148$

FIGURE 2.   Path diagram of intercept-only model (i.e., one-sample t-test). The intercept parameter (β_0) and error variance (σ_e^2) in this model equal the mean and variance of effort, respectively. The error, or influences on effort not captured by the model, is shown by a circle consisting of e. To provide further context, the mathematical equation is shown for the model at the bottom of the figure. The models associated with traditional techniques assume $e_i \sim N(0, \sigma_e^2)$. To simplify the path diagrams, e is no longer shown in the path diagrams and the error variance is represented by the curved bidirectional arrow under effort. In the Less Constrained (LC) Model, all parameters are freely estimated with the resulting estimates displayed on the figure. In the More Constrained (MC) Model, to visually indicate that β_0 is not estimated but set equal to a value of three, the color of the path was set to grey. Because the More Constrained Model is nested within the Less Constrained Model, the models can be statistically compared via an F test or likelihood ratio test. $SSE =$ sum of squares error; $DFE =$ degrees of freedom error.

equals a particular value. To illustrate, the parameter of the model was estimated using ordinary least squares (OLS) estimation, which is typical in introductory courses. Parameter estimates can be computed using a host of different estimators, one of which, maximum likelihood, will be illustrated later in the chapter. The resulting OLS parameter estimate is shown visually in Figure 2 under the heading "Less Constrained Model." The mean of *effort* is 3.70, which is the OLS parameter estimate of the intercept ($\hat{\beta}_0$). The variance of *effort* ($\hat{\sigma}_e^2$) is computed and equals 0.61. One use of the model is to obtain a significance test and confidence interval for $\hat{\beta}_0$. A significance test can be obtained by dividing the difference between $\hat{\beta}_0$ and the null value by the estimated standard error (*SE*) of the parameter, as shown in Equation 1:

$$\frac{\text{Parameter Estimate} - \text{Null Value}}{SE} \tag{1}$$

The resulting value is a *t*-distributed statistic that can be used to test the null hypothesis that β_0 equals zero. When employing OLS estimation, the degrees of freedom for this test are *n-k*-1, where *n* equals sample size and *k* equals number of predictors, which here equals zero. That is, the degrees of freedom are *n*-1 because only one population parameter (the population mean) is being estimated. Using this single parameter *t*-test and the value of 0.010 for the estimated standard error, the null hypothesis is rejected, $t(6147) = 371.63$, $p < 0.001$. Had we been interested in a value for the null hypothesis other than zero, we could have easily used that value as the null value in the single parameter *t*-test. For instance, using a null value of three, we obtain $t(6147) = 70.42$, $p < 0.001$ and reject the null hypothesis that β_0 equals three.

In Figures 3 and 4, differing numbers and types of predictors are added to the intercept-only model. Although σ_e^2 is represented in all diagrams, it now has a different interpretation and represents the amount of variance in *effort* that remains after controlling for the predictors. Relative to the intercept-only model, it is hoped that the value of σ_e^2, also known as mean square error and a function of the sum of squared error (*SSE*), is greatly reduced when predictors are included in the model. A familiar index used to capture the extent the error is reduced is R^2, which represents the reduction in error variance relative to the intercept-only model when predictors are included in the model. Parameters of interest include the coefficients associated with the predictors (e.g., β_1, β_2, β_3), as they indicate the direction and size of the relationship between the predictor and *effort* after controlling for all other predictors in the model.

Because path diagrams are infrequently utilized to represent traditional techniques, it may not be obvious that the diagrams in Figures 3 and 4 align with traditional statistical methods. Within the left column of Figure 3, diagrams with continuous predictors are arranged from simpler (less predictors) to more complex (more predictors) and visually depict simple linear regression (3.A), multiple regression with two predictors (3.B), and multiple regression with two predictors and their interaction (3.C). Within the right column of Figure 3, diagrams with categorical predictors[1] are arranged from simpler to more complex and graphi-

---

[1] There are a variety of different ways to portray group comparisons using path diagram. For example, Green and Thompson (2012) use a cell means approach, which entails including a dummy-coded variable for each group in the model and omitting the intercept. Because our approach uses g-1 contrast codes, where g equals the number of groups, the intercept is included in the models and path diagrams.

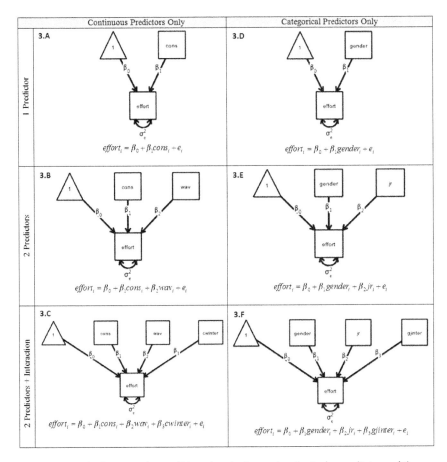

FIGURE 3. Path diagrams for traditional techniques that include predictors of the same type (all continuous or all categorical). To provide further context for the parameters depicted in the path diagrams, a general equation is presented for each model. The models associated with traditional techniques assume $e_i \sim N(0, \sigma_e^2)$. The variables in the figure are described in Table 1. The traditional statistical techniques aligning with each diagram include: simple linear regression (3.A), multiple regression with two predictors (3.B), multiple regression with two predictors and their interaction (3.C), an independent samples t-test (3.D), a two-way ANOVA without an interaction (3.E), and a two-way ANOVA with an interaction (3.F).

cally represent an independent samples *t*-test (3.D), two-way ANOVA without an interaction (3.E), and two-way ANOVA with an interaction (3.F). Figure 4 presents diagrams with both continuous and categorical predictors, which depict ANCOVA, where the interaction is absent (4.A), and the assessment of the homogeneity of regression assumption in ANCOVA, where the interaction is included (4.B).

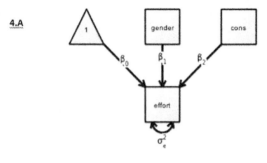

$$effort_i = \beta_0 + \beta_1 gender_i + \beta_2 cons_i + e_i$$

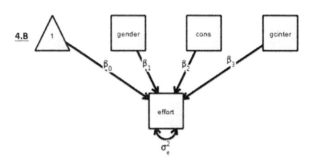

$$effort_i = \beta_0 + \beta_1 gender_i + \beta_2 cons_i + \beta_3 gcinter_i + e_i$$

FIGURE 4. Path diagrams for traditional techniques that include predictors of different types (categorical and continuous). To provide further context for the parameters depicted in the path diagrams, a general equation is presented for each model. The models associated with traditional techniques assume $e_i \sim N(0, \sigma_e^2)$. The variables in the figure are described in Table 1. The traditional statistical techniques aligning with each diagram include: ANCOVA (4.A), where the interaction is absent, and the analysis used to assess the homogeneity of regression lines assumption in ANCOVA (4.B), where the interaction is included.

Notice how these visuals highlight the extreme similarities between models typically referred to as "regression" techniques (models 3.A though 3.C) versus "ANOVA" techniques (models 3.D though 3.F). That is, a comparison of the diagrams within the same row in Figure 3 (e.g., 3.A compared to 3.D) makes it evident that the only difference between "regression" and "ANOVA" techniques is the nature of the independent variables. Students might be told that the same model underlies "ANOVA" and "regression" techniques, but the conversation often ends there. The addition of equations to this conversation along with the path diagrams in Figure 3 elucidates the connection between these seemingly disparate techniques. In short, the visuals make it obvious that these "different" techniques actually represent the same model.

Similarly, a comparison of models 3.B, 3.E, and 4.A highlights the correspondence between techniques typically referred to as multiple regression (3.B), two-way ANOVA without an interaction (3.E), and ANCOVA (4.B). Again, the fact that the same model underlies these techniques is easily communicated via diagrams. The interaction between predictors is added in models 3.C, 3.F, and 4.B. The similarity of these models highlights how the interaction term serves the same purpose in all three contexts: it assesses whether the relationship between a predictor and an outcome differs across the levels of the other predictor. Thus, the representation of the model using path diagrams conveys that the interaction term in an ANCOVA model is more than just a means by which to test an assumption; it represents what is often considered an important research question. According to Harlow (2013), "Quantitative understanding is increased when common ideas are revealed that occur in many statistical procedures" (p. 109). As evident from an examination of the diagrams in Figures 2 through 4, visuals are a powerful tool for conveying such commonalities.

USING VISUALS TO FACILITATE A MODELING APPROACH TO RESEARCH

Not only are the visuals in Figures 2 through 4 useful in teaching students about the similarities and differences among traditional techniques, but early use of diagrams to visually represent statistical models encourages a model-oriented approach to research. In a model-oriented approach to research, the emphasis is placed on creating a set of theoretically based models to describe relationships among variables. As an example, all models in Figures 3 and 4 could be thought of as competing models, with some models providing simple explanations (e.g., model 3.D) and others providing more complex explanations (e.g., model 4.B). Statistical evaluation of these models entails gauging whether models represent the data well and then advocating for models that not only accomplish this task, but that also provide parsimonious explanations of the phenomena under study. The use of path diagrams to describe traditional statistical techniques emphasizes that such techniques are merely a subset of a large number of mathematical models that can be used to explain relationships among variables.

Using Path Diagrams to Highlight Single Parameter Model Comparisons

Path diagrams of traditional statistics are very helpful when introducing the idea of evaluating competing models. A simple example is provided in the context of the intercept-only model to illustrate the model-comparison approach with the simplest of techniques. The same null hypotheses evaluated with the intercept-only model using Equation 1 are reframed as a comparison of models. Recall that the single parameter t-test in Equation 1 was used to assess two null hypotheses: (a) H_0: $\beta_0 = 0$ and (b) H_0: $\beta_0 = 3$. An equivalent approach to obtaining the same information is to compare the model where β_0 is freely estimated to the model that constrains β_0 to equal a particular value. To illustrate, consider the diagram under the heading "More Constrained Model (MC)" in Figure 2. Rather than freely estimating the intercept, we are fixing the intercept to a value of three. To visually indicate the intercept parameter is not estimated the color of the path was set to grey and displays only the value at which the intercept is fixed. The "Less Constrained Model (LC)" is more complex than the "More Constrained Model (MC)" because it requires the estimation of an additional parameter, in this case the mean of *effort*. We can compare the two models using the following F-test:

$$F(DFE_{MC} - DFE_{LC}, DFE_{LC}) = \frac{(SSE_{MC} - SSE_{LC})/(DFE_{MC} - DFE_{LC})}{SSE_{LC}/DFE_{LC}}$$

(2)

Like σ_e^2 in Figure 2 (which is equal to SSE/DFE for a model), the sum of squares error (SSE) for each model represents how "off" we are when using each model to predict *effort*, and thus lower values are desirable. The SSEs for the two models indicate that the supplied mean of three does a worse job representing the average of *effort* than the estimated mean of 3.70. The F-test is evaluating whether the reduction in error (i.e., improvement in fit) obtained by estimating the mean is worth the cost of using a more complex model (Rodgers, 2010a). More specifically, substituting the sum of squares error (SSE) and degrees of freedom error (DFE) for both models into Equation 2, we arrive at $F(1,6147) = 4959.32$, $p < .001$, indicating the SSE for the less constrained model is significantly smaller than the SSE for the more constrained model. On the basis of this alone, we would advocate for the more complex model where the mean is estimated. This model comparison is equivalent to the one-sample t-test results of the null hypothesis that the mean equals three (recall that $t^2 = F$; thus, $70.42^2 = 4959.32$). This illustration demonstrates that there are two equivalent approaches to testing the null hypothesis that a single parameter equals a particular value. One approach involves the single parameter t-test, where the null value is set equal to zero or some other value of interest. The other approach involves an overt model comparison, which entails comparing a model with the parameter freely estimated to a model in which it is constrained to zero or some other value of interest. This model-comparison approach is facilitated by visuals of the competing models.

This same model-comparison approach to testing the significance of a single parameter can be applied to the models in Figures 3 and 4. For instance, the F-test can be used to assess whether β_3 in model 3.C is significantly different from a particular value, where model 3.C serves as the less constrained model and the same model with β_3 fixed to the null value serves as the more constrained model. Note that if the more constrained model restricts β_3 to zero, the model comparison test is simply evaluating whether model 3.C, where the interaction is included in the

TABLE 2.   Model Comparison Results

Model Comparison (LC vs. MC)	Interaction Included vs. No Interaction	Interaction Included vs. Intercept-Only
Null Evaluated	$H_0: \beta_3 = 0$	$H_0: \beta_1 = \beta_2 = \beta_3 = 0$
OLS with predictors fixed	$\dfrac{(3504.97 - 3504.54)/(6145 - 6144)}{3505.54/6144} = 0.76$	$\dfrac{(3748.91 - 3504.54)/(6147 - 6144)}{3505.54/6144} = 142.81$
	$F(1, 6144) = 0.76, p = 0.39$	$F(3, 6144) = 142.81, p < 0.001$
ML with predictors fixed	$-2(-6996.22 - (-6995.84)) = 0.76$	$-2(-7203.04 - (-6995.84)) = 414.40$
	$\chi^2(1) = 0.76, p = 0.39$	$\chi^2(3) = 414.40, p < 0.001$
ML with predictors random	$-2(-29784.59 - (-29784.22)) = 0.76$	$-2(-29991.42 - (-29784.22)) = 414.40$
	$\chi^2(1) = 0.76, p = 0.39$	$\chi^2(3) = 414.40, p < 0.001$

Note. LC = Less Constrained Model. MC = More Constrained Model. The *F*-test and *LR* test for comparing nested models are asymptotically equivalent and have the following relationship: $LR = (DFE_{MC} - DFE_{LC}) * F$.

model, does a better job explaining variance in *effort* than model 3.B, where the interaction is omitted. These same models, along with their estimated parameters, *SSE*s and *DFE*s, are presented in Figure 5. Model 3.C, which includes the interaction, is in the first row and model 3.B, which omits the interaction, is shown in in the second row. In Figure 5's representation of model 3.B, the interaction is included, but its path is constrained to zero. Although the diagram for the model differs from model 3.B in Figure 3, it is the same model. The *F*-test comparing the *SSE*s of the model including the interaction to the model that does not (i.e., constrains it to zero) is shown in Table 2 and indicates that the *SSE* for the less constrained model (Interaction Included) is not significantly smaller than the *SSE* for the more constrained model (No Interaction). The more parsimonious model without the interaction is therefore favored. The diagrams in Figure 5 highlight how the single parameter *t*-test and *p*-value for β_3 is actually a comparison of competing models (recall that $t^2 = F$; thus, $-0.87^2 = 0.76$). Clearly, visuals are a powerful tool to orient learners to model comparisons, even in the context of a *p*-value for a single effect

Using Path Diagrams to Highlight the Null Hypothesis Being Tested

In addition to conducting single parameter model comparisons, researchers are often interested in multiparameter model comparisons. When these more complex comparisons are of interest, visual comparisons of path diagrams assist in determining what null hypothesis is being evaluated by the statistical test. To illustrate, consider the Interaction Included model in Figure 5. It might be questioned

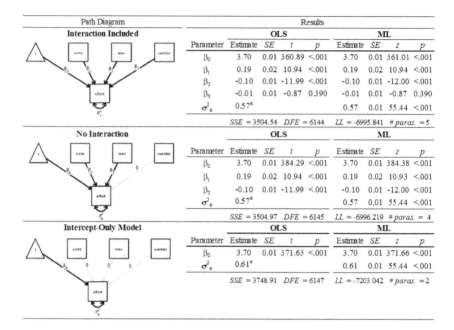

Path Diagram	Results								

Interaction Included

	OLS				ML			
Parameter	Estimate	SE	t	p	Estimate	SE	z	p
β_0	3.70	0.01	360.89	<.001	3.70	0.01	361.01	<.001
β_1	0.19	0.02	10.94	<.001	0.19	0.02	10.94	<.001
β_2	-0.10	0.01	-11.99	<.001	-0.10	0.01	-12.00	<.001
β_3	-0.01	0.01	-0.87	0.390	-0.01	0.01	-0.87	0.390
σ^2_e	0.57[a]				0.57	0.01	55.44	<.001

SSE = 3504.54   DFE = 6144   LL = -6995.841   # paras. = 5

No Interaction

	OLS				ML			
Parameter	Estimate	SE	t	p	Estimate	SE	z	p
β_0	3.70	0.01	384.29	<.001	3.70	0.01	384.38	<.001
β_1	0.19	0.02	10.94	<.001	0.19	0.02	10.93	<.001
β_2	-0.10	0.01	-11.99	<.001	-0.10	0.01	-12.00	<.001
σ^2_e	0.57[a]				0.57	0.01	55.44	<.001

SSE = 3504.97   DFE = 6145   LL = -6996.219   # paras. = 4

Intercept-Only Model

	OLS				ML			
Parameter	Estimate	SE	t	p	Estimate	SE	z	p
β_0	3.70	0.01	371.63	<.001	3.70	0.01	371.66	<.001
σ^2_e	0.61[a]				0.61	0.01	55.44	<.001

SSE = 3748.91   DFE = 6147   LL = -7203.042   # paras. = 2

FIGURE 5. Path diagrams and model results under OLS and ML estimation when predictors are treated as fixed. The variables in the figure are described in Table 1. The No-Interaction model is the same model as Model 3.B in Figure 3 and the intercept-only model is the same model as the Less Constrained (LC) Model in Figure 2. SSE = sum of squares error; DFE = degrees of freedom error, LL = log likelihood, # paras. = number of parameters estimated. [a]Although regression coefficients are estimated using OLS, the error variance is not and is instead calculated as SSE/n-k-1, where n equals sample size and k equals number of predictors.

whether this complex model for explaining individual differences in *effort* has any benefit over no predictors at all, a state of affairs captured by the intercept-only model. A visual comparison of the diagrams for the Interaction Included and intercept-only model elucidates the null hypothesis being evaluated, which is H_0: $\beta_1 = \beta_2 = \beta_3 = 0$. Stated in words, this null hypothesis evaluates whether the coefficients associated with all predictors in the Interaction Included model are equal to zero. Recall that the model comparison is evaluating whether the *SSE* of the less constrained model (which here is the Interaction Included model) is significantly smaller than the *SSE* of the more constrained model (which here is the intercept-only model). In this specific model comparison, we are assessing whether the set of three predictors are better than no predictors at all, which is a test of whether the R^2 for the Interaction Included model is different than zero. Using the *SSE*s and *DFE*s for the models in Figure 5, the *F*-test[2] for this comparison was calculated and the results shown in Table 2. The results indicate that R^2 for the Interaction Included model is significantly different than zero. Framed in the context of model comparisons, the results indicate that the intercept-only model fits significantly worse than the Interaction Included model. The results of this test are presented in almost all outputs for regression models but may not have been cast as a comparison of competing models (the model in question vs. the intercept-only model). Use of path diagrams clarifies what is meant by this often examined null hypothesis and associated significance test, and the visuals do so in a manner that orients learners to model comparisons.

Using Path Diagrams to Determine if Models are Nested

It may not be obvious, but all of the model comparisons conducted this far have involved nested models. Models are nested when one model is obtained by applying constraints to the parameters of another model. For the *F*-test, these models were referred to as the more constrained and less constrained models, respectively. Path diagrams are incredibly helpful for identifying if two models are nested and thus, whether the *F*-test is appropriate for determining if the *SSE* or R^2 of one model is significantly different from the other. For example, suppose two models of interest were models 3.C (*SSE* = 3504.97; R^2 = 0.065) and 4.B (*SSE* = 3584.41, R^2 = 0.044). Although the difference between the *SSE*s and R^2s of those models indicates model 3.C is doing a superior job, the *F*-test to evaluate whether the difference is significant cannot be used because the models are not nested.[3] That is, there are no restrictions we could place on one model to obtain the other, as easily evidenced by a visual comparison of the two path diagrams. In contrast, all models in Figure 5 are nested as highlighted by comparing their path diagrams, where the No Interaction and intercept-only models are simply the Interaction Included model with the constraints $\beta_3 = 0$ and $\beta_1 = \beta_2 = \beta_3 = 0$, respectively.

---

[2] An equivalent formulation for the *F* statistic when the model in question (considered the less constrained model) is compared to the intercept-only model (considered the more constrained model) is

$$F = \frac{R^2(n-k-1)}{(1-R^2)k}$$

with $df = k$, n-k-1. In this equation, R^2 is the proportion of variance in the dependent variable explained by the less constrained model and is equal to

$$R^2 = \frac{SSE_{MC} - SSE_{LC}}{SSE_{LC}}$$

In the equation, k equals the number of predictor variables and n equals sample size.

[3] Nonnested models can be statistically compared, but the comparison cannot be conducted using the *F*-test in Equation 2. Models 3.C and 4.B could be compared, for example, using Steiger's approach of comparing the two multiple correlation coefficients using a *z*-test (Steiger, 1980; Steiger & Browne, 1984).

SOFTWARE PROGRAMS FOR CREATING PATH DIAGRAMS

Researchers intending to create path diagrams when planning and presenting research or instructors hoping to employ these diagrams in their teaching might consider the effort needed to create nice-looking path diagrams as a barrier to their use. Fortunately, there are several software programs available for creating path diagrams and we refer readers to Beaujean (2013) for a review. The path diagrams in this chapter were created using the free program Ωnyx (von Oertzen, Brandmaier, & Tsang, 2014, 2015), which we found incredibly easy to use.

If SEM programs are used for analyses, path diagrams are often (but not always) available as part of the output. Several SEM programs allow the user to construct the model as a path diagram, as opposed to writing syntax. This option is available in Ωnyx, along with the option to export the program-generated syntax associated with the path diagram for use in another SEM program, such as OpenMx (Boker et al., 2011, 2012) and Mplus (Muthén & Muthén, 1998–2012). We agree with von Oertzen et al. (2014, p. 1) that programs such as Ωnyx can be powerful teaching tools because "modeling can be taught in a graphical approach without the need to teach a specific modeling language. In the progress of a course, a transition from the purely graphical approach to a specific modeling language can be made."

Using SEM programs for the analysis and creation of path diagrams is more efficient than the approach we took to acquiring the results presented thus far. The results in the previous section were obtained using PROC REG in SAS, which doesn't offer a path diagram representing the model. Our process therefore required two steps: creating the visual in one program and then estimating the model in another program. The same would be true had we used other popular programs for our analyses, such as SPSS. Clearly, there are advantages to using a single program that produces both the diagrams and the parameter estimates. Although both tasks can be accomplished using many SEM programs, the results of traditional techniques will differ from those obtained using more popular statistical software programs (e.g., SPSS). Because it would be irresponsible to guide readers to these useful SEM programs without noting and demonstrating these differences, the section below utilizes path diagrams to describe and illustrate why the results differ. We conclude our discussion of SEM software by noting many ancillary advantages such programs have to offer in addition to the creation of the path diagrams.

Differences in Results When SEM Software is Used

There are two primary reasons why the results for traditional statistics will differ when obtained using SEM software versus popular statistical software (e.g., SPSS, SAS). First, results differ because of differences between the programs in the default estimation methods. OLS estimation is typically the default estimator in the popular statistical software programs, whereas ML is the default estimator in SEM programs. As we will demonstrate, the differences in results due the use of OLS versus ML estimation are slight. Second, the results differ due to the different analytical orientations of the two software programs and this difference in orientation is, by and large, the reason why the results appear discrepant. For the more popular programs, the analytical orientation involves estimating a model to re-create scores on the dependent variable, whereas the orientation for covariance-based SEM programs involves estimating a model to re-create information associated with *all* variables in the model (i.e., the dependent variable *and* predictors). To demonstrate the differences, the three models in Figure 5 were estimated using ML and the same orientation as popular programs (results shown in Figure 5) and again using ML and the orientation utilized in SEM programs (path diagrams and results shown in Figure 6).

Differences Due to Estimator

Figure 5 shows the difference in the results obtained due to the use of a different estimator only.[4] The fact that a single set of path diagrams are shown in Figure 5 emphasizes that the same models are being estimated, only the estimation technique differs (OLS vs. ML). The OLS and ML values are the same, with the exception of the error variances (σ_e^2), which were slightly smaller when computed via ML. This difference is not obvious from Figure 5 because results are only reported out to two decimal places, but it is obvious when estimates of σ_e^2 are reported with increased precision (for the Interaction Included model, the values equal 0.57040 and 0.57003 for OLS and ML, respectively). It is well established that when model assumptions are met, the results obtained using OLS and ML are the same (Eliason, 1993), with the exception of the difference between OLS and ML variance values. ML estimates of variances and covariances are known to be smaller than OLS values[5] because of differences in what is used in the denominator. In computing σ_e^2 for example, ML uses *n* in the denominator, whereas OLS uses *n-k-1*, where *n* equals sample size and *k* equals the number of predictors in the model. When *n* is large, as it is in our example, the differences between OLS and ML estimates of variances and covariances are slight.

Another minor difference when using ML instead of OLS estimation involves the single parameter significance tests. Although Equation 1 can still be used to evaluate the departure of a parameter estimate from some null value when em-

---

[4]Although PROC MIXED in SAS or the MIXED procedure in SPSS could be used for this purpose, we used Mplus, which might be considered an SEM program. In Mplus, the model can be specified in a way that aligns with the traditional analytical orientation (i.e., where predictors are treated as fixed variables).

[5]This is true of limited or full information maximum likelihood. A different kind of ML estimation known as restricted maximum likelihood (REML) takes into account the degrees of freedom when estimating variances and covariances. Variance and covariance estimates obtained using REML are not negatively biased. Because REML is not as widely available in SEM software packages, it was not used in this example.

ploying ML estimation, the resulting statistic is normally distributed, not t-distributed, when sample sizes are large (as indicated by a z for the statistic instead of t in Figure 5). This test is commonly referred to as the single parameter Wald test. Given our large sample size, no differences were found between the single parameter t-tests using OLS estimation and the single parameter Wald tests using ML estimation.

There are also differences between OLS and ML in how nested models are compared. Nested models can be compared when ML is used, but instead of using the F-test, the log-likelihoods (LLs) associated with each model are used to obtain the likelihood ratio (LR) statistic, where $LR = -2(LL_{MC} - LL_{LC})$. The LL represents the likelihood of the data given the parameters estimated for that specific model. Models that better represent data have higher (i.e., more positive) LL values. To demonstrate, consider the models with and without the interaction in Figure 5. The LR test comparing these models is evaluating the same null hypothesis (H_0: β_3 = 0) as the F-test when OLS estimation was used. In words, the LR test is evaluating under which of the two models the data are more likely: one which includes the interaction or one that does not. When sample size is large, LR statistics are χ^2 distributed with degrees of freedom equal to the difference in the number of parameters being estimated in each model. As visually depicted by the path diagrams, the more constrained model is estimating one less parameter than the less constrained model, thus the difference in the number of parameters is one. The results of the LR test shown in Table 2 align with the F-test results and indicate that the more constrained model does not fit significantly worse than the less constrained model (i.e., the interaction term is not statistically significant).

Differences Due to Analytical Orientation

The three models in Figure 5 were modified and re-presented in Figure 6 to reflect the different orientation used in SEM programs.[6] Because path diagrams are incredibly helpful for conveying the difference in the analytical orientation utilized by popular statistics software programs (Figure 5) versus SEM programs (Figure 6), we recommend that instructors use the diagrams for this very purpose. A notable difference between the two figures is the presence of more paths and bidirectional curved arrows in Figure 6, reflecting the estimation of more parameters in the SEM orientation. The reason more parameters are estimated resides in the treatment of all variables as *random variables* in the SEM orientation, which is in contrast to the typical assumptions of most traditional techniques (e.g.,

---

[6] Most SEM programs utilize a covariance-based SEM framework, which is the analytical orientation of SEM programs described here. In fact, SEM is often called mean and covariance structure modeling to reflect the focus on analyzing and trying to reproduce summary statistics (covariances, variances, and means) of *all* the variables being modeled. Readers interested in an alternative SEM framework known as partial least squares SEM are referred to Hair, Ringle, and Sarstedt (2011).

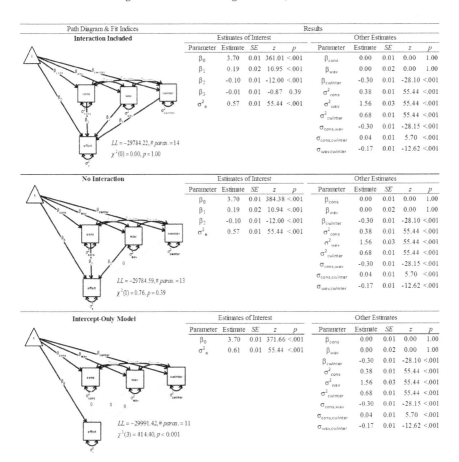

Interaction Included

| Path Diagram & Fit Indices | | | | | Results | | | | |

Estimates of Interest

Parameter	Estimate	SE	z	p
β_0	3.70	0.01	361.01	<.001
β_1	0.19	0.02	10.95	<.001
β_2	-0.10	0.01	-12.00	<.001
β_3	-0.01	0.01	-0.87	0.39
σ^2_e	0.57	0.01	55.44	<.001

Other Estimates

Parameter	Estimate	SE	z	p
β_{cons}	0.00	0.01	0.00	1.00
β_{wav}	0.00	0.02	0.00	1.00
$\beta_{cwinter}$	-0.30	0.01	-28.10	<.001
σ^2_{cons}	0.38	0.01	55.44	<.001
σ^2_{wav}	1.56	0.03	55.44	<.001
$\sigma^2_{cwinter}$	0.68	0.01	55.44	<.001
$\sigma_{cons,wav}$	-0.30	0.01	-28.15	<.001
$\sigma_{cons,cwinter}$	0.04	0.01	5.70	<.001
$\sigma_{wav,cwinter}$	-0.17	0.01	-12.62	<.001

$LL = -29784.22$, # *paras.* = 14
$\chi^2(0) = 0.00$, $p = 1.00$

No Interaction

Estimates of Interest

Parameter	Estimate	SE	z	p
β_0	3.70	0.01	384.38	<.001
β_1	0.19	0.02	10.94	<.001
β_2	-0.10	0.01	-12.00	<.001
σ^2_e	0.57	0.01	55.44	<.001

Other Estimates

Parameter	Estimate	SE	z	p
β_{cons}	0.00	0.01	0.00	1.00
β_{wav}	0.00	0.02	0.00	1.00
$\beta_{cwinter}$	-0.30	0.01	-28.10	<.001
σ^2_{cons}	0.38	0.01	55.44	<.001
σ^2_{wav}	1.56	0.03	55.44	<.001
$\sigma^2_{cwinter}$	0.68	0.01	55.44	<.001
$\sigma_{cons,wav}$	-0.30	0.01	-28.15	<.001
$\sigma_{cons,cwinter}$	0.04	0.01	5.70	<.001
$\sigma_{wav,cwinter}$	-0.17	0.01	-12.62	<.001

$LL = -29784.59$, # *paras.* = 13
$\chi^2(1) = 0.76$, $p = 0.39$

Intercept-Only Model

Estimates of Interest

Parameter	Estimate	SE	z	p
β_0	3.70	0.01	371.66	<.001
σ^2_e	0.61	0.01	55.44	<.001

Other Estimates

Parameter	Estimate	SE	z	p
β_{cons}	0.00	0.01	0.00	1.00
β_{wav}	0.00	0.02	0.00	1.00
$\beta_{cwinter}$	-0.30	0.01	-28.10	<.001
σ^2_{cons}	0.38	0.01	55.44	<.001
σ^2_{wav}	1.56	0.03	55.44	<.001
$\sigma^2_{cwinter}$	0.68	0.01	55.44	<.001
$\sigma_{cons,wav}$	-0.30	0.01	-28.15	<.001
$\sigma_{cons,cwinter}$	0.04	0.01	5.70	<.001
$\sigma_{wav,cwinter}$	-0.17	0.01	-12.62	<.001

$LL = -29991.42$, # *paras.* = 11
$\chi^2(3) = 414.40$, $p < 0.001$

FIGURE 6. Path diagrams, fit indices, and ML parameter estimates when all variables are treated as random. The variables in the figure are described in Table 1. *LL* = log likelihood, # *paras.* = number of parameters estimated.

ANOVA, regression) where predictors are treated as *fixed variables* and only the dependent variable is treated as random.

Fixed versus random variables are typically distinguished by whether one wishes to make inferences only to the levels of the variables observed in the study ("fixed") versus the larger populations from which the levels were sampled ("random," with random referring to the assumption that the levels of the variable were randomly sampled from a population of levels; for more information, see Maxwell and Delaney (2004, ch. 10)). When predictors are fixed, we assume their values don't change across samples; thus, there is no need to assume population distributions or estimate parameters for the predictors. This assumption is in contrast to assuming that predictors are random variables, where population distributions are assumed and corresponding parameters are estimated. It is this different treatment of predictors that results in the different number of parameters being estimated in Figures 5 and 6.

This different treatment of the predictors reflects different analytical orientations, which is illuminated by the visuals (Figures 5 and 6). In Figure 5, where predictors are treated as fixed variables, the variable of interest with respect to estimation is the dependent variable *effort*, regardless of whether OLS or ML estimation is used. In OLS estimation, the goal is to estimate parameters that minimize the distance between observed and model-implied *effort* scores, whereas in ML estimation, the goal is to select parameters most likely for the *effort* data, which is equivalent to selecting parameters that minimize the distance between observed and model-implied summary statistics for *effort*. Thus, in our example, when predictors are treated as fixed, the analytical orientation or focus is on estimating model parameters to best represent information about our one dependent variable, *effort*.

When predictors are treated as random, as in Figure 6, the variables of interest with respect to estimation are now both the predictors and the dependent variable. That is, the goal is to reproduce information pertaining to *all* variables in the model, not just the dependent variable. This analytical orientation is more comprehensive in that it switches the focus of modeling away from solely how the predictors relate to the dependent variable and toward how all variables relate to one another. Importantly, this shift in analytical orientation also means that any variable can serve as a predictor and an outcome in the model, as illustrated by the variable *cons* in models 1.C. and 1.D in Figure 1.

Moving from an orientation where the interest is in reproducing information associated with one variable (Figure 5) to an orientation where the interest is in reproducing information associated with a set of variables (Figure 6) has implications for the comparisons of nested models. As an example, consider the comparison of the Interaction Included and No Interaction models in Figure 5 that was used to test H_0: $\beta_3 = 0$. Recall that when the predictors were fixed, the No Interaction model in Figure 5 was the same as model 3.B in Figure 3, which essentially is the Interaction Included model with the interaction variable *removed*. Because these two models are the same, either could be used in the nested model comparison with the Interaction Included model. A model that sets the parameter to zero (Figure 5) is equivalent to one that *doesn't include the predictor at all* (Figure 3) because only one model parameter (the regression parameter) is associated with a predictor when it is treated as fixed. Thus, there are two ways to conceptualize the no interaction effect in the context of fixed predictors: (a) setting the slope parameter associated with the interaction to zero or (b) not including the interaction variable at all. These two approaches can be explained during instruction most easily via path diagrams similar to those presented in Figures 3 and 5.

On the other hand, when predictors are treated as random, the appropriate model comparison when evaluating whether the interaction is necessary (e.g., test H$_0$: $\beta_3 = 0$) is one that compares the Interaction Included and No Interaction models in Figure 6. Note how the path diagrams for these two models in Figure 6 clearly convey that the variables included in both models are the *same*; the only difference is the constraint of $\beta_3 = 0$ in the more constrained model. When predictors are random, the Interaction Included model in Figure 6 with the interaction variable removed does *not* result in the same model as the No Interaction model in Figure 6. In short, when predictors are random, there are several parameters associated with the predictor (as showcased in Figure 6), thus the appropriate model comparison test of whether that predictor's regression coefficient equals zero is one that sets only that parameter to zero, not one that removes the variable entirely from the model.

Similarly, when all variables are treated as random, the appropriate model comparisons to evaluate H$_0$: $\beta_1=\beta_2=\beta_3=0$ is that between the Interaction Included model and the intercept-only model in Figure 6. Comparing the Interaction Included model to a model that does not include any predictors would not be appropriate when predictors are treated as random. The use of visual displays such as those in Figure 6 emphasize how the appropriate intercept-only model when predictors are treated as random includes all predictors, but with their regression coefficients constrained to zero. The *LR* test is conducted as usual to compare nested models when variables are treated as random (i.e., to compare the nested models in Figure 6). As shown in Table 2, the conclusions drawn from these model comparison tests are the same as those obtained when predictors were treated as fixed coupled with either ML or OLS estimation.

Clearly, the visuals are incredibly helpful for revealing how different software packages treat the data due to different analytic orientations. That is, when introducing fixed versus random variables, an instructor can easily compare and contrast figures similar to Figures 3, 5, and 6 to facilitate understanding of the models being estimated. Moreover, instructors can use the diagrams to introduce the idea of model-data fit, which is often emphasized in SEM and explained below.

Differences in the Use of Fit Indices

Another difference in the results obtained when using SEM software is the presence of model-data fit indices[7] in the output for each model. Fit indices summarize the alignment between the observed and model-implied summary statistics. As opposed to comparing competing theoretical models, fit indices address how well any one particular model fits (i.e., reproduces) the data. To convey the utility of fit indices and highlight the effectiveness of path diagrams for understanding them conceptually, a fit index known as the goodness-of-fit χ^2 is presented for each model in Figure 6. Importantly, most other fit indices are simply transformations of this χ^2 value.

---

[7] For a thorough review of fit indices and their functioning, consult Hu and Bentler (1998).

Saturated Model

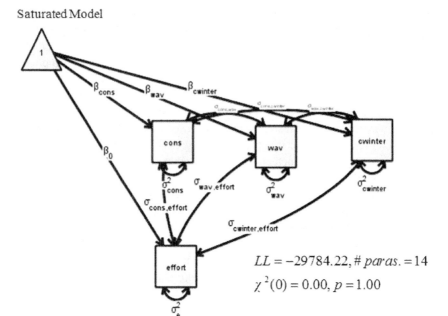

$$LL = -29784.22, \# paras. = 14$$
$$\chi^2(0) = 0.00, p = 1.00$$

FIGURE 7.   Path diagrams for the saturated model associated with the models in Figure 6. The variables in the figure are described in Table 1. LL = log likelihood, # *paras.* = number of parameters estimated.

The goodness-of-fit χ^2 is a *LR* test between two nested models: the model in question and the saturated model, where all variables are allowed to covary. Because the saturated model perfectly reproduces the observed summary statistics, the comparison of the theoretically based model to the saturated model addresses how well the theoretically based model reproduces the data. The saturated model associated with all diagrams in Figure 6 is presented in Figure 7. That is, the same saturated model applies to all theoretically based models in Figure 6 because all three hypothesized models are attempting to reproduce the same data. Because a nonsignificant χ^2 value[8] indicates the model fits the data, the results suggest that the No Interaction model fits the data, but that the intercept-only model does not.[9] When models do not fit the data, they are often rejected by the researcher as a plausible explanation of the phenomena under study and are not further in-

---

[8] Several factors (e.g., sample size, model complexity, violation of assumptions) influence fit indices (Hu & Bentler, 1998) and these factors should always be taken into consideration during the interpretation of fit indices.

[9] The astute reader may have recognized that the goodness-of-fit χ^2 values for the No Interaction and intercept-only models in Figure 6 are the same as the *LR* test results in Table 2 using these models. The reason these results align is because the less constrained model in those comparisons, which is

terpreted. In contrast, models that fit the data, like the No Interaction model,[10] are considered as possible explanations for the phenomena under study (with the caveat that there may be other models that fit the data just as well or better).

The Interaction Included model is notably absent from our interpretation of the χ^2 values in Figure 6. Fit cannot be assessed for this model because it has zero degrees of freedom. Models with zero degrees of freedom, also known as just-identified models, are equivalent to saturated models and thus not falsifiable (as evidenced by zero degrees of freedom). Thus, even though fit indices are provided in the output for models where $df = 0$, the fit of these models to the data cannot be meaningfully evaluated.

Models for traditional statistics estimated in SEM software (regardless of whether predictors are treated as fixed or random) are just-identified and there-fore, traditional SEM fit indices are of little use in evaluating their utility. Just-identified models may still be appropriate for the data, but unlike models that have positive degrees of freedom (known as overidentified models), just-identified models cannot be tested for model-data fit. In contrast, fit indices are incredibly informative for models having positive degrees of freedom, as demonstrated by the retention and rejection of the No Interaction and intercept-only models, re-spectively, based on their goodness-of-fit χ^2 values.

Ancillary Advantages of Using SEM Software

Clearly, our primary purpose of promoting SEM software is to facilitate the creation of path diagrams. However, we would be remiss if we didn't briefly note a major reason people employ SEM software programs to conduct what would be deemed traditional techniques—the ability to easily accommodate ill-behaved data. One advantage of using SEM programs is the flexibility offered when the assumption of normality is violated. When this assumption is violated, both OLS and ML parameter estimates remain unbiased, but standard errors are affected. Fit indices are also affected, thus impacting tests of significance and evaluation of model-data fit (Finney & DiStefano, 2013). Importantly, nonnormality can be addressed by either choosing a more appropriate data distribution (Skrondal & Rabe-Hesketh, 2004) or by assuming multivariate normality and applying a cor-rection to the ML standard errors and fit indices (Satorra & Bentler, 1994). This correction is effortlessly accomplished by simply including a short line of syntax when employing an SEM software program. In contrast to employing ML estima-tion and correcting biased values due to the violation of nonnormality, the use of SEM software packages also affords the additional option of employing differ-

---

the Interaction Included model, is statistically equivalent to the saturated model (thus yielding the same *LL* and same *LR* test results).

[10] Despite the fact the No Interaction model fits or reproduces the summary data, the R^2 value indicates that only 6.5% of the variance in *effort* is explained by the two predictors. Importantly, adequate model-data fit doesn't imply a large R^2 or significant parameter estimates.

ent estimators that make no assumptions about normality (e.g., weighted least squares).

SEM programs are also useful in addressing violations of the homogeneity of error variance assumption made by traditional statistical techniques. For instance, all models that include a categorical variable in Figures 3 and 4 assume that the error variance is equal across groups. These models (Figures 3 and 4) are known as multiple-indicator multiple-cause models in the SEM framework (Jöreskog & Goldberger, 1975; Muthén, 1989). Structured means modeling within the SEM framework (Sörbom, 1974) is an alternative approach (associated with path diagrams that are different than those shown in Figures 3 and 4) that does not make this assumption. Both approaches for group comparisons are available in most SEM programs and have been described and illustrated in the context of traditional univariate and multivariate techniques by several methodologists (Green & Thompson, 2006, 2012; Hancock, 2010). Researchers have also demonstrated that the use of robust means modeling within SEM programs, which is the combination of structured means modeling with techniques to overcome problems with normality, is advantageous over traditional "fixes" to these assumption violations (e.g., adjustments in OLS, robust statistics; Fan & Hancock, 2012).

Another advantage has to do with the options for handling missing data available in many SEM programs (for a thorough review of approaches to missing data, see Enders, 2010). Common approaches to handling missing data (e.g., listwise deletion, pairwise deletion, mean substitution) are not recommended because they work well in only a limited number of situations (Wilkinson & Task Force on Statistical Inference, 1999). For this reason, researchers are often encouraged to employ more modern approaches to missing data. Fortunately, these approaches are available in many of the commercially available SEM software programs and often the programming required for their implementation is minimal (e.g., a line or two in the syntax).

The most commonly noted advantage of SEM software is the ability to estimate a variety of models, including models that incorporate "error-free" latent variables. Measurement error associated with "error-prone" observed variables affects results associated with traditional statistical techniques. In our examples (Figures 2 to 6), relationships among observed variables were modeled; however, using SEM software, it would be fairly easy to instead model relationships among latent variables. For instance, instead of predicting effort scale scores (i.e., error-prone composite of five effort items), a measurement model consisting of the individual effort items could be incorporated into any of the models, as illustrated in Figure 1. Similarly, measurement models could be utilized for predictors (e.g., conscientiousness). Demonstrations of the incorporation of latent variables into traditional "ANOVA" techniques are provided by Green and Thompson (2006, 2012), Hancock (2003, 2004, 2010) and Thompson and Green (2013). In short, employing SEM programs for their path diagram capabilities has the ancillary benefits of introducing students to additional analytic orientations to modeling, ease in accommodating ill-behaved data, and the capability to model a host of variables and relationships not afforded in other software programs. Thus, we recommend the introduction of these diagrams and the accompanying software early in the instructional process.

CONCLUSION

Given that all traditional techniques are subsumed within SEM, it would seem that approaches to planning, presenting, and teaching SEM that have proven useful would apply to planning, presenting, and teaching traditional statistical techniques. More specifically, if, when employing or learning SEM, path diagrams reduce cognitive load, organize information into a coherent representation, provide novel information that text cannot communicate, and activate prior knowledge, the same advantages would be realized when employing or learning traditional techniques. Thus, we believe supplementing equations and verbal descriptions with path diagrams has clear advantages that align with tenets of cognitive processing, and their adoption is long overdue for these reasons.

Moreover, we believe that adoption of path diagrams, along with SEM software, early in training is likely to facilitate students' transition to more sophisticated models, because the "techniques" won't be perceived as disparate, but rather just different "flavors" of the same modeling approach. Thus, familiarity with path diagrams, ML estimation, and the software should ease the transition from multiple regression models to path models, full structural models, latent growth models, mixture models, and beyond.

Finally, although there are benefits to understanding a large number of techniques, we would argue that even more important is engaging in a model-oriented approach to research, which is facilitated by the use of visuals. If this approach is used throughout statistical training, each technique will be viewed as a mathematical model that *might* be appropriate for analyzing data, depending on the theoretical relationships among variables that are proposed. This focus on the model via the visual should train students to consider the theory first and the analytical technique second. The culmination of this training is likely to result in the realization that some theories are not represented well by the models aligning with traditional or existing statistical techniques. In other words, the advanced student who is trained under a model-oriented approach to research will realize that some phenomena require the development of new mathematical representations to be well understood.

REFERENCES

Aiken, L. S., West, S. G., & Millsap, R. E. (2008). Doctoral training in statistics, measurement, and methodology in psychology: Replication and extension of Aiken, West, Sechrest, and Reno's (1990) survey of PhD programs in North America. *American Psychologist, 63,* 32–50.

American Psychological Association (APA). (2010). *The publication manual of the American Psychological Association* (6th ed.). Washington, DC: Author.

Aron, A., Aron, E. N., & Coups, E. (2013). *Statistics for psychology* (6th ed.). Boston, MA: Pearson.

Barry, C. L., & Finney, S. J. (in press). *Modeling change in effort across a low-stakes testing session: A latent growth curve modeling approach.*

Barry, C. L., Horst, S. J., Finney, S. J., Brown, A. R., & Kopp, J. (2010). Do examinees have similar test-taking effort? A high-stakes question for low-stakes testing. *International Journal of Testing, 10,* 342–363.

Beaujean, A. A. (2013, December). *Creating path model diagrams.* Retrieved from http://blogs.baylor.edu/rlatentvariable/files/2013/12/AppendixCreatingPathModels-211jclc.pdf

Boker, S. M., Neale, M. C., Maes, H. H., Wilde, M. J., Spiegel, M., Brick, T. R., . . . Brandmaier, A.M. (2012). *OpenMx user guide.* Retrieved from http://openmx.psyc.virginia.edu/docs/OpenMx/latest/OpenMxUserGuide.pdf

Boker, S. M., Neale, M. C., Maes, H. H., Wilde, M. J., Spiegel, M., Brick, T. R., Spies, J., . . . Fox, J. (2011). OpenMx: An open source extended structural equation modeling framework. *Psychometrika, 76,* 306-317.

Bollen, K. A. (1989). *Structural equations with latent variables.* New York, NY: Wiley.

Boomsma, A. (2000). Reporting analyses of covariance structures. *Structural Equation Modeling, 7,* 461–483.

Bray, J. H., & Maxwell, S. E. (1985). *Multivariate analysis of variance.* Beverly Hills, CA: Sage.

Cohen, J., Cohen, P., West, S. G., & Aiken, L. S. (2003). *Applied multiple regression/correlation analysis for the behavioral sciences* (3rd ed.). Mahwah, NJ: Erlbaum.

Cooper, H. M. (2011). *Reporting research in psychology: How to meet journal articles reporting standards.* Washington, DC: American Psychological Association.

DeMars, C. E., Bashkov, B. M., & Socha, A. B. (2013). The role of gender in test-taking motivation under low-stakes conditions. *Research & Practice in Assessment, 8,* 69–82.

Denis, D. J. (2003). Alternatives to null hypothesis significance testing. *Theory & Science, 4,* 1–21. Retrieved June 5, 2013 from http://theoryandscience.icaap.org/content/vol4.1/02_denis.html

Dwyer, J. H. (1983). *Statistical models for the social and behavioral sciences.* New York, NY: Oxford University Press.

Eliason, S. R. (1993). *Maximum likelihood estimation: Logic and practice.* Newbury Park, CA: Sage.

Elliot, A. (1999). Approach and avoidance motivation and achievement goals. *Educational Psychologist, 34,* 169–189.

Enders, C. K. (2010). *Applied missing data analysis.* New York, NY: Guilford.

Fan, W., & Hancock, G. R. (2012). Robust means modeling: An alternative for hypothesis testing of independent means under variance heterogeneity and nonnormality. *Journal of Educational and Behavioral Statistics, 37,* 137–156.

Fan, X. (1997). Canonical correlation analysis and structural equation modeling: What do they have in common? *Structural Equation Modeling, 4,* 65–79.

Feingold, A. (1994). Gender differences in personality: A meta-analysis. *Psychological Bulletin, 116,* 429–456.

Field, A. (2013). *Discovering statistics using IBM SPSS Statistics* (4th ed.). London, UK: Sage.

Finney, S. J., & DiStefano, C. (2013). Nonnormal and categorical data in structural equation models. In G. R. Hancock & R. O. Mueller (Eds.), *A second course in structural equation modeling* (2nd ed., pp. 439–492). Charlotte, NC: Information Age.

Graham, J. M. (2008). The general linear model as structural equation modeling. *Journal of Educational and Behavioral Statistics, 33*, 485–506.

Granaas, M. (2012, May 14–18). Modeling in undergraduate statistics. Poster presented at the Electronic Conference on Teaching Statistics, Online. *CAUSEweb.org*. Retrieved June 6, 2013 from https://www.causeweb.org/ecots/ecots12/posters/21

Green, S. B., & Thompson, M. S. (2006). Structural equation modeling for conducting tests of differences in multiple means. *Psychosomatic Medicine, 68*, 706–717.

Green, S. B., & Thompson, M. S. (2012). A flexible structural equation modeling approach for analyzing means. In R. H. Hoyle (Ed.), *Handbook of structural equation modeling* (pp. 393–416). New York, NY: Guilford.

Hair, J. F., Ringle, C. M., & Sarstedt, M. (2011). PLS-SEM: Indeed a silver bullet. *Journal of Marketing Theory and Practice, 19*, 139–151.

Hancock, G. (2003). Fortune cookies, measurement error, and experimental design. *Journal of Modern Applied Statistical Methods, 2*, 293–305.

Hancock, G. (2004). Experimental, quasi-experimental, and nonexperimental design and analysis with latent variables. In D. Kaplan (Ed.), *The Sage handbook of quantitative methodology for the social sciences* (pp. 317–334). Thousand Oaks, CA: Sage.

Hancock, G. (2010, May). *Life after ANOVA: Reframing and extending analysis of variance using a likelihood/information paradigm.* Paper presented at the Structural Equation Modeling Interest Group of the American Educational Research Association, Denver, CO.

Harlow, L. L. (2010). On scientific research: The role of statistical modeling and hypothesis testing. *Journal of Modern Applied Statistical Methods, 9*, 348–358.

Harlow, L. L. (2013). Teaching quantitative psychology. In T. Little, (Ed.), *Oxford handbook of quantitative methods* (pp. 105–117). New York, NY: Oxford University Press.

Henson, R. K., Hull, D. M., & Williams, C. S. (2010). Methodology in our education research culture: Toward a stronger collective quantitative proficiency. *Educational Researcher, 39*, 229–240.

Ho, M., Stark, S., & Chernyshenko, O. (2012). Graphical representation of structural equation models using path diagrams. In R. H. Hoyle (Ed.), *Handbook of structural equation modeling* (pp. 43–55). New York, NY: Guilford.

Hoyle, R. H., & Panter, A. T. (1995). Writing about structural equation models. In R. H. Hoyle (Ed.), *Structural equation modeling: Concepts, issues, and applications* (pp. 158–176). Thousand Oaks, CA: Sage.

Hu, L.-T., & Bentler, P. M. (1998). Fit indices in covariance structure modeling: Sensitivity to underparameterized model misspecification. *Psychological Methods, 3*, 424–453.

John, O. P., & Srivastava, S. (1999). The Big Five trait taxonomy: History, measurement, and theoretical perspectives. In L. A. Pervin & O. P. John (Eds.), *Handbook of personality: Theory and research* (2nd ed., pp.102–138). New York, NY: Guilford.

Jöreskog, K. G. (1973). A general method for estimating a linear structural equation system. In A. S. Goldberger & O. D. Duncan (Eds.), *Structural equation models in the social sciences* (pp. 85–112). New York, NY: Academic.

Jöreskog, K. G., & Goldberger, A. S. (1975). Estimation of a model with multiple indicator and multiple causes of a single latent variable. *Journal of the American Statistical Association, 70,* 631–639.

Keesling, J. W. (1972). *Maximum likelihood approaches to causal analysis.* (Doctoral dissertation). University of Chicago, IL.

Kelly, K., & Maxwell, S. E. (2010). Multiple regression. In G. R. Hancock & R. O. Mueller (Eds.), *The reviewer's guide to quantitative methods in the social sciences* (pp. 281–297). New York, NY: Routledge.

Kline, R. B. (2011). *Principles and practice of structural equation modeling* (3rd ed). New York, NY: Guilford.

Klockars, A. J. (2010). Analysis of variance: Between-groups designs. In G. R. Hancock & R. O. Mueller (Eds.), *The reviewer's guide to quantitative methods in the social sciences* (pp. 1–13). New York, NY: Routledge.

Lix, L. M., & Keselman, H. J. (2010). Analysis of variance: Repeated measures designs. In G. R. Hancock & R. O. Mueller (Eds.), *The reviewer's guide to quantitative methods in the social sciences* (pp. 15–27). New York, NY: Routledge.

Maxwell, S. E., & Delaney, H. D. (2004). *Designing experiments and analyzing data: A model comparison perspective* (2nd ed). New York, NY: Taylor & Francis.

McDonald, R. P., & Ho, M. (2002). Principles and practice in reporting structural equation analysis. *Psychological Methods, 7,* 64–82.

Mueller, R. O., & Hancock, G. R. (Eds.). (2010). *The reviewer's guide to quantitative methods in the social sciences.* New York, NY: Routledge.

Muthén, B. O. (1989). Latent variable modeling in heterogeneous populations. *Psychometrika, 54,* 525–543.

Muthén, L. K., & Muthén, B. O. (1998–2012). *Mplus user's guide* (7th ed.). Los Angeles, CA: Muthén & Muthén.

Nicol, A. M., & Pexman, P. M. (2010). *Displaying your findings: Practical guide for creating figures, posters, and presentations* (6th ed.). Washington, DC: American Psychological Association.

Olejnik, S. (2010). Multivariate analysis of variance. In G. R. Hancock & R. O. Mueller (Eds.), *The reviewer's guide to quantitative methods in the social sciences* (pp. 315–327). New York, NY: Routledge.

Pastor, D. A., & Finney, S. J. (2013). Using visual displays to enhance understanding of quantitative research. In G. Schraw, M. McCrudden, & D. Robinson (Eds.), *Learning through visual displays* (pp. 387–415). Charlotte, NC: Information Age.

Pieper, S. (2003). Refining and extending the 2 x 2 achievement goal framework: Another look at work-avoidance (Doctoral dissertation, James Madison University, Harrisonburg, VA). *Dissertation Abstracts International, 64,* 4436A.

Rodgers, J. L. (2010a). The epistemology of mathematical and statistical modeling: A quiet methodological revolution. *American Psychologist, 65,* 1–12.

Rodgers, J. L. (2010b). Statistical and mathematical modeling versus NHST? There's no competition! *Journal of Modern Applied Statistical Methods, 9,* 340–347.

Rutherford, A. (2011). *ANOVA and ANCOVA: A GLM approach* (2nd ed.). Hoboken, NJ: Wiley.

Satorra, A., & Bentler, P. M. (1994). *Corrections to test statistics and standard errors in covariance structure analysis.* In A. von Eye & C. C. Clogg (Eds.), Latent variables analysis: Applications for developmental research (pp. 399–419). Thousand Oaks, CA: Sage.

Schraw, G., McCrudden, M. T., & Robinson, D. (2013). *Learning through visual displays.* Charlotte, NC: Information Age.

Skrondal, A., & Rabe-Hesketh, S. (2004). *Generalized latent variable modeling: Multilevel, longitudinal, and structural equation models.* Boca Raton, FL: Chapman & Hall.

Sörbom, D. (1974). A general method for studying differences in factor means and factor structure between groups. *British Journal of Mathematical and Statistical Psychology, 27,* 229–239.

Spirtes, P., Richardson, T., Meek, C., Scheines, R., & Glymour, C. (1998). Using path diagrams as a structural equation modeling tool. *Sociological Methods & Research, 27,* 182–225.

Steiger, J. H. (1980). Tests for comparing elements of a correlation matrix. *Psychological Bulletin, 87,* 245–251.

Steiger, J. H., & Browne, M. W. (1984). The comparison of interdependent correlations between optimal linear composites. *Psychometrika, 49,* 11–24.

Sweller, J. (2005). Implications of cognitive load theory for multimedia learning. In R. E. Mayer (Ed.), *The Cambridge handbook for multimedia learning* (pp. 19–30). New York, NY: Cambridge University Press.

Tabachnick, B. G., & Fidell, L. S. (2013). *Using multivariate statistics* (6th ed.). Boston, MA: Pearson.

Tanaka, J. S., Panter, A. T., Winborne, W. C., & Huba, G. J. (1990). Theory testing in personality and social psychology with structural equation models: A primer in 20 questions. In C. Hendrick & M. S. Clark (Eds.), *Review of personality and social psychology* (Vol. 11, pp. 217–241). Newbury Park, CA: Sage.

Thelk, A., Sundre, D. L., Horst, J. S., & Finney, S. J. (2009). Motivation matters: Using the Student Opinion Scale (SOS) to make valid inferences about student performance. *Journal of General Education, 58,* 131–151.

Thompson, M. S., & Green, S. B. (2013). Evaluating between-group differences in latent variable means. In G. R. Hancock & R. O. Mueller (Eds.), *A second course in structural equation modeling* (2nd ed., pp. 163–218). Greenwich, CT: Information Age.

van Merriënboer, J. J. G., & Sweller, J. (2010). Cognitive load theory in health professional education: Design principles and strategies. *Medical Education, 44,* 85–93.

von Oertzen, T., Brandmaier, A. M., & Tsang, S. (2014, July 1). Ω*nyx user's guide.* Retrieved from http://onyx.brandmaier.de/userguide.pdf

von Oertzen, T., Brandmaier, A. M., & Tsang, S. (2015). Structural equation modeling with Ωnyx. *Structural Equation Modeling, 22,* 148–161.

Vekiri, I. (2002). What is the value of graphical displays in learning? *Educational Psychology Review, 14,* 261–312.

Wiley, D. E. (1973). The identification problem for structural equation models with unmeasured variables. In A. S. Goldberger & O. D. Duncan (Eds.), *Structural equation models in the social sciences* (pp. 69–83). New York, NY: Academic.

Wilkinson, L., & Task Force on Statistical Inference. (1999). Statistical methods in psychology journals: Guidelines and explanations. *American Psychologist, 54,* 594–604.

Wise, S. L., & DeMars, C. E. (2005). Examinee motivation in low-stakes assessment: Problems and potential solutions. *Educational Assessment, 10,* 1–17.

Wise, S. L., & Smith, L. F. (2011). A model of examinee test-taking effort. In J. A. Bovaird, K. F. Geisinger, & C. W. Buckendahl (Eds.), *High-stakes testing in education: Science and practice in K–12 settings* (pp. 139–153). Washington, DC: American Psychological Association.

Wright, S. (1934). The method of path coefficients. *Annals of Mathematical Statistics, 5,* 161–215.

CHAPTER 6

USING JOINT DISPLAYS AND MAXQDA SOFTWARE TO REPRESENT THE RESULTS OF MIXED METHODS RESEARCH

Tim Guetterman, John W. Creswell, and Udo Kuckartz

ABSTRACT

Mixed methods research involves the collection and analysis of qualitative and quantitative data and their integration. This defining feature, integration, is one of the challenges to conducting mixed methods research. Building on the existing work of mixed methods scholars on the issue of integration, this chapter discusses 11 joint displays that researchers can use to represent integration in mixed methods research. Joint displays array quantitative and qualitative results together in a single display to represent integration. The chapter presents one computer application, MAXQDA, to illustrate the creation of these joint displays. We link the visual displays to six mixed methods research designs to assist researchers in selecting an appropriate display for their mixed methods study.

Use of Visual Displays in Research and Testing: Coding, Interpreting, and Reporting Data,
pages 145–175.

INTRODUCTION

Researchers across the world and in diverse disciplines (Denscombe, 2008; Plano Clark, 2010) have been increasingly using mixed methods research, which involves the systematic and rigorous collection and analysis of both quantitative and qualitative data within a single study (Creswell & Plano Clark, 2011). Mixed methods research further includes a characteristic, the mixing or integration of the quantitative and qualitative data, which is a defining element of it as a research approach. The premise of mixed methods is simply that this combination and integration of data leads to more than merely the sum of its parts, yielding a more complete understanding of a research problem. Mixed methods research achieves this purpose through leveraging the strengths of qualitative and quantitative approaches and by systematically integrating the databases. Integration, however, is one of its most challenging features to execute.

Building on mixed methods literature that addresses integration, visual displays, and computer applications, the next step is to relate visual displays to the types of mixed methods designs discussed in the literature and the procedures of analyzing data within designs. Thus, the purpose of this chapter is to present how to create joint displays, assisted computer applications, and connect the displays to six common mixed methods designs. A mixed methods joint display represents quantitative and qualitative data analysis or results interpretation in a single visual display (Creswell, 2015). For each of the designs, we will discuss the relevant joint displays to represent the integration of qualitative and quantitative data along with procedures to create each type of display using a particular application, MAXQDA[1] (Version 11), for illustrative purposes. Although joint displays might also be used for planning purposes, the focus of this chapter is the analysis and results stage of research. In this chapter, we aim to address a practical problem for researchers needing to integrate data and communicate it to readers.

The Need for Integration and Representing Integration in Mixed Methods

The challenges associated with integration reduce to two particular issues: how to integrate data and how to represent the integration in published mixed methods studies (Bryman, 2006). The mere collection of qualitative and quantitative data without their integration is not mixed methods research (Creswell, 2015); integration is a defining and critical component. For instance, integrating the results of an instrument in light of the stories of participants can illuminate a topic of interest and add a valuable perspective. Although the topic of integration has continually received attention from mixed methods scholars, it continues to be one of the more perplexing aspects of conducting mixed methods research. Perhaps a reason

---

[1] MAXQDA is a software for qualitative and mixed-data analysis. The software is developed by Verbi GmbH/ Berlin, Germany. More information and a free 30-day trial version can be obtained from the website www.maxqda.com

for the difficulty is the lack of available mixed methods software tools, relative to other research approaches.

The emergence of these computer applications with mixed methods features is beginning to address the second difficulty with integration—its representation. Procedures are available for the detailed analysis of both qualitative and quantitative data. Quantitative programs such as SPSS emerged during the 1970s and have been refined and developed since inception. Qualitative software programs, such as MAXQDA (Version 11), NVivo (Version 10), and ATLAS.ti (Version 7) originated in the late 1980s and have been used by an increasingly wider audience worldwide for the analysis of textual and image data. Unfortunately, mixed methods research has seen less linkage to software applications that facilitate the integration of data. Some efforts have emerged recently, such as SPSS's text analysis add-on (IBM SPSS Statistics for Windows, Version 22.0), the Canadian software QDA Miner 4 (Version 4) from Provalis, which includes within its program both a text analysis and a statistical program, and the German software MAXQDA (Version 11), which has a collection of mixed methods features. These features facilitate the integration of qualitative and quantitative data. Furthermore, they give the researcher tools to create tables and figures to represent the integration visually for readers. Representation of integration in mixed methods research is accomplished through *joint displays* (Creswell & Plano Clark, 2011; Dickinson, 2010). Although we have examples of joint displays in published studies, the body of literature has not connected them in depth to methods of integration for the various mixed methods designs.

What Has Been Done on This Problem to Date

The evolution of data analysis and computer applications in mixed methods has proceeded through six key developments. It began with the early strategies for data analysis and continued with the development of frameworks for the analysis of data in mixed methods research. Third, software applications emerged that provided tools for intersecting quantitative and qualitative data. Fourth, these software applications and their features then became connected to particular mixed methods procedures. Fifth was the detailed identification of types of mixed methods designs and data analysis within the types of designs. Finally, recent innovations in the use of computer-assisted data joint displays or matrices hold potential for analyzing, representing, and interpreting data. The following section traces this evolution in detail to encourage and define a substantive discussion about computer applications to develop mixed methods joint displays.

Early and evolving strategies for mixed methods data analysis.

Early discussions about data analysis in mixed methods identified general approaches to integrate qualitative and quantitative data during analysis. These approaches were not related to specific designs but viewed as generic approaches to analyzing data. An important development in mixed methods was the discussion of four analytic strategies by Caracelli and Greene (1993). The first of their four strategies was to suggest that data might be converted or transformed from one type into another type, a procedure called data transformation. A second strategy was to analyze one type of data so that it would yield a typology or set of categories that then could be used as a framework, such as guiding the development and analysis of a survey in a follow-up strand. A third form of data analysis was to analyze one type of data to identify "extreme cases" and then to use the other form of data to test and refine the initial explanations about the extreme cases. A fourth type was called "data consolidation," which involved merging both types of data to create new or consolidated variables or datasets useful for further analyses. Caracelli and Greene (1993) then linked these strategies of integrated analysis to the purpose (i.e., rationale) for using a mixed methods design. The four strategies provided an initial set of promising strategies for data analysis in mixed methods research based on the intent of mixing. Data analysis procedures in mixed methods research have further evolved from general strategies to approaches embedded within specific stages in the data analysis process.

Data analysis and the process of research.
Following these initial efforts, a substantive conversation was taking place around data analysis that linked closely to the process of conducting research. Onwuegbuzie and Teddlie (2003) discussed a model for mixed methods data analysis around seven stages in the data analysis process:

1. Data reduction—reducing data collected through statistical analysis of quantitative data or writing summaries of qualitative data
2. Data display—reducing the quantitative data to, for example, tables and the qualitative data to, for example, charts and rubrics
3. Data transformation—transforming qualitative data into quantitative data (i.e., quantitizing qualitative data) or vice versa (i.e., qualitizing quantitative data)
4. Data correlation—correlating the quantitative data with quantitized qualitative data
5. Data consolidation—combining both data types to create new or consolidated variables or datasets
6. Data comparison—comparing data from different sources
7. Data integration—integrating all data into a coherent whole.

The first two steps in this process of analysis follow logical steps in data analysis, but the last five steps (from transformation to integration) in this list of procedures appear to be alternative options for analysis rather than steps that follow one after the other. This model was a fundamental development that enabled further work to relate analysis to particular mixed methods designs or software applications.

Software applications that link quantitative and qualitative data.
Bazeley (2009) reviewed the range of software packages that might be used in mixed methods research. She cited Excel for mixed methods tasks and then highlighted two software programs primarily designed for qualitative analysis that might be used for mixed methods analysis—NVivo and Provalis. Concurrently, Bazeley discussed emerging ways to consider mixed methods data analysis. Researchers might consider mixed methods analysis through a substantive common purpose for a study. For instance, the purpose can consist of intensive case analysis, extreme or negative cases, or inherently mixed analysis (e.g., social network analysis). In addition, mixed methods analysis can occur through the employment of the results in one analysis in approaching the analysis of another form of data (e.g., typology development, instrument development). Through synthesis of data from several sources for joint interpretation, such as comparing theme data with categorical or scaled variables using matrixes, researchers can tackle mixed methods data analysis. In other instances, researchers convert data from one form of data into the other in the procedure called *data transformation* or to create blended variables. Finally, the purpose of the study can require data analysis through multiple, sequenced phases of iterative analyses. With a clear set of purposes for mixed methods data analysis, it is natural to then consider how computer software can assist the researcher with analysis.

Data analysis within the types of mixed methods designs.
Bazeley's (2009) discussion foreshadowed the more substantive linking of visual displays in mixed methods data analysis to research designs. The conversation about the types of research designs available to the investigator has been underway for many years with multiple typologies of designs available. What has changed recently is the move toward specific procedures of data analysis within types of designs, an innovation that paved the way for specific discussions about the current software and how it might be altered or applied to assist in the mixed methods data analysis process. In their chapter on analyzing and interpreting data in mixed methods analysis, Creswell and Plano Clark (2011) advanced strategies of integrated analysis and joint displays based on the type of mixed methods design and whether the intent is to merge qualitative and quantitative data concurrently or connect sequentially. They offered detailed strategies to use visual displays for merged data analysis, which is used with convergent designs, as follows (Creswell & Plano Clark, 2011):

- Side-by-side comparison for merged data analysis
- Joint displays for merged data analysis
    - Category/theme display
    - Typology and statistics display
    - Convergent and divergent findings display
    - Case-oriented display
- Data transformation merged analysis

TABLE 1. Mixed Methods Designs, Questions, Integrated Data Analysis, and Joint Displays

Type of Design	Mixed Methods Questions (illustrative questions)	Merging or Connected Data Analysis	Types of Joint Displays that Can be Developed that Link Quantitative and Qualitative Data
Convergent Design	To what extent do the quantitative and qualitative results converge?	Merging analysis	• A display that places quantitative results side by side with qualitative themes • A display that combines qualitative codes/themes with quantitative categorical or continuous variable data • A display relating qualitative themes to quantitative ratings for transforming qualitative data into quantitative scores
Explanatory Design	In what ways do the qualitative data help to explain the quantitative results?	Connected analysis	• A display that links quantitative results and demographic characteristics to participants purposefully selected for the follow-up sample • A display at the end of the study that links qualitative themes to quantitative results for the purpose of explanation
Exploratory Design	In what ways do the quantitative results generalize the qualitative findings?	Connected analysis	• A display of quotes, codes, and themes that match proposed items, variables, and scales for instrument development • A display at the end of the study to show how the quantitative results generalize the qualitative themes and code
Intervention Design Social Justice Design Multistage Evaluation Design	How do the qualitative findings provide enhanced understanding of the quantitative results?	Merging or connected analysis	• A display that links the qualitative themes to recruitment strategies for an intervention trial • A display that links qualitative themes to specific intervention activities • A display that compares themes about the processes individuals have experienced with outcome data • A display that compares the statistical results with qualitative follow-up themes • A display that compares qualitative themes with significant correlations at each stage in the research study

Table 1 presents an updated conceptualization of their work that links the latest (Creswell, 2015) mixed methods design typology, research questions, integration, and potential visual joint displays.

What This Chapter Will Address

The next step to build on these efforts is to relate joint displays to the types of mixed methods designs discussed in the literature and the procedures of analyzing data within designs. Thus, the purpose of this chapter is to present how to create joint displays, assisted by a computer application, and connect the displays to the six common mixed methods designs identified in Table 1. A *mixed methods joint display* represents quantitative and qualitative data, analysis, results, or interpretation in a single visual display (Creswell, 2015). For each of the designs, we will discuss the relevant joint displays to represent the integration of qualitative and quantitative data along with procedures to create each type of display, using MAXQDA software for illustrative purposes. Through this chapter, we aim to address a practical problem for researchers needing to integrate data and communicate it to readers.

BRIEF INTRODUCTION TO MIXED METHODS RESEARCH

What Mixed Methods Is

Although we can look at mixed methods researchers through different perspectives, such as philosophically or methodologically, a concrete way to discuss it is to focus on the methods involved. It is an approach to research that involves collecting quantitative and qualitative data, integrating the two, and interpreting the results based on these combined strengths to understand a research problem (Creswell, 2015). Mixed methods research has four core characteristics: (a) the collection and analysis of qualitative (i.e., open ended) and quantitative (i.e., closed ended) data, (b) the use of rigorous qualitative and quantitative methods, (c) the use of a mixed methods design to integrate data, and (d) the occasional incorporation of a philosophy of theory to frame the design.

When Mixed Methods Developed

Early conceptualizations of mixed methods trace to the multitrait, multimethod matrix as conceived by Campbell and Fiske (1959). However, as a research approach, mixed methods began in earnest in the late 1980s through the early 1990s (Creswell & Plano Clark, 2011). Throughout this period, researchers in fields such as evaluation (e.g., Greene, Caracelli, & Graham, 1989), sociology (e.g., Fielding & Fielding, 1986; Hunter & Brewer, 1993), management (e.g., Bryman, 1988), education (e.g., Creswell, 1994), medicine (Stange, Miller, Crabtree, O'Connor, & Zyzanski, 1994), and nursing (e.g., Morse, 1991) began to conduct the pioneering work to develop mixed methods research (Creswell & Plano Clark, 2011).

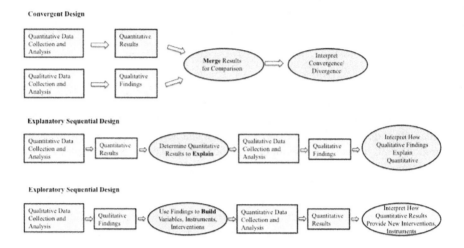

FIGURE 1. Three Basic Mixed Methods Designs adapted from Creswell (2015). In these figures, ovals represent integration, rectangles represent data, and arrows represent the flow of procedures.

Six Types of Designs

It would be useful to identify the types of mixed methods designs and discuss the procedures that have unfolded in the literature about their data analysis steps. Three basic mixed methods designs serve as the foundation for mixed methods studies. The basic designs are a convergent design, an explanatory sequential design, and an exploratory sequential design. A visual diagram of the basic mixed methods designs appears in Figure 1. Researchers can build on the basic designs and employ an advanced mixed methods design. Three popular advanced designs are the intervention design, the social justice design, and the multistage evaluation design. The following section provides an introduction to six mixed methods designs. Table 2 summarizes analysis features by design.

In the **convergent design**, the researcher collects both quantitative and qualitative data concurrently, analyzes the information separately, and then merges the two databases. The analysis is conducted in order to merge the results by comparing the two datasets or to merge the data after the researcher transforms one of the datasets. *Data analysis* in this design occurs at three distinct points in one phase of the research: with each dataset independently, when the comparison or transformation of the data occurs, and after the comparison or transformation is completed. Interim steps may occur between these points, such as identifying the dimensions on which the data will be compared, defining what variable will be transformed, and representing the comparisons in data displays or in discussions. In the end, the researcher compares the merged results with the research ques-

TABLE 2. Data Analysis and Key Decisions for the Six Primary Mixed Methods Designs

Type of Design	Data Analysis	Key Data Analysis Decisions	Example
Convergent Design	One phase at three points: with each dataset, when comparing data sets, and after comparing	How to compare two datasets, how to present the combined analyses, what if results diverge	DeVoe, Baez, Angier, Krois, Edlund, & Carney (2007)
Explanatory Design	Three phases: quantitative phase, qualitative phase, address how qualitative helped explain quantitative results	How to identify participants for follow-up, what results to explain qualitatively	Zeng, North, & Kent (2012)
Exploratory Design	Three phases: initial qualitative phase, quantitative phase, address how quantitative extended or generalized qualitative findings	How to move from qualitative findings to quantitative follow up, psychometric properties of instruments developed	Stoller et al. (2009)
Intervention Design	Depends on how and at what point qualitative data enters the study	Follow the basic design at the core of the study, how qualitative data will flow into the study	Plano Clark et al. (2013)
Social Justice Design	Typically depends on the underlying basic design	Follow the basic design at the core of the study, how to thread the overall social justice lens	Marcellus, MacKinnon, Benoit, Phillips, & Stengel (2014)
Multistage Evaluation Design	May occur at multiple phases: developing instruments, psychometric analysis, to explain quantitative findings	Follow the basic design at the core of the study, how to logistically connect multiple stages of qualitative and quantitative results	Nastasi, Hitchcock, Sarkar, Burkholder, Varjas, & Jayasena (2007)

tions. *Key data analysis decisions* in this design relate to deciding how to compare the two datasets, how to present the combined analyses, and what further analysis to conduct if the results diverge.

The data analysis procedures in the **explanatory design** involve first collecting quantitative data, analyzing the data, and using the results to inform the follow-up qualitative data collection. The *data analysis* occurs in three phases: the analysis of the initial quantitative data, an analysis of the follow-up qualitative data, and an analysis of the mixed methods question as to how the qualitative data help to explain the quantitative data. In this design, the data analysis of the initial quantitative phase connects into the data collection phase of the follow-up qualitative phase. At the interpretation stage in this design, the analysis is used to address the mixed methods question about whether and how the qualitative data help to explain the quantitative results. *Key data analysis decisions* relate to the point of interface between the quantitative and qualitative analysis, such as how to use the quantitative analysis to identify participants and to determine what results will be explained qualitatively.

In an **exploratory design**, the researchers first collect qualitative data, analyze it, and then use the information to develop a follow up quantitative phase of data collection. The quantitative strand thus connects to the initial qualitative strand. Like the explanatory design, three *data analyses* are conducted: after the initial qualitative data collection, after the follow-up quantitative data collection, and at the interpretation phase when the researcher connects the two databases to address how the follow-up analysis helps to generalize or extend the initial qualitative exploratory findings. *Key data analysis decisions* in this design relate to the point of interface when the initial qualitative findings are used for the data collection in the follow-up quantitative phase. Other decisions need to be made about the psychometric quality of the instrument, how to analyze data from it, and how the quantitative results build or expand on the initial qualitative findings.

As noted, the researcher might use one of the basic designs to underlie the study and then develop it into an advanced mixed methods design. Three popular advanced designs are the intervention design, the social justice design, and the multistage evaluation design (Creswell, 2015). Figure 2 presents a basic procedural diagram for three advanced designs. Each of these designs has one of the basic designs at its core, depending on the intent of the design. In the **intervention design**, the researcher might add qualitative components to a larger experimental trial. In this case, analysis could occur before the experiment to recruit participants or develop the intervention (i.e., planning), during the intervention to examine how participants experience the intervention, or after the intervention to explain the outcomes. *Data analysis* then depends on how and when the qualitative data enters the study. In the **social justice design**, the intent is to investigate a research problem through an overarching social justice lens, such as a racial, a disability, or a gender lens. The researcher threads this social justice framework through the study that builds on one of the basic designs. *Data analysis* is contingent upon the basic design at the core of the study. Finally, in the **multistage evaluation design**, the intent is to evaluate a program or set of activities in a particular setting over a period. These designs often involve a series of multiple qualitative and quantitative phases that connect sequentially. For instance, the evaluator may begin with a needs assessment (qualitative), next, develop a program theory, then specify instruments to test the program (quantitative), and finally conduct follow-up to explain the program outcomes (qualitative). Phases could also consist of mixed methods studies that connect over the course of inquiry. *Data analysis* will focus the development of measures from the needs assessment and program theory, the psychometric properties of instruments, and what results need further explanation.

For all of the advanced designs, *key data analysis decisions* follow those of the basic designs (e.g., how to compare two datasets in convergent designs, how to connect in sequential designs), and relate to the particular intent of the advanced design. The researcher, however, first decides how to use the additional dataset and how to

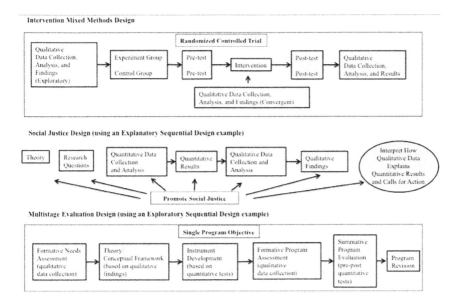

FIGURE 2. Three Advanced Mixed Methods Designs adapted from Creswell (2015). In these figures, ovals represent integration, rectangles represent data, and arrows represent the flow of procedures.

incorporate it into the basic design. In general, the focus of mixed methods analysis within the designs has been on strategies to merge or connect the data.

Points Where Integration and Representation Can Occur in the Designs

Integration can occur in the planning stages of research, during analysis, or at the conclusion of research for interpretation. It will generally consist of three integration strategies for the basic designs: (a) merging (convergent design), (b) explaining (explanatory sequential design), or (c) building (exploratory sequential design). The latter two are sometimes collectively considered "connecting" strategies for integration. The advanced designs rely on the integration strategies of the underlying basic designs but also involve (a) embedding qualitative data (intervention design), (b) threading a theoretical lens (social justice design), and (c) expanding (multistage evaluation design) (Creswell, 2015).

For studies employing a convergent basic design, merged integration strategies involve bringing quantitative and quantitative data (or results) together, assessing whether results converge or diverge, and reconciling divergent results. Although a discussion with comparison of qualitative and quantitative results in prose is a common approach to merged integration, Creswell and Plano Clark (2011) provided three options for comparing the results of quantitative and qualitative analysis. The options are (a) a side-by-side display, (b) a joint display comparison in results or interpretation, or (c) data transformation. In side-by-side displays, a table brings results together by arraying qualitative themes and quantitative statistical results along with a column to account for discrepancies. Creswell and Plano Clark further presented practical methods to integrate qualitative and quantitative data using *joint displays*. The defining feature of a joint display is the representation of a combination of quantitative and qualitative data, analysis, results, or interpretation in a single visual display (Creswell, 2015). Types of joint displays include a typology development, convergent and divergent findings, a case-oriented merged analysis, and a category/theme display. An example category/theme joint display is a matrix with quantitative categorical data levels arrayed as rows and qualitative themes arrayed horizontally as columns. The cells within the matrix then contain illustrative quotes. The third integration strategy for convergent designs is data transformation (Creswell & Plano Clark, 2011). Data transformation involves converting data from one type to another (e.g., qualitative to quantitative). Generally, this approach involves creating a dichotomous variable for the theme or code based on whether it is present (e.g., 1 = Yes, 2 = No) or obtaining the frequencies of codes or themes.

Creswell and Plano Clark (2011) further discussed ways to connect data sequentially. Analysis in the first phase guides the selection of participants in the follow-up phase. For sequential designs, joint displays link qualitative and quantitative strands by showing how the results from one phase proceeded to data collection in the subsequent phase. In an explanatory design, the researcher determines what quantitative results need further explanation and then conducts a qualitative follow-up phase. Similarly, in an exploratory sequential design, themes, codes, and quotes may be useful to design items, variables, and scales. A table may be useful for mapping the analysis and demonstrating mixed methods integration in either type of sequential design.

For the advanced designs, integration and representation strategies generally follow the underlying basic designs. However, we do have useful additional integration options: embedding, threading, and expanding. In an intervention study, for example, qualitative data is *embedded* into an experiment to assist in participant recruitment, informing the intervention, or explaining outcome results. A researcher can also *thread* a philosophical view or theory throughout a social justice study. In this type of integration, the framework becomes a continuous focus (i.e., through planning, data collection, analysis, interpretation, and reporting) with the goal of improving the lives of individuals (Creswell, 2015). Finally, in a multistage evaluation design, integration involves *expanding* from stage to stage within a line of inquiry. The stages themselves could consist of mixed methods stages or individual qualitative and quantitative strands. Thus, integration occurs both within the individual phases and by connecting phases over time.

The Use of MAXQDA to Represent Integration

Although joint displays help the researcher with integration and help the reader of mixed methods studies to understand integration, developing joint displays can be challenging. Addressing this challenge, Kuckartz (2009) linked the joint displays to the use of computer assisted qualitative data analysis software (CAQ-DAS). Originally conceived as qualitative programs, the mixed methods features of these applications allow the user to store qualitative and quantitative data, conduct analysis, and generate visual displays. Kuckartz (2009, 2014) noted that the applications may be used to: (a) import and export data, (b) selectively retrieve text based on quantitative variables, (c) compare results of different studies by use of thematic coding, (d) transform qualitative into quantitative data through counts of code occurrences, and (e) create joint displays of themes and variables. We can then extend these functions across mixed methods designs to create visual displays tailored to the particular intent of the study.

Kuckartz (2009, 2014) went into detail about the qualitative and quantitative data links that a user can forge using MAXQDA (Version 11) software. This software program can link, code, and memo; transform qualitative data into quantitative data; and create visual representations of code distributions for exporting to statistical software. Some specific qualitative and quantitative data analysis procedures available in MAXQDA are

- quantifying qualitative data—counting the number of times that a code occurs;
- linking text and variables using text codes and the "attributes" features (demographic or other quantitative variables);
- exporting and importing data into a statistical program—a researcher can create a data display of demographic variable names on the horizontal axis and themes on the vertical axis with counts in the cells and export this display into a statistical computer program; and
- using word counts—analyzing the qualitative data for the frequency of words used and linking the word counts to the codes or to the variables.

Through these features, researchers are able to integrate qualitative and quantitative data. Furthermore, MAXQDA provides researchers with a tool to create displays to represent integration.

In the preceding section, we provided a brief introduction to mixed methods research. Mixed methods research involves the collection, analysis, and integration of qualitative and quantitative data to better understand research problems. It is accomplished through six major research designs: convergent, explanatory sequential, exploratory sequential, intervention, social justice, and multistage evaluation designs. The design then determines when and where integration can occur. Computer software, such as MAXQDA, can assist researchers with integration and representation. We will now focus on using and creating joint displays to address and represent mixed methods integration.

ADDRESSING INTEGRATION AND REPRESENTATION THROUGH JOINT DISPLAYS

What are Joint Displays?

A mixed methods joint display represents integration or mixing in a single visual display (Creswell, 2015). The overall intent is to represent integration and assist the reader in understanding the study. The content may consist of quantitative and qualitative data, analysis, results, or interpretation. It is important, however, that the display includes both qualitative and quantitative data and clearly labels each for the reader. The joint display should be consistent with the mixed methods design of the study, the stage in which integration occurred, and the type of integration used. Table 3 contains a checklist for the researcher in creating joint displays and suggests the features that should be present in mixed methods joint displays.

Joint displays are valuable in mixed methods research because they can assist the researcher and reader alike in thinking about the integration of qualitative and quantitative data. Joint displays may facilitate the cognitive process involved with mixing and adding perspectives. This process of mixed methods analysis and interpretation then provides a better understanding of a research problem than either approach alone would yield.

Types of Joint Displays Useful in Mixed Methods Designs

The next section of this chapter will present 11 joint displays in detail along with procedures to create each type of display using computer software. The intent of this section is to illustrate the types of joint displays that can aid in planning, analyzing, and interpreting mixed methods data. To illustrate the procedures

TABLE 3.   Checklist for Creating Joint Displays

☐ Joint Display Feature

☐ Clear title to indicate what is presented

☐ Includes both qualitative and quantitative data

☐ Clearly identifies qualitative and quantitative data sources

☐ Demonstrates the integration of qualitative and quantitative data

☐ Consistent with the selected mixed methods design

☐ Consistent with the stage of integration (e.g., planning, analysis, conclusion)

☐ Consistent with the type of integration: merging, building, explaining

☐ A description in the text accompanies the display

involved, we will use MAXQDA (Version 11) as a computer tool and identify the steps involved in conducting the procedure. We include figures to provide an example of each display and how to create it. The displays are all modifiable, based on the needs of the researcher and the intent of the communication. Table 4 presents a summary of the mixed methods joint displays, along with their description, mixed method designs in which they are applicable, and the MAXQDA application features to create the display.

Comparing results display in a convergent design.

The researcher may need to highlight the extent to which qualitative findings are congruent with the quantitative results. In the comparing results display, the investigator works with the results from the quantitative and qualitative analysis of a research study. Using thematic coding, the interesting themes in both findings—the qualitative and the quantitative—have to be coded (Kuckartz, 2014). The display then facilitates the integrated mixed methods analysis. This type of integration is especially useful in studies using convergent designs. The purpose of the display is to present the convergent and divergent findings side-by-side. Highlighting divergence and convergence might be useful for several reasons: to bring attention to diverse perspectives or to present evidence in test validation studies. For example, Lee and Greene (2007) studied the predictive validity of test scores with academic criterion measures. They created a joint display to link the predictive validity of test scores to qualitative data that identifies congruent and discrepant findings. The display consists of a matrix. Rows represent the relationship between the test score and criterion while the columns displayed the qualitative findings. The cells then contain example quotes that confirmed the predictive validity of the test next to those that presented the alternative, disconfirming view.

Figure 3 illustrates the comparing results display (for a concrete example, see Lee & Greene, 2007, Table 5). In this configuration, the convergent and divergent qualitative findings appear side-by-side, with rows representing the quantitative results. The cells contain quotes to illustrate the convergence and divergent findings. Depending on the emphasis, we could reverse the orientation to examine convergent and divergent quantitative results by theme and cells could contain numbers. Regardless of the format, this display showcases differing perspectives.

To create the comparing results display in MAXQDA (Version 11), we will use the quote matrix and summary grid. First, it may be necessary to activate the documents we are interested in by variable (e.g., by a level of a categorical variable or range for a continuous variable). Next, we will create a quote matrix or summary grid (Kuckartz, 2014). A quote matrix contains the original text passages from the data sources (i.e., all text passages concerning a particular topic from the reports of both qualitative and quantitative strands). The summary grid allows the researcher to summarize these text passages and work on the more abstract level of summaries. Specifically, with the summary grid we can view coded segments for only those activated variables of interest. We can then edit the summary column

TABLE 4. Types of Joint Displays for Mixed Methods Designs

Design Joint Display	Description	Stage/Type of Integration	Constructing the Joint Display Using MAXQDA
Convergent			
Comparing Results Display	Highlight the extent to which qualitative findings are congruent with the quantitative results	Conclusion/ Merging	Quote matrix, Summary grid, Summary table
Side-by-Side Display	Array quantitative and qualitative data together by questions, statistical results, or themes	Analysis/ Merging	Quote matrix Summary grid, Summary table
Statistics-by-Themes Display	Array quantitative data by qualitative themes	Analysis/ Merging	Crosstabs, Configuration table
Geocoding-by-Themes Display	Array geographic location data by qualitative themes	Analysis/ Merging	Geolinks, Summary grid, Summary table
Explanatory sequential			
Participant Selection Display	Link quantitative results to participants purposefully selected for the follow-up sample	Planning/ Connecting (Explaining)	Typology table
Interview Questions Display	Link the initial quantitative findings to the follow-up qualitative results for the purpose of explanation	Planning/ Connecting (Explaining)	Quote matrix Summary grid, Summary table
Exploratory sequential			
Instrument Development Display	Quotes, codes, or themes that match proposed items, variables, or scales for instrument development purposes	Planning/ Connecting (Building)	Typology table, Crosstabs
Generalizing Themes Display	Indicate how the quantitative results generalize the qualitative findings	Conclusion/ Connecting (Explaining)	Crosstabs, Summary table
Intervention			
Adding Qualitative Data into an Experiment Display	Represent the points in which qualitative data entered the larger experimental trial	All stages/ Embedding	Quote matrix Summary grid, MAXMaps
Social Justice			
Adding a Theoretical Lens Display	Present the integration of data in light of a theoretical lens undergirding the study	All stages/ Threading	Quote matrix Summary grid, Summary table
Multistage Evaluation			
Linking Stages Display	Indicate integration at multiple points throughout the evaluation study	All stages/ Expanding	Quote matrix Summary grid, Summary table Crosstabs, typology table, MAXMaps

Survey Scale Score	Convergent Findings	Divergent Findings
1	Illustrative quotes	
2		
3		
4		

FIGURE 3.   A sample template for comparing results display

by extracting the convergent and divergent findings. Figure 4 displays a summary grid with coded segments and the summary completed. We can select a code and then view its segments and summary. We can then build a table in a report or export our summary to Excel by creating a grid table (click the grid table icon). The table will represent the mixed methods integration for the reader.

Side-by-side display in a convergent design.

The purpose of the side-by-side display is to array quantitative and qualitative data together. It is applicable for studies based on convergent mixed methods designs, but it may also be useful for a final integration step in sequential designs. The display presents the combined of quantitative and qualitative results systematically. Specifically, it could focus the reader on research questions, quantitative results, qualitative themes, or a theoretical framework. For instance, within a particular thematic finding, the display can present the related codes or an explana-

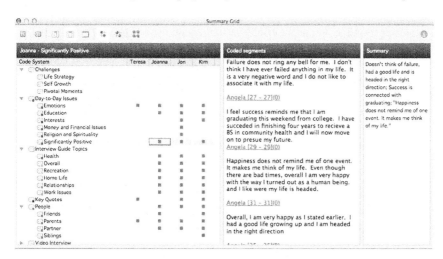

FIGURE 4.   The summary grid in MAXQDA is an initial step in creating the comparing results display.

	Qualitative	Quantitative
Theme	**Interview Findings**	**Results of Survey**
Theme 1	Descriptive summary, codes, quotes, et.	Summary of results related to the theme
Theme 2		
Theme 3		
Theme 4		

FIGURE 5.   A template for a side-by-side display

tion of the theme next to the relevant quantitative results. Thus, the presentation is parallel. In a variation of this type of display, Fetters, Curry, and Creswell (2013) presented a box plot of the quantitative scale results along with illustrative qualitative text to the side of the figure. They color-coded the joint display such that the participant response box plot was the same color as the corresponding text.

Figure 5 presents an example of a side-by-side display comparing results by themes (for an example, see Fetters, Curry, & Creswell, 2013). Each row consists of a theme and the columns consist of the interview findings and survey findings, respectively. The cells within the qualitative column contain the description of the theme emerging from the interviews, and the cells within the quantitative column contain the major survey results. Thus, it reduces the comparison of major results from each strand to a concise visual for the reader.

Statistics-by-themes display in a convergent design.

In convergent designs, a common merging strategy is to create a joint display to integrate data by arraying the qualitative data as one dimension and the quantitative data as another dimension in a matrix. Although numerous variations exist, the researcher often arrays quantitative categorical data by qualitative themes. The categorical data might consist of actual quantitative results from a categorical variable (e.g., educational level) or it might consist of a continuous quantitative variable that has then been stratified into levels (e.g., high, medium, low severity of risk) to facilitate integration. The cells within the matrix then contain illustrative quotes. In another variation, Wittink, Barg, and Gallo (2006) created a display with rows of variables, columns of themes, and cells of descriptive statistics for each variable-theme combination. Their display merged the data to represent a typology for the reader. Alternatively, we could array cases as columns and statistics as rows to present a complete picture of cases. Figure 6 presents a general template for the statistics-by-themes display (see Wittink et al., 2006). The researcher

	Variable-level 1	Variable-level 2	Variable-level 3
Theme 1	Illustrative quotes; statistical results		
Theme 2			
Theme 3			
Theme 4			

FIGURE 6. Example statistics-by-themes joint display

could transpose the rows and columns based on the variables, themes, available space and the intended communication. Although the purpose of the display is to represent the merged analysis, the overall intent could be to communicate a typology, as in Wittink et al. (2006), or to portray a more complete and complex understanding of a concept.

We can create the statistics-by-themes display using the crosstabs function of MAXQDA (Kuckartz, 2014, pp. 98–99). First, it is important set up variables for each "document" (i.e., qualitative data source) in MAXQDA. We can enter these manually or import numerical data for combination with qualitative data. By selecting the variable of interest and values of interest, we can gather themes or codes by variable. Figure 7 displays a crosstab of codes (vertically as rows) by the emotions scale score. Here it displays counts of coded segments for each variable-code combination. We could also request percentages by document or by code. Clicking on any of the numbers will retrieve the coded text segments.

Geocoding-by-themes display in a convergent design.
In convergent designs, the quantitative data may be in the form of geographical location references (e.g., GPS coordinates). With this type of data, the research-

	emotion = 1	emotion = 2	emotion = 3
Emotions	44,4%	44,4%	11,1%
Education	50,0%	50,0%	
Interests	50,0%	50,0%	
Money and Financial Issues	33,3%	66,7%	
Religion and Spirituality		100,0%	
Σ SUM	42,3%	53,8%	3,8%
# N (Documents)	36,4%	36,4%	27,3%

FIGURE 7. The MAXQDA crosstab function can help us generate a statistics-by-themes display.

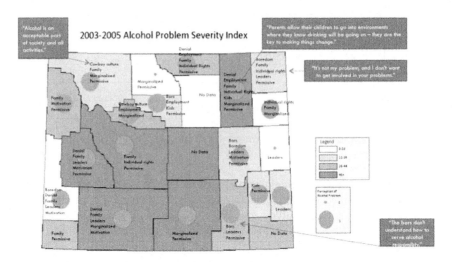

FIGURE 8. An example a geocoding-by-themes display. Reprinted from "State Level Assessments, Graphic Displays, and Mixed Method" by P.A. Minugh, 2012, Invited presentation at the Eighth International Congress of Qualitative Inquiry: Mixed Methods Day, University of Illinois at Urbana-Champaign. Reprinted with permission.

er might integrate the location references with qualitative data using software (Fielding, 2012). The qualitative data might consist of text from interviews or observations or images and photographs. The researcher can geocode the data, obtaining GPS coordinates from mapping software and tagging the data with the code. Many digital cameras and smartphones automatically tag images with GPS coordinates. However, manual geocoding might also be useful for tagging observation locations, open responses to surveys, or text documents to place events in their spatial setting (Yeager & Steiger, 2013). This geographical information can then be integrated with qualitative data and presented in a visual image, such as a map of a geographical area (e.g., Crooks, Shuurman, Cinnamon, Castleden, & Johnston, 2010; Dickinson, 2010). Figure 8 presents a joint display that Minugh (2012) created to integrate Alcohol Problem Severity Index scores (color coded by county) and community perception of problem (size of dots) with qualitative community perception categories and example quotes. Minugh overlaid this integrated data onto a state map.

Participant selection display in an explanatory sequential design.

In sequential designs, the results of one phase connect to the sampling of another phase. The researcher might use the findings from a quantitative analysis to guide sampling and participant selection by determining what results need fur-

	Group 1 (Participant)	Group 2 (Participant)	Group 3 (Participant)
Age	19 or less	20 – 25	over 25
Gender	Female	Male	Female
Race	White	White	Non-White
Geographic Location	Indiana	New York	New York

FIGURE 9. An example participant selection joint display using individual groups and demographic characteristics.

ther explanation in the subsequent qualitative phase. The qualitative sampling could be based on certain demographics, important variables, surprising results, or outliers. A similar procedure can occur when the qualitative phase precedes the quantitative phase. For example, Koops and Lindley (2002) began with a quantitative survey and qualitative focus group exploration to develop better and more ethically acceptable recruitment procedures for a planned randomized controlled trail. The researcher could also use a visual display to depict this selection and recruitment process as the integration of qualitative and quantitative data. Although the possibilities abound, we will demonstrate a concrete example of a planning display for selecting a qualitative sample.

In an explanatory sequential design, the researcher faces an integration challenge in connecting quantitative results to the subsequent qualitative explanation. A participant selection display links the quantitative results or demographic characteristics to the participants purposefully selected for the follow-up sample. Figure 9 presents an example of this display similar to one presented by Ivankova, Creswell, and Stick (2006). The figure contains a matrix of participant selection using purposeful sampling based on demographic characteristics. The organization of the table is to array demographic characteristics (rows) by participant (columns), and the cells contained the characteristics of each participant. The rows, however, can be whatever is meaningful to select participants for the study, such as instrument scores or other measures.

Although MAXQDA (Version 11) does not perform statistical procedures other than frequency tables, bar charts, and pie charts, the user can import an existing data matrix into MAXQDA in order to use it in combination with the qualitative data. The file must contain the variables textgroup and text name. These variables must also correspond to the appropriate text. The variables then attach to documents. Using this data, the researcher can construct a typology table to assist with participant selection. Figure 10 displays a section of a typology table. The researcher will then need to determine the selection of participants and create the table with appropriate data within each cell.

	Type – A (N=5)	Type – B (N=4)	Type – C (N=2)
Gender: Female, Number (%)	3 (60.0)	2 (50.0)	2 (100.0)
Age: 19 or less, Number (%)	2 (40.0)	3 (75.0)	1 (50.0)
Race Ethnicity: White, Number (%)	4 (80.0)	3 (75.0)	1 (50.0)
relations, friends, Mean (SD)	28.6 (6.3)	35.5 (7.9)	48.5 (18.5)
career, Mean (SD)	17.0 (6.0)	15.2 (7.3)	23.0 (5.0)
religion, Mean (SD)	0.2 (0.4)	1.8 (1.8)	0.0 (0.0)

FIGURE 10.   A MAXQDA typology table as the initial step for a participant selection joint display.

Interview questions display in an explanatory sequential design.

An interview questions display links the initial quantitative findings to the follow-up quantitative results for the purpose of explanation. This type of joint display appears at the end of the study to portray integration in explanatory sequential designs. For example, Zeng et al.'s (2012) study of depression among older adults includes a visual display "mapped" (p. 162), the categories derived from the qualitative interviews onto the related quantitative indicators from various scales. Each row in the matrix contained one category next to the corresponding indicators to demonstrate the combination. Figure 11 presents a template for an interview questions display (for a concrete example, see Zeng et al., 2012). In this template, the results of each scale is mapped to the interview question to understand that particular result.

Ideally, the explanation display, as in Figure 11, consists of two components: a column that displays the quantitative results and a column that displays the qualitative follow-up question (Creswell, 2015). Depending on space and esthetic needs, the display could also be oriented vertically. Moreover, the researcher has options for each component. The information presented in the quantitative results area depends on the researcher's selection of what data needed further explanation. It could contain the significant, nonsignificant, unexpected, or outlier result (Creswell & Plano Clark, 2011). Regardless of these options, the overall intent of this display is to communicate how the qualitative strand was specifically con-

Quantitative Results	**Qualitative Follow-up Questions**
Scale 1	Related questions
Scale 2	
Scale 3	

FIGURE 11.   Template for an explanation display

Qualitative Finings		Quantitative Instrument	
Qualitative Theme	**Codes**	**Instrument Scale**	**Instrument Variables**
Day-to-Day Issues	Emotions Education Interests Money and Finances Religion and Spirituality Significantly Positive	Day-to-Day Issues	Emotions Education Personal Interests Money Religion Positivity
Interview Guide Topics	Health Recreation Home Life Relationship Work Issues Overall	Satisfaction Scale	Health Satisfaction Recreation Satisfaction Home Life Satisfaction Relationship Satisfaction Work Satisfaction Overall Satisfaction
People	Friends Parents Partner Siblings	People and Relationships	Friends Parents Partner Siblings

FIGURE 12.   Instrument development display

nected to explain the quantitative results. A summary table, such as the summary grid in MAXQDA (Version 11) might be useful for creating the explanation display.

Instrument development display in an exploratory sequential design.

The reason for using mixed methods is often to develop an instrument with the exploratory sequential mixed methods design. A primary challenge of this design, regarding the integration of qualitative and quantitative databases, is how to use the qualitative findings to build an instrument. A way to visually depict this process is the instrument development display. The instrument development display involves a display of quotes, codes, or themes that match proposed items, variables, or scales for instrument development purposes. The sample in Figure 12 presents qualitative findings next to the related aspects of the qualitative instrument.

Alternatively, the instrument development display could depict how particular quotes informed the language of items. The purpose of this display is to align the qualitative findings with the resulting quantitative instrument to depict how the researcher used the findings to inform the instrument development.

Although MAXQDA (Version 11) cannot create the display fully, several features are available as initial steps to creating it. Specifically, retrieved segments, the typology table, and the closely related crosstabs can assist the researcher. First, by activating codes of interest and ordering by code system, the retrieved segments window will display the coded text. The user can then export the segments to word processing or spreadsheet programs for further work, such as selecting quotes that will inform item language in an instrument. Second, the typology table and crosstabs functions are useful to analyze by document variable. Perhaps the interest is in tailoring an instrument for certain ethnic groups of individuals. We could use crosstabs and the typology table to examine coding differences among ethnicities and use this to inform specific language on the instrument. A similar process would hold when using themes to inform instrument scales or codes to inform variables.

Generalizing themes display in an exploratory sequential design.

A generalization display at the end of the study shows how the quantitative results generalize the qualitative findings. So, it represents integration in an exploratory sequential mixed methods design. In this design, the researcher begins qualitatively, develops an instrument or intervention, and then follows with a final quantitative phase to test what was developed. This display is a variation of a side-by-side display with qualitative findings next to qualitative results. However, it includes a final column comparing the results and indicating the extent to which the quantitative testing supported the qualitative findings. Figure 13 presents a template of this display organized by the thematic findings of the first phase of the study. Options for this display include organizing the display by theme or by research question. For example, Zhou (2014) conducted a study of Chinese scholars' perceptions and intention to use mixed methods. She created a joint display organized by research question, with qualitative findings presented side-by-side with quantitative findings followed by a final column indicating whether the quantitative results confirmed qualitative findings (see Zhou, 2014, Table 5.2). Thus, the reader can easily visualize the results together along with an indication of whether we can generalize qualitative findings to a population.

Using CAQDAS, we can compare the relationship of codes to variables. By adding variables into MAXQDA (Version 11), for instance, it is possible to compare codes (or themes) by variable using cross tabulation or summary tables. However, most likely it will be necessary to create the display manually based on this output. Therefore, we will take the crosstabs or summary table and export the display for further combination with statistical results, such as regression results

Qualitative Findings (n =)	Statistical results (n =)	Generalization
Theme 1	Scale results, surveys, intervention outcome measures, etc.	The quantitative results confirmed (or did not confirm) the qualitative findings
Theme 2		
Theme 3		

FIGURE 13.   Generalizing themes display template

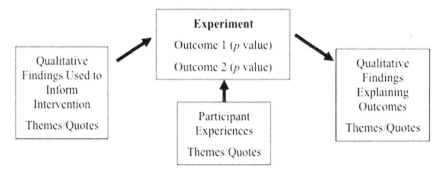

FIGURE 14. A template to represent embedding for an adding qualitative data into an experiment display

or factor loadings. We can then indicate the extent to which quantitative analysis generalized the qualitative.

Adding qualitative data into an experiment display in an intervention design.

In an intervention design, the focus is an experimental trial. Mixed methods brings qualitative data into this study by embedding it throughout the process of the intervention. Visually, we can represent the embedded qualitative data by demonstrating where the qualitative findings added to the experimental data. For example, researchers could collect qualitative data prior to an experiment to inform an intervention, during the intervention to understand participants' experiences, or at the end of trial to help explain outcomes. Although developing a joint display based on the underlying basic design is one option (see Shaw et al., 2013), the researcher should also consider a joint display to communicate integration as it occurred throughout the process. Betancourt et al. (2011, Fig. 1) included a diagram of the overall flow of qualitative data into an intervention study. Additional text boxes could be easily added to this type of figure to represent themes and statistical results. Figure 14 provides a template for this type of display. In this display, the overall procedural process appears along with where qualitative data added to the experiment. Supporting themes, codes, and perhaps quotes can appear in the display. For example, the box below "Experiment" shows how qualitative data flows into the experiment and contains the themes with quotes gathered from participants during the experiment to understand their experience of the intervention.

To develop a joint display to represent the addition of qualitative data to an experiment, we will likely rely on the tools used to integrate data for the basic designs. Software like NVivo, Atlas.TI, or MAXQDA offer mapping features that can also assist with creating this type of display. The researcher can add text to the

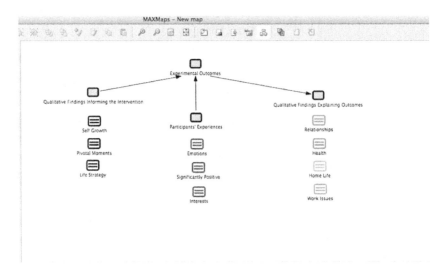

FIGURE 15.   Using MAXQDA's MAXMaps to represent qualitative data added into an experiment

map manually, bring in codes and themes from the program, or include segments of coded text (i.e., quotes). Figure 15 presents an example using MAXQDA to develop a concept map. Adding text boxes, we can represent outcome data along with our themes. We can save the map as a picture for including in papers or presentations.

Adding a theoretical lens into a social justice design display.

Mixed methods researchers often thread a theoretical framework throughout the study to guide data collection, analysis, or the interpretation of results. Social justice designs involve an overarching theoretical lens or framework to bring attention to a social issue or problem. For example, researchers might add a feminist or critical race theory to guide the study. The theoretical lens or framework is then threaded throughout the study. This threading of a theory can be incorporated into a joint display. The structure of a joint display will likely follow the basic design that forms the foundation of a study. For example, Meysenburg, Albrecht, Litchfield, and Ritter-Gooder (2014) threaded the Health Belief Model into a convergent parallel mixed methods design that brought attention to the issue of food safety. They presented a side-by-side joint display of findings organized by each construct of the model. For each construct, their display included focus group findings and related survey results. The goal of this display is to depict both the integration of data and a theoretical lens or conceptual framework. Figure 16 presents a template for this type of display, based on an underlying convergent basic design (for an example, see Meysenburg et al., 2014, Table 4). The joint display is

Constructs of Theory	Qualitative Findings	Quantitative Results
Construct 1	Interview quotes	Survey descriptive statistics
Construct 2		
Construct 3		
Construct 4		

FIGURE 16. A template for adding a theoretical lens into a social justice design display

similar to a side-by-side display but organized by the constructs of the theory or framework guiding the study.

To create this display in MAXQDA (Version 11), follow the relevant merging approach for the basic design at the foundation of the study. Using the previous example of a social justice design with an underlying convergent design, constructing a side-by-side display will represent the merged integration. To construct this table, we can compare codes (or themes) by variable using crosstabs or the summary table features of MAXQDA. Then, using the summary grid, we can add the components of the relevant theoretical lens to frame the results with the theory. For social justice mixed methods designs using a sequential approach, the researcher would engage in a similar process of representing integration while adding the relevant theoretical lens to the display.

Linking a stages display in a multistage evaluation design.

The final example of a mixed methods visual display is one that captures a complex multistage evaluation design. This design involves multiple points of integration that expand from stage to stage over time. Consider a program evaluation study that begins with a qualitative needs assessment and development of a program theory followed by instrument development and eventually to program implementation and impact evaluation. Multiple joint displays can represent the points of integration. Although we have not yet found an example in the literature, one display might be an instrument development display to show how the evaluator used the qualitative program theory development phase to build to the instrument development. Figure 17 aligns the program theory with the quantitative instrument to assess program outcomes. The left side contains the outcomes and codes derived from thematic text analysis of interviews with stakeholders and potential participants. The right side contains the related instrument scales in addition to items or variables. The researcher can build upon this template by entering the appropriate aspects of the model and the mixed methods findings related to each aspect. A second display might then represent the merging of qualitative and quantitative data during the program impact evaluation. The researcher can

Program Theory		Impact Evaluation Instrument	
Program Outcomes	**Qualitative Codes**	**Scale**	**Instrument Items**
Outcome 1	Codes (derived from thematic text analysis of interviews)	Scale 1	Items or variables measured
Outcome 2	Codes	Scale 2	Items or variables measured
Outcome 3	Codes	Scale 3	Items or variables measured

FIGURE 17. Linking stages display in a multistage evaluation to represent integration building to an instrument

develop additional displays based on the particular types of integration occurring within the evaluation.

To construct a linking stages display, the researcher would follow the same procedures the basic underlying design requires. As noted, multiple joint displays may be necessary. The researchers can use many of the MAXQDA (Version 11) features: crosstab, summary tables, summary grids, code relations browser, typology table. In a variation, a concept map is often useful to display a complex type of design or model or evaluation. The MAXMaps feature can assist with developing this type of display. In an evaluation for instance, the researcher could present a model of the program theory (i.e., a logic model) with integrated qualitative and quantitative data. Although the focus of this chapter has been on displaying analysis and results, other display types might be used for planning. Using a logic model of program inputs, outputs, outcomes, and impact, the researcher could indicate where qualitative and quantitative components will flow into the proposed evaluation.

CONCLUSIONS AND RECOMMENDATIONS

Scholars have addressed mixed methods integration throughout the history of the field. Among many developments, the early data analysis strategies of Caracelli and Greene (1993) and continuing work to connect strategies to the research process (e.g., Onwuegbuzie & Teddlie, 2003) provided the initial foundation for mixed methods data analysis. As methodologists continued to expound upon that work, connecting visual displays (Creswell & Plano Clark, 2011) and computer applications (Bazely, 2009; Kuckartz, 2009) to mixed methods analysis, we have a larger toolkit today to create interesting and engaging joint displays. A joint display is important because it includes the representation of quantitative and qualitative data, analysis, results, or interpretation into a single visual display. Thus, a joint display represents integration, which is a defining feature of mixed methods research. Ultimately, the joint display will assist the reader in understanding the study.

We have presented 11 examples of mixed methods joint displays, but future refinement and creations are needed. Researchers continue to create new mixed methods joint displays. The displays are particularly important because the defining feature of mixed methods is integration. A visual depiction is a primary method of representing the integration. More research is needed on the process of integration, and scholars should continue to explore those areas. Potential developments include finding new ways to reduce complexity and engage the reader. Further developments are needed by design. For instance, by comparison, existing visual displays for explanatory sequential designs seem somewhat rudimentary. More work and creativity is needed to display how the researcher decided on what needs explanation and link to what the follow-up qualitative findings revealed. We encourage researchers to build on existing displays, create variations to meet the needs of studies, and share those displays with the community of scholars.

REFERENCES

ATLAS.ti (Version 7) [Computer software]. Berlin, Germany: Scientific Software Development GmbH. Retrieved from http://atlasti.com/

Bazeley, P. (2009). Integrating data analyses in mixed methods research [Editorial]. *Journal of Mixed Methods Research, 3*, 203–207. doi:10.1177/1558689809334443

Betancourt, T., Myers-Ohki, S. E., Stevenson, A., Ingabire, C., Kanyanganzi, F., Munyana, M., . . . & Beardslee, W. R. (2011). Using mixed-methods research to adapt and evaluate a family strengthening intervention in Rwanda. *African Journal of Traumatic Stress, 2*, 32–45.

Bryman, A. (1988). *Quantity and quality in social research.* London, UK: Unwin Hyman.

Bryman, A. (2006). Integrating quantitative and qualitative research: How is it done? *Qualitative Research, 6*, 97–113. doi: 10.1177/1468794106058877

Campbell, D. T., & Fiske, D. W. (1959). Convergent and discriminant validation by the multitrait-multimethod matrix. *Psychological Bulletin, 56*, 81–105.

Caracelli, V. J., & Greene, J. C. (1993). Data analysis strategies for mixed-method evaluation designs. *Educational Evaluation and Policy Analysis, 15*, 195–207. doi:10.3102/01623737015002195

Creswell, J. W. (1994). *Research design: Qualitative and quantitative approaches.* Thousand Oaks, CA: Sage.

Creswell, J. W. (2015). *A concise introduction to mixed methods research.* Thousand Oaks, CA: Sage.

Creswell, J. W., & Plano Clark, V. L. (2011). *Designing and conducting mixed methods research* (2nd ed.). Thousand Oaks, CA: Sage.

Crooks, V. A., Schuurman, N., Cinnamon, J., Castleden, H., & Johnston, R. (2011). Refining a location analysis model using a mixed methods approach: Community readiness as a key factor in siting rural palliative care services. *Journal of Mixed Methods Research, 5*, 77–95.

Denscombe, M. (2008). Communities of practice: A research paradigm for the mixed methods approach. *Journal of Mixed Methods Research, 2,* 270–283. doi:10.1177/1558689808316807

DeVoe, J. E., Baez, A., Angier, H., Krois, L., Edlund, C., & Carney, P. A. (2007). Insurance + access ≠ health care: Typology of barriers to health care access for low-income families. *The Annals of Family Medicine, 5*(6), 511–518. doi:10.1370/afm.748

Dickinson, W. B. (2010). Visual displays for mixed methods findings. In A. Tashakkori & C. Teddlie (Eds.), *Sage handbook of mixed methods in social & behavioral research* (2nd ed.). Thousand Oaks, CA: Sage.

Fetters, M. D., Curry, L. A., & Creswell, J. W. (2013). Achieving integration in mixed methods designs—Principles and practices. *Health Services Research, 48,* 2134–2156. doi: 10.1111/1475-6773.12117

Fielding, N. G. (2012). Triangulation and mixed methods designs: Data integration with new research technologies. *Journal of Mixed Methods Research, 6,* 124–136. doi: 10.1177/1558689812437101

Fielding, N. G., & Fielding, J. L. (1986). *Linking data: The articulation of qualitative and quantitative methods in social research.* Beverly Hills, CA: Sage.

Greene, J. C., Caracelli, V. J., & Graham, W. F. (1989). Toward a conceptual framework for mixed-method evaluation designs. *Educational evaluation and policy analysis, 11,* 255–274. doi:10.3102/01623737011003255

Hunter, A., & Brewer, J. (2003). Multimethod research in sociology. In A. Tashakkori & C. Teddlie (Eds.), *Handbook of mixed methods in social and behavioral research* (pp. 577–594). Thousand Oaks, CA: Sage.

IBM SPSS Statistics for Windows (Version 22.0) [Computer software]. Armonk, NY: IBM Corp.

Ivankova, N. V., Creswell, J. W., & Stick, S. L. (2006). Using mixed-methods sequential explanatory design: From theory to practice. *Field Methods, 18,* 3–20. doi:10.1177/1525822X05282260

Koops, L., & Lindley, R. I. (2002). Thrombolysis for acute ischaemic stroke: Consumer involvement in design of new randomised controlled trial. *BMJ, 325*(7361), 415. doi:10.1136/bmj.325.7361.415

Kuckartz, U. (2009). *Realizing mixed-methods approaches with MAXQDA.* Marburg, Germany: Philips-Universität Marburg.

Kuckartz, U. (2014). *Qualitative text analysis: A guide to methods, practice, & using software.* Thousand Oaks, CA: Sage.

Lee, Y.-J., & Greene, J. C. (2007). The predictive validity of an ESL placement test: A mixed methods approach. *Journal of Mixed Methods Research, 1,* 366–389. doi:10.1177/1558689807306148

MAXQDA (Version 11) [Computer software]. Berlin, Germany: Verbi GmbH. Retrieved from http://www.maxqda.com/

Marcellus, L., MacKinnon, K., Benoit, C., Phillips, R., & Stengel, C. (2014). Reenvisioning success for programs supporting pregnant women with problematic substance use. *Qualitative Health Research.* doi:10.1177/1049732314551058

Meysenburg, R., Albrecht, J. A., Litchfield, R., & Ritter-Gooder, P. K. (2014). Food safety knowledge, practices and beliefs of primary food preparers in families with young children. A mixed methods study. *Appetite, 73,* 121–131. doi:10.1016/j.appet.2013.10.015

Minugh, P. A. (2012, May 16). *State level assessments, graphic displays, and mixed methods.* Invited presentation at the 8th International Congress of Qualitative Inquiry: Mixed Methods Day, University of Illinois at Urbana-Champaign.

Morse, J. M. (1991). Approaches to qualitative-quantitative methodological triangulation. *Nursing Research, 40*, 120–123.

Nastasi, B. K., Hitchcock, J., Sarkar, S., Burkholder, G., Varjas, K., & Jayasena, A. (2007). Mixed methods in intervention research: Theory to adaptation. *Journal of Mixed Methods Research, 1*, 164–182. doi:10.1177/1558689806298181

NVivo (Version 10) [Computer software]. Melbourne, Australia: QSR International. Retrieved from http://www.qsrinternational.com/

Onwuegbuzie, A. J., & Teddlie, C. (2003). A framework for analyzing data in mixed methods research. In A. Tashakkori & C. Teddlie (Eds.), *Handbook of mixed methods in social & behavioral research* (pp. 351–383). Thousand Oaks, CA: Sage.

Plano Clark, V. L. (2010). The adoption and practice of mixed methods: U.S. trends in federally funded health-related research. *Qualitative Inquiry, 16*, 428–440. doi:10.1177/1077800410364609

Plano Clark, V. L., Schumacher, K., West, C., Edrington, J., Dunn, L. B., Harzstark, A., . . . Miaskowski, C. (2013). Practices for embedding an interpretive qualitative approach within a randomized clinical trial. *Journal of Mixed Methods Research, 7*, 219–242. doi:10.1177/1558689812474372

QDA Miner (Version 4) [Computer software]. Montreal, Canada: Provalis Research. Retrieved from http://provalisresearch.com/

Shaw, E. K., Ohman-Strickland, P. A., Piasecki, A., Hudson, S. V., Ferrante, J. M., McDaniel, R. R., . . . Crabtree, B. F. (2013). Effects of facilitated team meetings and learning collaboratives on colorectal cancer screening rates in primary care practices: A cluster randomized trial. *The Annals of Family Medicine, 11*(3), 220–228. doi:10.1370/afm.1505

Stange, K. C., Miller, W., Crabtree, B. F., O'Connor, P. J., & Zyzanski, S. J. (1994). Multimethod research. *Journal of General Internal Medicine, 9*, 278–282. doi:10.1007/BF02599656

Stoller, E. P., Webster, N. J., Blixen, C. E., McCormick, R. A., Hund, A. J., Perzynski, A. T., . . . Dawson, N. V. (2009). Alcohol consumption decisions among nonabusing drinkers diagnosed with Hepatitis C: An exploratory sequential mixed methods study. *Journal of Mixed Methods Research, 3*, 65–86.

Vrkljan, B. H. (2009). Constructing a mixed methods design to explore the older driver-copilot relationship. *Journal of Mixed Methods Research, 3*, 371–385. doi:10.1177/1558689809336843

Wittink, M. N., Barg, F. K., & Gallo, J. J. (2006). Unwritten rules of talking to doctors about depression: Integrating qualitative and quantitative methods. *Annals of Family Medicine, 4*, 302–309. doi:10.1370/afm.558

Yeager, C. D., & Steiger, T. (2013). Applied geography in a digital age: The case for mixed methods. *Applied Geography, 39*, 1–4.

Zeng, W., North, N., & Kent, B. (2011). Methodological challenges to research among Chinese: Using mixed methods to investigate older persons with depression in Macau. *Journal of Mixed Methods Research, 6*, 154–165. doi:10.1177/1558689811419513

Zhou, Y. (2014). *The adoption of mixed methods in China: An exploratory instrument design.* Retrieved from ProQuest Dissertations and Theses (Order No. 3628357)

CHAPTER 7

THE USE OF VISUAL DISPLAYS IN MIXED METHODS RESEARCH

Strategies for Effectively Integrating the Quantitative and Qualitative Components of a Study

Vicki L. Plano Clark and Khahlia Sanders

ABSTRACT

Mixed methods research is an approach to research in which the researcher meaningfully integrates quantitative and qualitative approaches to address a research problem. Achieving meaningful integration is challenging. Visual displays that explicitly combine the quantitative and qualitative components of a study (known as joint displays) may facilitate the integrative process, but little guidance exists for their use. We examined researchers' use of joint displays in published mixed methods articles to identify the different ways they are used, their key features, and to offer practical recommendations. From our analysis, we identified four major categories of joint displays: conceptual, research process, connection/development, and integrated results. These joint displays portrayed different types of integration information, were formatted as matrices and figures, and varied in terms of their or-

Use of Visual Displays in Research and Testing: Coding, Interpreting, and Reporting Data,
pages 177–206.

ganization and means for depicting integration. Based on our review, we offer a set of templates and recommendations to help researchers design and use joint displays to facilitate the integration within their applications of mixed methods research.

OBJECTIVES

Specific objectives for this chapter include:

- Articulating the role of integration in mixed methods research.
- Distinguishing different ways that researchers use visual displays to facilitate integration within mixed methods research.
- Identifying key features and decisions associated with the effective use of visual displays in mixed methods research.
- Advancing recommendations for scholars using visual displays within mixed methods research.

Researchers across the educational, social, and health sciences disciplines are increasingly turning to mixed methods research to address the complex problems of interest today (Alise & Teddlie, 2010; Ivankova & Kawamura, 2010; Plano Clark, 2010). We define mixed methods in this chapter as an approach to research in which the researcher explicitly combines quantitative and qualitative research to address the problem under study (Creswell & Plano Clark, 2011). The overall reason researchers use mixed methods is to combine the different perspectives, research questions, methods, data, and results commonly associated with both quantitative and qualitative research to develop more complete, nuanced, valid, and useful understandings than could be obtained by using a single research approach (Bryman, 2006; Creswell, Klassen, Plano Clark, & Smith, 2011; Greene, Caracelli, & Graham, 1989). Therefore, the potential and quality of any mixed methods research approach depends on the researcher's ability to effectively combine, or *integrate*, the quantitative and qualitative components of a study in a meaningful way (Bazeley & Kemp, 2012; Teddlie & Tashakkori, 2006). Despite the clear importance of integration within mixed methods studies, researchers across disciplines who use mixed methods struggle with meaningfully integrating their study components (e.g., Bryman, 2006, 2007; O'Cathain, Murphy, & Nicholl, 2007; Plano Clark et al., 2014).

One strategy to facilitate meaningful integration is the use of visual displays, which can help researchers connect and/or synthesize the quantitative and qualitative components of a mixed methods study (e.g., Creswell & Plano Clark, 2011; Dickinson, 2010; Ivankova, Creswell, & Stick, 2006; Teddlie & Tashakkori, 2006). Just as visual displays can be useful in responding to the unique challenges involved in quantitative and qualitative research studies (see chapters in this volume), visual displays can also be effective tools in the context of mixed methods research. Mixed methods studies frequently incorporate visual displays within the quantitative and qualitative components of the studies, but they also call for visual displays that *integrate* these two components. These so-called *joint displays* are visual displays that explicitly integrate the quantitative and qualitative components of a mixed methods study within one visual representation. Although joint displays offer great promise for helping researchers navigate the integration demands of mixed methods studies, there is currently little practical guidance available to assist researchers with the process of using joint displays in mixed methods research.

The intent of this chapter, therefore, is to advance a set of practical strategies for effectively using joint displays to conceptualize, implement, and report integration within mixed methods research. We begin with a brief introduction to the concept of integration within mixed methods research. We then discuss our process for systematically examining scholars' use of joint displays within the published mixed methods literature. From this examination, we describe four overarching categories that describe the many ways that scholars make use of joint displays within mixed methods research. Our descriptions highlight major variations, key features, and important decisions for each of the major categories. We conclude with recommendations for the use of joint displays to advance the planning, implementation, and reporting of mixed methods studies.

INTEGRATION IN MIXED METHODS RESEARCH

Our definition of integration guides this examination of the use of joint displays within mixed methods research. *Integration* is the explicit combination of the quantitative and qualitative components of a mixed methods study (Creswell & Plano Clark, 2011). Integration within mixed methods has been likened to a conversation or dialogue between the study components, where the quantitative and qualitative components interact with each other in some explicit and meaningful way so that their combination results in a more comprehensive understanding than the two separate components in isolation (Greene, 2007; Morse & Neihaus, 2009). Although early mixed methods writings considered studies that simply had separate quantitative and qualitative components, the importance of integration has evolved so that it is now a central aspect of most current definitions of mixed methods research (Johnson, Onwuegbuzie, & Turner, 2007; Tashakkori & Creswell, 2007; Teddlie & Tashakkori, 2006).

Integration can take on many forms and definitions. For example, Bazeley and Kemp (2012) advanced 12 metaphors to describe the different ways that researchers integrate their quantitative and qualitative study components during data analysis, ranging from jigsaw puzzles and sprinkling to fusion and DNA. Despite the wide range of perspectives about integration within mixed methods, there is general agreement that it can be best described in terms of (a) when it occurs in a mixed methods study and (b) what strategies are used to accomplish the integration (Creswell & Plano Clark, 2011; Guest, 2013). Morse and Niehaus (2009) used the term *point of interface* to describe the places in a study when the quantitative and qualitative components are in direct conversation with each other.

Scholars emphasize many different points of interface for mixed methods, including at the design stage (e.g., Creswell & Plano Clark, 2011; Greene, 2007), at the research question stage (e.g., Tashakkori & Teddlie, 1998), at the data collection stage (e.g., Creswell, Plano Clark, Guttman, & Hanson, 2003), at the analysis stage (e.g., Bazeley & Kemp, 2012), at the stage of drawing conclusions (e.g., Teddlie & Tashakkori, 2009), and between phases of a study or program of studies (e.g., Creswell & Plano Clark, 2011).

There are also many strategies discussed in the literature for accomplishing the integration at the different possible points of interface. At a minimum, researchers who use mixed methods need to integrate during the stage of drawing conclusions at the end of the study, and Teddlie and Tashakkori (2009) discuss strategies for obtaining meta-inferences drawn from a study's quantitative and qualitative components. Creswell and Plano Clark (2011) advanced a framework to describe three types of integration strategies that occur during a mixed methods study: merging, connecting, and embedding. *Merging* is the set of strategies that researchers use to align, compare, relate, or blend the quantitative and qualitative data and results during data analysis and interpretation. *Connecting* is the set of strategies that researchers use to apply results obtained from the implementation of one method to the design of the other method in a subsequent phase of the study. *Embedding* is the set of strategies that researchers use to integrate at the design level when the quantitative and qualitative study components are shaped by a guiding methodological or theoretical framework.

The diversity of views about when and how integration occurs within mixed methods research both encourages researchers' creativity and provides researchers with significant challenges for designing, implementing, and reporting integration in rigorous ways. Joint displays are one useful tool for supporting creativity and navigating the challenges of mixed methods integration. For the purposes of this chapter, we use the term *integration* as broadly as possible to capture the many different perspectives found in the literature. Likewise, as stated earlier, our definition of *joint displays* includes any visual display that explicitly conveys the integration of the quantitative and qualitative components of a mixed methods study within one visual representation. Although some definitions of joint displays found in the literature limit their application to integrating results at the data analysis point of interface of a study, we are interested in the many possible ways that researchers integrate within mixed methods and how joint displays can help to plan, implement, and report these many forms of integration.

EXAMINATION OF RESEARCHERS' USE OF JOINT DISPLAYS IN MIXED METHODS RESEARCH

As a faculty member who specializes in mixed methods (VPC) and a doctoral student particularly interested in the use of visualization within research (KS), our examination of the use of joint displays builds from three semesters of coursework together and our collective interest in integration within mixed methods research and how it is visually displayed to various audiences. We chose to examine the mixed methods literature to develop a typology of different ways that scholars currently use joint displays in published empirical study reports and methodological discussions. Our examination was guided by three research questions:

- How do experienced mixed methods scholars use joint displays to integrate quantitative and qualitative study components?
- What are the key features of mixed methods joint displays?
- What recommendations are suggested based on our review?

To address our questions, we studied the use of joint displays within published mixed methods research literature. Our primary source of information was a systematic review of the use of joint displays within the *Journal of Mixed Methods Research* (*JMMR*). Additional documents that we examined included examples of joint displays from published mixed methods empirical studies gathered serendipitously over several semesters of the mixed methods course and methodological literature about the use of visual displays within mixed methods.

JMMR, published by Sage Publications, is the premier peer-reviewed journal for scholarly works (empirical and methodological) that contribute to our understanding of mixed methods research. Therefore, we decided that this journal would be a good source of documents to learn about effective and innovative practices related to the use of joint displays in mixed methods research. Due to the challenge of locating specific types of visual displays when using keyword searches, we examined every issue of *JMMR* by hand, starting from the debut of the journal in January 2007 to the time of our final search in June 2014 (196 articles in total). KS was the primary reviewer and VPC independently examined a randomly selected subsample of articles. Agreement was high, and we discussed any discrepancies until agreement was reached. Through the review process, we identified all visual displays (figures, matrices, etc.) that appeared to explicitly combine information related to the quantitative and qualitative components of the study/argument.

Once we identified the sample of visual displays, we conducted an emergent thematic analysis to describe the many ways in which researchers used joint displays. We conducted separate analyses of the visuals and then discussed the emergent categories and agreed on four major themes that emerged from our analysis. We further examined the features of the visuals to give in-depth descriptions of the subcategories within the major themes. As we refined our analyses, we examined the additional example empirical documents to verify and refine the emergent categories and the additional methodological documents to gain further insights into the categories. Finally, we developed templates that portrayed the major features and uses of the joint displays within each of the categories to aid our descriptions.

USE OF JOINT DISPLAYS IN MIXED METHODS RESEARCH

From our emergent analysis of 196 articles published by *JMMR* between January 2007 and June 2014, we identified 75 articles (38%) that contained at least one joint display. Authors of the articles used these 110 joint displays in four major ways, including:

1.   to convey conceptual frameworks for mixing methods ($n = 20$),
2.   to describe a study's overall research design and process ($n = 61$),
3.   to indicate the connection and development occurring from one set of results to other method decisions ($n = 6$), and
4.   to present and interpret integrated results and meta-inferences ($n = 23$).

A total of 23 articles included more than one joint display, and 12 of those articles included joint displays that fell within two or more of the four categories.

Table 1 provides an overview of the four categories that emerged to describe the use of joint displays in mixed methods research. In the sections that follow, we describe each of the categories, including prominent variations within the categories and key features and important decisions associated with the categories and variations. We also provide general templates for each of the prominent variations based on notable exemplars identified within our database.

Conceptual Joint Displays: Articulating Frameworks for Mixing Methods

The first way we found *JMMR* authors using joint displays was to highlight or present conceptual frameworks for mixed methods. Scholars used conceptual joint displays to depict the overarching concepts that inform the mode of thinking and theoretical approaches to consider and use within mixed methods research. Specifically, this category of joint displays provided representations of rationales, paradigms, definitions, theoretical frameworks, and ranges of possible options that explained and justified the use of mixed method approaches. These types of joint displays conveyed to readers the conceptual approaches that the scholars envisioned as a mode of thinking to guide understanding within a specific mixed methods study or mixed methods research as a whole. This category included the second smallest number of joint displays ($n = 20$) among the four categories that emerged from our analysis. Within this category of joint displays, both tables and figures were present although most were composed of figures.

It was interesting to discover that researchers used visual displays to conceptualize mixed methods. Researchers' use of these displays to define what they meant by mixed methods speaks to the emergent and evolving nature of this relatively new field and the different perspectives that exist as to the meaning of mixed methods research. The conceptual joint displays also tended to focus on larger methodologically and theoretically oriented concepts as opposed to the details specific to a particular study. Therefore, it is likely that the small but notable

TABLE 1. Overview of Scholars' Use of Joint Displays in the *Journal of Mixed Methods Research*

Major Category	Description of Use	Prominent Variations
Conceptual	Joint displays used to conceptualize and define mixed methods research	• Figures used to describe frameworks for integrating qualitative and quantitative elements • Tables and figures used to describe the range of options available in mixed methods research
Research process	Joint displays used to provide an overview of a study's research process including the quantitative, qualitative, and integration study components	• Figures used to diagram the flow of procedures in a study • Tables used to summarize the procedural details in a study • Figures used to diagram the logic of a study's design
Connection / development	Joint displays used to apply findings from one phase of a mixed methods study to inform decisions about the methods used for the next phase of the study	• Matrices used to explain findings-to-methods decisions • Matrices used to generate questionnaire items
Integrated results	Joint displays used to directly compare or relate results from the quantitative strand with findings from the qualitative strand of a mixed methods study	• Matrices used to juxtapose quantitative results and qualitative findings • Matrices used to interrelate specific quantitative results and qualitative findings • Figures used to depict relationships among quantitative results and qualitative findings

occurrence of the conceptual joint displays reflects the methodological focus of *JMMR*.

We identified two major variations among the sample of conceptual joint displays. These variations included figures used to describe frameworks for integrating qualitative and quantitative elements as well as tables and figures used to describe the range of options available in mixed methods research

Figures used to describe frameworks for integrating qualitative and quantitative elements.

A few conceptual joint displays depicted the framework or conceptual approach for mixed methods research as a whole or as relates to a specific research study. Examples of how researchers applied joint displays of conceptual frameworks included perspectives to justify thinking, designing, and approaching mixed methods research or concepts. Researchers used these displays to give graphic representations of the nature of the approach that influenced the use of mixed methods. These joint displays were mostly depicted using shapes, such as circles, squares, and rectangles that overlapped in ways to convey the integration of different perspectives. Although typically simple in construction, these figures incorporated phrases and descriptions to describe or highlight the concepts of the display. For example, Woolley (2009) used overlapping circles to conceptualize how methods were integrated to study the phenomenon of interest. Additionally, Hall and Howard (2008) used an overlapping circle and square to conceptualize how two different paradigms were mixed in a study to produce quantitative, qualitative, and mixed results.

Tables and figures used to describe the range of options available in mixed methods research.
The bulk of conceptual joint displays in our sample provided a range of options for researchers to consider when constructing frameworks for thinking about and approaching mixed methods research. Researchers used both tables and figures to summarize the range of options available, such as options for paradigmatic perspectives (e.g., Johnson et al., 2007), options for sampling (e.g., Teddlie & Yu, 2007), and options for making generalizations (e.g., Collins, Onwuegbuzie, & Jiao, 2007). We noted two major styles for the joint displays that conveyed a range of available options: representing the options as a set of discrete categories or representing the options as falling along continua. Table 2 provides a template for a table that depicts a discrete set of options for mixing methods. The organization of these tables necessarily depended on the content that was being portrayed, but many of them included options associated with quantitative, qualitative, and mixed approaches. Although tables are a good way of listing a set of discrete options, several authors chose to use figures to depict a set of options, such as depicting four quadrants to portray the different combination of options for drawing

TABLE 2. Template for a Conceptual Joint Display to Describe a Discrete Set of Options Available in Mixed Methods Research

Concept	Quantitative Aspect	Qualitative Aspect	Mixed/Combined Aspect
Conceptual dimension 1	Option(s) for the quantitative perspective/ approach for dimension 1	Option(s) for the qualitative perspective/approach for dimension 1	Option(s) for how and where the concepts mix for dimension 1
Conceptual dimension 2	Option(s) for the quantitative perspective/ approach for dimension 2	Option(s) for the qualitative perspective/approach for dimension 2	Option(s) for how and where the concepts mix for dimension 2
Conceptual dimension 3	Option(s) for the quantitative perspective/ approach for dimension 3	Option(s) for the qualitative perspective/approach for dimension 3	Option(s) for how and where the concepts mix for dimension 3

Note. Exemplars of this template include: Collins et al. (2007), Figure 3; Morgan (2007), Table 2; and Teddlie and Yu (2007), Table 3.

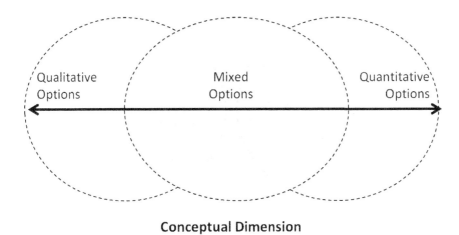

Conceptual Dimension

FIGURE 1.   Template for a Conceptual Figure to Describe the Range of Options Considered for a Mixed Methods Study. Note. Exemplars of this template include: Flick, Garms-Homolová, Herrmann, Kuck, and Röhnsch (2012), Figure 1; Johnson et al. (2007), Figure 1; and Teddlie and Yu (2007), Figure 3.

generalizations from the quantitative and qualitative study components (Collins et al., 2007). Figure 1 provides one template that illustrates how some authors depicted the range of options for mixing methods along one or more continua. In these figures, the researchers emphasized the many possibilities available. For example, Johnson et al. (2007) represented the different paradigms for research along a continuum from "pure qualitative" to "pure quantitative" with many mixed methods possibilities between the ends.

The use of conceptual joint displays can be a very practical way for a research-er to convey her/his definition of mixed methods in the context of a study or to explain the possible options for integration and how her/his approach fits within those options. We offer the following questions to guide the decisions that are required when using a conceptual joint display:

1.   What concept related to the use of mixed methods needs to be explained or defined?
2.   What is the nature of and/or options for the relationships among the quantitative, qualitative, and mixed aspects of the concept?
3.   How is the concept best defined and expressed (as one overall frame-work, one of several categories, or a point along a continuum)?
4.   What shapes, dimensions, and/or categories best describe, convey, or amplify the concept within mixed methods research or the specific study?

Research Process Joint Displays: Describing the Designs for Mixed Methods Studies

The most prevalent way ($n = 61$) that we found *JMMR* authors using joint displays was to visually depict and summarize the methods and procedures that made up the study's research process. The scope of these research process joint displays varied extensively as authors used them to depict the procedures implemented in a single stage of a study (e.g., sampling *or* integration), across multiple stages of a study (e.g., data collection, analysis, *and* interpretation), or across multiple connected studies. The level of detail in the displays also varied in terms of whether authors provided a general overall picture of the flow of procedures in a study or an extensive amount of detail about the procedures and products that occurred for each individual step in the study. Although the scope and level of detail included in the visuals varied, all of the joint displays in this category portrayed procedural information about how researchers designed, implemented, and integrated the quantitative and qualitative methods of their studies. A few of the research-process joint displays were presented in table form, but the examples we reviewed were overwhelmingly presented as figures.

The use of visual displays to depict the quantitative, qualitative, and integration procedures used in mixed methods studies has been discussed nearly as long as the field of mixed methods (e.g., Steckler, McLeroy, Goodman, Bird, & McCormick, 1992; Tashakkori & Teddlie, 1998). From the early times, authors have used visual displays to organize and convey the complexity of mixed methods designs. Scholars continue to write about the use of visual displays to convey mixed methods procedures, referring to them by terms such as "procedure diagrams" (Creswell, 2010, p. 59) and "methodological maps" (Christ, 2010, p. 652). Ivankova et al. (2006) and Teddlie and Tashakkori (2006) published guidelines for constructing and reading these diagrams, offering advice regarding layout and notations. Several authors note the importance of design planning, rigor, and transparency for the quality of the use of mixed methods, and explicitly link the utility of visuals for planning and communicating this critical aspect of any mixed methods study (Creswell, 2010; Morse, 2010; O'Cathain, 2010).

We identified three variations among the sample of research-process joint displays, some of which introduced features that went beyond those previously discussed in the literature. These variations included:

- Figures used to diagram the flow of procedures in a study
- Tables used to summarize the procedural details in a study
- Figures used to diagram the logic of a study's design

Figures used to diagram the flow of procedures in a study.

The vast majority of the research process joint displays in our sample provided an overview of the flow of the quantitative, qualitative, and integration procedures in a study. Researchers used these displays to provide concise descriptions of what took place in the study or a specific stage in the research design over time. Although it is impossible to advance a single template that can encompass the wide range of procedural options available in mixed methods studies, the templates in Figures 2 and 3 highlight many of the common features that we noted in our review. As both figures illustrate, researchers generally used shapes (e.g., rectangles, circles, or triangles) to depict the major steps of the study and basic arrows to indicate the temporal order in which the steps took place. Researchers used text within and around the shapes and arrows to provide details (minimal to extensive) about the steps. We designed Figures 2 and 3 to illustrate two common mixed methods approaches: concurrent and sequential, respectively. In addition, these templates demonstrate two different visual styles. Figure 2 depicts a style that emphasizes the interactions between the quantitative and qualitative strands by highlighting points of integration in the middle of the figure. Although this figure happens to describe a concurrent mixed methods approach, researchers also used this style for sequential approaches (e.g., Brown, Kennedy, Tucker, Golinelli, & Wenzel, 2013; Knaggs, Sondergeld, & Schardt, 2013). Figure 3 is an example of a style that emphasized the temporal order of the procedures, where the points of integration are positioned at the time in the sequence when they happened to occur.

The templates in Figures 2 and 3 demonstrate many features that we found to be effective for creating research-process joint displays that were clear, concise, and easy to interpret. These effective strategies included the use of labels that provide an organizational framework to the display (e.g., Step 1, Step 2) and the incorporation of a timeline into the display. Effective research-process joint displays also made careful choices for the format of shapes and arrows used to represent different elements of the process and used these formats consistently throughout the figure, which aided readers in interpreting the presented information. For example, many figures purposefully used different shapes or shading to indicate different components (i.e., quantitative, qualitative, and integration) and different styles of arrows for different aspects (e.g., flow of time and integration). It was particularly helpful when researchers included notes that explicitly identified different shapes and styles represented within the figure. Among the many figures we reviewed, we also noted several design features that did not work as well for these joint displays because they made the figures less clear and harder to interpret. For example, when authors used the same shape (e.g., a rectangle) to depict the study components and to provide supplemental information or used the same style of arrow for multiple purposes (such as to indicate flow of procedures and to point at a highlighted features), it was sometimes difficult to distinguish between the different elements of the figure. In contrast, if authors used too great a variety of shapes and style of arrows without clear reason, then the figure became busy and difficult to follow. Likewise, the readability of some figures was diminished when authors used fonts and shading combinations that were difficult to read (such as a small white font on a light gray background).

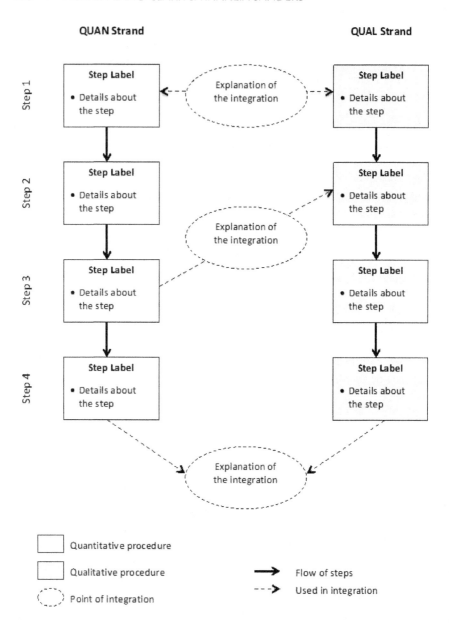

FIGURE 2. Template for a Research Process Figure that Emphasizes Points of Integration for a Concurrent Mixed Methods Approach. Note. Exemplars of this template include: Arnon and Reichel (2009), Figure 4; Brown, Kennedy, Tucker, Golinelli, and Wenzel (2013), Figure 1; von der Lippe (2010), Figure 1; and Vrkljan (2009), Figure 2.

Timeline

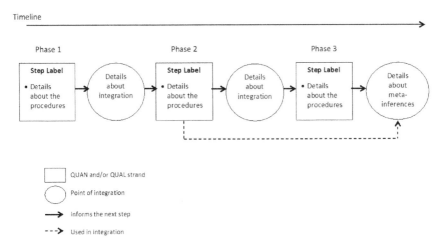

FIGURE 3.   Template for a Research Process Figure that Emphasizes the Temporal Order for a Sequential Mixed Methods Approach. Note. Exemplars of this template include: Farmer and Knapp (2008), Figure 1; Ivankova (2014), Figure 1; Sosulski and Lawrence (2008), Figures 1 and 2; and Wesely (2010), Figure 1.

Tables used to summarize the procedural details in a study.

In a handful of examples, researchers summarized their research procedures in a table instead of a figure. These tables summarized procedural details such as strand designation (quantitative, qualitative, or some combination), research questions, types of data sources, time of data collection, analysis techniques, and integration procedures. They were typically organized by time (e.g., phase 1, phase 2, etc.), data collection sources (e.g., interviews, questionnaires, etc.), or theoretical concepts (e.g., concept 1, concept 2, etc.). These research-process tables worked well for providing an extensive amount of detail about the complex procedures used in a mixed methods study, although they did not convey the flow of these procedures as well as was captured within figures. Interestingly, Robinson and Mendelson (2012) combined the advantages of figures and tables by including both a general procedural diagram and a table of corresponding detailed information within one joint display about their study's procedures.

Figures used to diagram the logic of a study's design.

A few of the reviewed articles included figures that visually depicted the logic of their study's mixed methods design. Although these figures conveyed information about the procedures used in a mixed methods study, these figures organized the procedures in a logical or conceptual way instead of as determined by the flow of procedures over time. For example, Christ (2009) included logic diagrams that explained the logical connections among the study's research questions, purpose, conceptual framework, methods, and validity considerations. Castro, Kellison, Boyd, and Kopak (2010) included a figure that presented how the different stages of their study fit within the theory they used.

Mixed methods designs are complex, and researchers need to successfully navigate through their quantitative, qualitative, and integration steps. The use of research-process joint displays, such as Figures 2 and 3, provide a good strategy for both designing and describing a study's procedures. The use of research-process joint displays requires researchers to consider the following decisions within the context of their studies:

1. What scope of the study's research process (one stage, one phase, or multiple phases) needs to be conveyed?
2. What level of detail about the research process is appropriate for the joint display's purpose?
3. What shapes, arrows, and shading will be used to convey the quantitative, qualitative, and integration aspects of the study?
4. What labels and fonts will be most clear for conveying the organization of the shapes and the information within the shapes?

Connection/Development Joint Displays: Linking Results to Methods Decisions

The third way that we found authors using joint displays was to visually depict how results from one phase of a mixed methods study connected to or informed the development of a subsequent phase of the study. These connection/development joint displays explicitly linked certain results (e.g., qualitative findings) to specific programmatic or methods decisions (e.g., determination of quantitative variables and questionnaire items). This category included the smallest number of joint displays ($n = 6$) among the four categories that emerged from our analysis. With one exception, all the joint displays classified within this category were constructed as matrices. In addition, all examples of connection/development joint displays were from studies in which researchers connected qualitative results to decisions for a subsequent phase (such as intervention development or questionnaire development). Somewhat surprisingly, we did not locate any examples of joint displays that described how researchers linked quantitative results to qualitative methods decisions (e.g., purposeful sampling procedures or protocol development), despite their potential usefulness in studies using such approaches.

The mixed methods literature emphasizes the importance of researchers making a strong connection between phases in mixed methods studies with sequential components (Creswell & Plano Clark, 2011; Howell Smith, 2011; Ivankova, 2014). This process of integrating from one phase of a mixed methods study to the next is referred to as connecting, building, development, and linking (Creswell & Plano Clark, 2011; Fetters, Curry, & Creswell, 2013; Greene et al., 1989). The quality of a sequential mixed methods approach depends upon the strength of the connection made between the two phases of a study; however, this is a challenging process because researchers cannot know the actual results from the first phase until it is complete and therefore cannot know in advance what connections will need to be made within the study. When the resulting connection is strong, then the researcher builds on initial findings in meaningful ways. When the connection is weak, then the researcher does not make adequate use of the initial findings and the subsequent logic of and conclusions from the study's design may be brought into question.

We identified two major variations of connection/development joint displays: matrices used to explain findings-to-methods decisions and matrices used for the generation of questionnaire items.

Matrices used to explain findings-to-methods decisions.

Several connection/development joint displays provided an overview of major findings that had been obtained from a qualitative phase of the study and how the researchers used those findings to shape the design of subsequent phases of the study. Examples of how researchers applied the findings from an initial qualitative phase to the procedures for a subsequent phase included making decisions about the development of a program or intervention that would be tested (e.g., Peterson et al., 2013) and about the data collection procedures that would be implemented (e.g., Collins & Dressler, 2008). Table 3 provides a template that illustrates how researchers organized this type of joint display to describe the connections being made within their mixed methods studies. As Table 3 indicates, the rows of these tables were typically organized by the major findings that emerged from the initial phase of the research. The columns in Table 3 indicate three possible ways that researchers connect from initial findings to subsequent methods decisions (e.g.,

TABLE 3. Template for a Connection/Development Matrix to Explain Findings-to-Methods Decisions

Overall Major Findings	How Major Findings Inform Program	How Major Findings Inform Sampling Decisions	How Major Findings Inform Data Collection Decisions
Finding 1	Decision regarding program development based on finding 1	Decision regarding sampling procedures based on finding 1	Decision regarding data collection methods based on finding 1
Finding 2	Decision regarding program development based on finding 2	Decision regarding sampling procedures based on finding 2	Decision regarding data collection methods based on finding 2
Finding 3	Decision regarding program development based on finding 3	Decision regarding sampling procedures based on finding 3	Decision regarding data collection methods based on finding 3

Note. Exemplars of this template include: Collins and Dressler (2008), Table 1; and Peterson et al. (2013), Tables 2 and 3.

to inform programmatic, sampling, and data collection decisions); however, most joint displays that we examined included only one of these possible dimensions. These matrices were most effective at explaining the study connections when the researchers clearly identified specific key findings from the initial phase and included an explanation of how those findings were applied in the decisions for subsequent phases. The matrices were less effective when the researcher only referred to findings in a general way (e.g., "qualitative findings") because then there was insufficient information for the reader to understand which specific results led to which subsequent methods decisions.

Matrices used to generate questionnaire items.

Several of the connection/development joint displays were specifically tailored to the purpose of using qualitative findings to generate quantitative questionnaire items. Table 4 provides a template for such an "item generation matrix" (Howell Smith, 2011, p. 69). As the template illustrates, the most effective examples of these joint displays started with columns on the left side that summarized key qualitative findings, including the different major themes and corresponding participant quotes that represented different perspectives within each of the major themes. These qualitative columns provided the organizational structure for the table. The right-side columns then demonstrated how the qualitative findings were applied to generate items for a new or revised quantitative questionnaire. In some examples, the researchers clearly identified the quantitative construct/scale that they developed from the major qualitative findings as well as the wording of specific items derived from the example quotes (e.g., Crede & Borrego, 2013). This was a particularly effective strategy because it documented the overarching connection of qualitative theme to quantitative variable in addition to the development of specific questionnaire items. It was also useful when researchers who were modifying an existing instrument provided clear indicators as to which items were kept, changed, added, or eliminated based on qualitative findings (e.g.,

TABLE 4. Template for a Connection/Development Matrix to Generate Questionnaire Items

Overall Major Qualitative Findings	Specific Qualitative Findings	Quantitative Constructs Developed	Quantitative Items Developed
Theme 1	Salient quote(s) for theme 1	Variable 1 (based on theme 1)	Item(s) for variable 1 based on quote(s) for theme 1
Theme 2	Salient quote(s) for theme 2	Variable 2 (based on theme 2)	Item(s) for variable 2 based on quote(s) for theme 2
Theme 3	Salient quote(s) for theme 3	Variable 3 (based on theme 3)	Item(s) for variable 3 based on quote(s) for theme 3

Note. Exemplars of this template include: Crede and Borrego (2013), Table 2; Stoller et al. (2009), Table 1; and Howell Smith (2011), Table 5.

Stoller et al., 2009) because this made the connection explicit and easy to follow. One practice that we found to be less effective was when researchers organized the columns of the matrix by placing the quantitative items in the first (left-most) column (even though the qualitative findings occurred first). We found this to be less effective because the authors organized the information in ways that did not follow the logic of their overall mixed methods approach. It was also less effective when researchers only provided participant quotes and questionnaire items in the matrix. Although conveying some useful details, this approach did not explicitly identify the larger substantive frameworks (themes and constructs) that provide the context for and meaning of the quotes and items.

Connecting two phases of a study is an important and challenging form of integration in sequential mixed methods research. Researchers develop connection/development joint displays such as Tables 3 and 4 to facilitate and document this process. Decisions required of the researcher when using connection/development joint displays include:

1. Which findings of the current study phase provide the best insights and are most useful to inform the subsequent phase of the study and organize the matrix?
2. What aspects of the next phase of the study will be informed by the current findings?
3. How will the current findings be used to inform the program/methods used in the next phase?
4. What specific decisions occurred in the next phase based on the findings of the initial phase and need to be documented?

Integrated Results Joint Displays: Mixing Results and Interpreting Meta-Inferences

The fourth way that authors used joint displays was to explicitly combine results from the quantitative strand of a study with findings from the qualitative strand. These integrated-results joint displays served to mix the two sets of results and provided evidence of the researchers' process for drawing meta-inferences and new insights based on the combination. Joint displays that integrated results were the second most common category ($n = 23$) in our *JMMR* review, next to the research-process category. We also had numerous examples on hand from the larger empirical literature due to our interest in gathering examples of these specific types of displays over several years. Across these documents, matrices were the most prevalent form for the integrated-results joint displays, but we also had examples of figures that incorporated graphical or conceptual representations of combined study results. The visuals in this category originated from studies using many different mixed methods designs, but they were most often associated with concurrent approaches.

No matter the mixed methods approach used, scholars agree that researchers need to meaningfully integrate the two sets of results in their studies and draw meta-inferences from the combination in order to fulfill the potential offered by a mixed methods approach (e.g., Teddlie & Tashakkori, 2009). The importance of this form of integration is noted because a key consideration for assessing the quality of mixed methods studies is the rigor and extent to which the authors have meaningfully integrated and interpreted the combined results (O'Cathain, 2010; Teddlie & Tashakkori, 2009). Indicative of this importance, the majority of the literature that discusses the use of joint displays in mixed methods research has focused on their use for integrating the two strands of a study during data analysis and interpretation (e.g., Creswell & Plano Clark, 2011; Dickson, 2010; O'Cathain, Murphy, & Nicholl, 2010).

Three major variations emerged to describe the integrated-results joint displays within our sample of documents:

- Matrices used to juxtapose quantitative results and qualitative findings
- Matrices used to interrelate specific quantitative results and qualitative findings
- Figures used to depict relationships among quantitative results and qualitative findings

Matrices used to juxtapose quantitative results and qualitative findings.

In several of the integrated-results joint displays reviewed, the researchers directly compared the quantitative results and qualitative findings within a mixed methods study. Table 5 provides a template for a joint display that juxtaposed the two sets of results to facilitate this direct comparison. To accomplish the comparison, researchers organized the two sets of results in a matrix along specific dimensions, such as by topic domains (e.g., Spencer, Creswell, Reed, Young, & Mark, 2013) or by cases (e.g., Sedoglavich, Akoorie, & Pavlovich, 2014). The matrix then included separate columns to summarize the quantitative results and the qualitative findings for each of the specific organizational dimensions. These columns included specific results (e.g., statistical values or salient quotes) or statements that summarized key results. Some researchers also included a final column that provided their interpretations of the combination of the results and findings (see right-most column in Table 5). We found this to be a particularly effective strategy for this style of matrix because it provided a clear articulation of the authors' conclusions and indicated the evidence that formed the basis for those conclusions. The effectiveness of this style of matrix was reduced when the organization of the information did not match the logic of the mixed methods design (such as starting the matrix with the conclusion column) or the information presented in the cells did not include sufficient detail for the results and/or findings being compared. The utility of matrices such as Table 5 to juxtapose results as a

TABLE 5. Template for an Integrated Results Matrix to Juxtapose Quantitative Results and Qualitative Findings

Organizational dimensions[a]	Qualitative findings[b]	Quantitative results[c]	Authors' interpretations[d]
Dimension 1	Qualitative findings for dimension 1	Quantitative results for dimension 1	Interpretation of combined results for dimension 1
Dimension 2	Qualitative findings for dimension 2	Quantitative results for dimension 2	Interpretation of combined results for dimension 2
Dimension 3	Qualitative findings for dimension 3	Quantitative results for dimension 3	Interpretation of combined results for dimension 3

Note. Exemplars of this template include: Sosulski and Lawrence (2008), Table 3; Sedoglavich et al. (2014), Table 4; and Spencer et al. (2013), Table 2.
[a]Organizational dimensions examples: research questions, topic domains, cases, themes, or variables
[b]Qualitative findings examples: quotes, codes, themes, theme prevalences, story lines, or summary statements
[c]Quantitative results examples: variables, descriptive statistics (e.g., %, M, SD), inferential statistics (e.g., correlations, regression coefficients), or summary statements
[d]Authors' interpretations examples: level of agreement, examples of complementarity, dimensions of convergence and divergence, or substantive insights

means to enhance integration and the development of meta-inferences has been previously discussed in the literature as a useful strategy for implementing side-by-side comparisons (Creswell & Plano Clark, 2011) and triangulation protocols (O'Cathain et al., 2010).

Matrices used to interrelate specific quantitative results and qualitative findings.

Several of the integrated results joint displays in our sample went beyond comparing major quantitative and qualitative results to interrelating specific aspects of the two sets of results within a matrix. As illustrated in Table 6, one format for interrelation matrices involved arraying two or more quantitatively derived variables or levels of one variable in the matrix rows by two or more qualitatively derived themes or categories in the matrix columns. Examples of such displays included arraying qualitative themes by levels of a quantitative grouping variable (e.g., Kennett, O'Hagan, & Cezer, 2008), qualitative themes by quantitative variables (e.g., Jang, McDougall, Pollon, Herbert, & Russell, 2008), quantitative variables by qualitative typology categories (e.g., Wittink, Barg, & Gallo, 2006), and the association between scores on two variables by qualitative responses that converge or diverge with the association (e.g., Lee & Greene, 2007). As indicated in the notes below Table 6, researchers included a wide range of quantitative and qualitative information within the cells of the matrices to uncover the interrelationships among the dimensions. Although arraying the information within a

TABLE 6. Template for an Integrated Results Matrix to Interrelate Quantitative Results and Qualitative Findings

	Qualitative category A [b]	Qualitative category B [b]	Qualitative category C [b]
Quantitative level/ variable 1 [a]	Information for level/ variable 1 and category A [c]	Information for level/ variable 1 and category B [c]	Information for level/ variable 1 and category C [c]
Quantitative level/ variable 2 [a]	Information for level/ variable 2 and category A [c]	Information for level/ variable 2 and category B [c]	Information for level/ variable 2 and category C [c]
Quantitative level/ variable 3 [a]	Information for level/ variable 3 and category A [c]	Information for level/ variable 3 and category B [c]	Information for level/ variable 3 and category C [c]

Note. Exemplars of this template include Lee and Greene (2007), Table 5; Kennett et al. (2008), Table 3; and Palak and Walls (2009), Table 4.
[a] Quantitative dimension examples: key variables or levels for one or more variables (e.g., low, medium, and high; control and treatment)
[b] Qualitative dimension examples: participants, categories within an emergent typology, themes, different perspectives (e.g., congruent and discrepant)
[c] Cell information examples: scores, frequencies, percentages, means and standard deviations, correlations, characteristics, key perspectives, quotes, and/or summary statements

matrix is potentially straightforward, the effective application of this type of joint display clearly depends on researchers identifying quantitative and qualitative dimensions that are substantively relevant and potentially related to each other. It also demands that the researcher integrate during analysis by organizing one dataset (e.g., the quantitative data gathered for multiple variables) based on dimensions associated with the other dataset (e.g., qualitative typology categories that emerged from a thematic analysis) to examine potential relationships among the dimensions.

Figures used to depict relationships among quantitative results and qualitative findings.

The last notable variation within the integrated results category was the use of figures to depict relationships among the quantitative results and qualitative findings from a study. Interestingly, few examples of such figures emerged from our review of *JMMR*, but several examples had been published in other sources. Most of these examples included some sort of a graphical display of quantitative results along a one- or two-dimensional plot, which provided the overall organization of the figure. As illustrated in Figure 4, qualitative information (such as illustrative quotes) that corresponded to specific quantitative results was linked to the specific plotted results. This qualitative information was most often positioned around the border of the graphical display and required that the researcher help the reader understand which qualitative information is linked to which quantitative plotted

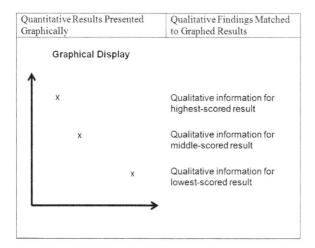

Quantitative Results Presented Graphically	Qualitative Findings Matched to Graphed Results
Graphical Display	

FIGURE 4. Template for an integrated results figure to interrelate quantitative results and qualitative findings. Note. Exemplars of this template include Mendlinger and Cwikel (2008), Figure 3; and Fetters et al. (2013) Figure 2.

information. Effective strategies for visually linking the qualitative information to the corresponding quantitatively graphed information included aligning the position of the two types of information (e.g., Mendlinger & Cwikel, 2008) and/or using different font colors for each pair of information (e.g., Fetters et al., 2013).

Researchers also used integrated results figures to present conceptual models that portrayed relationships among substantive findings derived from the quantitative and qualitative results. These figures used shapes (such as boxes and circles) to represent the major quantitative results and qualitative findings and arrows to depict the relationships among the results and findings. For example, Plano Clark et al. (2013) depicted the nested nature of the qualitatively described contexts and the quantitatively measured outcomes in their mixed methods study and used double-headed arrows to indicate how the contexts dynamically shaped and were shaped by the outcomes. Howell Smith (2011) advanced a revised version of her grounded-theory model based on the combination of her qualitative findings and subsequent quantitative results. When well designed, these figures summarized substantively relevant results and indicated how the results, and relationships among the results, were based on the integration of the different strands of the mixed methods study. As the substantive results became more abstract and integrated, however, it seemed that it became more challenging for researchers to indicate how they were based on the quantitative and qualitative strands within the model without making the figure too busy and distracting.

Integrating the results from the quantitative and qualitative strands is an essential but challenging process in every mixed methods study. Researchers may find integrated joint displays such as Table 5, Table 6, and Figure 4 as useful models for undertaking this process. When applying the templates, researchers need to consider the following decisions within the context of their studies:

1. If needing to compare the quantitative results and qualitative findings, what dimensions (topics, cases) can be used to juxtapose the two sets of results?
2. If needing to interrelate the quantitative results with the qualitative findings, what quantitative dimensions and qualitative dimensions can be expected to be related?
3. What quantitative and/or qualitative information will be most useful to examine for each of the dimensions identified for the integrative analyses?
4. How will the integrated results be interpreted for meta-inferences, such as identifying agreement, disagreement, complementary results, patterns, or new insights?

DISCUSSION

Integrating the quantitative and qualitative components of a mixed methods study is a challenging process. Based on our review, we found that many researchers have used joint displays to help capture the integrative aspects of their scholarly works. Just as there are different ways to integrate within mixed methods, researchers used joint displays in a variety of ways. We advanced four major categories based on the ways that researchers used joint displays in our sample. These categories included the use of joint displays to convey conceptualizations of mixed methods research, to describe the overall mixed methods research process, to document the connections between two phases, and to develop and interpret integrated results and conclusions. Although we did not start with these four categories in mind, in hindsight it is not surprising that they emerged. Collectively they represent important ways in which researchers need to grapple with integration in the context of mixed methods research, from conceptualizing mixed methods, to designing and implementing the process and procedures in mixed methods studies, to analyzing and using results that emerge in mixed methods studies to make connections or draw integrated conclusions and meta-inferences. Each of the categories presents different ways for researchers to plan, implement, and report integration within mixed methods studies, and therefore it appears that researchers may find joint displays to be useful for planning, implementing, and reporting mixed methods research.

Although our examination of the use of joint displays provides evidence for their utility, we were somewhat surprised that we did not find even more examples. Even though *JMMR* is the premier journal for cutting-edge work in mixed methods research and supports the extensive use of tables and figures, less than 50% of the articles included at least one visual display that explicitly integrated quantitative and qualitative components of the study/argument. That is, all 196 articles explicitly addressed the integration of quantitative and qualitative components within the text of the articles (or they would not be published in *JMMR*), but less than half did so with the use of joint displays. This may be partly related to the overall methodological focus of the articles in *JMMR*, but we suggest it may also be indicative of the fact that developing joint displays is a challenging process.

Of the joint displays we reviewed, research-process joint displays were by far the most common. This makes sense considering the methodological focus of *JMMR*. In addition, it is likely that research-process joint displays were common because this type of joint display has been discussed the longest and most extensively within the mixed methods literature (e.g., Ivankova et al., 2006; Teddlie & Tashakkori, 2006). Similarly, integrated-results joint displays were the next most prevalent, which may also reflect the fact that they have received more discussion in the literature than the other two categories (e.g., Creswell & Plano Clark, 2011; Dickinson, 2010). Although prevalent within our sample, less than 15% of the *JMMR* articles reviewed included a joint display that integrated results. Therefore, we conclude that researchers are not yet making extensive use of these displays to integrate results despite the literature advocating for their use.

Since integration is an essential but challenging element of mixed methods research (Bryman, 2007; Creswell & Plano Clark, 2011; O'Cathain et al., 2007; Teddlie & Tashakkori, 2006), it was interesting to note the different ways that researchers represented integration across the different categories of joint displays. When using figures, researchers portrayed integration as (a) an area of overlap between two shapes, (b) as an arrow that connects two shapes that represent study components, (c) as an intermediate box/shape coming between two study components, and (d) as the physical space located between the quantitative and qualitative "sides" of the study. In addition, researchers used (e) certain lines (e.g., dashed or double-headed) and (f) certain shading (e.g., an intermediate shade or two-tone shade) to highlight the integration aspects of their joint display figures. When using joint displays in a table format that listed the quantitative, qualitative, and mixed aspects of study, researchers generally provided one or more columns that explicitly addressed the integration. This column was placed between or after the quantitative and qualitative columns of the table. When using joint displays in an integrated-results matrix format, the integration occurred within the information placed in the cells as organized by specific dimensions of the quantitative results and the qualitative findings.

After reviewing this collection of joint displays, we conclude that joint displays have value for mixed methods researchers because they are a tool that facilitates the understanding of integration within mixed methods research. Across the categories we identified, we note that the development and use of any joint display demands that the researcher explicitly consider and portray the integrative aspects of a mixed methods study. It is by making the integration explicit, and therefore potentially more rigorous, that joint displays bring great potential value to the process of conducting mixed methods research. To obtain these benefits, researchers need to consider integration throughout the conceptualization/ planning, implementation, and interpretation/reporting stages of a study. Therefore, we argue that researchers should consider applying joint displays throughout these stages as a means for focusing their attention on the integrative aspects of their mixed methods studies.

In Box 1, we offer a few recommendations for researchers who are conducting mixed methods research and may benefit from using joint displays to plan, implement, and report the integrative aspects of their studies. These recommendations emerged from our reflections about the different categories of joint displays used by researchers as well as the features that made their use more or less effective. Using joint displays during study planning may help researchers conceptualize integration within the context of the study and better anticipate and plan for the integrative aspects that will occur. During implementation, joint displays may help researchers work through the complex tasks of integrating during the research, connection, and integrated results process. Using tables and figures to explicitly document the integrative processes may help researchers think about the decisions more thoughtfully and ensure that the decisions meaningfully integrate the quantitative and qualitative components within the purpose and context of the study. Once the mixed methods study is implemented, then joint displays may also be a valuable strategy for documenting for readers how the integration occurred and what resulted from the integration. By including conceptual, research-process, connection/development, and integrated-results joint displays in a study report, researchers can provide clear evidence of the integration process, including how it was implemented in the study and what was produced by it. This provides readers with the opportunity to better understand the process and make their own assessments as to the quality of the integration within the study.

It is important to note that the joint display categories described within this chapter are based on a purposefully selected sample of joint displays from one journal augmented by a convenient sample of joint displays on hand. Therefore, the categories may not generalize to all uses of joint displays within mixed methods research. However, our goal was to advance some practical strategies to help researchers think about how joint displays can be used and examples of how they might be constructed. Therefore, we believe the categories and templates that emerged from this review provide mixed methods researchers with a helpful starting place for designing joint displays that facilitate planning, implementing, and reporting meaningful integration within mixed methods research studies. We are certain that researchers will continue to bring their creativity and innovation to mixed methods research and will develop additional joint displays that go well beyond the basic templates described here. Let the integration possibilities flourish!

Recommendations for Planning Mixed Methods Research

- Clearly articulate your definition of mixed methods and develop a conceptual joint display that conveys your guiding framework for integrating methods.
- Develop a research process joint display early in the study planning and clearly indicate the points of interface where integration is expected to occur and needs to be considered.
- For each point of interface in the study, imagine how you might integrate the study components by connecting phases or merging results and develop hypothetical connection/development and integrated results joint displays to plan how you will undertake these integration processes.

Recommendations for Conducting Mixed Methods Research

- Revisit your framework for integrating methods as depicted in a conceptual joint display and use the framework to inform and guide your implementation decisions.
- Continually refine your research process joint display with the details of your study implementation (such as sample sizes, data collection tools, and analytic strategies), paying particular attention to the procedures occurring at the points of interface of your study.
- When implementing sequential mixed methods approaches, develop a connection/development joint display to work through and document the specific decisions that connect from one set of results to the other methods.
- When integrating results, consider using multiple forms of integrated-results joint displays to facilitate comparing and relating the quantitative results and qualitative findings and drawing meta-inferences in response to the study's research questions.

Recommendations for Reporting Mixed Methods Research

- Use joint displays from each of the four categories to clearly communicate the framework for, procedures for, and decisions/results/interpretations from integrating the quantitative and qualitative study components.
- Make joint displays as simple and concise as possible, but also include sufficient detail so that readers can follow the information and make their own assessment of the quality of the integration that occurred in the study.
- Choose shapes, fonts, lines, and shading features carefully to make certain that the information is easily readable in printed and electronic forms.
- Use shapes, fonts, lines, and shading features consistently and identify their meaning in notes.
- Organize your joint displays logically to follow the flow of activities and information that occurred in the mixed methods study.

BOX 1. Recommendations for the use of joint displays to facilitate integration in mixed methods research.

SUMMARY

Achieving meaningful integration in mixed methods research is both important and challenging. Joint displays that explicitly combine the quantitative and qualitative components of mixed methods can provide researchers with a useful tool for planning, implementing, and reporting this essential aspect of mixed methods research. From our review, we found that researchers have used joint displays in a variety of ways to convey integration within the context of mixed methods. The four identified categories, with variations, provide researchers with models of different types of joint displays that may be useful for supporting integration within their mixed methods studies. Within and across the conceptual, research-process, connection/development, and integrated-results categories, we noted several features of mixed methods joint displays that need to be considered. The most prominent features included the type of information depicted (i.e., conceptual framework, research-process procedures, methods decisions, or results and interpretations), overall format (i.e., table/matrix and/or figure), and how the quantitative, qualitative, and integrative aspects were organized and represented. From this review, we conclude that joint displays are a useful tool for considering integration within mixed methods research. Researchers interested in developing joint displays for their own mixed methods studies can examine the nine joint display templates that we advanced in this chapter as well as our recommendations for using joint displays throughout the stages of planning, implementing, and reporting mixed methods research. It is our hope that these models will provide a useful starting point that encourages and supports researchers to use joint displays to enhance meaningful integration within their mixed methods studies.

NOTE

This work was supported in part by a Graduate Student and Faculty Research Mentoring Grant from the College of Education, Criminal Justice, and Human Services, University of Cincinnati. We also thank Rachael Clark and Peggy Shannon-Baker for their feedback on early drafts of this chapter.

REFERENCES

Alise, M., & Teddlie, C. (2010). A continuation of the paradigm wars? Prevalence rates of methodological approaches across the social/behavioral sciences. *Journal of Mixed Methods Research, 4*(2), 103–126.

Arnon, S., & Reichel, N. (2009). Closed and open-ended question tools in a telephone survey about "the good teacher": An example of a mixed methods study. *Journal of Mixed Methods Research, 3*(2), 172–196.

Bazeley, P., & Kemp, L. (2012). Mosaics, triangles, and DNA: Metaphors for integrated analysis in mixed methods research. *Journal of Mixed Methods Research, 6*(1), 55–72.

Brown, R. A., Kennedy, D. P., Tucker, J. S., Golinelli, D., & Wenzel, S. L. (2013). Monogamy on the street: A mixed methods study of homeless men. *Journal of Mixed Methods Research, 7*(4), 328–346.

Bryman, A. (2006). Integrating quantitative and qualitative research: How is it done? *Qualitative Research, 6,* 97–113.

Bryman, A. (2007). Barriers to integrating quantitative and qualitative research. *Journal of Mixed Methods Research, 1*(1), 8–22.

Castro, F. G., Kellison, J. G., & Kopak, A. (2010). A methodology for conducting integrative mixed methods research and data analyses. *Journal of Mixed Methods Research, 4*(4), 342–360.

Christ, T. W. (2009). Designing, teaching, and evaluating two complementary mixed methods research courses. *Journal of Mixed Methods Research, 3*(4), 292–325.

Christ, T. (2010). Teaching mixed methods and action research: Pedagogical, practical, and evaluative considerations. In A. Tashakkori & C. Teddlie (Eds.), *Sage handbook of mixed methods in social & behavioral research* (2nd ed., pp. 643–676). Thousand Oaks, CA: Sage.

Collins, C. C., & Dressler, W. W. (2008). Cultural consensus and cultural diversity. *Journal of Mixed Methods Research, 2*(4), 362–387.

Collins, K. M. T., Onwuegbuzie, A. J., & Jiao, Q. G. (2007). A mixed methods investigation of mixed methods sampling designs in social and health science research. *Journal of Mixed Methods Research, 1*(3), 267–294.

Crede, E., & Borrego, M. (2013). From ethnography to items: A mixed methods approach to developing a survey to examine graduate engineering student retention. *Journal of Mixed Methods Research, 7*(1), 62–80.

Creswell, J. W. (2010). Mapping the developing landscape of mixed methods research. In A. Tashakkori & C. Teddlie (Eds.), *Sage handbook of mixed methods research in social & behavioral research* (2nd ed., pp. 45–68). Thousand Oaks, CA: Sage.

Creswell, J. W., Klassen, A. C., Plano Clark, V. L., & Smith, K. C. (2011, August). Best practices for mixed methods research in the health sciences. *U.S. Department of Health and Human Services.* Retrieved from http://obssr.od.nih.gov/mixed_methods_research

Creswell, J. W., & Plano Clark, V. L. (2011). *Designing and conducting mixed methods research* (2nd ed.). Thousand Oaks, CA: Sage.

Creswell, J. W., Plano Clark, V. L., Guttman, M., & Hanson, W. (2003). Advanced mixed methods research designs. In A. Tashakkori & C. Teddlie (Eds.), *Handbook of mixed methods in social and behavioral research* (pp. 209–240). Thousand Oaks, CA: Sage

Dickinson, W. B. (2010). Visual displays for mixed methods findings. In A. Tashakkori & C. Teddlie (Eds.), *Handbook of mixed methods in social and behavioral research* (2nd ed., pp. 469–504). Thousand Oaks, CA: Sage.

Fetters, M. D., Curry, L. A., & Creswell, J. W. (2013). Achieving integration in mixed methods designs: Principles and practices. *HSR: Health Services Research, 48,* 2134–2156.

Flick, U., Garms-Homolová, V., Herrmann, W. J., Kuck, J., & Röhnsch, G. (2012). "I can't prescribe something just because someone asks for it . . .": Using mixed methods in the framework of triangulation. *Journal of Mixed Methods Research, 6*(2), 97–110.

Greene, J. C. (2007). *Mixed methods in social inquiry.* San Francisco, CA: Jossey-Bass.

Greene, J. C., Caracelli, V. J., & Graham, W. F. (1989). Toward a conceptual framework for mixed-method evaluation designs. *Educational Evaluation and Policy Analysis, 11*(3), 255–274.

Guest, G. (2013). Describing mixed methods research: An alternative to typologies. *Journal of Mixed Methods Research, 7*(3), 141–151.

Hall, B., & Howard, K. (2008). A synergistic approach: Conducting mixed methods research with typological and systemic design considerations. *Journal of Mixed Methods Research, 2*(3), 248–269.

Howell Smith, M. C. (2011). Factors that facilitate or inhibit interest of domestic students in the engineering PhD: A mixed methods study. *University of Nebraska - Lincoln.* Paper AAI3466518. Retrieved from http://digitalcommons.unl.edu/dissertations/AAI3466518

Ivankova, N. V. (2014). Implementing quality criteria in designing and conducting a sequential QUAN —> QUAL mixed methods study of student engagement with learning applied research methods online. *Journal of Mixed Methods Research, 8*(1), 25–51.

Ivankova, N. V., Creswell, J. W., & Stick, S. (2006). Using mixed methods sequential explanatory design: From theory to practice. *Field Methods, 18*(1), 3–20.

Ivankova, N., & Kawamura, Y. (2010). Emerging trends in the utilization of integrated designs in social, behavioral, and health sciences. In A. Tashakkori & C. Teddlie (Eds.), *Sage handbook of mixed methods in social & behavioral research* (2nd ed., pp. 581–611). Thousand Oaks, CA: Sage.

Jang, E. E., McDougall, D. E., Pollon, D., Herbert, M., & Russell, P. (2008). Integrative mixed methods data analytic strategies in research on school success in challenging circumstances. *Journal of Mixed Methods Research, 2*(3), 221–247.

Johnson, R. B., Onwuegbuzie, A. J., & Turner, L. A. (2007). Toward a definition of mixed methods research. *Journal of Mixed Methods Research, 1*(2), 112–133.

Kennett, D. J., O'Hagan, F. T., & Cezer, D. (2008). Learned resourcefulness and the long-term benefits of a chronic pain management program. *Journal of Mixed Methods Research, 2*(4), 317–339.

Knaggs, C. M., Sondergeld, T. A., & Schardt, B. (2013). Overcoming barriers to college enrollment, persistence, and perceptions for urban high school students in a college preparatory program. *Journal of Mixed Methods Research.* doi:10.1177/1558689813497260

Lee, Y. J., & Greene, J. (2007). The predictive validity of an ESL placement test: A mixed methods approach. *Journal of Mixed Methods Research, 1*(4), 366–389.

Mendlinger, S., & Cwikel, J. (2008). Spiraling between qualitative and quantitative data on women's health behaviors: A double helix model for mixed methods. *Qualitative Health Research, 18*(2), 280–293.

Morgan, D. L. (2007). Paradigms lost and pragmatism regained: Methodological implications of combining qualitative and quantitative methods. *Journal of Mixed Methods Research, 1*(1), 48–76.

Morse, J. M. (2010). Procedures and practice of mixed method design: Maintaining control, rigor, and complexity. In A. Tashakkori & C. Teddlie (Eds.), *Sage handbook of mixed methods research in social & behavioral research* (2nd ed., pp. 339–352). Thousand Oaks, CA: Sage.

Morse, J. M., & Niehaus, L. (2009). *Mixed methods design: Principles and procedures.* Walnut Creek, CA: Left Coast.

O'Cathain, A. (2010). Assessing the quality of mixed methods research: Toward a comprehensive framework. In A. Tashakkori & C. Teddlie (Eds.), *Sage Handbook of mixed methods in social & behavioral research* (2nd ed., pp. 531–555). Thousand Oaks, CA: Sage.

O'Cathain, A., Murphy, E., & Nicholl, J. (2007). Integration and publications as indicators of "yield" from mixed methods studies. *Journal of Mixed Methods Research, 1*(2), 147–163.

O'Cathain, A., Murphy, E., & Nicholl, J. (2010). Three techniques for integrating data in mixed methods studies. *British Medical Journal, 341,* c4587

Palak, D., & Walls, R. T. (2009). Teachers' beliefs and technology practices: A mixed-methods approach. *Journal of Research on Technology in Education, 41*(4), 417–441.

Peterson, J. C., Czajkowski. S., Charlson, M. E., Link, J. B., Wells, M. T., Isen, A. M., . . . Jobe, J. B. (2013, April). Translating basic behavioral and social science research to clinical application: The EVOLVE mixed methods approach. *Journal of Consulting and Clinical Psychology, 81*(2), 217–230.

Plano Clark, V. L. (2010). The adoption and practice of mixed methods: U.S. trends in federally funded health-related research. *Qualitative Inquiry, 16*(6), 428–440.

Plano Clark, V. L., Anderson, N., Zhou, Y., Wertz, J., Schumacher, K., & Miaskowski, C. (2014). Conceptualizing longitudinal mixed methods designs: A methodological review of health sciences research. *Journal of Mixed Methods Research.* doi:10.1177/1558689814543563

Plano Clark, V. L., Schumacher, K., West, C., Edrington, J., Dunn, L. B., Harzstark, A., . . . Miaskowski, C. (2013). Practices for embedding an interpretive qualitative approach within a randomized clinical trial. *Journal of Mixed Methods Research, 7*(3), 219–242.

Robinson, S., & Mendelson, A. L. (2012). A qualitative experiment: Research on mediated meaning construction using a hybrid approach. *Journal of Mixed Methods Research, 6*(4), 332–347.

Sedoglavich, V., Akoorie, M. E. M., & Pavlovich, K. (2014). Measuring absorptive capacity in high-tech companies: Mixing qualitative and quantitative methods. *Journal of Mixed Methods Research.* doi:10.1177/1558689814523677

Sosulski, M. R., & Lawrence, C. (2008). Mixing methods for full-strength results: Two welfare studies. *Journal of Mixed Methods Research, 2*(2), 121–148.

Spencer, D. B., Creswell, J. W., Reed, K. E., Young, J. M., & Mark, J. (2013, April 26). Coherent implementation of mathematics instructional materials: A multilevel mixed methods study. *Education Development Center.* Paper presented at the American Educational Research Association annual meeting. Retrieved from http://ltd.edc.org/mixed-method-study

Steckler, A., McLeroy, K. R., Goodman, R. M., Bird, S. T., & McCormick, L. (1992). Toward integrating qualitative and quantitative methods: An introduction. *Health Education Quarterly, 19*(1), 1–8.

Stoller, E. P., Webster, N. J., Blixen, C. E., McCormick, R. A., Hund, A. J., Perzynski, A. T., . . . Dawson, N. V. (2009). Alcohol consumption decisions among nonabusing drinkers diagnosed with hepatitis C: An exploratory sequential mixed methods study. *Journal of Mixed Methods Research, 3*(1), 65–86.

Tashakkori, A., & Creswell, J. W. (2007). The new era of mixed methods [Editorial]. *Journal of Mixed Methods Research, 1*(1), 3–7.

Tashakkori, A., & Teddlie, C. (1998). *Mixed methodology: Combining qualitative and quantitative approaches.* Thousand Oaks, CA: Sage.

Teddlie, C., & Tashakkori, A. (2006). A general typology of research designs featuring mixed methods. *Research in the Schools, 13*(1), 12–28.

Teddlie, C., & Tashakkori, A. (2009). *Foundations of mixed methods research: Integrating quantitative and qualitative approaches in the social and behavioral sciences.* Thousand Oaks, CA: Sage.

Teddlie, C., & Yu, F. (2007). Mixed methods sampling: A typology with examples. *Journal of Mixed Methods Research, 1*(1), 77–100.

von der Lippe, H. (2010). Motivation and selection processes in a biographical transition: A psychological mixed methods study on the transition into fatherhood. *Journal of Mixed Methods Research, 4*(3), 199–221.

Vrkljan, B. H. (2009). Constructing a mixed methods design to explore the older drive-copilot relationship. *Journal of Mixed Methods Research, 3*(4), 371–385.

Wesely, P. M. (2010). Language learning motivation in early adolescents: Using mixed methods research to explore contradiction. *Journal of Mixed Methods Research, 4*(4), 295–312.

Wittink, M. N., Barg, F. K., & Gallo, J. J. (2006). Unwritten rules of talking to doctors about depression: Integrating qualitative and quantitative methods. *Annals of Family Medicine, 4,* 302–309.

Woolley, C. M. (2009). Meeting the mixed methods challenge of integration in a sociological study of structure and agency. *Journal of Mixed Methods Research, 3*(1), 7–25.

CHAPTER 8

USE OF CONCEPT MAPS TO FACILITATE STUDENT LEARNING IN RESEARCH AND MEASUREMENT COURSES

Florian Feucht, Gwen Marchand, and Lori Olafson

ABSTRACT

This chapter introduces concept maps as visual displays that researchers can use to depict processes and outcomes of research and concept mapping as an instructional tool that instructors can use to foster graduate students' learning in doctoral research method courses. In the context of a theory-driven typology of visual displays, we describe the nature of concept maps and their use to facilitate student learning. Two applications of concept maps are provided to illustrate these ideas: creating visual models of research designs in an advanced qualitative research course and facilitating shared understanding of research designs in an evaluation research method course. The use of concept maps between the two courses is compared and contrasted and the chapter concludes with general recommendations for practice.

Use of Visual Displays in Research and Testing: Coding, Interpreting, and Reporting Data,
pages 207–234.

INTRODUCTION

In considering the ways in which visual displays can impact learning, a substantial body of research has focused on the use of visual displays for instructional purposes. In their review of practices, Schraw and Paik (2013) described four common properties of instructional visual displays that facilitate learning in classrooms, such as helping learners identify important information. Learners encounter many of these visual displays in their textbooks or other instructional materials. These include visual devices such as underlining, headings, and indentations that are used to direct the learner's attention, as well as concept maps, geographical maps, temporal sequences, and causal diagrams. These visual displays are meant to help learners identify and organize important information, incorporate external information into a mental model, and reduce cognitive load (Schraw & Paik, 2013).

This chapter focuses specifically on concept maps, a type of visual display that impacts student learning. Concept maps are diagrams that represent concepts and the relationships between these concepts. These can be used to present information to students, to assess what students know, and to provide ways for students to represent their knowledge (Nesbit & Adesope, 2013). In particular, we sought to extend this work by investigating whether student-constructed concept maps facilitate understanding of course material that graduate students encounter in research methods classes. To do so, we explored two instructional applications of concept maps: creating visual models of research designs and facilitating shared understanding of research designs.

In this chapter, we describe how graduate students developed and used concept maps in the context of their coursework to further their understandings of research methods. The chapter begins by providing a brief overview of previous work on the topic, including a description of the theory-driven typology of visual displays that were developed by the authors. Next, the two instructional uses of concept maps are described, including the context of the courses, the concept map tasks, and key insights resulting from the analysis of the student-constructed maps. The chapter concludes with suggestions for enhancing the concept map tasks and identifying additional instructional applications for the use of concept maps.

VISUAL REPRESENTATIONS OF PROCESSES AND PRODUCTS IN QUALITATIVE RESEARCH

Olafson, Feucht, and Marchand (2013) noted that the use of visual displays in qualitative research was limited, despite extensive use of graphs, charts, and histograms in quantitative research. They developed a theory-driven 3 x 2 typology of visual displays to categorize representations by the type of format (*Text, Table,* and *Graphic*) and its intended function (*Process* and *Product*) (see Table 1). Working from Tufte's (2001) typology of visual displays of quantitative data, they identified three primary levels to best represent qualitative data: Text, Table,

TABLE 1. Types of Visual Displays by Function

	Process	**Product**
Text @ Level 1	*Text: Process*	*Text: Product*
Table @ Level 2	*Table: Process*	*Table: Product*
Graphic @ Level 3	*Graphic: Process*	*Graphic: Product*

and Graphic. *Text* is the most common way of presenting qualitative data in a sequential, rather than simultaneous, way (e.g., interview excerpts). The second level is a *Table* that includes labels and explanatory sentences (e.g., data ordered by time and sequence). The third level is a *Graphic* that describes the integration of words and pictures (e.g., flow chart). They also added the intended function of visual display—*Process* and *Product*—to their framework based on Creswell's (2013) work. Distinguishing between the function of a visual display as process (e.g., an excerpt of a coded text transcript) or product (e.g., a graphical network representing an emerging theory) was also noted by Tufte (2001). The six cells in their typology permit a more precise classification of visual displays in qualitative research.

Their framework yielded a 3 x 2 matrix that allowed us to look at how level one, two, and three visual displays are used in the processes of qualitative analysis and how they are used to create products of analysis. The authors believe that the six cells of this matrix provide a more complete representation of the uses of visual displays in qualitative analyses. Table 1 illustrates an overview of different types of visual displays by function, and Table 2 provides examples accordingly.

Olafson et al. (2013) provided extensive examples to illustrate the processes and products of qualitative analysis represented by visual displays. Visual displays are used to improve researchers' understanding of components and processes of the research cycle, such as data organization, analysis, and interpretation.

TABLE 2. Typology of Visual Displays With Examples in Qualitative Research

	Process	**Product**
Text @ Level 1	• Taking field notes • Transcribing data • Selecting quotations	• Interview excerpts and quotations to illustrate written results • Outline of case summary
Table @ Level 2	• Operationalizing coding schemes • Maintaining a code book and category list	• Code hierarchies • Code occurrence across participants • Summary of themes
Graphic @ Level 3	• Mapping data analysis • Charting of data and method triangulation • Demonstrating relationships between codes and categories	• Concept map of key findings • Conceptual framework • Process model • Paradigm model

Similarly, they play an important role in conveying this information to readers and consumers in publications and presentations. In this chapter, they extend this work by considering the development and use of concept maps, a particular type of Level 3 visual display, as a specific instructional tool in teaching graduate courses in research methods.

CONCEPT MAPS AS LEVEL 3 VISUAL DISPLAYS

Maps or models are considered graphical displays (Level 3). Concept maps are two-dimensional diagrams that represent concepts and relationships between concepts (Cañas et al., 2004; Nesbit & Adesope, 2013). Concept maps are an effective way of representing a person's understanding of a domain of knowledge (Novak, 1997).

As described in Olafson et al. (2013), concept maps have several uses in qualitative analysis. They can be used to reduce data, create a coding system, and analyze themes (Daley, 2004). These uses are all related to processes and products of analyses. However, the strength of concept mapping is seen in its utility to create products of analysis by visually displaying the associations between multiple themes and ideas (Burke et al., 2005). This application of concept maps is relevant across all forms of research, ranging from qualitative, quantitative, and mixed research designs, including program evaluation and action research. Therefore, the use of concept maps as visual displays to illustrate products and processes of a diverse body of research has become a common practice in professional publications and other scientific outlets of research, such as conferences, professional development and training, and policy guidelines.

INSTRUCTIONAL USE OF CONCEPT MAPS

Concept maps have been used for their instructional applications. As a way of expressing and building knowledge, concept mapping promotes elaborative processing by activating more associations between new information and prior knowledge (Nesbit & Adesope, 2013). In this section of the chapter, we describe the use of concept maps to create visual models of qualitative and evaluation research designs. More specifically, in the context of two graduate research courses, concept maps (product) and concept mapping (process) were used as instructional tools with a goal to help students better understand the methodological steps and components of the research cycle and their idiosyncratic derivations and pragmatic workflows when cycling through the actual act of designing, conducting, and reporting a research study. Figure 1, as an example, represents steps and components of a general research cycle with varying usage and workflows of theory, data, and technology (e.g., analysis software, video cameras) throughout a research project.

From an instructional perspective, concept mapping can be used as a formative assessment tool to evaluate students' understanding of the methodologies of

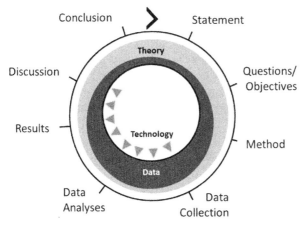

FIGURE 1.   Steps and components of the research cycle with usage of theory, data, and technology.

research design and program evaluation described and explained in various text-books, as well as their ability to transfer these narratives and scripts into the ac-tuality of the professional practice of a researcher or program evaluator. Therein, the instructional use of concept mapping can also encourage students to raise their own awareness of professional competencies (e.g., knowledge, skills, attitudes) and reflect on the professional expectations required from the conceptualization of a research project to the acceptance of a manuscript or approval of a research report for dissemination. From a social constructivist perspective, concept maps allow students to reconstruct the knowledge presented in textbooks and other in-structional materials into their own understanding of research and program evalu-ation, contextualized within their own research interest and emerging expertise. Hence, concept maps can be considered to be visual displays of students' owner-ship of the reconstructed course content, interlaced with their own interest and expertise. Finally, generating concept maps allows students to practice the profes-sional use of visual displays as it is culturally expected in the field of education sciences (Olafson et al., 2013).

Example 1: Use of Concept Maps in the Process of Developing a Qualitative Research Proposal

The course.

This first example focuses on the use of concept mapping as an advanced 3-credit seminar entitled, *Qualitative Research II – Design and Analysis*. Most students who enroll in this advanced elective course are motivated to pursue a qualitative research study for their dissertations and are often at the end of their doctoral programs of study. The objectives of the course focus on students' ability to design, conduct, and report sections of qualitative studies and therein simulate various steps and processes of a typical qualitative research cycle. In the context of their emerging research agendas, students establish theoretical frameworks and justify suitable qualitative research designs that allow them to investigate a research problem of their choice. They strategize on how to establish rapport with participants and maintain working relationships with gatekeepers in their data collection fields. Students collect different types of qualitative data (e.g., narratives, videos, artifacts) using different collection techniques (e.g., interviews, classroom observation, document collections). They analyze and interpret data using different types of coding schemes and finally verbalize/present and report key sections of their research studies.

In this course, the method of concept mapping was used as an instructional scaffold to help students in the developmental process of conceptualizing, verbalizing, and formalizing their research proposals in writing and to familiarize them with the use of visual displays to illustrate aspects of their written research proposals and future work. That is, it was intended that students learn to become users of concept maps as examples to visually represent processes and products of qualitative research at the third level of the typology of visual displays (see Table 1). The following five steps were part of the instructional scaffold:

Step 1: Individually, use concept mapping as a brainstorming process to generate and sort ideas for an unspecified research proposal. Focus on students' idea generation.

Step 2: Individually, use concept maps to visualize and pinpoint components and processes of an emerging research proposal without being distracted by the writing process of a full proposal. Focus on students' thinking by means of graphical conceptualization.

Step 3: In small groups, presenting and talking through the research proposal using concept maps as starting points and for illustration purposes of components and process. Focus on students' thinking by means of verbalizations; also in anticipation of the readiness for the writing process.

Step 4: In small groups and/or individually, write feedback on a copy of the concept maps. Focus on students' rethinking through alternatives and/or specifications of processes or components.

Step 5: Individually, use concept maps as structures or outlines in the writing process of the final research proposal. Focus on students' thinking by means of their writing.

The underlying purpose of the scaffold is to extend students' thinking and writing along five different steps. From a cognitive processing perspective, the use of concept mapping can decrease students' cognitive load by allowing them to focus on each step of the conceptualization, verbalization, and formalization of their proposal in writing; thus, they can avoid cognitive overload when trying to accomplish this multifaceted thinking task the night before the due date of the assignment (Moreno & Mayer, 1999; Pass, Renkel, & Sweller, 2004; Schraw & Paik, 2013). From a learning-to-write perspective, the use of concept mapping can help students improve the quality of their written research proposals by asking them to identify the content, structure, and logical flow before engaging in the actual writing process (Emig, 1977; O'Rourke, Clavo & McNamara, 2011; Villalon & Calvo, 2011). From a socioconstructivist perspective, the creation of concepts maps allows students to (a) have ownership in the to-be-learned knowledge by reconstructing the generic concepts and processes of the research cycle in light of their own research interests and topical expertise, (b) become enculturated in the use of visual displays as communication tools and artifacts common in the scientific community, and (c) improve their proposals based on peer and instructor feedback to a level that they might not have achieved on their own, but are more likely to with the help of a more experienced learner or methodologist (Vygotsky, 1978).

The task.

While the scaffold, with its five steps and its theoretical underpinnings, seems to be quite complex, the wording of the actual task is very basic (see in italics below). Most of the task's description provides students with information about the purpose and context of the task rather than identifying specifics on the content of the concept maps:

> In preparation of your research proposal, *please bring the following items to the next class meeting: a) a written research question (draft), with sub questions, if needed; b) three concept maps that describe your planned research design, data collection, and data analyses, respectively; and c) a paper copy of these items with your name on it.* We will use these items to discuss your research ideas and provide you with feedback as a group. . . . While you can still adjust/change your research question(s) and the three concept maps until the due date of the assignment, these items will be part of your written research proposal.

Leaving the task open-ended to a certain extent allows the instructor to assess students' conceptual readiness to engage in the actual writing process and to provide them with systematic and timely feedback before writing their proposals. Typically, the three concept maps provide insight into following areas: (a) level of conceptual detail and areas of emphasis (including conceptual framework/literature review, rationalization of the research objective, and alignment of research questions and research methods), (b) use of itemized and/or procedural outlines, (c) order of components and processes along the research cycle, and (d) use of expert terminology.

The context.

Eight students in the *Qualitative Research II – Design and Analysis* course consented that their work could be used to illustrate how concept maps can benefit students in strengthening their conceptual thinking and writing of a research proposal. These students were female, ranging between 25 and 60 years of age, and were close to completing their doctoral coursework in the departments of Curriculum and Instruction, Early-Childhood and Special Education, and Foundations of Education and Leadership.

Halfway through the course, students were asked to complete the above described task of identifying their research questions and outlining their research designs, data collection, and data analysis in the form of concept maps. During the following class meeting, students pitched their proposal ideas in small groups using these materials and changed groups until everybody had the chance to present, listen, and provide feedback to all research proposals. The instructor participated in different groups to give all students additional feedback. This activity lasted about two and a half hours, was full of positive energy, and demonstrated student excitement, as demonstrated by the high noise levels that required several reminders to calm down.

The analyses.

The following analyses focus retrospectively on issues that the instructor addressed during verbal and written feedback to students in the course. Analyses of the concept maps were divided into two areas: a content analysis and a structural analysis. The content analysis was used to identify whether students included all components and processes typical of a research proposal in their concept maps, including but not limited to a literature review/framework, research questions, rationales to provide reasoning for the research objective and/or chosen methodology, data collection, and data analysis. During the course, this analysis and the instructor's provision of feedback to students were driven primarily by a mental checklist based on American Psychological Association (APA) style expectations for research proposals. For example, does a rationale for the importance of the study exist, are the participants and population of the study identified, and what analytical procedures are anticipated? If certain components and processes were missing, students were encouraged to integrate them into their concept maps in a meaningful manner. Again, it is important to note that because the task was designed to be open-ended, the concept maps could be used strategically to assess whether students were able to apply the methodological knowledge that they acquired to this point in the course.

The structural analysis of the concept maps appeared to be most meaningful in the feedback for students to strengthen the conceptualization of the proposed research study and for the instructor to gain an understanding of the students' readiness to engage in the writing process. The structural analysis focused on the graphical representation of concepts and lines/arrows depicted on the maps to

TABLE 3.   Analytical Frameworks to Assess Conceptualization of Research Proposals

		Content Analysis			
		Research design			Data collection	Data analysis
Structural Analysis	**Components and processes**	**Integrated framework**	**Integrated questions**	**Integrated rationales**	**Components and processes**	**Components and processes**
Providing conceptual details in concept map	High: 4 Medium: 2 Low: 2	Yes: 3 No: 5	Yes: 3 No: 5	Yes: 2 No: 6	High: 3 Medium: 2 Low: 2	High: 4 Medium: 1 Low: 2
Using procedural and/or itemized outlines	Procedural outline: 4 Itemized outline: 4				Procedural outline: 4 Itemized outline: 4	Procedural outline: 6 Itemized outline: 2
Following the sequence of research cycle	Yes: 5 Yes, but with mistakes: 1 No: 2				Yes: 5 Yes, but with mistakes: 1 No: 2	Yes: 5 Yes, but with mistakes: 1 No: 2
Using expert terminology	Yes: 6 No: 2				Yes: 6 No: 2	Yes: 6 No: 2
Example concept maps	Figures 2 and 3				Figures 4 and 5	Figures 6 and 7

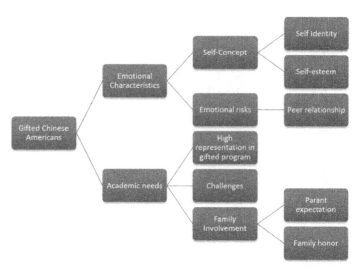

FIGURE 2. Research design concept map—Student 1.

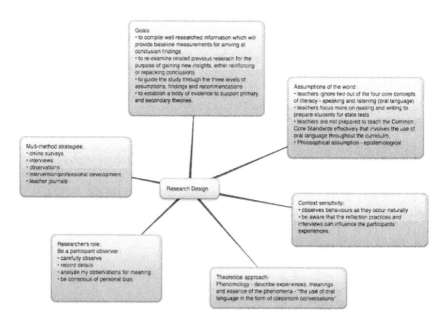

FIGURE 3. Research design concept map—Student 2.

visually represent students' knowledge and understanding of their proposed research ideas. The following areas were of particular interest for student feedback: (a) provision of conceptual details, (b) use of procedural or itemized outlines, (c) organization following the sequence of the research cycle, and (d) use of expert terminology. Table 3 depicts a brief quantified analysis of the content and structural analyses. Figures 2 through 7 provide visual examples of the concept maps representing research design, data collection, and data analysis. Figures 2, 4, and 6 represent the concept maps from a single student (Student 1) to demonstrate variations within the same proposal, while Figures 3, 5, and 7 were chosen from different students to illustrate the overall diversity of concept maps generated for this task.

Providing conceptual details.

Each concept map can be analyzed for its numbers of graphical concepts and links to better understand the depth and breadth of the proposal's conceptualization. Some concept maps had a low level of conceptual detail (fewer than 10 concepts; e.g., Figure 6), some had a medium level (11–20 concepts; e.g., Figure 2), and most had a high level (20 concepts and more; e.g., Figure 3). Lower levels of conceptualization didn't necessarily mean lack of quality. For example, one concept map made use of conceptual content and link labels to precisely identify key components and processes of data analysis (one of three branches: "Data Analysis—Thematic Analysis—Collaborative Analysis—Determine Essentials Themes vs. Incidental Themes"), while another concept map was not well-thought-out at all (circular alignment of: "Literature—Interview transcripts—Observation field notes"). A close screening of the concept maps that represented the research design provided insight into the complexity of the proposed research studies. Some students represented their (a) theoretical framework stemming from an emerging literature review, (b) their research questions, and (c) rationales for the research objective or for their methodological choices and integrated those into their overall research design. Interestingly, none of these students had all three of these essential components represented on their research-design concept maps. Hence, the feedback to the class was to consider a meaningful integration of these components into their concept maps before beginning the writing process.

Using procedural or itemized outlines.

Two different outline structures could be identified in the concept maps. One outline followed a procedural structure that connected different concepts with arrows to indicate a step-by-step progression of components (e.g., Figure 5). The other outline represented concepts more like an itemized list using lines to indicate the conceptual (but not procedural) relationship of the components (e.g., Figure 2). Across the research-design concept maps and the data-collection concept maps, both types of outlines occurred equally, while the procedural outline was more utilized in the data-analysis concept maps. For each individual concept

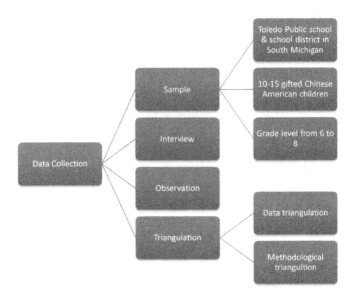

FIGURE 4.   Data collection concept map—Student 1.

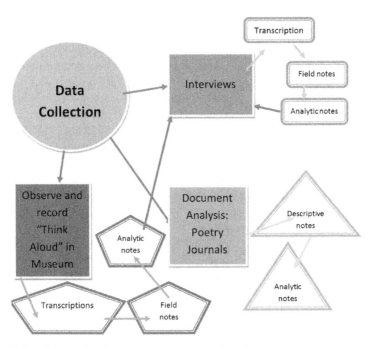

FIGURE 5.   Data collection concept map—Student 3.

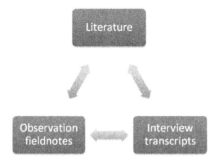

FIGURE 6.   Data analysis concept map—Student 1.

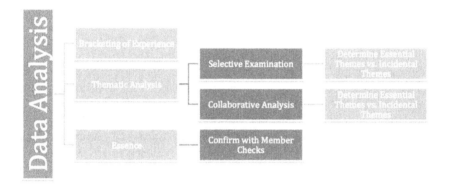

FIGURE 7.   Data analysis concept map—Student 4.

map, students choose either a procedural or an itemized outline. Many students, however, chose different outlines across their three concept maps (e.g., Student 1, Figures 2, 4, and 6), while some maintained the procedural or itemized outline across all three concept maps. It was interesting to note that in the written draft version of the proposals, students who had used only a procedural outline seemed to struggle with the Material section, listing individual materials, while the students who exclusively made use of an itemized structure had problems providing a Procedure section to identify the step-by-step application of the materials. Hence, feedback to these students was to balance both components (itemized outline) and processes (procedural outline) of the research cycle in their conceptual proposal.

Following the sequence of the research cycle.

Most students dispersed the methodological components and processes of the research cycle appropriately across the three concept maps, accounting for design, data collection, and data analysis. Similarly, most of the students also depicted them appropriately within each concept (e.g., Figure 5). Two students simply spread out/brainstormed their content within each map without accounting for any structure. One student who followed a procedural outline to depict the sequence of the research cycle had several components in the wrong locations. That is, the design concept map depicted many detailed *analytical* components and procedures, while the data-analysis concept map included the *research question* and *research objective*. The correct conceptual order would have required that this information be transposed. Again, in the written draft, the student seemed to have misarranged the overall outline of the concept maps into the outline of her written proposal, which required her later to restructure certain areas. This error in the direct transfer from the concept map outline into the written proposal outline was obvious. Hence, feedback on getting the sequencing of the research proposal in the appropriate order within and across the concept maps seemed to be crucial for developing an effective outline for written proposals.

Using expert terminology.

From the perspective of symbolic interactionism, the use of terminology to communicate in the structural environment of a concept map can be quite powerful and insightful (Herman-Kinney & Reynolds, 2003). Without going into philosophical detail, a basic screening was used to simply identify terminology in the concept maps that demonstrated the knowledge of components and processes an expert qualitative researcher would use and that were acquired within the context of this advanced graduate course. The majority of students used expert terminology, such as phenomenology, bracketing experiences, selective examination, snowball sampling, adductive coding, observe and record think-aloud, textual descriptions, and methodological triangulations, to name a few (e.g., Figure 7). Correct use of terminology seemed to be an indicator of students' conceptual depth and breadth of the field of qualitative research and demonstrate at least a more professional presentation of their research proposals. Hence, students who did not use expert terminology sufficiently and appropriately were asked to increase and improve their terminology usage. All students were encouraged to use the terminology proactively when presenting their proposed studies within the course and beyond.

Summary.

Overall, it appeared that concept maps in this advanced qualitative research course could be utilized as a formative assessment to gain a better understanding of students' conceptual understanding of their proposed studies and their readiness to engage in the writing process. The findings of the study showed that students differed in their ability to provide conceptual details in their concept maps, use procedural and/or itemized outlines, follow the sequence of the research cycle, and use expert terminology. Some of these aspects of the concept maps and the underlying thinking or nonthinking seemed to have an influence on the quality of the written proposals, which could be influenced through timely feedback (Emig, 1977; O'Rourke et al., 2011; Villalon & Calvo, 2011).

Finding the right balance between the open-endedness of the assessment and student readiness to write a proposal seems to be the key to the overall task. On one hand, if the task provides too much detail with respect to proposal components and processes, then content and structural analyses of students' understanding would not be possible, as too much information (or too many expectations) is given away upfront. On the other hand, if students have not developed sufficient knowledge, skills, and attitudes toward research and research design at the time of the task, they fail in developing a successful research proposal. While the immanent logic of the scaffold would apply to many situations, the actual task description would need to accommodate the anticipated student readiness to conceptualize, verbalize, and formalize a written research design. Then again, the main purpose of concept mapping was to use it as an instructional and formative assessment tool to identify student readiness to start the process of writing their research proposals.

Example 2: Use of Concept Maps in the Process and Outcomes of Mixed Evaluation Research Studies in Group Projects

The course.

In this second example, the use of concept maps was situated in the second of a two-course series on program evaluation. The series is designed to provide doctoral-level graduate students a working knowledge of program evaluation tools and theories. The course, *Evaluation Research Methods*, exposes students to common concepts in program evaluation. Working in teams of 3–5, students gain real-world evaluation experience by selecting a project and developing a proposal for an evaluation. The second semester course, *Advanced Evaluation Research Methods*, is focused on developing a more in-depth understanding of program evaluation theories and models and applying that knowledge to refine the first-semester proposal and guide the implementation of the proposed evaluation. The students who enroll in the second-semester course tend to be those who are interested in a career in program evaluation or who are seeking a specialty for their doctoral work. Teams from the first semester may not be intact in the continuation course, leading to some necessary realignment of teams.

The team nature of these evaluation projects is critical to the course for several reasons. Most notably, in real-world settings, evaluations for larger programs are commonly conducted by teams assembled to specifically meet the demands of an evaluation. These teams may include a lead evaluator, project manager, research assistants charged with data collection, methodological or analytic specialists, and other support level staff (Skolits, Morrow, & Burr, 2009). Thus, students need to develop skills for working in different roles as a member of a research team, such as skills to negotiate ideas and responsibilities and effective communication skills. The second rationale for teamwork is that the course sequence is designed to give participating clients an actionable evaluation product. The scope of the work is limited by student expertise and constrained by the academic year, yet the projects typically exceed what any individual student could reasonably undertake in one year. Finally, the instructor for this course believes that constructive peer collaboration is a critical aspect of developing research expertise (Marchand, Schraw, & Olafson, 2013) and students learning a new craft may feel more comfortable first vetting ideas with student colleagues rather than the instructor.

The task.

At the most general level, concept maps are tools used to visually display the associations between themes and ideas (Burke et al., 2005; Olafson et al., 2013). Concept mapping is a common tool used in program evaluation for both the planning of the research process as well as communication of findings to end-users. For example, logic models may be considered a visual display used to represent the theory of change underlying programs, program implementation processes, and other purposes (W.K. Kellogg Foundation, 2004). Evaluators tend to embrace the art of visual displays for planning projects and communicating results; however, the use of concept maps to facilitate shared understanding of the evaluation design, methods, and analyses among evaluation team members is perhaps an underutilized activity.

As evaluation teams may be assembled quickly, may add members as needed throughout the evaluation process, and may draw from a range of formal training disciplines and experience levels, tools to uncover different assumptions about the evaluation process and build consensus as to the evaluation design and research process are critical. In this course setting, concept maps were used to elucidate individual group member's perceptions of their project's evaluation design, the data-collection process, and analytic plan. Members shared and discussed the individual maps within their groups. Each group drew upon the individual maps and associated discussion to construct a shared concept map that represented the final agreed-upon research design, data-collection process, and analytic plan.

In the language of the typology for visual displays presented earlier in this chapter, this task represented a visual display for *Graphic @ Process* level (see Table 1) in that students constructed concept maps to represent the evaluation design, methodological, and analytic processes. The group-level maps demonstrated consensus that grew out of the process phase of the map development and were used as a communication tool to be used to facilitate understanding of the evaluation design with other class members, the instructor, and the evaluation client, thus representing a *Graphic @ Product* level (see Table 1). The figures described in the following sections represent both individual-level maps and group-level maps. Figures 8 and 9 illustrate individual maps from one team. Figures 10–12 represent the group-level maps produced by a different team and are the outcome of the consensus-building process.

The process.

This illustration focuses on three groups of students. The first group consisted of three students who were developing an evaluation of a community college tutorial services program (TSP). This group was intact from the first semester and will be referred to as the TSP team. The second group consisted of four students conducting an evaluation on a reading program at a local elementary-level charter school (Charter team). The project proposal was developed during the first semester by two students, one of whom continued on in the second semester, but the other students were new to the group. The final group consisted of four students who were working on an evaluation of a new professional development course developed by a university-based center (UC team). This group was also newly composed, with only one individual involved from the previous semester. Taken together, these teams represented three very different dynamics in terms of group composition, evaluation content area, and methodological approaches to evaluation. All three team projects used some form of mixed methods (Plano Clark & Creswell, 2011) for their evaluation project.

Students were given the task of constructing three concept maps during class-time to represent the research design, data collection, and analytic plan. Students were given approximately 30 minutes during class to work on the assigned concept map as individuals, after which time the groups met, discussed, and developed a shared concept map over another 20–30 minutes. This process was strongly encouraged and followed by all groups for the first concept map. The process was more flexible for the remaining two maps as the groups experimented with finding the most effective communication process for their teams. The following section describes each team's experience with the concept maps to illustrate how the maps impacted the development and communication of the research process.

Assumptions revealed.

Recall that the groups were using existing evaluation plans that included proposed evaluation questions, design, data collection, and analyses. The concept maps from two members of the TSP team revealed a sharp contrast in the level from which the individuals approached the design map (see Figures 8–9). The individual map in Figure 8 included three distinct research topics, but did not explicitly link any particular sampling approach or data-collection process with an individual question. In contrast, the individual map in Figure 9 took a more hierarchical approach, leading with one broad, overarching research question and then differentiating method, specific questions, and data-collection processes. The final group map was more consistent with the second individual, albeit with greater detail. The team used this process to ensure that each research question was linked to a data source, ended up rephrasing some questions, and added a link called "concept" between question and data-collection tool to demonstrate conceptual understanding of the overall question.

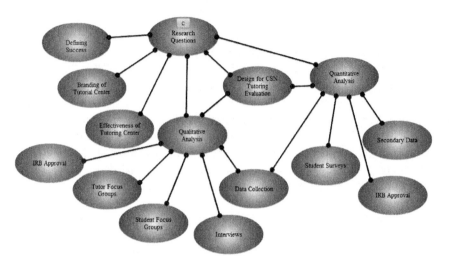

FIGURE 8. Research design map—TSP individual 1.

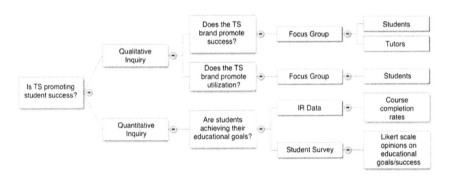

FIGURE 9.   Research design map—TSP individual 2.

The individual students expressed surprise at the many different assumptions that arose across team members not only in design (mixed methods) but also in goals of evaluation. As this team had worked together for several months already and had contact in their workplace, they felt so immersed in the project that they assumed they were on the same page in terms of the evaluation. They determined that because they had designed their project with different individuals contributing different parts of the evaluation plan, they had lost sight of the overall sense of the project.

Finding Direction.

The Charter team faced substantial challenges during their evaluation process, including strong internal disagreement on the direction of the evaluation and a client with whom it was difficult to connect. The team was forced to renegotiate the data-collection plan at several points during the semester and it was clear that the group struggled to enact an effective plan for data collection. A review of the individual and team data-collection maps revealed the range of changes to the evaluation plan. For example, one team member separated their data-collection map into three different sections to include program implementation questions measured by performance data collected at two time points, program outcome questions measured by using a matrix tool called CARMA (Putney, Wink, & Perkins, 2006) to compare expected versus evident program implementation, and program impact questions, investigated through a case study methodology. Yet another team member included only implementation and outcome components with less detail as to how the data collection would actually occur (e.g., number of interviews). The final group map did not include the proposed case study, but did include an explicit treatment of how the evaluation team reflections fit into the data-collection process when using the CARMA tool. This team used the maps to find direction for their evaluation data collection.

Organizing complexity.

The UC team appeared to have the most cohesion in terms of shared understanding of the evaluation process as the concept map task began. The team also had designed the most complex evaluation, with a stated convergent parallel mixed methods design, including both quantitative and qualitative components to answer both program implementation and outcome questions. After completing the first concept map task, the team spent only about half the allowed time working on individual maps, preferring to verbally contribute individual perspectives to develop and refine the group map. The team clearly preferred to use the specialized technical skills of one team member to free up time for the group to collaborate. The team turned in at least two versions of a group concept map for each task. Maps from all three tasks are included in Figures 10–12. The team expressed that maps helped them cull aspects from the design that they were not able to address during the semester due to time limitations. The team also found that the maps served as a focal point for grounding the data collection and analysis processes during the data collection and reporting time frame. Individual team members focused on different aspects of the project used the maps to reorient themselves to the way their individual tasks contributed to the overall project.

Summary.

When considering the development and use of the maps across individual students as well as teams, there emerged some clear areas of benefit, but also areas in need of change or improvement. Several benefits were observed. First,

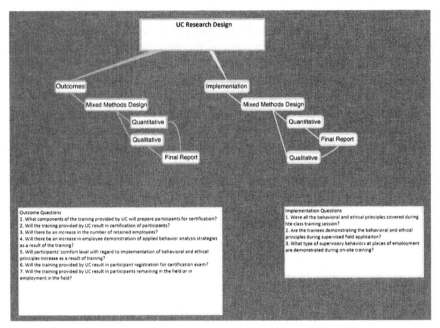

FIGURE 10.   Research design map—UC group.

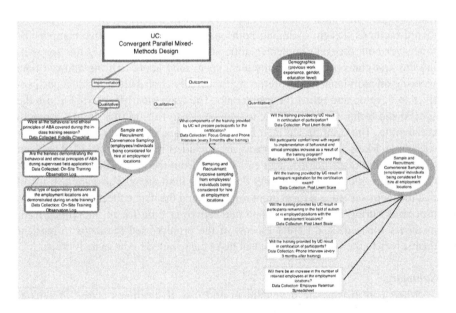

FIGURE 11.   Data collection map—UC group.

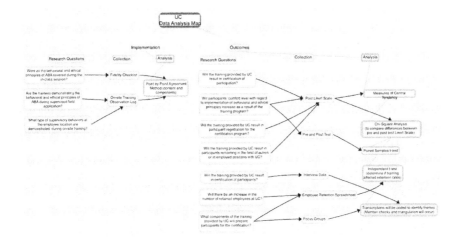

FIGURE 12.   Analysis map—UC group.

the concept maps were a useful tool for helping individual students confront their own gaps in knowledge and understanding of the existing research design and methodology. In particular, the maps showed disconnects between research questions and the appropriateness of tools and methods to answer those questions. Second, consensus across all groups was that discussing the individual maps revealed compartmentalized teamwork. In other words, different individuals had been responsible for writing different parts of the evaluation proposal (e.g., introduction, rationale for evaluation questions, measures, and tools), which led to a rather murky understanding of the holistic nature of proposed evaluation on the part of the team members. Simply put, group members were surprised to learn that they had different conceptualizations of the purpose, process, and product of their evaluation. Next, discussing the individual concept maps also revealed different metatheoretical assumptions about the fundamental nature of evaluation research, which were rooted in individual epistemological worldviews (Mertens & Wilson, 2012). Within groups, some individuals held more constructivist views of knowledge, whereas others approached evaluation research from a postpositivist perspective. Students were forced to confront how these assumptions guided their choice of research questions, design, data collection, and analyses. By making these assumptions explicit, groups could address their differences and attempt to find a path forward. Finally, groups agreed that creating a group map for the design and data-collection aspects of their project helped to develop shared understanding of the way the evaluation questions would be answered from a methodological standpoint as well as how the team would work together to complete the evaluation.

There were also aspects of this process that were less successful, yielding the following reflections and suggestions for amending this process in the future. The quality of the maps were highly divergent, ranging from extremely simple to highly detailed. The course did not include instruction on the construction of concept maps per se. In future applications, students should be assigned read-ings or receive explicit instruction on concept mapping (e.g., Novak & Cañas, 2008). Further, the individuals and teams submitted fewer concept maps for the analytic process than for the first two assigned maps. This could be due to fatigue on the part of the students as this was the third assigned map; lack of need as students became more skilled at communication within their groups; or a failure to comprehend how to use concept maps to plan for data analysis. This process also suggests that concept maps for team planning of the research-based evalu-ation process should be an ongoing and living process. Evaluation teams must respond to changes in the evaluation design, data collection, and analyses that are often due to conditions in the field. Finally, because all teams proposed to use mixed methods, a map that explicitly detailed at what stage(s) during the research process data were to be integrated across the qualitative and quantitative com-ponents and what form the integration would take may have been useful to pro-vide a more clear understanding of why the mixed methods design was proposed (Creswell, Clark, Gutmann, & Hanson, 2008). These evaluations were undertaken with a pragmatic lens. The assumptions underlying the appropriateness for using a mixed methods approach were not discussed in detail in this class.

DISCUSSION

The two examples provided in this chapter demonstrated how concept mapping and concept maps were used for instructional purposes in graduate-level research methods courses. Students in both courses were given the assignment of using concept mapping as a tool to illustrate the research design, data collection, and analyses steps of the research cycle (see Figure 1). The instructor in the first ex-ample used student concept maps to assess conceptual readiness to engage in the actual process of writing a research proposal, as well as to provide students with a structure for delivering feedback before writing proposals. In other words, the concept mapping process and analyses of the maps focused on both the content and structure of the maps themselves as a tool for formative assessment. The instructor in the second example focused on the function of the maps for helping to refine and clarify the research process and facilitate group consensus for team projects. Taken together these examples demonstrate a multilevel perspective on the use of concept mapping and maps during instruction to consider the overall function of the maps, the specific structural elements of the maps to delineate process, and the research-related content of the maps.

The examples revealed several areas for discussion based primarily on com-monalities found across the examples, but also those based on divergent details associated with concept maps as both process and product types of visual displays (see Table 1).

Concept Mapping to Promote Student Engagement and Active Understanding

The examples both presented concept mapping as an example of visual displays of the type *Graphic @ Process*, which facilitated active cognitive engagement in conceptualizing and planning research and evaluation. Concept mapping allowed for both groups of students to actively construct their own representation of different phases of the research process. By constructing a different map for distinct phases of the research cycle (see Figure 1), the instructors provided a method for disentangling the "work" phases of research from each other, but also a method for unpacking processes within different phases. For example, in our experience, students sometimes bypass design or conflate design with data-collection processes rather than treating design as the guide for the methods and analytic phases of the project. Further, in research-methods classes, we often ask students to carefully consider the structure of the data-collection process to ensure adequate coverage of the phenomena under study and how data-collection activities are interrelated. By asking students to construct these three separate but related maps, we found that students achieved conceptual clarity and sophistication that helped prepare them for the next steps of their projects. Moreover, students were immersed in the concept-mapping process, demonstrating a deep level of cognitive engagement (Creswell et al., 2008; Emig, 1977; O'Rourke et al., 2011; Schraw & Paik, 2013).

Concept Mapping to Facilitate Communication about Research

Individual concept maps were used in both examples to facilitate communication in small group settings. The first example situated sharing the concept maps as a way to demonstrate strengths and gaps in developing plans. The maps were used as a foundation to garner feedback from other students to improve individual plans, and students were able to receive feedback from all peers in the course via small groups. In this way, students developed the critical skill of sharing ideas with groups that might have diverse, different, or divergent perspectives, thus leading to a more thoughtful and complete conceptualization of the student projects. In the second example, students were working from program evaluation proposals that were already in existence, thus the individual concept maps were used to reveal misalignment amongst group members in conceptual and practical understanding of the proposed evaluation. The individual maps were used to refine and clarify the proposed group evaluation plan.

Considering that these product-oriented maps formed the basis for communication about research both during the early stages of the planning cycle (example 1) and later stages of proposal development and project implementation (example

2), we consider these visual displays as a potential integral part of an iterative cycle of both process and product for learning about and sharing research. The concept-mapping process can be used to describe research ideas and methods. These early concept maps can be shared for the purposes of gaining feedback to improve the design. Feedback is reinvested during subsequent concept-mapping activities to shape the research or evaluation methodology. Concept maps of the data-collection process can be given to other group members or research sites to ensure shared understanding and to make adjustments to meet site needs. Researchers may then use concept mapping to describe the analytic process or may create a map of the relations amongst research findings. Finally, findings may be shared in a visual display to facilitate discussion as to the meaning of the research findings or potential use of the findings (Olafson et al., 2013). This iterative process/product feedback cycle may be particularly helpful when working on a complex, multisite project or with research or evaluation teams, when shared understanding is paramount for a successful project (Skolits et al., 2009). Sharing research activities in the form of concept maps also might be particularly effective with those unfamiliar with the research process due to content area differences/ specialization that might rely on particular methods or with individuals who are truly novices to research, such as program staff in an evaluation context (Marchand et al., 2013; Vygotsky, 1978).

Considering Graphic @ Process and Graphic @ Product During Instruction

Concept mapping for different purposes.

The two examples illustrate multiple applications on the use concept mapping to facilitate development of understanding and communication about the research process. The first example demonstrated what may be a more standard use of concept mapping for aiding student understanding. Students were in early stages of the development of individual projects, thus the concept-mapping process was used to create a conceptually cohesive vision for research. In the second example, the mapping process was used to facilitate personal reflection and peer collaboration around an existing evaluation plan. Students in the first example completed all maps and shared them in small groups, whereas in the second example, in some cases only group-level maps were developed. These minor distinctions associated with the final product may very well have reflected the underlying purpose for which the mapping process was created. Thus, we encourage instructors to consider using a mapping process to both yield the physical artifact of a completed concept map of phases of the research process, but also to encourage hierarchical and relational conceptual thinking even if the process does not yield a formalized map. We found that valuing both the mapping process as well as the map led to conceptual clarity amongst our students that was represented in the quality of research plans, the interpretation of findings (evaluation course), and communication of the research process and findings (Emig, 1977; O'Rourke et al., 2011; Villalon & Calvo, 2011).

"Road maps" to guide next steps.

The instructor in the first example held a clear expectation that the finalized concept maps would act as a tool to organize the complexity of the research process in a way that would guide writing during proposal development. In contrast, the finalized concept maps in the second example were proposed as a tool to refine the evaluation plan and for communicating the research process to consumers, clients, and current/future evaluation team members. In a way, the final product maps represented a snapshot of the state of the project at a particular point in time and as such, were important artifacts of the history of the project. In both instances, the instructors expected final maps to be products that would guide the next steps of the research or evaluation process (Nesbit & Adesope, 2013; Schraw & Paik, 2013). Thus, beyond the confines of the course, the students were able to have a clear road map even in the absence of immediate instructor input.

Implementing concept mapping during instruction.

Finally, we were struck with the range of ways that students chose to represent their conceptual process in the concept map graphics. In some cases, the maps were extremely detailed, whereas other graphics were quite simple. Maps for both examples represented both procedural and nonprocedural conceptual relationships, but they certainly differed in form. This led us to consider the potential benefits or drawbacks of templates or formalized concept mapping instruction. On the one hand, perhaps concept maps should derive from a natural, creative process that is customized to an individual's way of knowing. On the other hand, some students may focus more on the actual construction of the graphic, worrying that the graphic is not "perfect," which may interfere with the generative conceptual process that is the actual goal. In this case, provision of templates may be beneficial. Therefore, during instruction it may be particularly important to recognize individual differences among students in their comfort level for constructing concept maps.

CONCLUSION

Helping graduate students to develop into competent researchers is a primary emphasis of graduate instruction. Competencies needed to become graduate researchers include an accurate understanding and skills for conceptualizing research, designing research, analyzing data, and technical writing (Marchand et al., 2013). The examples described in this chapter demonstrate how visual displays may serve as a tool to nurture conceptual understanding, planning, guide writing, and communicate research processes and outcomes (Olafson et al., 2013). Table 4 includes some recommendations for how concept maps may be used to facilitate these competencies in practice. Whether and how the use of visual displays facili-

TABLE 4. Concept Maps in Practice

Competency	Description	Recommendations for Practice
Demonstrate Conceptual Understanding	Concept maps develop and demonstrate understanding of relations amongst study constructs and how design will address research questions.	• Distinguish between central and peripheral constructs and activities • Determine nature of relationships among research components and processes • Using only the information in concept maps, describe the study to peers; revise map components that are conceptually unclear or missing
Plan Research	Concept maps create a graphical representation of the research process; check for consistency amongst procedures, sampling, measurement, and analytic approach.	• Link specific actions of the design, data collection, and analyses processes in map • Discard planned collection of data not included in concept map • Create different layers of map to illustrate activities within the data collection process
Guide Writing	Concept maps serve as a roadmap for the writing process; researchers translate graphical representation of ideas to technical writing in formal text.	• Use concept map to develop argument structure of text • Ensure literature review includes constructs and processes displayed in concept maps • Check to ensure text is in line with logic of connections displayed in concept maps
Communicate Process & Outcomes	Concept maps function as an aid when describing the research process and components of research studies.	• Create opportunities to share maps with a research novice to check logical consistency of process and results • Use maps to negotiate shared understanding of studies involving multiple group members

tates the development of research competencies in graduate researchers compared to instructional methods not guided by visual displays would be an excellent avenue for future research.

REFERENCES

Burke, J., O'Campo, P., Peak, G., Gielen, A., McDonnell, K., & Trochim, W. (2005). An introduction to concept mapping as a participatory public health research method. *Qualitative Health Research, 15*(10), 1392–1410.

Cañas, A. J., Hill, G., Carff, R., Suri, N., Lott, J., Eskridge, T., Gómez, G., . . . Carvajal, R. (2004). In A. J. Cañas, J. D. Novak, & F. M. González (Eds.), *Concept maps: Theory, methodology, technology. Proceedings of the First International Conference on Concept Mapping* (pp. 125–133). Pamplona, Spain: Universidad Pública de Navarra.

Creswell, J. (2013). *Qualitative inquiry and research design: Choosing among five approaches* (3rd ed.). Los Angeles, CA: Sage.

Creswell, J., Clark, J., Gutmann, V., & Hanson, W. (2008). An expanded typology for classifying mixed methods research into designs. *The Mixed Methods Reader*, 159–196.

Daley, B. J. (2004). Using concept maps in qualitative research. *Proceedings of the First International Conference on Concept Mapping*, pp. 14–17.

Emig, J. (1977). Writing as a mode of learning. *College Composition and Communication, 28*, 122–128.

Herman-Kinney, N., & Reynolds, L. (2003). *Handbook of symbolic interactionism*. New York, NY: AltaMira.

Marchand, G. C., Schraw, G., & Olafson, L. (2013). The role of deliberate practice in the development of graduate researchers. In M. Shaugnessey (Ed.), *Developing skills, talents and abilities*. Hauppauge, NY. Nova Science.

Mertens, D. M., & Wilson, A. T. (2012). *Program evaluation theory and practice: A comprehensive guide*. New York, NY: Guilford.

Moreno, R., & Mayer, R. (1999). Cognitive principles of multimedia learning: The role of modality and contiguity. *Journal of Educational Psychology, 91*(2), 358–368.

Nesbit, J., & Adesope, O. (2013). Concept maps for learning: Theory, research, and design. In G. Schraw & M. McCrudden (Eds.), *Learning through visual displays* (pp. 303–328). Charlotte, NC: Information Age.

Novak, J. D. (1977). *A theory of education*. Ithaca, NY: Cornell University Press.

Novak, J. D. & Cañas, A. J. (2008). The theory underlying concept maps and how to construct and use them. *CMAP*. Retrieved from http://cmap.ihmc.us/Publications/ResearchPapers/TheoryUnderlyingConceptMaps.pdf

Olafson, L., Feucht, F., & Marchand, G. (2013). A typology of visual displays in qualitative analyses. In G. Schraw & M. McCrudden (Eds.), *Learning through visual displays* (pp. 359–385). Charlotte, NC: Information Age.

O'Rourke, S. T., Calvo, R. A., & McNamara, D. S. (2011). Visualizing topic flow in students' essays. *Educational Technology & Society, 14* (3), 4–15.

Paas, F., Renkel, A., & Sweller, J. (2004). Cognitive load theory: Instructional implications of the interaction between information structures and cognitive architecture. *Instructional Science, 32,* 1–8.

Plano Clark, V. L., & Creswell, J. W. (2011). *Designing and conducting mixed methods research*. Thousand Oaks, CA: Sage.

Putney, L. G., Wink, J., & Perkins, P. (2006). Teachers as researchers: Using the critical action research matrix application (CARMA) for reflexive classroom inquiry. *Florida Journal of Teacher Education, 9,* 23–36.

Schraw, G., & Paik, E. (2013). Toward a typology of instructional visual displays. In G. Schraw, M. McCrudden, & D. Robinson (Eds.), *Learning through visual displays* (pp. 97–129). Charlotte, NC: Information Age.

Skolits, G. J., Morrow, J. A., & Burr, E. M. (2009). Reconceptualizing evaluator roles. *American Journal of Evaluation, 30*, 275–295.

Tufte, E. (2001). *The visual display of quantitative information* (2nd ed.). Cheshire, CT: Graphics.

Villalon, J., & Calvo, R. A. (2011). Concept maps as cognitive visualizations of writing assignments. *Educational Technology & Society, 14*(3), 16–27.

Vygotsky, L. (1978). *Mind in society: The development of higher mental processes*. Cambridge, MA: Harvard University Press.

W. K. Kellogg Foundation (2004). Logic model development guide. *W. K. Kellogg Foundation*. Retrieved from http://www.wkkf.org/resource-directory/resource/2006/02/wk-kellogg-foundation-logic-model-development-guide

SECTION IV

VISUAL DISPLAYS TO REPORT TESTING AND ASSESSMENT DATA

CHAPTER 9

THE GRAPHIC REPRESENTATION OF FINDINGS FROM THE NATIONAL CENTER ON ASSESSMENT AND ACCOUNTABILITY FOR SPECIAL EDUCATION

Keith Zvoch and Joseph J. Stevens

ABSTRACT

In recent years, the collection and analysis of longitudinal data has become more widespread and technically sophisticated. At the same time, there has been a push for greater communication between researchers and practitioners. One means for translating and more broadly sharing the results of complicated longitudinal data analyses is use of the visual display. Visual displays incorporate many features that provide a summarization of major data patterns and trends, and facilitate the com-

Use of Visual Displays in Research and Testing: Coding, Interpreting, and Reporting Data,
pages 237–264.
237

munication of information to diverse audiences. In this chapter, visual displays are used as a vehicle to demonstrate graphing principles and illustrate a subset of the research findings obtained by the National Center on Assessment and Accountability for Special Education, a federally funded research center charged with investigating the achievement growth of students with and without disabilities.

Keywords: visual displays, longitudinal data analysis, special education

The collection and analysis of longitudinal data have become increasingly widespread and technically sophisticated (Zvoch, 2014). At the same time, there is an increasing need for research results to be expressed and communicated in ways that are more meaningful and actionable for practitioners and diverse stakeholder groups. The accessibility of complex findings has recently been taken up by federal funding agencies. Applicants for federal funding are now required to directly address how research findings and products will be disseminated and utilized by a range of audiences (Institute for Education Sciences, 2014; National Science Foundation, 2013). Under the new guidelines, researchers are expected to create products and convey findings in less technical publications designed for practitioners and policymakers as well as in traditional peer-reviewed journal publications and academic conference presentations. In light of the push toward greater accessibility, the purpose of this chapter is to demonstrate how visual displays can serve as a mechanism for translating complex analytic results into a form that is informative and easily understandable for diverse stakeholders. Data from the National Center on Assessment and Accountability for Special Education (NCAASE), a federally funded research center, provide the basis for each of the displays.

Brief Historical Overview

The use of visual displays to illustrate complex patterns and trends has a long history that predates modern quantitative analysis of longitudinal data structures. Playfair (1786) is widely cited as providing the groundbreaking examples of how to transform tabular data into rich and informative graphic representations. Playfair is most recognized for his foundational work on the descriptive display of quantitative time series data by virtue of development, refinement, and/or creative use of pie, line, and bar charts (Tufte, 2001; Wainer, 2005, 2009). His contemporary, John F. W. Hershel, is credited with inventing the scatterplot that was later popularized by Francis Galton and is now ubiquitous throughout all fields of science (Friendly & Denis, 2005; Tufte, 2001; Wainer, 2009). Further development and innovative use of graphical data displays continued throughout the 19th century. Publication of a variety of climatic, military, and public health charts, maps, and plots (see Tufte, 1990, 1997, 2001; Wainer, 1997, 2005, 2009) offered rich two-dimensional representations of multivariate relationships and demonstrated the utility that the visual display held for scientific description and inference. However, it was not until the early 20th century that the first formal guidelines for the creation and use of graphs were developed by a group of academic and governmental representatives. The Joint Committee on Standards for Graphic Presentation (1915) provided 17 elementary design principles that were to serve as uniform standards for the orientation, scaling, and presentation of graphs.

Modern guidelines and recommendations regarding the use and misuse of data displays and their production have been articulated in a number of sources (Bertin, 1983; Cleveland, 1985, 1995; Huff, 1954; Schmid, 1983; Tufte, 1997, 2001; Wainer, 1984, 1997, 2005). These works provide rich examples that extensively illustrate how graphs and charts can be used to represent or distort the presentation of data. For some authors, graphical excellence is achieved when data density is maximized (i.e., the greatest number of ideas is presented in the shortest time and space), substantive multivariate relationships are accurately conveyed, and meaningful patterns and trends are displayed clearly and precisely (Tufte, 2001). For others, graphics and graphical forms logically derive from a grammatical structure that follows formal mathematical and aesthetic rules for representing data (Wilkinson, 2005). Conversely, graphical distortion emerges when labeling is sparse and inaccurate, consistency in scaling and proportionality is not observed, and meaning is convoluted by the inclusion of artistic decoration or "chartjunk" (Tufte, 2001; Wainer, 1984, 1997, 2005).

In addition to the development of rules and guidelines for the construction and use of visual displays, attention has also been devoted to elucidating theories of graphical perception. Much of this work centers on the perceptual tasks involved in the coding of visual information (Cleveland & McGill, 1984) and the manner in which components of memory facilitate or hinder graph comprehension (Kosslyn, 1994; Pinker, 1990). Another area of graphics research has focused on identifying general design principles that reduce cognitive load and complexity and boost information processing capacity (e.g., Hoffman & Schraw, 2010; Lane & Sándor, 2009; Robinson & Kiewra, 1995). This research draws heavily on learning theory and the ways in which the graphical display of data can be used to activate new and existing schema, promote integration and transfer of information across cognitive domains, and enable the construction of mental models that facilitate deeper comprehension of focal concepts and contextual information (see Schraw, McCrudden, & Robinson, 2013).

Contemporary Applications

Although visual displays are now commonly used to illustrate the results of descriptive data analyses, some of the key advances in exploratory graphical techniques have occurred relatively recently. The innovations (e.g., stem and leaf display, box-and-whisker plot) that allow the researcher to quickly organize, summarize, and present major characteristics of a dataset are attributable to John Tukey. Tukey's descriptive data displays (Tukey, 1977) form an integral part of the contemporary data-screening process (e.g., evaluating distributional shape, identification of unique or outlying values) and serve as an invaluable means for communicating descriptive statistical information (Wainer, 2005). In addition to their use in descriptive data presentations, visual displays are also increasingly used to evaluate and convey the results of more complex model-based data analyses. For example, residual plots enable analysts to visually detect outlying cases and evaluate the extent to which certain statistical model assumptions are met (e.g., Pedhazur, 1997). Similarly, the visual display of group-specific regression functions offers a convenient and straightforward means for illustrating and contrasting group performance at one measurement occasion or over multiple points in time (e.g., Singer & Willett, 2003).

Graphical display also plays a central role in the presentation and validation of results obtained from regression discontinuity (RD) and interrupted time series (ITS) designs, two increasingly popular alternatives to the randomized experiment. RD and ITS designs derive strength of interpretation from knowledge and analysis of the selection mechanism used to assign individuals or units to treatment (Shadish, Cook, & Campbell, 2002). The designs are conceptually similar in that a specific point along a continuum serves as a basis for the counterfactual. In RD designs, the treatment effect (if present) is observed at the cutoff score used to assign participants to the treatment and control groups. In ITS designs, the treatment effect is observed at a point in time contiguous with the onset of treatment. In both designs, strength of inference depends on the absence of a spurious relationship coincidental with the cut point and statistical conclusion validity in modeling the pre-post relationship (Shadish et al., 2002).

In practice, the examination of RD/ITS data begins with a scatterplot of pretest and posttest scores. If a treatment effect is present, visual evidence of a discontinuity at the cutpoint should be observed. Figure 1 illustrates an RD design with a pretest cutoff score of 30. In the example, treatment is delivered to those who scored < 30 on the pretest. The figure on the left shows absence of treatment, the figure on right shows a hypothetical treatment effect. The solid line(s) in the interior of the figures are the lines of best fit for each group. The dashed line in the figure on the right represents the unobserved, theoretical counterfactual (i.e., the result that would have occurred if the treatment group had not received the intervention). The size of the discontinuity (at the cutpoint) in the figure on the right represents the magnitude of the treatment effect. The visual presentation of results contextualizes the design and score distributions, and simultaneously scales the treatment effect. The visual presentation also makes the RD (and ITS) design and associated analyses more accessible to those who are more accustomed to thinking about a group mean contrast rather than intercept (or slope) differences.

Beyond its communicative value, graphical analysis serves a particularly useful role in the detection of failures of RD model assumptions and/or the identification of irregularities or complexities of functional form that may not be apparent in model-based statistical analysis. To evaluate, different smoothing and fitting functions are applied to the data and separate graphs are fitted on either side of the cutpoint. Smoothing and fitting functions make different assumptions about

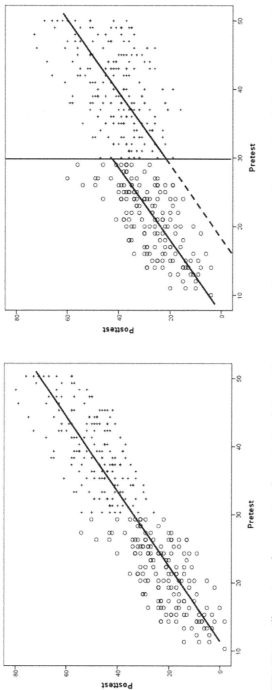

FIGURE 1.   Illustration of a regression discontinuity design with a pretest cutoff score at 30. The figure on the left shows absence of treatment, the figure on right shows a treatment effect. The solid line(s) in the interior of the figures are the lines of best fit for each group. The dashed line represents the unobserved, theoretical counterfactual.

the data and apply different methods and/or algorithms to summarize the data. In practice, nonparametric regression techniques are used to create a variety of local scatterplots using different bandwidths or "bins" (Imbens & Lemieux, 2008). Bins are created by dividing the assignment variable distribution into smaller intervals on the premise that any relationship between variables, even if complex, can be well fitted within a small interval. Nonparametric regression fits a function within the bin, and then repeats the process across all nonoverlapping bins in the region of the cutpoint. A variety of figures are then created to demonstrate RD design results using different bins or bandwidths. This procedure ensures that there is no influence locally that occurs from more distal data points. Figure 2 presents two local linear regressions for an RD design with a cutoff score of 30 with 30% smoothing on the left and 60% smoothing on the right. Across the two figures, it can be seen that there is more irregularity in the pretest-posttest relationship with less smoothing. However, most importantly, the figures demonstrate that regardless of the degree of smoothing, a clear discontinuity, and therefore a treatment effect remains evident at the cutpoint of 30. The use of graphical displays thus provides mechanisms for visualizing relationships as well as evaluating the tenability of more complex statistical model-based analyses.

National Center on Assessment and Accountability for Special Education (NCAASE)

As visual displays have begun to play an increasingly important role in the descriptive presentation of data and the evaluation of model-based analyses, they can also serve as a vehicle to enhance communication between producers and consumers of research. Visual displays are particularly helpful when the results of technically sophisticated research designs and statistical analyses must be conveyed to diverse stakeholder groups or when results are too complex to be easily described or summarized in text or tables. The displays that follow demonstrate and highlight several of the key findings that have emerged from NCAASE, a federally funded research center in the United States. NCAASE has been funded to conduct research that provides evidence about the developmental achievement progress of students with disabilities, and the technical properties of alternative accountability models where student academic growth is used to describe and evaluate school effectiveness.

NCAASE's 5-year program of growth modeling research draws on summative annual test scores from four states (North Carolina, Arizona, Oregon, and Pennsylvania) to model and compare student learning outcomes using different longitudinal procedures, including growth models, transition matrices, as well as residual gain and value-added models. Formative and interim assessments are also used to document developmental progress when measurement of performance occurs more frequently than once per year, as is currently the case in most high-stakes accountability testing under the No Child Left Behind Act of 2001 (NCLB, 2002). NCAASE researchers also conduct growth modeling studies using covari-

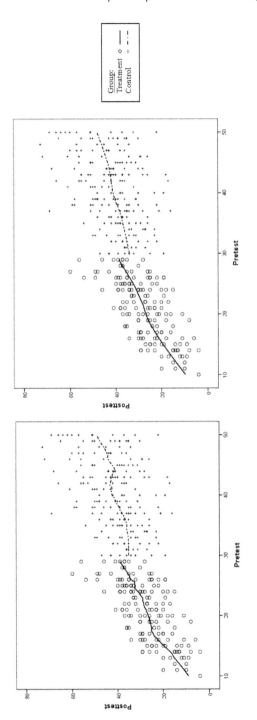

Figure 2. Two local linear regressions for an RD design with a cutoff score of 30 with 30% smoothing on the left and 60% smoothing on the right.

ates that provide teachers and school leaders with contextual information about students' knowledge and skills that may be useful in designing interventions to change the trajectory of growth.

A particular focus of NCASSE's work is on the learning outcomes of students with disabilities (SWD), one of the targeted subgroups in NCLB. The interest in the achievement progress of SWD stems in part from the impact particular assessment and accountability choices can have on the reliability and validity of disaggregated test scores at the school or higher levels (e.g., Kiplinger, 2008; Linn, 2008). Further, numerous investigators have drawn attention to schools' poor performance with this group of students and the implications of low performance for schools' ability to meet accountability expectations (McDonnell, McLaughlin, & Morison, 1997; Schulte, Osborne, & Erchul, 1998). For example, in a 3-state study of schools that failed to make their adequate yearly progress (AYP) targets, schools' failure with the performance of SWD was the most frequent reason (Eckes & Swando, 2009). With many states now reporting that over 70% of students with disabilities are below expectations in reading and mathematics on annual statewide achievement tests, there is a critical need to provide accurate information to schools about whether their practices with this subgroup are effective. Moreover, the extent to which student achievement performance and growth differs not only on the basis of disability status, but also on exceptionality classification and whether special education performance trends represent a closing, widening, or maintenance of the achievement gap continues to receive attention (see Morgan, Farkas, & Wu, 2009, 2011; Shin, Davison, Long, Chan, & Heistad, 2013).

Summary and Purpose

The rate and variability of student achievement growth remains a central issue in educational research and educational policy. For researchers and practitioners, questions regarding how students learn and why performance varies across population subgroups are at the heart of conceptual and methodological efforts that seek to elucidate the contextual environments and instructional conditions that promote effective and equitable achievement outcomes (Raudenbush, 2004; Raudenbush & Williams, 1995). However, the same design and modeling advances that have transformed how researchers conceptualize the collection and analysis of longitudinal data have also made the communication of analytic findings more challenging. With this backdrop, the current chapter draws on selected results from one NCAASE data source to demonstrate the visual presentation of a series of longitudinal data analyses. The graphical displays are used to highlight and communicate several of the key findings that have emerged from the Center's work.

Data Source

Although NCAASE is working with data from four partner states, the illustrations presented in this chapter are all based on data drawn from the North Carolina state assessment system. These data were collected by the state as part of operational accountability testing conducted in the spring of each school year in grades 3–8. Currently, multiple cohorts of data are being analyzed by NCAASE researchers. Each academic year cohort (2001–2002 to 2012–2013) consists of over 100,000 students before exclusions are made to create analytic samples without missing data or untested students. From North Carolina state master files, NCAASE researchers have created different analytic samples in order to answer a series of research questions that center on the academic performance of students and the variability of student outcomes within and between schools with a particular focus on the performance of special education students with specific exceptionalities. The examples below stem from several of the investigations and analyses that have been conducted to date. Details on methods and procedures for data preparation and construction of the analytic samples can be found in the original studies (Biancarosa & Zvoch, 2013; Schulte & Stevens, in press; Stevens, Schulte, Elliott, Nese, & Tindal, 2015).

Outcome Measure

In the examples provided below, the outcome measure was student scale scores on the state reading or mathematics test. Scale scores were constructed based on vertical linking using a common items design, making longitudinal growth analysis appropriate. Technical manuals are available that provide reliability and validity data for the End of Grade (EOG) Reading and Mathematics Tests, as well as information about scaling and standard setting (North Carolina Department of Public Instruction, 2004, 2006). For reading, internal consistency estimates from .92 to .94 for grades 6–8; for mathematics, the estimates were above .90 for all grades studied (i.e., grades 3–7). Criterion validity was investigated by correlating scores and achievement levels with teacher judgments of student achievement and expected grade. Evidence of criterion-related validity was demonstrated through moderate to strong Pearson correlation coefficients with associated variables (e.g., assigned achievement level by expected grade, teacher judgment of achievement by assigned achievement level, teacher judgment of achievement by expected grade, teacher judgment of achievement by reading and math scale score, and expected grade by reading and math scale score).

Predictor Variables

Students' exceptionality classifications serve as the main predictor variable in the following examples. During the period of the study, the state utilized 14 disability classifications, plus a code for students designated as academically gifted.

The classifications in order of prevalence were academically or intellectually gifted (AIG; ~10%), specific learning disabled (SLD; ~6%), other health impairment (OHI; ~1.5%), educable mentally handicapped (EMH; ~0.7%), emotional impairment (EH; ~0.5%), speech-language impairment (SLI; ~0.4%), autism (ASD; ~0.2%), hearing impairment (HI; ~0.1%), orthopedic impairment (OI; ~0.1%), visual impairment (VI; < 0.1%), and traumatic brain injured (TBI; < 0.1%). Three additional classifications each represented a very small number of students: deaf, severe/profound mentally disabled, and multiple impairments. Dichotomous indicators were created to represent the disability/exceptionality classifications with sufficient group membership. General education students served as the reference group for most comparisons. In other comparisons, students without disabilities (SWoD), consisting of general education and academically gifted students, were contrasted with the group of students who had a disability classification (SWD). An indicator contrasting specific learning disabled students (LD) with general education students (GE) was also created. Learning disability status (LD/GE) was then crossed with select sociodemographic characteristics in a subset of analyses.

Analytic Models

Descriptive and inferential analyses have been used to summarize and estimate the reading and mathematics achievement growth of students with and without disabilities. Descriptive methods have been used to report mean performance and year-to-year growth outcomes for all students by exceptionality category. Two- and three-level multilevel models have been used to estimate growth trajectories and relationships between growth parameters and exceptionality classifications at the student and school level. In multilevel growth models, the first level is used to represent measurement occasions and estimate a growth trajectory for each student. The second level in the structure represents student characteristics, and the third level represents school context, characteristics, and programs. An important feature of the multilevel model is that variation in performance can be separated out into the student and school levels. Another feature of the model is the ability to estimate an intercept and a slope for each individual and each school. Equation 1 describes a Level-1 model that specifies linear and quadratic growth parameters. In the equation, Y is the expected scale score for student i at time t, π_{0i} is the initial status or intercept for student i at time 0, π_{1i} is the linear rate of change, π_{2i} is the quadratic curvature term that represents the acceleration or deceleration in each student's growth trajectory, and e_{ti} is the residual for each student.

$$\text{Level-1 Model:} \quad Y_{ti} = \pi_{0i} + \pi_{1i}*(\text{Time}_{ti}) + \pi_{2i}*(\text{Time2}_{ti}) + e_{ti} \quad (1)$$

At Level-2, the Level-1 parameters are modeled using multiple dichotomous vectors to represent student disability/exceptionality classifications. The Level-2 equations for the initial status and growth rate parameters are as follows:

Level-2 Model: $\pi_{0i} = \beta_{00} + \beta_{01}*(\text{Exceptionality Classification}_i) + r_{0i}$ (2)

$\pi_{1i} = \beta_{10} + \beta_{11}*(\text{Exceptionality Classification}_i) + r_{1i}$ (3)

$\pi_{2i} = \beta_{20} + \beta_{21}*(\text{Exceptionality Classification}_i) + r_{2i}$ (4)

In 3-level models, student growth trajectories are estimated as above but with explicit recognition of the nesting of students within schools. In the 3-level model, the outcome is the expected scale score at time t for student i in school j. The nesting of students in schools requires that variation in student growth trajectory parameters be modeled as a function of associated school means and residual terms at Level 2 and variation in school growth parameters be modeled as a function of associated grand means and residual terms at Level 3. The 3-level models enable the estimation of a mean achievement score and mean growth rate for each school in each subject area.

To further contextualize the descriptive and inferential presentations and provide a benchmark for interpreting students' achievement growth, year-to-year growth effect sizes and achievement gap effect sizes between student exceptionality groups and students without disabilities have been calculated. Year-to-year effect sizes (ES) for general education students and students from each exceptionality category are identified by computing the mean difference from one academic year to the next in ratio to the pooled standard deviation for the 2 years. To estimate achievement gaps between SWD and SWoD, the mean performance in reading and mathematics each year for students in a particular exceptionality category is compared to the mean performance of either all students without disabilities (general education and academically/intellectually gifted students combined) or general education students. Achievement gap ES is computed by taking the mean difference of interest and dividing by the standard deviation of the scores for all students in that grade (Bloom, Hill, Black, & Lipsey, 2008).

Summary of Results

In the subset of NCAASE's work that was drawn from the North Carolina database, several consistent patterns and trends have emerged. In brief, analytic results indicate that (a) student academic performance tends to be best described by a decelerating growth function; (b) status-based differences between exceptionality groups and students without disabilities tend to be large while growth rates remain relatively constant; (c) portrayals of student performance vary on the basis of how special education membership is defined; (d) academic performance may depend in part on the joint relationship between learning disability status and demographic background characteristics; (e) academic performance and growth varies widely within and between schools; (f) school mean performance is generally not associated or weakly associated with school mean growth; and (g) statistical distinctions in school performance are difficult to identify. For teachers, school leaders, and policymakers, summary statements regarding the shape of growth functions, the amount of within and between-school variability, and/or the presentation of tables of coefficients may not strongly resonate or provide an actionable basis for reform. Yet, when presented in a visual medium, a range of stakeholders may be able to gain a thorough understanding of key data patterns and trends and begin to consider the implications the findings have for directing policy efforts. The displays that follow are used to augment the textual and tabular presentation of results and provide visual depictions that represent and convey the meaning of NCAASE findings.

Mean Observed Growth by Exceptionality Category

The most fundamental representation of longitudinal achievement outcomes is a time series plot of student scores or group means. The time series plot is a simple descriptive presentation that specifies the outcome of interest (e.g., mean mathematics performance) on the y-axis and a time metric (e.g., grade) on the x-axis. Distinctive markers and lines are used to identify each student subgroup or exceptionality classification. The time series plot conveys the general learning trend as well as status and growth-based differences between the subgroups of interest. Its greatest strength and value is the concise summarization of complex statistical results. The straightforward summary enables consumers to grasp key data patterns and trends that may not be readily evident in a table of coefficients, including status and growth-related group comparisons. However, when creating a time series graph, it is important to keep the ratio of y- to x-axis proportional. Exaggerating one axis can make the performance gains appear more or less impressive and group differences more or less stark. Distinct markers and labels are also requisite in order to facilitate the identification and comparison of subgroups.

In Figure 3, the mean mathematics performance by student group and grade is presented. In the figure, it can be seen that most trajectories are typically curvilinear in form, with decelerating growth across grades. All student groups demonstrated growth over time, although there are some differences in both rate of change and rate of curvature for some groups. In terms of level of performance at Grade 3, the order of growth trajectories from highest to lowest performing was Academically Gifted to Educable Mentally Handicapped.[1] Over time, there was some crossing of growth trajectories, but by the end of Grade 6, the initial performance level differences were largely preserved. It should also be noted that with the exception of the educable Mentally Handicapped Group and those with an Emotional Disturbance at Grade 3, all other student groups' average performance was above the North Carolina proficiency cutpoint at each assessment occasion.

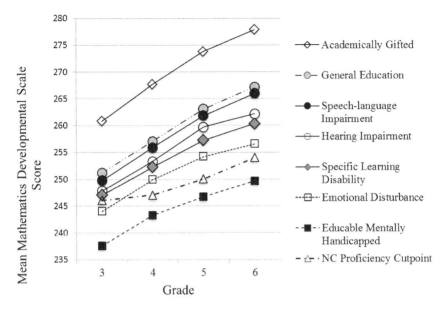

FIGURE 3. Mean mathematics achievement by grade and exceptionality category.

Growth Effect Sizes

Additional context for interpretation of student performance trends can be provided by calculating and graphically representing the change in achievement growth from year to year expressed as an effect size. Effect size estimates provide a means for interpreting the substantive impact of an intervention or the standardized change between two measurement occasions. Once calculated, effect size estimates can be compared between subgroups, samples, or studies to provide an empirical benchmark (e.g., normative growth expectations) for interpreting results (Hill, Bloom, Black, & Lipsey, 2008; Lipsey et al., 2012). Figure 4 shows year-to-year standardized growth in mathematics for general education students, students who were academically gifted, and students in each exceptionality category. Mathematics achievement growth effect size is represented on the y-axis and the time variable adjacent grade transitions are represented on the x-axis. Figure 4 demonstrates that learning growth from Grade 3 to Grade 4 is positive for all student groups, ranging from 0.75 for the Hearing Impairment and Learning Disabilities groups to 1.19 for the Educable Mental Handicapped students. Figure 4 also reveals that grade transition effect sizes generally diminish across grades, a result similar to that reported in other studies (Bloom et al., 2008; Hill et al., 2008). For general education students, the negative trend results in a decrease in ES from 0.78 in grade transition 3–4 to 0.48 in grade transition 5–6. It can

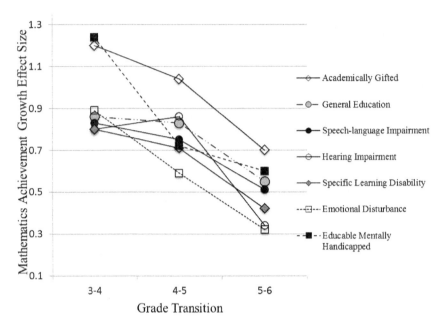

FIGURE 4. Mathematics achievement growth effect size at each grade transition by exceptionality category.

also be seen that students who were Academically Gifted and Educable Mental Handicapped students both maintained relatively higher growth throughout the grades studied, while students with an Emotional Disturbance had a particularly steep learning decline.

Time-Varying Special Education Status

Participation in special education can be defined in multiple ways and portrayals of achievement growth for students with disabilities (SWD) may vary depending on how and when analysts identify special education status (Schulte & Stevens, in press). In most longitudinal studies, special education status is identified on the first wave or measurement occasion (Grade 3 here) and there is no accounting of entrances to or exits from special education status in later grades. Schulte and Stevens (in press) identified special education status in four ways: (a) whether a student was in special education at wave 1, (b) whether a student was ever in special education in any grade; (c) whether a student was always in special education in every grade; or (d) their current-grade special education status (which could vary from one grade to another).

Using these criteria for defining special education status, Figure 5 depicts the mathematics achievement gap for students in special education across grades 3 to 6 using effect sizes. In the figure, achievement gap effect size is represented

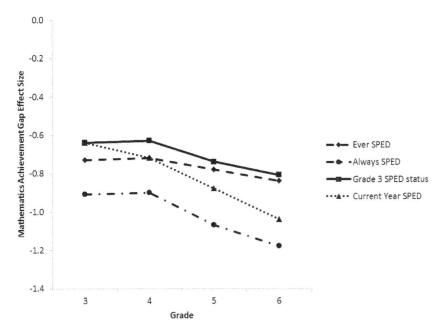

FIGURE 5. Mathematics achievement gap effect sizes between SWoD and SWD when SWD is identified at Wave 1, Ever, Always, or in the Current Year.

on the y-axis and grade is represented on the x-axis. Students without disabilities (SWoD) serve as the referent. Achievement gap effect sizes are computed by subtracting the mean for the special education group from the mean for the referent group and dividing by the pooled standard deviation (Bloom et al., 2008). Achievement gap effect sizes provide direct indication of the magnitude of group differences and their display allows quick assessment of the size and direction of disparate performance outcomes. Inspection of Figure 5 reveals that while the mathematics achievement gap increases over time, achievement gap group differences remain relatively stable across the period of study. The one exception is for students identified using the Current Year definition. Using this definition, the gap in performance steadily increases through grade 6. Otherwise, students who were classified on the basis of receiving special education services in Grade 3 had the smallest gap and students who were classified on the basis of receiving special education services every academic year had the largest disparity in mathematics performance. In comparison to the referent group of SWoD, student exceptionality group performance ranged from two thirds to over one standard deviation across the study period. The variability in performance outcomes thus suggests that ignoring the time-varying entry and exits of students into or out of special education may lead to nonrepresentative results and interpretations.

Interactions Between Disability Status and Sociodemographic Characteristics

In addition to disability classification, academic performance can be contextualized by examining whether student achievement growth is moderated by sociodemographic characteristics. For example, evidence indicates that economically disadvantaged students start school behind their peers and learn at a somewhat slower rate than students from more advantaged backgrounds (Jordon, Kaplan, & Hanich, 2002; Lee & Burkam, 2002). However, what is typically not investigated or known is whether student background characteristics and disability status interact. When simply added as predictors in models of achievement growth, student sociodemographic and disability status indicators identify the partial regression relationship between each predictor and outcome, but do not directly assess either the "main effects" or the interaction of the factors of interest (see Hayes, 2013; Jaccard & Turrisi, 2003). Only by explicitly including product-interaction terms can one test whether disability status and sociodemographic characteristics interact in the prediction of growth outcomes in the longitudinal model.

As an example, Figure 6 presents the interaction between learning disability status (LD-general education, GE) and ethnic minority status (White-Native American) on the mathematics achievement growth of a sample of students in North Carolina. When presenting the results of interaction effects, data displays can be particularly revealing as the interrelations among variables in interactions are typically complex and may often be easier to visualize than to describe in text. In Figure 6, mean mathematics achievement is represented on the y-axis and the time variable (grade) is represented on the x-axis. The interior of the figure displays the growth trajectories for each of the four groups (i.e., GE-White; GE-Native American, LD-White, LD-Native American). As can be seen, ethnic minority status interacted with learning disability status for intercepts, slopes, and the curvature of growth. More specifically, Figure 6 demonstrates that while all subgroups showed positive growth over grades, the learning rate was greatest for GE-White students and lowest for LD-Native American students. It should also be noted that after fourth grade, the growth trajectories of the two disability groups were quite similar. The nature and extent of the similarities and differences in group performance thus become readily evident with aid of a data display.

School Performance

The desire to hold schools accountable for their effects on student achievement has led to interest in design and analytic approaches that facilitate more precise and less biased estimates of school performance (see Castellano & Ho, 2013; Goldschmidt et al., 2005; Heck, 2006; Stevens, 2005). The challenge for researchers and analysts is to identify and apply methodologies that aid in overcoming the nonrandom selection processes that sort families into neighborhoods and students into schools. Evidence that school performance cannot be estimated without bias

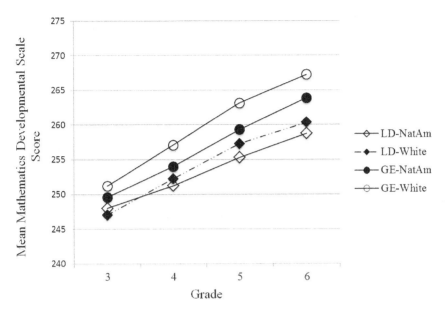

FIGURE 6.   Interaction of learning disability and ethnic minority status on mathematics achievement.

when student test scores are examined at a single point in time or with precision when successive student cohorts are compared has led a number of authors to argue for the use of longitudinal analyses of individual student performance as a more direct and accurate estimate of school effects (Downey, von Hippel, & Hughes, 2008; Raudenbush, 2004; Schulte & Villwock, 2004; Stevens, 2005; Zvoch & Stevens, 2003, 2006, 2008). Longitudinal growth models provide a degree of control over confounding factors that are stable characteristics of students over time and may enable a more valid comparison of schools that differ in the intake characteristics of their student bodies. In a series of investigations, NCAASE researchers have modeled and compared student learning outcomes using different longitudinal procedures, including growth models, transition matrices, as well as residual gain and value-added models. The following figures provide a translation of some of the modeling results that have been obtained from analysis of a subset of data from one North Carolina student cohort.

School Growth Trajectories

A companion to the descriptive time series plot is the model-based representation of individual or unit-level longitudinal performance outcomes. A model-based display represents the fitted trajectories that emerge from estimated growth parameters. Figure 7 displays a random sample of school growth trajectories ob-

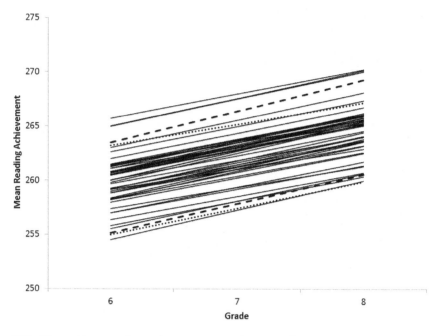

FIGURE 7.   Mean reading achievement as a function of grade level and school building.

tained from analysis of North Carolina middle school data. School mean performance is represented on the y-axis and grade is placed on the x-axis. Each line in Figure 7 shows the trajectory of reading achievement at 1 of 50 middle schools. As can be seen, there is variation from school to school both in initial status (i.e., grade 6 reading level) and in the average rates of growth over time. The variation in reading achievement is captured by the distribution of intercepts while variation in growth rates is represented in part by the crossing lines in the figure. Alternative line styles are used to highlight schools with relatively high or low growth rates at either end of the Grade 6 reading achievement distribution. Schools with a high growth rate are represented by the broken line pattern. Schools with a low growth rate are represented by the broken dot pattern. Figure 7 demonstrates that relatively strong or weak reading growth can be found throughout the reading performance distribution, an assessment that would be more difficult to derive from examination of tabular data.

School Mean Status vs. School Mean Growth

To further illustrate the school level differences in reading performance, the model-based estimates of the 50 middle school mean achievement (y-axis) and mean growth rates (x-axis) are presented in the scatterplot in Figure 8. In the figure, each circle represents a school, and its location reflects the school's mean reading achievement and growth, concisely summarizing the bivariate relationship between the two variables. For additional context, the horizontal line in the interior of the figure represents grand mean achievement in reading; the vertical line grand mean growth in reading. The two grand mean reference lines classify schools into four quadrants of school performance. The upper right quadrant contains schools with above average reading achievement in grade 6 and above average reading growth from grades 6 to 8. The lower right quadrant contains schools with below average mean scores but above average growth. The two quadrants on the left side of the figure contain schools with below average growth and either high or low mean achievement.

In Figure 8, it can be seen that schools with low mean scores have a range of growth outcomes, including some of the strongest and weakest in the sample. The same is also true for schools with relatively high 6th-grade reading achievement. These results suggest that the characterization of school performance can differ depending on whether mean achievement or mean growth is examined. Overall,

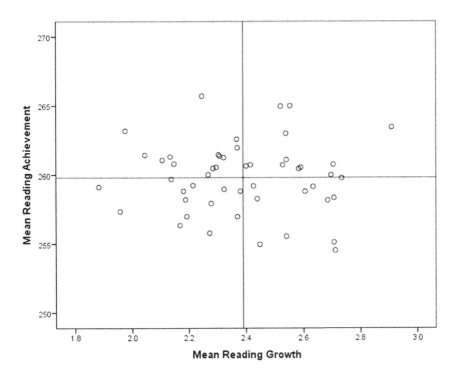

FIGURE 8.   Mean reading achievement as a function of mean reading growth.

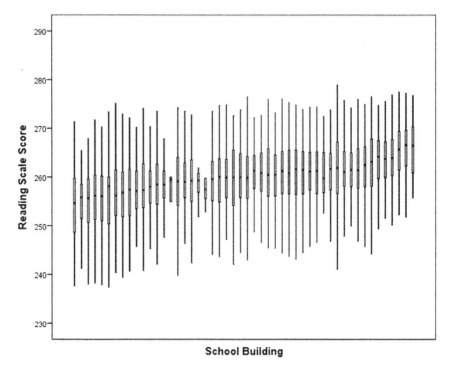

FIGURE 9.   Within- and between-school variability in 6th-grade reading achievement.

there was a slight negative relationship between mean reading achievement and growth.

Within- and Between-School Variability

In addition to displaying status and growth point estimates, it is also important to provide an indication of how much variability in achievement outcomes exists within and between schools. The "caterpillar" plots presented in Figures 9 and 10 usefully summarize and convey the achievement distribution of a sample of North Carolina middle schools. In the interior of each figure, a box and whisker plot (Tukey, 1977) is presented for each school. These plots display key information (i.e., central tendency, variability) regarding the distribution of student performance within each school. The box represents the first, second (i.e., the median), and third quartiles; the whiskers extend to 1.5x the interquartile range. The box plot is a particularly effective tool for simultaneously comparing multiple distributions. When presented as a rank ordered function of the outcome metric, unit differences in performance can easily be evaluated. The caterpillar plots demon-

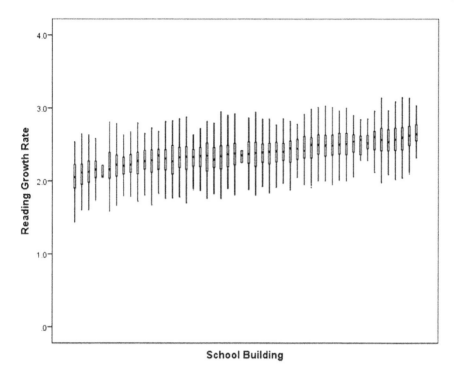

FIGURE 10. Within- and between-school variability in middle school reading achievement growth.

strate that (a) within-school variability in reading outcomes was greater than the variability observed between schools, (b) there was larger within-school variation in reading achievement (Figure 9) than in reading achievement growth (Figure 10), and (c) the heterogeneity in performance within schools makes it difficult to distinguish one school from another.

Cross-Level Interactions

Another way to evaluate school performance is to examine school differences in the relationship between a student characteristic and an achievement outcome. In the multilevel model, allowing the predictor-outcome relationship (i.e., intercept or slope) to vary randomly enables investigation of between-school differences in within-school outcomes. As an example, Figure 11 displays the relationship between special education status and reading achievement growth across the sample of 50 North Carolina middle schools. Mean reading growth is represented on the y-axis and special education status is placed on the x-axis. The slopes that relate special education status to reading growth at each of 50 middle schools

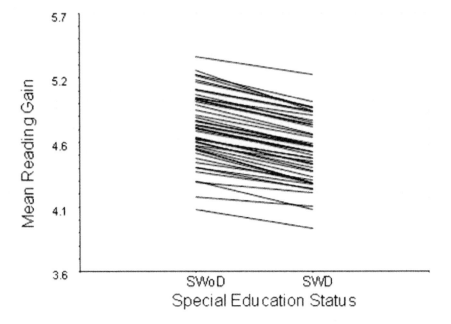

FIGURE 11. Relationship between disability status and achievement growth across a sample of North Carolina middle schools.

are presented in the interior of the figure. As can be seen, there is variation in the level and steepness of slopes. In general, the relationship is negative (i.e., SWoD advantage), but in some schools the relationship is relatively flat while in others the relationship is quite strong. It is also notable that within-schools SWoD demonstrate average reading growth that is larger than their peers with an identifiable disability, but across schools, SWD demonstrate a reading growth rate that is larger than that attained by SWoD in several instances.

SUMMARY AND CONCLUSIONS

The visual display of data is an integral part of the data screening process and is invaluable for evaluating model assumptions and presenting the results of sophisticated statistical analyses. Visual displays enable presentation of complex patterns and trends that otherwise would be difficult to describe in words and thereby promote understanding and facilitate communication with diverse stakeholder groups. Table 1 outlines some of the analytic contexts in which visual displays can be particularly useful. The contexts range from basic exploratory data applications to the evaluation and dissemination of complex model-based results.

TABLE 1. Contexts in Which Visual Displays are Particularly Useful

Analytic context	Purpose
Exploratory Data Analysis	Identify distributional form, patterns and relations in data, and outlying values
Statistical Model Assumptions	Evaluate functional form, distributional problems or dependencies, or identify influential cases
Group Contrasts	Illustrate group performance differences at a single time point or over multiple assessment occasions
Trajectories of Change	Demonstrate the shape of a growth function and patterns of change over time
Nested Designs	Display within and between group/unit variation

In general, visual displays tend to be most helpful when they can be used to illustrate distributional form, identify influential cases, and/or reveal patterns that may be obscured otherwise (e.g., comparing subpopulations of students, comparing within and between schools). Visual displays are also germane when summarizing results from technical research designs and analyses like RD and ITS, which are not as commonly known but which often offer compelling visual representation of results.

Greater appreciation of the functionality of data displays has come at an opportune time as federal grant solicitations now contain language that requires applicants to outline the manner in which research results will be disseminated. To be considered responsive, applications must contain a plan for communicating results to various constituent groups. Products can take a variety of forms (e.g., academic publications, informational websites, webinars), but researchers must explicitly address how products will be accessed and utilized by audiences that range from educational researchers to practitioners and policymakers as well as the general public. In light of recent research that demonstrates how well-constructed visual displays can serve to reduce cognitive load and complexity and boost information processing capacity (Schraw et al., 2013), the graphic representation of data may serve as a general mechanism for translating analytic results and facilitating widespread understanding among various stakeholder groups.

In this chapter, a variety of displays were used to demonstrate the use of graphics in the communication of analytic findings from NCAASE, a federal research center funded to study the achievement growth of students with and without disabilities as well as the performance of schools. The visual displays presented herein summarize the results of a subset of the work conducted by NCAASE researchers. The displays included depictions of the average trajectory of growth for different population subgroups, standardized gaps in group performance, and a demonstration of the joint relationship between a student background characteristic and mathematics growth. Displays that contrasted performance on the basis of the application of different group membership definitions (i.e., time invariant based on one occasion, multiple occasions, or time varying) and achievement outcomes (i.e., status vs. growth) were also presented. The message that emerges is that student performance varies within and across school buildings, across population subgroups, and achievement outcomes. Overall, population subgroups tend to differ with respect to achievement level, but otherwise acquire academic skills and knowledge at a relatively similar (nonlinear) rate over time. At the school level, differences in performance and growth were also observed, but the variability within schools tends to outweigh the differences between schools. Nonetheless, the data indicate that some schools are more adept at promoting effective and equitable outcomes than others.

The developments in longitudinal research design and analysis that underlie the work of NCAASE researchers have made it possible to link analytic method with the time-dependent process of academic learning. The use of longitudinal growth models enables analysts to capture the fundamental output of the educational process, the academic growth that students achieve over time. Measures of students' academic progress thus have great value for schools, districts, and the educational community as they provide some indication of the effectiveness of schooling policy and practice. However, the design and modeling advances that have transformed how researchers conceptualize the collection and analysis of longitudinal data have also made the communication of analytic findings more difficult. As demonstrated here, the graphical display of data provides a straightforward means for translating and communicating the results of complex statistical models. When displays are used to illustrate analytic findings derived from specialized data-modeling processes, the results become more meaningful and actionable. In light of the added value that visual displays offer to producers and consumers of research, greater use of graphic representation in technical and nontechnical research products and presentations is recommended.

ACKNOWLEDGEMENT

This research was funded in part by a Cooperative Service Agreement from the Institute of Education Sciences (IES) establishing the National Center on Assessment and Accountability for Special Education – NCAASE (PR/Award Number R324C110004); the findings and conclusions expressed do not necessarily represent the views or opinions of the U.S. Department of Education.

Footnote

[1] "Educable mentally handicapped" is the term used by the state of North Carolina to refer to higher performing students with intellectual disabilities who take the state's general assessment. Other students with intellectual disabilities take an alternate assessment and are not included in these analytic results.

REFERENCES

Bertin, J. (1983). Semiology of graphics: Diagrams, networks, maps. Madison: University of Wisconsin.

Biancarosa, G., & Zvoch, K. (2013, April). *School effects on the middle school reading achievement of students with disabilities: A multilevel, longitudinal analysis.* Paper presented at the annual meeting of the National Council on Measurement in Education, San Francisco, CA.

Bloom, H. S., Hill, C. J., Black, A. R., & Lipsey, M. W. (2008). Performance trajectories and performance gaps as achievement effect-size benchmarks for educational interventions. *Journal of Research on Educational Effectiveness, 1,* 289–328.

Castellano, K. E., & Ho, A. D. (2013). *A practitioner's guide to growth models.* Washington, DC: Council of Chief State School Officers.

Cleveland, W. S. (1985). *The elements of graphing data.* Summit, NJ: Hobart.

Cleveland, W. S. (1995). *Visualizing data.* Summit, NJ: Hobart.

Cleveland, W. S., & McGill, R. (1984). Graphical perception: Theory, experimentation, and application to the development of graphical methods. *Journal of the American Statistical Association, 79,* 531–554.

Downey, D. B., von Hippel, P. T., & Hughes, M. (2008). Are "failing" schools really failing? Using seasonal comparisons to evaluate school effectiveness. *Sociology of Education, 81*(3), 242–270.

Eckes, S., & Swando, J. (2009). Special education subgroups under NCLB: Issues to consider. *Teachers College Record, 111,* 2479–2504.

Friendly, M., & Denis, D. (2005). The early origins and development of the scatterplot. *Journal of the History of the Behavioral Sciences, 41*(2), 103–130.

Goldschmidt, P., Roschewski, P., Choi, K., Auty, W., Hebbler, S., Blank, R., & Williams, A. (2005). *Policymakers' guide to growth models and school accountability: How do accountability models differ?* Washington, DC: Council of Chief State School Officers.

Hayes, A. F. (2013). *Introduction to mediation, moderation, and conditional process analysis: A regression-based approach.* New York, NY: Guilford.

Heck, R. (2006). Assessing school achievement progress: Comparing alternative approaches. *Educational Administration Quarterly, 42,* 667–699.

Hill, C. J., Bloom, H. S., Black, A. R., & Lipsey, M. W. (2008). Empirical benchmarks for interpreting effect sizes in research. *Child Development Perspectives, 2*(3), 172–177.

Hoffman, B., & Schraw, G. (2010). Conceptions of efficiency: Applications in learning and problem-solving. *Educational Psychologist, 45,* 1–14.

Huff, D. (1954). *How to lie with statistics.* New York, NY: Norton.

Imbens, G. W., & Lemieux, T. (2008). Regression discontinuity designs: A guide to practice. *Journal of Econometrics, 142,* 615–635.

Institute of Education Sciences. (2014). *Request for applications: Education research grants.* Washington, DC: U. S. Department of Education.

Jaccard, J., & Turrisi, R. (2003). *Interaction effects in multiple regression* (2nd ed.). Thousand Oaks, CA: Sage.

Joint Committee on Standards for Graphic Presentation. (1915). Preliminary report published for the purpose of inviting suggestions for the benefit of the committee. *Journal of the American Statistical Association, 14,* 790–797.

Jordon, N. C., Kaplan, D., & Hanich, L. B. (2002). Achievement growth in children with learning difficulties in mathematics: Findings of a two year longitudinal study. *Journal of Educational Psychology, 94,* 586–597.

Kiplinger, V. (2008). Reliability of large-scale assessments and accountability systems. In K. Ryan & L. Shepard (Eds.), *The future of test-based educational accountability* (pp. 93–114). New York, NY: Routledge.

Kosslyn, S. M. (1994). Understanding charts and graphs. *Applied Cognitive Psychology, 3,* 185–225.

Lane, D. M., & Sándor, A. (2009). Designing better graphs by including distributional information and integrating words, numbers, and images. *Psychological Methods, 14,* 239–257.

Lee, V. E., & Burkam, D. T. (2002). *Inequality at the starting gate.* Washington, DC: Economic Policy Institute.

Linn, R. (2008). Educational accountability systems. In K. Ryan & L. Shepard (Eds.), *The future of test-based educational accountability* (pp. 3–24). New York, NY: Routledge.

Lipsey, M. W., Puzio, K., Yun, C., Hebert, M. A., Steinka-Fry, K., Cole, M. W., . . . Busick, M. D. (2012). *Translating the statistical representation of the effects of education interventions into more readily interpretable forms.* (NCSER 2013-3000). Washington, DC: National Center for Special Education Research, Institute of Education Sciences, U.S. Department of Education.

McDonnell, L. M., McLaughlin, M. J., & Morison, P. (Eds.). (1997). *Educating one and all: Students with disabilities and standards-based reform.* Washington DC: National Academies Press.

Morgan, P. L., Farkas, G., & Wu, Q. (2009). Five-year growth trajectories of kindergarten children with learning difficulties in mathematics. *Journal of Learning Disabilities, 42,* 306–321.

Morgan, P. L., Farkas, G., & Wu, Q. (2011). Kindergarten children's growth trajectories in reading and mathematics: Who falls increasingly behind? *Journal of Learning Disabilities, 44,* 472–488.

National Science Foundation (NSF). (2013). *Proposal and award policies and procedures guide* (NSF 14-1). Arlington, VA: Author

No Child Left Behind (NCLB) Act of 2001, Pub. L. No. 107–110, § 115, Stat. 1425 (2002).

North Carolina Department of Public Instruction. (2004). *The North Carolina reading comprehension tests: Technical report.* Raleigh, NC: Author. Retrieved from http://www.ncpublicschools.org/docs/accountability/testing/readingtechmanual.pdf

North Carolina Department of Public Instruction. (2006). *The North Carolina mathematics tests: Technical report.* Raleigh, NC: Author. Retrieved from http://www.ncpublicschools.org/docs/accountability/testing/mathtechmanual.pdf

Pedhazur, E. J. (1997). *Multiple regression in behavioral research* (3rd ed.). New York, NY: Harcourt Brace

Pinker, S. (1990). A theory of graph comprehension. In R. Freedle (Ed.), *Artificial intelligence and the future of testing* (pp. 73–126). Hillsdale, NJ: Erlbaum.

Playfair, W. (1786). *The commercial and political atlas.* London, UK: Curry.

Raudenbush, S. W. (2004). Schooling, statistics, and poverty: Can we measure school improvement? *ETS.* Paper presented at the William H. Angoff Memorial Lecture Series, Princeton, NJ. Retrieved from http://www.ets.org/research/

Raudenbush, S. W., & Williams, J. D. (1995). The estimation of school effects. *Journal of Educational and Behavioral Statistics, 20*, 307–335.

Robinson, D. H., & Kiewra, K. A. (1995). Visual argument: Graphic organizers are superior to outlines in improving learning from text. *Journal of Educational Psychology, 87*(3), 455–467.

Schmid, C. (1983). *Statistical graphics: Design principles and practices.* New York, NY: Wiley.

Schraw, G., McCrudden, M. T., & Robinson, D. (2013). *Learning through visual displays.* Charlotte, NC: Information Age.

Schulte, A. C., Osborne, S. S., & Erchul, W. P. (1998). Effective special education: A United States dilemma. *School Psychology Review, 27*, 66–76.

Schulte, A. C., & Stevens, J. J. (in press). Once, sometimes, or always in special education: Mathematics growth and achievement gaps. *Exceptional Children.*

Schulte, A., & Villwock, D. (2004). Using high-stakes tests to derive school-level measures of special education efficacy. *Exceptionality, 12*, 107–127.

Shadish, W. R., Cook, T. D., & Campbell, D. T. (2002). *Experimental and quasi-experimental designs for generalized causal inference.* Boston, MA: Houghton Mifflin.

Shin, T., Davison, M. L., Long, J. D., Chan, C.-K, & Heistad, D. (2013). Exploring gains in reading and mathematics achievement among regular and exceptional students using growth curve modeling. *Learning and Individual Differences, 23*, 92–100.

Singer, J. D., & Willett, J. B. (2003). *Applied longitudinal data analysis.* New York, NY: Oxford University Press.

Stevens, J. J. (2005). The study of school effectiveness as a problem in research design. In R. Lissitz (Ed.), *Value-added modes in education: Theory and applications* (pp. 166–208). Maple Grove, MN: JAM.

Stevens, J. J., Schulte, A. C., Elliott, S. N., Nese, J. F. T., & Tindal, G. (2015). Mathematics achievement growth of students with and without disabilities on a statewide achievement test. *Journal of School Psychology, 53*, 45–62.

Tufte, E. R. (1990). *Envisioning information.* Cheshire, CT: Graphics.

Tufte, E. R. (1997). *Graphical explanations.* Cheshire, CT: Graphics.

Tufte, E. R. (2001). *The visual display of quantitative information.* Cheshire, CT: Graphics.

Tukey, J. W. (1977). *Exploratory data analysis.* Reading, MA: Addison-Wesley.

Wainer, H. (1984). How to display data badly. *American Statistician, 38*, 137–147.

Wainer, H. (1997). *Visual revelations: Graphical tales of fate and deception from Napoleon Bonaparte to Ross Perot.* New York, NY: Springer-Verlag.

Wainer, H. (2005). *Graphic discovery: A trout in the milk and other visual adventures.* Princeton, NJ: Princeton University Press.

Wainer, H. (2009). *Picturing the uncertain world: How to understand, communicate, and control uncertainty through graphical display.* Princeton, NJ: Princeton University Press.

Wilkinson, L. (2005). *The grammar of graphics* (2nd ed.). New York, NY: Springer.

Zvoch, K. (2014). Modern quantitative methods for evaluation science: Recommendations for essential methodological texts. *American Journal of Evaluation, 35*(3), 430–440.

Zvoch, K., & Stevens, J. J. (2003). A multilevel, longitudinal analysis of middle school math and language achievement. *Educational Policy Analysis Archives, 11*(20).

Zvoch, K., & Stevens, J. J. (2006). Successive student cohorts and longitudinal growth models: An investigation of elementary school mathematics performance. *Educational Policy Analysis Archives, 14*(2).

Zvoch, K., & Stevens, J. J. (2008). Measuring and evaluating school performance: An investigation of status and growth-based achievement indicators. *Evaluation Review, 32*(6), 569–595.

CHAPTER 10

TAILORING VISUAL DISPLAYS TO IMPROVE TEST SCORE INTERPRETATION

Including Indicators of Uncertainty

Brett P. Foley

ABSTRACT

For all educational and psychological tests, there is uncertainty (i.e., error) associated with the results. The purpose of this chapter is to describe ways of using visual displays to improve the presentation and understanding of assessment results by integrating measures of uncertainty (e.g., confidence bands, error bars) that are used with assessments (e.g., student score reports, state reports comparing demographic groups) into visual displays. The chapter is divided into three primary sections. First, several sources of error that can contribute to the uncertainty of assessment results are defined and described. The second section provides examples of visual displays that can be used in the test development and reporting process that can help to convey this uncertainty to test users/consumers. Specific areas of emphasis include the determination of cut scores, individual score reporting, and aggregate score reporting. The third section provides guidance on choosing among multiple display

Use of Visual Displays in Research and Testing: Coding, Interpreting, and Reporting Data,
pages 265–298.

options. The chapter concludes with recommendations for ways assessment developers can use visual displays to better convey uncertainty to test users/consumers.

For all educational and psychological tests, there is uncertainty (i.e., error) associated with the results. Uncertainty associated with test scores can arise from many sources (e.g., testing conditions, content/construction decisions, scoring, student instruction) and may result in reduced score precision and reliability. This uncertainty is a primary reason that the *Standards for Educational and Psychological Testing* (hereafter, *The Standards*; AERA, APA, & NCME, 2014) note that critical decisions should not be based on the results of a single test alone (Standard 12.10, 2014) and call for the precision/reliability of test scores to be reported along with other interpretive information:

> When test score information is released, those responsible for testing programs should provide interpretations appropriate to the audience. The interpretations should describe in simple language what the test covers, what scores represent, *the precision/reliability of the scores*, and how scores are intended to be used. (Standard 6.10, 2014, p. 119; emphasis added).

In practice, however, test users/consumers often are not provided with any information about the uncertainty associated with test scores. In a review of educational score reports, Goodman and Hambleton (2004) reported that a majority of score reports did not include information about the precision of scores at either the total score or subscore level. When test scores are reported without clearly communicating the uncertainty associated with the scores, test users/consumers have no way to evaluate their precision, resulting in an increased risk of misinterpretation or overinterpretation of test results.

One reason why uncertainty measures are not included with test results may be that many test users/consumers have difficulty understanding the mathematical concepts and statistical jargon related to the quantification of uncertainty in test scores (Hambleton & Slater, 1997; Impara, Divine, Bruce, Liverman, & Gay, 1991). The effective use of visual displays may help address this issue. Visual displays that accurately and clearly portray the precision (or imprecision) of test results may help test users/consumers better understand the uncertainty that accompanies test results and subsequently encourage more appropriate use of test results.

The purpose of this chapter is to describe ways of using visual displays to improve the presentation and understanding of assessment results by integrating measures of uncertainty (e.g., confidence bands, error bars) that are used with assessments (e.g., student score reports, state reports comparing demographic groups) into visual displays. The chapter is divided into three primary sections. First, several sources of error that can contribute to the uncertainty of assessment results are defined and described. The second section provides examples of visual displays that can be used in the test development and reporting process that can help to convey this uncertainty to test users/consumers. Specific areas of emphasis include the determination of cut scores, individual score reporting, and aggregate score reporting. The third section provides guidance on choosing among multiple display options. The chapter concludes with recommendations for ways assessment developers can use visual displays to better convey uncertainty[1] to test users/consumers.

SOURCES OF ERROR

Uncertainty can enter into assessment results in several ways that judicious use of visual displays can help to ameliorate. One form of uncertainty is random error, which is introduced by taking a sample from a population. When discussing the results of a survey, the "margin of error" is one way of referring to random error. For example, consider a newspaper that reports the favorability ratings of a political candidate. The newspaper reports that the candidate has a 47% favorability rating, the estimate was based on a survey of 500 registered voters, and the survey has a margin of error of plus or minus 4%. Because readers are likely interested in the overall opinion of the full population of voters (rather than just the 500 people who responded to the survey), the 500 survey respondents are a considered a sample of the full population of registered voters. Similarly, the 47% favorability rating is considered an estimate of the actual favorable rating that would have been observed if all registered voters had participated in the survey. If a different sample of 500 respondents was collected in the same way, the favorability rating would likely be similar to, but not necessarily equal to, the estimate of 47%. The margin of error is included to present the estimate as a range (i.e., 43%–51%) in order to help quantify the uncertainty in the estimate that results from taking a sample. All things being equal, a larger sample will result in a smaller margin of error. If the entire population participated in the survey, there would not be random sampling error because the sample would be the same as the population of interest. Therefore, when we discuss random error, the word "error" is not being used to refer to a "mistake," but rather as an indication of the uncertainty of our estimate.

Similarly, most assessments are made up of a set of items or tasks that can be thought of as a sample from the population of possible questions that could have been asked about the particular domain being assessed. And like the newspaper survey mentioned above, aggregated test results may be based on a sample (rather than a full population) of examinees. Several of the ways that random error can enter into assessment results are defined in the subsequent subsections.

---

[1] Precision and uncertainty are two sides of the same coin. They are two different ways of talking about the amount of confidence one should have in results. We have less uncertainty when our measures are very precise and more uncertainty when our measures are less precise. If one overestimates the precision of a measure, they are, in turn, underestimating the uncertainty associated with that measure. Because precision and uncertainty simply reflect different perspectives on the same issue, the two terms are used interchangeably in this chapter.

Measurement Error

Most assessments, whether they are for educational or credentialing purposes, represent samples of larger domains. For example, consider an end-of-course exam for a high school geometry course. Within the scope of content for such a course, although the specific learning goals may be necessarily limited to a finite number of specific objectives (e.g., calculating the area of an irregular polygon; applying theorems for similar triangles), a potentially infinite number of test items could be written to assess students' understanding of the objectives. A given set of test items can be thought of as a sample of the population of items that make up the larger domain of interest. A student could be tested using several geometry tests built to the same content and statistical specifications, and while we would expect the student's scores to be similar across the tests, it would not be surprising for the scores to vary slightly across the tests. This is because each assessment is an imperfect representation of the full domain of interest. Broadly speaking, measurement error can be thought of as the variability in test scores across multiple hypothetical test administrations. For additional information about measurement error, see Haertel (2006) and Thorndike and Thorndike-Christ (2011).

Sampling Error

In some cases, test users/consumers are interested in assessment results that are aggregated across groups (as opposed to scores for individual examinees). For instance, the National Assessment of Educational Progress (NAEP) is an assessment that is based on a nationally representative sample that is intended to "[inform] the public about the academic achievement of elementary and secondary students in the United States" (National Assessment of Educational Progress, National Center for Education Statistics, National Assessment Governing Board, Institute of Education Sciences, & U.S. Department of Education, Institute of Education Sciences, National Center for Education Statistics, n.d.). NAEP results are not provided at the student level, but aggregate information is reported at the state and national levels (and for some very large urban districts). If summary statistics for the NAEP assessments were based on an equally representative but different sample of students, the results would likely be similar, but not necessarily the same as the results from the original sample. Sampling error can be thought of as the variability introduced into the estimation process by taking a sample (rather than a census). The magnitude of the sampling error is affected by sample size and the sampling design. For additional information about sampling error and sampling designs, see Mazzeo, Lazer, and Zieky (2006) and Schaeffer, Mendenhall, Ott, and Gerow (2011).

Equating Error

From time to time, testing programs produce new test forms that consist of (at least partially) new test items. One reason to do this is to limit the exposure of test items in order to help maintain test security. These newer forms are built to the same content specifications and are of similar difficulty to the older form, but because the items on the forms are not identical, small differences in form difficulty are expected. In other words, new forms may be slightly easier or more difficult than the old test form.

Consider a hypothetical licensure testing program that is producing a new test form. In order to be fair to all test takers, the passing score is adjusted on each test form to account for these differences in form difficulty. This is standard practice in the testing industry and follows the guidelines presented in *The Standards*. In practical terms, this means that if a new form is more difficult than the old form, the passing score is adjusted downwards; if a new form is less difficult than the old form, the passing score is adjusted upwards. These adjustments are calculated using a statistical process called equating. Some equating methods use information obtained from items that appear across multiple forms to identify a statistical relationship between the forms that helps to ensure that the passing score on each form reflects an equivalent expectation. The estimated statistical relationship can vary based on, among other things, the sample of examinees taking the tests, the items on the test, and the extent to which the underlying assumptions of the particular equating methodology in question are satisfied. For example, the equating relationship across forms can vary based on the number of items in common across the two test forms. Equating error can be thought of as the uncertainty introduced into test scores through the estimation of the statistical relationships between test forms. Equating error can affect both the scores of individual examinees and aggregated examinee information. For addition information about equating error, see Holland and Dorans (2006) and Kolen and Brennan (2014).

Other Sources

Error affecting the uncertainty of test results can arise from other sources as well. One important source of uncertainty is nonresponse error. Nonresponse error can affect test results at both the item and person level. That is, an examinee may choose not to answer some questions on a test while answering others. Alternatively, a person selected to be a member of the tested sample may chose not to participate, or a parent may choose to opt their child out of a school's standardized testing program. Nonresponse might increase sampling error by reducing sample size. Nonresponse may also introduce systematic biases into the assessment process. For example, if parents of low-ability students are more likely to opt out of a school district's testing program, then the average score for the district will be biased: it will no longer be an accurate estimate for the population in the district because the underrepresentation of low-ability students will result in a district average that is too high. Missing data caused by nonresponse can also complicate the analysis of assessment data. For additional explanations of missing data mechanisms and guidance on analyses, see Enders (2010).

Other sources of error include processing and response errors. Processing errors can occur when the correct response for an item is miscoded or a scoring machine malfunctions (Moore, 2000). Response errors can occur in psychological or personality assessments when a person does not respond honestly or accurately (Moore, 2000). An example of a response error is a test taker responding to a question by choosing a socially desirable response.

Broadly speaking, the validity of a test's uses and interpretations is reduced whenever a factor unrelated to the underlying construct has an effect on the test scores (i.e., construct irrelevant variance). Examples of sources of construct irrelevant variance include cheating, guessing, lack of motivation, inadequate opportunity to learn, excessive reading difficulty (on a nonreading test), uncomfortable testing conditions, and unclear scoring rubrics. Test developers work to design tests and testing processes that minimize the effect of these (and other) sources of error.

For any given testing situation, multiple sources of error can come into play, each to a greater or lesser extent. Although it may not be necessary or possible to account for all sources of error, it is essential to identify the primary (i.e., largest) sources of error because they will have the greatest effect on the overall uncertainty of the results (Kane, 2013). The quantification of the sources of error described in this section can be a very complex task for many test/sampling/equating designs, requiring support from trained psychometricians and/or statisticians. Additionally, the degree to which each source of error affects test scores will vary depending on assessment design decisions. It is beyond the scope of this chapter to provide specific methods for calculating estimates for the sources of error described here. However, the interested reader can find additional information about these calculations in the references noted in this section. The remainder of this chapter discusses how the uncertainty caused by sources of error like those described in this section can be communicated to test users/consumer through visual displays, assuming that the relevant source(s) of error have been identified and quantified.

USING VISUAL DISPLAYS TO ILLUSTRATE UNCERTAINTY

The Standards refer to the sources of error described above in terms of "reliability/precision" of test scores, and note that, "For each total score, subscore, or combination of scores that is to be interpreted, estimates of relevant indices of reliability/precision should be reported" (Standard 2.3, 2014, p. 43). Although some have expressed concern that (at least in cases like college admission tests) test takers/users don't care about receiving such information (e.g., Wainer, 2005), it is a professional expectation that such information be provided and to present the information in such a way as to make it accessible and useful to test users/consumers. In this section, we discuss ways that visual displays can help illustrate the uncertainty associated with test scores. Specifically, examples of ways to indicate uncertainty will be shown with respect to (a) performance level recommendations, (b) individual score reporting, and (c) aggregate score reporting.[2]

Indicating Uncertainty in Performance Level Recommendations

In many testing programs, it is necessary to divide test score ranges into categories (i.e., performance levels) that are ascribed some additional meaning or interpretation. Examples of such programs are licensure and certification (sometimes referred to together as "credentialing programs"). The most consequential use of test scores for credentialing programs is identifying examinees who pass the test and those who fail. The pass/fail decision may be intended to separate those who are qualified to practice from those who are unqualified, especially if the test is for an initial credential allowing someone to enter a profession. In the case of an advanced credential, the pass/fail decision may be intended to separate masters from nonmasters.

In educational assessments, examinees can also be assigned into categories that help test users/consumers to interpret the test scores. Such categories might include basic/proficient/advanced, below grade level/at grade level/above grade level, or eligible for graduation/not eligible for graduation. In either case (credentialing or education), for the performance levels to be meaningful, they should be determined using a systematic, defensible process. As a group, these processes are referred to as "standard setting" (for detailed descriptions of several standard setting methodologies see, for example, Cizek, 2012; Cizek & Bunch, 2007; Hambleton & Pitoniak, 2006; Zieky, Perie, & Livingston, 2008). Subject matter experts (i.e., those who are experts in the area being assessed; SMEs) are an integral part of the standard-setting process, because most standard-setting methodologies rely on the professional judgments of SMEs to determine the performance levels. Because consequential decisions are made based on the performance levels determined during standard setting studies, it is important that the SMEs who provide judgments are qualified and representative of the experts in the area being assessed and have knowledge of the population being tested. For example, in a credentialing context, SMEs may be selected from multiple constituencies: experienced practicing professionals (e.g., more than 5 years of experience), newly credentialed professionals (e.g. 5 or fewer years of experience), and educators who train new professionals. In education, SMEs often include teachers of the particular subject area being assessed.

Standard setting panels vary in the number of participating SMEs. A panel size of 12–18 participants has been recommended in the literature (Zieky et al., 2008).

---

[2] We argue in this chapter that augmenting visual displays in ways that help indicate uncertainty can help to make these displays accessible and useful to test users/consumers. The inclusion of indicators of uncertainty is only one of many design decisions that should be considered when constructing visual displays. There are several excellent resources that provide guidance on additional design considerations for effective visual displays, including, for example, Few (2012), Tufte (2001), and Wong (2010).

However, panel sizes may vary based on factors like the stakes involved for the test, the size of the SME population, and the number of stakeholder groups to be included. Additionally, multiple panels may be used to help evaluate panel-level variability or facilitator effects.

In most cases, the standard-setting panel(s) represent samples from the population of SMEs. Therefore, sampling error will affect the standard-setting results. In other words, a different but similarly qualified panel would likely provide similar but not necessarily identical cut score recommendations. This sampling variability provides both opportunities and challenges to the policymakers who must ultimately decide on the final performance levels: Because there is a margin of error associated with the SME recommendations, there is a "defensible" range for the policymakers to work within, giving the policymakers some flexibility; however, with a range of values, there is a challenge to the policymakers to choose the "best" value within the range. Figure 1 shows a visual display that could help to inform this type of challenging decision-making process. This hypothetical example is from a credentialing program that utilizes SMEs selected from the three constituencies described earlier: experienced professionals, newly credentialed professionals, and educators. The stacked dot plot shows the recommended cut scores from each of the 30 panelists (each dot represents one SME). This type of graph can be useful to policymakers because it helps illustrate the overall spread of recommendations (cut score recommendations range from 12 to 20) while also allowing the user to easily make comparisons across the constituency groups (experienced professionals tended to recommend a higher passing score than the newly credentialed professionals; educators tended to be more spread out in their recommendations than the other two groups). Similar graphs can be used in education settings when multiple performance levels are set (e.g., basic/proficient/advanced). By using these levels as rows of the graph (as opposed to SME

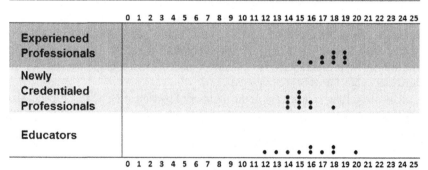

FIGURE 1. Example of stacked dot plots for comparing standard setting recommendations across SME groups.

constituency groups), policymakers can evaluate how recommendations compare both within and across performance levels (Foley & Buckendahl, 2013).

Different standard-setting procedures have different underlying assumptions and methodologies. Therefore, in some cases it is desirable to use multiple methodologies when determining performance levels. If each method is based on recommendations from a sample of SMEs, then each methodology will have margins of error associated with the results, with the same benefits and challenges mentioned above with an additional challenge: What should policymakers do when the results from the different methodologies do not agree? Figure 2 shows results from a hypothetical educational program in a way that could help policymakers answer this question. The hypothetical program in question has three performance levels (basic, proficient, and advanced), and five different standard-setting methodologies were used.

The graph below (Figure 2) shows 15 different error bars (three performance levels with five standard setting results each). Vertical lines help distinguish the

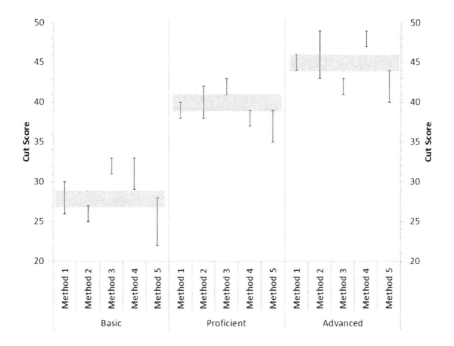

FIGURE 2. Example of parallel error bars for comparing results from multiple standard-setting methodologies. The vertical error bars indicate 95% confidence intervals around the mean recommended cut score for each method; the horizontal shaded bars illustrate the areas of greatest overlap among the different methodologies.

different performance levels. For each level, a shaded bar has been drawn (two points tall) that helps to illustrate the areas of greatest overlap among the different methodologies. This might be considered the "most defensible" range for selecting a passing score (assuming that all standard-setting methods were equally valued). If one standard-setting methodology was preferred over others, the shaded bar could be adjusted up or down to ensure the shaded bar passed through the error bar for that particular method. Graphs like this can also be useful for comparing standard-setting recommendations from different SME constituent groups: simply replace the methods listed on the horizontal axis with the constituent groups. This type of graph is useful for synthesizing many sets of results. It would take a large amount of numbers and narratives to describe these results, while the graph makes the results clear within a single glance.

A final example from education considers vertically moderated standard setting (VMSS). VMSS can be broadly defined as procedures to smooth standard-setting results across grades (Cizek & Bunch, 2007). VMSS grew from the underlying assumption that, for very large groups of students, it is unlikely that ability will vary widely across adjacent grades. Therefore, the percentage of students in a given performance level should be similar for adjacent grades, and the overall trend across all grades should make sense, given what is known about developmental processes. Put another way, one would not expect large swings in proficiency rates from grade to grade.

When standards are set in educational settings, it is common for SME panels to set performance levels for one grade a time. Additionally, SMEs might only work with a small subset of grades, or perhaps only one grade. Because the SMEs are only considering one grade at a time, they could unintentionally recommend cut scores that result in large changes in the percentage of students at each performance level, even for adjacent grades. VMSS procedures aim to help produce coherent standard-setting results across grades.

An example of one VMSS procedure is provided below. This procedure uses error bars around initial standard-setting results to help a VMSS panel make adjustments to help ensure coherence of expectations across grades. For this procedure, there are five steps:

1. Review target student descriptions and assessment tasks.
2. Make initial estimates for proficiency levels across grades.
3. Review standard-setting results and additional supporting information.
4. Revise individual proficiency level estimates.
5. Come to group consensus on proficiency levels recommendations. (Foley, 2014, p. 4)

In Step 3, VMSS panelists review the results of an earlier standard setting by viewing a set of parallel error bars that show the results across grades (see the top panel of Figure 3). This graph shows the standard-setting results as error bars, with one bar for each grade (i.e., grades 3–8 and 10) and performance level (i.e.,

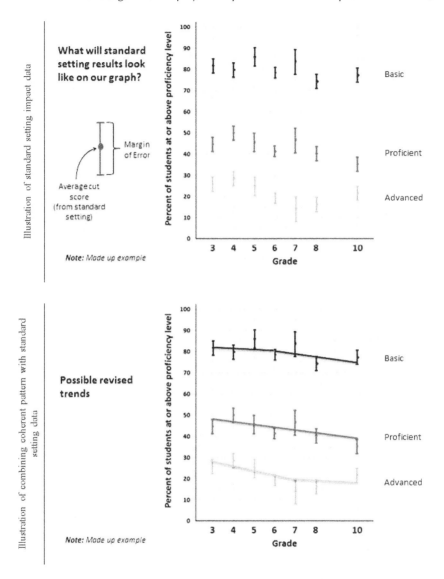

FIGURE 3. Illustrations of standard-setting results with 95% confidence intervals and possible coherent proficiency rate trends (from Foley, 2014, p. 10).

Basic/Proficient/Advanced). The VMSS panelists (who may be made up of SMEs from the initial standard-setting study or may be a stand-alone panel) use a graph like this as the starting point for Step 4 of the process. In Step 4, panelists draw a trend line for each performance level, attempting to pass the line through the error band for each grade level, deviating from these bands only when doing so would result in unreasonable differences between grade levels (see the bottom panel of Figure 3). After further revision, the percentages identified using this method are converted back to cut scores. In this way, visual displays of standard-setting results with error bands aid policymakers in setting performance levels that are coherent across grades.

Indicating Uncertainty in Individual Score Reporting

There has been a great deal of research and professional guidance on the subject of score reporting (see, for example, Cohen & Wollack, 2006; Deng & Yoo, 2009; Ryan, 2006; van den Heuvel, Zenisky, & Davis-Becker, 2014; Ysseldyke & Nelson, 2002). Rather than discussing the full breadth of issues related to score reports (a broad topic, worthy of its own volume), this subsection targets some specific aims of the standard mentioned previously: providing interpretations that are appropriate to the audience and using simple language to represent the uncertainty (or as the standards refer to it, precision/reliability) of test scores. Specifically, this section provides examples of visual displays that can help test users/consumers better understand individual score reports.

Uncertainty in total scores.

Total scores are often the primary outcome of interest for test users/consumers. Professional standards require that when these scores are reported, information about the uncertainty of these scores should be provided as well. Many score reports include additional documentation (i.e., an interpretive guide) that aides the test user/consumer in interpreting the score report. However, whenever possible, visual displays should be constructed in such a way that the user/consumer is provided the necessary information for understanding what is contained either within or in close proximity to the display itself. Ideally, the display should stand on its own, without relying on the user/consumer to look elsewhere to determine what is being conveyed. Figure 4a shows a graph and accompanying text that comes from a hypothetical score report (adapted from Foley & Buckendahl, 2013, p. 422). This graph provides a wealth of information in a single glance, including

- criterion-referenced information showing how the student performed relative to the performance standards,
- the range of scores that bound each performance level, and
- norm-referenced information in the form of the student's performance relative to the state average.

Information about the uncertainty of the student's test score is provided using a written explanation included in the upper right of the display.

An alternative design is shown in Figure 4b. The difference in this graphic is that the indicator for the student's score is shown as a range, bounded by arrows,

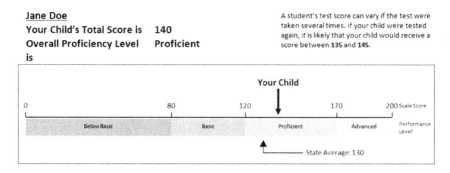

FIGURE 4a.   Excerpt from an individual score report with basic explanation of uncertainty.

indicating the uncertainty around the students score. This design may be preferable to Figure 4a, because both the explanation and score indicator illustrate uncertainty, providing an additional cue to the test user/consumer. The redundancy of the information will (hopefully) convey the idea of uncertainty in the score to readers who look at the graph but fail to read the accompanying text.

A variation of the design shown in Figure 4b can be seen in Figure 4c. In this design, the indicator for the error band is a diamond shape. This design is based on an example provided by Zwick, Zapata-Rivera, and Hegarty (2014). The diamond shape is useful in that it helps to convey to the user that not all scores in the error band are equally likely: values close to the observed score are more likely than values further away. Zwick et al. refer to this type of design as a "variable-width confidence band" (p. 120). A second variation drawing on the work of Zwick et al. is shown in Figure 4d. In this version, both the student's observed score and the end points of the error bar are labeled in the graph. An additional change is the

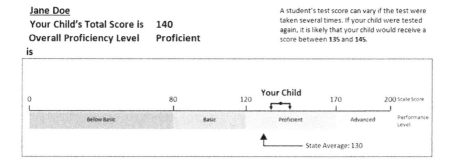

FIGURE 4b. Excerpt from an individual score report with arrows and basic explanation of uncertainty.

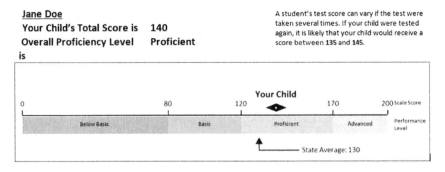

FIGURE 4c.   Excerpt from an individual score report with variable-width error band and basic explanation of uncertainty.

wording of the interpretation note included in the upper right. This wording uses the analogy of measuring weight and blood pressure to help test users/consumers understand the idea of measurement uncertainty (Zwick et al., 2014, p. 120).

Uncertainty in subscale scores.

Test users/consumers often desire more detailed test performance feedback than a total score alone can provide. Additionally, some professional guidelines for credentialing programs call for these programs to provide meaningful feedback to examinees who fail the test, when providing such information is psychometrically defensible (Institute for Credentialing Excellence, 2007). In many cases, testing programs use subscale scores—scores calculated based on a subset of items making up the full test—to provide such feedback. In order for this feedback to be meaningful, the subscores need to be based on a sufficiently large group of items for the subscores to have adequate reliability and should also be

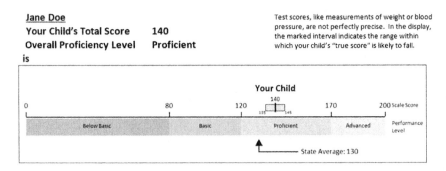

FIGURE 4d.   Excerpt from an individual score report with labeled error band and analogy-based explanation of uncertainty.

sufficiently different from the overall score (i.e., the subscore should have a relatively low correlation with the total score) so as not to provide redundant information (Haberman, 2008; Haberman, Sinharay, & Puhan, 2009; Sinharay, 2010; Sinharay, Haberman, & Puhan, 2007). In other words, the correlation between the total scores and the subscale score should be neither too high nor too low: if the correlation between the total scores and the subscale score is very high, it indicates that the two scores are essentially measuring the same thing, thus negating the utility of providing a subscore (i.e., no additional unique information is provided by the subscore); if the correlation between the total scores and the subscale score is very low, it indicates that the constructs being measured are so different that it may not be appropriate to use the subscore in the calculation of the total score (i.e., two substantially different constructs are being measured, so the examinee should be given two different scores).

If a testing program determines that providing subscores is appropriate, *The Standards* note that information about the precision of these scores should be provided to test users/consumers (Standard 2.3, 2014; see Haladyna and Kramer, 2004, for a framework for evaluating the validity of subscore uses and interpretations). This section provides several examples of how such information might be shown in a visual display.

Figure 5a illustrates a simple table that presents the information about five content areas (identified as A through E, for convenience; more descriptive labels should be used on real score reports) of a hypothetical test, as well as subscores for each area. The number of items for each content area is listed in the table (as recommended by Goodman and Hambleton, 2004), as well as the proportion of the total test score that the content area comprises. Individual performance is reported as percentage correct for each content area, but might also be displayed as a raw or scaled score (depending on the testing program design). Uncertainty is included in the visual display through the inclusion of the standard error (SE) of the examinee's percentage correct for each content area. Although the SE infor-

Content area information			Your Performance
Content area	# of items in area	% of total test	% correct (SE)
A	50	25	20 (10)
B	30	15	80 (15)
C	70	35	70 (7)
D	30	15	90 (15)
E	20	10	65 (16)

Note. SE = Standard error

FIGURE 5a.   Example of a subscore report, providing numerical representations of the percentage correct and standard errors for each subscore.

Content area information								
Content area	# of items in area	% of total test				Your Performance		

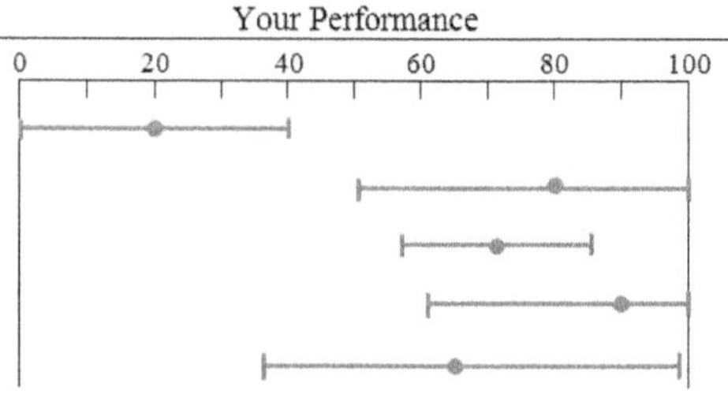

Note: Because content area scores are based on fewer items than the full test, the scores are less precise than the full test score. Therefore, your results are presented as score bands. Score bands that overlap are not significantly different. For example, performance in content area B was greater than content area A, but there was not a significant difference between performances in content areas B and C.

FIGURE 5b.   Example of a subscore report, illustrating the percentage correct and confidence bands for each subscore.

mation meets the professional requirement of providing information about uncertainty in subscale scores, it may not meet the requirement of providing information to test users in a way they can understand. Researchers have found that test users/consumers (including teachers and policymakers) are not familiar with statistical jargon and often misinterpret "standard errors" and "confidence intervals" (e.g., Hambleton & Slater, 1997; Impara et al., 1991). Therefore, an alternative presentation, such as that shown in Figure 5b, may be preferable.

Figure 5b shows the same information as Figure 5a, but presents subscores as points with error (i.e., score) bands on a scale. This representation has the ben-

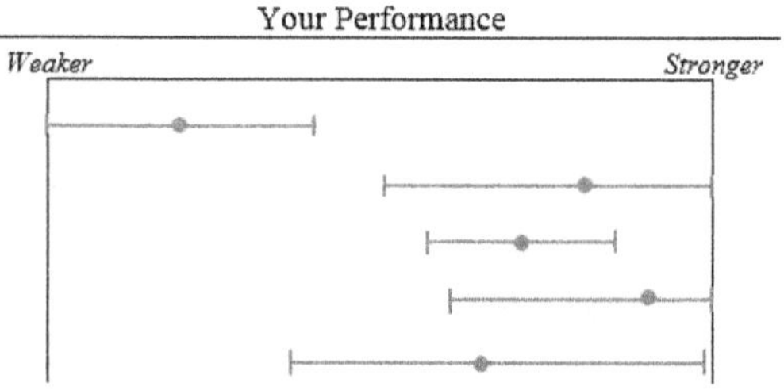

Note: Because content area scores are based on fewer items than the full test, the scores are less precise than the full test score. Therefore, your results are presented as score bands. Score bands that overlap are not significantly different. For example, performance in content area B was stronger than content area A, but there was not a significant difference between performances in content areas B and C.

FIGURE 5c.   Example of a subscore report, illustrating relative performance by using confidence bands for each subscore on an unnumbered scale.

Content area information			Your Performance		
Content area	# of items in area	% of total test	Level 1	Level 2	Level 3
A	50	25%			
B	30	15%			
C	70	35%			
D	30	15%			
E	20	10%			

Note: Because content area scores are based on fewer items than the full test, the scores are less precise than the full test score. Therefore your results are presented as score bands. Score bands that overlap are not significantly different. For example, performance in content area B was greater than content area A, but there was not a significant difference between performance in content areas B and C.

FIGURE 5d. Example of a subscore report, illustrating relative performance by using confidence bands for each subscore on a scale divided into performance categories.

efit of showing relative performance while also clearly indicating uncertainty. A note is added to help users/consumers interpret overlapping error bands. In order for such a display to make sense, it is necessary to place all of the subscores on a common scale. In this case, this scaling is accomplished by using percentage correct. Figure 5c shows a variation of figure 5b in which the value labels on the performance axis have been replaced with verbal end-point labels (i.e., Stronger, Weaker). Although this labeling adds ambiguity to the display, it may be preferable in some cases because it serves as an additional reminder to users/consumers of the uncertainty in the scores and might help to discourage overinterpretation of the subscale results (Wainer, 1996).

Figures 5d and 5e provide an alternative way of presenting results that divides the score scale into performance levels rather than a specific score scale. In some cases, performance categories may be more helpful/meaningful to test users/consumers. The levels may be given more descriptive names (e.g., below/borderline/meets, below average/average/above average, weaker/similar/stronger). This method requires additional work for the test producer in that the scoring categories must be created and procedures must be used to identify the cutoffs for each performance level. The test producer must determine whether these categories are criterion referenced (i.e., representative of some absolute level of performance) or norm referenced (i.e., related to the performance of other test takers). For example, a test program may want to provide feedback to candidates comparing their performance to those of passing candidates. The test taker should make sure that clear descriptions of the performance categories are provided to the test takers.

Figure 5d presents results using error bands. Figure 5e only shows which performance category to which the examinee was assigned for each content area. Al-

Content area information			Your Performance		
Content area	# of items in area	% of total test	Level 1	Level 2	Level 3
A	50	25%	X		
B	30	15%			X
C	70	35%			X
D	30	15%			X
E	20	10%		X	

FIGURE 5e. Example of a subscore report, illustrating the performance for each subscore using performance categories.

though uncertainty in test scores may be considered when identifying such placements (e.g., the examinee is placed in the middle category unless the error band falls completely above or below the middle category end points), this display does not do as well as the other options in this section in conveying the uncertainty of the subscale results. The choice of the best display from among those shown in this section will depend on the individual testing program and the needs of the particular group of test users/consumers that is the target audience for the results.

Indicating Uncertainty in Aggregate Score Reporting

The proceeding sections of this chapter provided examples of visual displays that helped to convey to test users/consumers the uncertainty in individual test scores, at both the total score and subscore level. This section focuses on situations where test scores are aggregated and reported for a group rather than for an individual. In many cases, the same visual displays shown above will work equally well for groups as they do for individuals. This is especially true when the results for a single group (e.g., one state, one school district, one ethnic group) are being considered in isolation. However, because the measurement, sampling, equating, and other forms of error mentioned above can effect aggregate scores in similar ways as they do for individuals, care is needed when presenting comparisons of different groups. Specifically, test users/consumers should be informed when group differences are small enough to be considered negligible based on the error inherent in the measures and when the differences are large enough to be considered meaningful (after accounting for error). These differences may compare one group over time (e.g., fourth graders in 2012 vs. fourth graders in 2014), compare multiple groups at a given point in time (e.g., males vs. females, students in Nebraska vs. students in Kansas, Hispanic examinees vs. non-Hispanic examinees), or compare combinations of groups and time points.

As mentioned earlier, NAEP is set of voluntary national assessments given to a sample of students in the United States. The NAEP exams are among the most extensively studied tests that have ever been produced. Excerpts from NAEP reports provide excellent examples of how one large testing program has chosen to indicate uncertainty in aggregated assessment results and how design preferences for the visual displays used have changed over time. Although the visual displays in this section are selected from various NAEP reports, the focus of the discussion is on the utility and design of the various displays, which can be applied to many other educational or credentialing exams.

Comparing One Group Over Time

Perhaps the simplest way to display comparisons is through a table. Figure 6 shows a comparison of reading scores at the national level for 1992 and 1994. Uncertainty is shown by including standard errors in parentheses following the average score for each year (in this case, also broken down by percentile to help show the overall distribution). Symbols ("<" and ">") are used to indicate differences across years that are significant (after accounting for uncertainty). Although this display presents relevant information, it also contains statistical language that may not be correctly interpreted by those without a strong statistical background. Figure 7 shows an alternate way of identifying significant changes over time. This visual display is meant to identify important changes in performance (at the state level) over time. No numbers or graphs are included; the table simply lists which states had meaningful changes in the average science performance from 2000 to 2005. This simplified design has the benefit of not requiring users/consumers to

	Average Proficiency	10th Percentile	25th Percentile	50th Percentile	75th Percentile	90th Percentile
Grade 12						
1992	292 (0.6)	249 (0.8)	271 (0.8)	294 (0.8)	315 (0.6)	333 (0.8)
1994	287 (0.7)<	239 (0.9)<	264 (0.9)<	290 (0.8)<	313 (0.9)	332 (1.3)

< The value for the 1994 assessment was significantly lower (> higher) than the value for 1992 at or about the 95 percent confidence level.

The standard errors of the estimated percentages and proficiencies appear in parentheses. It can be said with 95 percent certainty that for each population of interest, the value for the whole population is within plus or minus two standard errors of the estimate for the sample.

SOURCE: National Center for Education Statistics, National Assessment of Educational Progress (NAEP), 1992 and 1994 Reading Assessments.

FIGURE 6.   Average Reading Proficiency by Percentile, Grade 12 (National Center for Education Statistics, 1996a, p. 23).

Higher average scores	Lower average scores	Higher percentage of students at or above *Basic*	Lower percentage of students at or above *Basic*	Higher percentage of students at or above *Proficient*	Lower percentage of students at or above *Proficient*
California	Alabama	California	Arizona	California	None
Hawaii	Arizona	North Dakota		North Dakota	
Kentucky	Indiana	South Carolina		Virginia	
Louisiana	Nevada	Vermont		Wyoming	
Massachusetts		Virginia			
North Dakota		Wyoming			
South Carolina		DoDEA			
Vermont					
Virginia					
Wyoming					
DoDEA					

SOURCE: U.S. Department of Education, Institute of Education Sciences, National Center for Education Statistics, National Assessment of Educational Progress (NAEP), 2000 and 2005 Science Assessments.

FIGURE 7.   State changes in NAEP science performance from 2000 to 2005 at grade 8 (Grigg, Lauko, & Brockway, 2006, p. 26).

know anything about standard errors or confidence intervals in order to interpret the results. However, it provides less information than Figure 6, and does not provide users/consumers with any information about the magnitude of the changes across years. A third variation is shown in Figure 8, which combines aspects of Figures 6 and 7. Like Figure 6, it presents information for all comparisons (as

Characteristic	Change in average reading scale score		Change in average mathematics scale score
	Since 1992	Since 2005	Since 2005
Overall	▼	▲	▲
Race/ethnicity			
White	◆	▲	▲
Black	◆	◆	▲
Hispanic	◆	◆	▲
Asian/Pacific Islander	◆	▲	▲
American Indian/Alaska Native	‡	◆	▲
Gender			
Male	▼	▲	▲
Female	▼	◆	▲
Gaps			
White – Black	◆	◆	◆
White – Hispanic	◆	◆	◆
Male – Female	◆	◆	◆

FIGURE 8.   Changes in reading scores, math scores, and achievement gaps (National Center for Education Statistics, 2010, p. 2)

opposed to Figure 7, in which only cases with significant differences are displayed). Like Figure 7, it avoids using numbers, instead using symbols to identify increases, decreases, and situations with no differences over time.

The previous figures compare groups at one or two time points. Figures 9 and 10 show two ways to compare multiple years at once by showing trends over time. In Figure 9, uncertainty is shown by including error bands at each data point and by connecting these error bands across time for each age/grade displayed. Additionally, raw data (including standard errors) are included, as well as various symbols indicating significant differences. Although this display contains a wealth of information, it may have too much information (and statistical jargon in the notes) for nontechnical users/consumers, and it may be difficult to determine whether a specific yearly change is meaningful. Figure 10 presents an alternate format for conveying trend information. Rather than including numerical data, asterisks are used to identify years where scores were different from the most recent year (in the case of this graph, 2013). The symbols used for the data markers (circles and arrows) indicate whether each year is different from the previous year. Figure 10 displays concisely the trend over time while also identifying significant changes, comparing each year both to the most current and previous years.

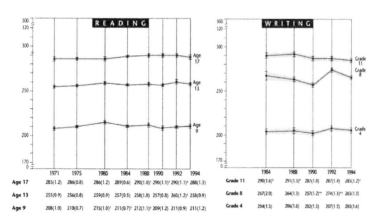

FIGURE 9. National trends in average scale scores in reading and writing (National Center for Education Statistics, 1996b, p. v).

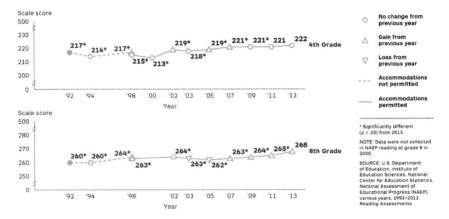

FIGURE 10. Trends in 4th- and 8th-grade NAEP reading average scores (National Center for Education Statistics, 2013, p. 5).

Comparing Multiple Groups

To this point, when error bands (or standard errors) have been displayed, it has been with respect to one score or one group average. Figure 11 is different in that it displays standard errors for the *difference* between two groups. Specifically, the figure shows a comparison of the reading performance of students in public schools versus students in nonpublic schools. For each state, the average score of students in each type of school is shown. An error band that shows the estimated difference between the school types (which is constructed using a 95% confidence interval around the average difference) conveys uncertainty about the estimated differences. Comparing Figure 11 to Figure 5b shows how similar displays can be adapted for very different purposes: Figure 5b shows how subscores compare for one test taker, while Figure 11 shows how different school types compare for different states. Both graphs use horizontal error bars (and their overlap with each other or a specific value) to show meaningful differences while also conveying the uncertainty inherent in the measures.

In a perfect world, all visual displays would stand on their own, with the correct interpretation of results intuitively obvious to the most casual observer. Sadly, however, not all visual displays are perfect, nor will every observer immediately be able to interpret a complex display. With this in mind, Figure 11 contains a feature that has not been seen previously in this chapter: instructions. Users/consumers are provided with instructions above the graph that explain that only cases where the error band does not include zero are significantly different. Rather than assuming the audience will understand and correctly interpret the graph, the creators of the display provide the audience with guidance for extracting meaning from the graph and examples of correct interpretations that can be drawn from

This figure presents average reading proficiencies for the 23 jurisdictions in which comparisons between students attending public and nonpublic schools are possible. The graphic to the right of the two averages illustrates *confidence bands* that, with 95 percent certainty, capture the true difference in average reading scores between the two types of schools within the state or jurisdiction. If the confidence band is completely on the "Higher for Nonpublic" or "Higher for Public" side of the dashed line, the difference between the two averages is significant. Therefore, it is correct to say that students from one type of school performed better or worse than the other on the NAEP reading assessment. However, if the confidence band crosses the dashed line (representing no difference), the average proficiencies of public and nonpublic school fourth graders are not significantly different. In the seven states with blue confidence bands, there was no significant difference in the performance of students attending public and nonpublic schools.

	Average Proficiency		Differences Between Public and Nonpublic Average Reading Proficiencies						
	Public	Nonpublic							
Nation	212	231							
State*									
Alabama**	208	237							
Arkansas	209	235							
Colorado†**	213	239							
Connecticut‡	222	228							
Delaware†	206	233							
Georgia†	207	234							
Hawaii‡	201	234							
Indiana	220	234							
Iowa	223	232							
Kentucky‡	212	237							
Louisiana†	197	227							
Maine**	228	238							
Massachusetts	223	238							
Minnesota	218	234							
Missouri	217	238							
New Jersey†	219	231							
New Mexico**	205	228							
North Dakota	225	238							
Pennsylvania††	215	228							
Rhode Island†	220	229							
Virginia†**	213	240							
West Virginia	213	235							
Other Jurisdiction									
Guam	181	213							

* Only jurisdictions with reportable public and nonpublic results are presented.
† Did not satisfy one of the guidelines for public school sample participation rates in 1994 (see Appendix A).
‡ Did not satisfy one of the guidelines for nonpublic school sample participation rates in 1994 (see Appendix A).
** Interpret the difference between public and nonpublic average proficiencies with caution. The nature of the sample does not allow for accurate determination of the variability of the difference.
SOURCE: National Center for Education Statistics, National Assessment of Educational Progress (NAEP), 1992 and 1994 Reading Assessments.

FIGURE 11. Comparison of Average Reading Proficiency for Public and Nonpublic Schools, Grade 4, 1994 Trial State Assessment in Reading (National Center for Education Statistics, 1996a, p. 35)

it. This interpretive guidance is proximate to the graph, rather than elsewhere in a score report or separate interpretive guide. By including such guidance as part of the display, the creators of Figure 11 are in keeping with the recommendations of visual display scholars who note that the interpretability and strength of a display can be enhanced though the inclusion of descriptive legends and annotations (Few, 2012; Playfair, 2005; Tukey, 1986; Wainer, 2005). The inclusion of interpretive information has the added benefit of expanding the audience for which the display will be appropriate by reducing the level of background/specialized knowledge necessary to extract meaning from the display.

Figure 12 provides an effective way to compare one group to many others. In this case, the state of Nebraska's average NAEP mathematics score is being com-

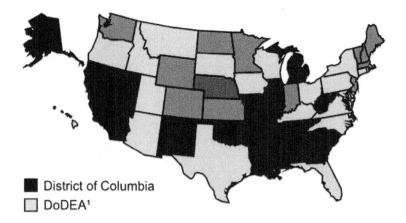

■ District of Columbia
☐ DoDEA¹

¹ Department of Defense Education Activity (overseas and domestic schools).
In 2013, the average score in Nebraska (243) was
▨ lower than those in 12 states/jurisdictions
■ higher than those in 17 states/jurisdictions
▨ not significantly different from those in 22 states/jurisdictions

FIGURE 12.   Comparison the 2013 average NAEP grade 4 mathematics score in Nebraska to other states/jurisdictions (U.S. Department of Education, Institute of Education Sciences, National Center for Education Statistics, 2014).

pared with all other states. Color shading is used to identify states that performed higher, lower, or similar to Nebraska. Although graphs like this one, which features geographical borders, are common, Cleveland and McGill (1984) note some cautions in their use: Large jurisdictions (e.g., Texas on a U.S. national map) or several states in close proximity with a similar shading (forming a large color block) can unintentionally overwhelm the viewer or result in inappropriate interpretations. One alternative they suggest is including equally sized graphs or symbols (such as those used in Figure 8) within each state instead of shading.

One limitation of Figure 12 is that it only allows direct comparisons between a reference jurisdiction/group (in this case, Nebraska) and the other jurisdictions. Figure 13, which compares average reading scores across jurisdictions in 1992, shows an alternative design where all jurisdictions can be compared to all others. Wainer (1996) refers to this type of display as a "pantyhose chart" (p. 106). By sorting jurisdictions from highest performing to lowest performing across the horizontal axis, and by using different shading to indicate higher, lower, no difference, it is easy to identify jurisdictions which differ in performance. This type of display allows for a huge number of comparisons (more than 1,700 in this case)

Instructions: Read down the column directly under a state name listed in the heading at the top of the chart. Match the shading intensity surrounding a state postal abbreviation to the key below to determine whether the average reading performance of this state is higher than, the same as, or lower than the state in the column heading.

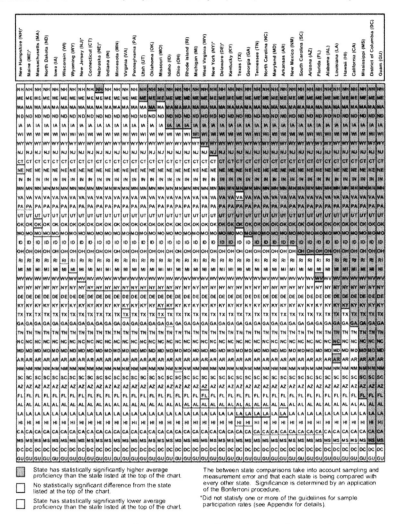

FIGURE 13. Comparisons of Average Overall Reading Proficiency for the 1992 Trial State Reading Assessment, Grade 4, Public Schools Only (National Center for Education Statistics, 1996a, p. 59)

to be concisely displayed in a relatively small area and in a way that should be interpretable to users with a wide range of backgrounds.

The visual displays shown in this section, although used for the NAEP exam, can be adapted easily for other testing scenarios. For example, a graph like Figure 13 could be constructed to compare pass rates at different testing centers for a licensure program. Figure 8 could be adapted to compare average scores over time, broken down by training school, for a certification program.

CHOOSING DISPLAYS

Principles for Designing and Selecting Displays

Display type.

In the sections above, various examples are shown for displaying measurement uncertainty. But what is the *best* way to display this information? First, the type of display must be appropriate for the question that it is intended to inform. For example, tables are most effective when the goal is to compare precise individual values. Graphs are more effective for evaluating trends or patterns in a set of data (Few, 2012). When selecting graphs, one must determine the type of relationship the graph is intended to feature. For example, a time series may best be shown through a line graph, whereas the correlation between two variables may be best illustrated with a scatterplot (see Few, 2012, p. 310 for an extensive discussion of graph type selection). Once a display type has been decided upon, there are several design decisions that can help improve the interpretability of the display.

Design decisions.

Pastor and Finny note that an effective visual display, "(a) reduces cognitive load, (b) selects and organizes relevant information, [and] (c) provides unique information not afforded by text alone" (2013, p. 411). Mayer (2013) identified three principles for helping to reduce extraneous cognitive processing: "coherence (reducing extraneous material), spatial contiguity (place printed words near corresponding part of visual display), and signaling (highlight essential material)" (p. 47). Mayer's principles parallel the recommendations of other visual display scholars (e.g., Bertin, 1983; Cleveland, 1985; Few, 2012; Lane & Sándor, 2009; Tufte, 2001; Wainer, 1997, 2005; Wong, 2010) for choosing and creating displays:

- **Aim for simplicity**—Visual displays should be simple, but complete. Graphical elements that do not directly convey information should be removed or minimized. Avoid the use of 3-D rendering for 2-D or 1-D information. Limit the number and type of fonts and symbols.
- **Integrate text, numbers, and figures**—Information necessary for interpretation should be proximate to the display. When labels are required, place them close to the elements they are describing, when possible (e.g., label lines directly, as opposed to in a separate legend). Place relevant annotations near the data when doing so will not obscure other important information. Describe conclusions that may be drawn. If appropriate for the audience, consider including inferential statistics as part of the display. Because error bars can be constructed in different ways, they should always be accompanied by an explanation.

- **Highlight what's important**—The important features of the graph should be salient. Nondata elements (e.g., grid lines, scales) should support interpretations, but should not be obtrusive. Intense colors should only be used to highlight important features. Use annotations to identify important data features. Items that are intended to be compared should be placed close to one another.
- **Do not intentionally mislead**—Graphical elements should not distort information. Labels should not be ambiguous. Choices of scales and aspect ratios should be defensible and appropriate; scales should be chosen so as not to bias interpretation. Clearly indicate projections or estimates. Units should be appropriate (e.g., actual values vs. percent change for stocks; inflation adjusted vs. unadjusted incomes; age-adjusted vs. unadjusted death rates).

Pairing the design with the audience.

In addition to reducing cognitive load, Tufte (2001) notes that attractive visual displays "display an accessible complexity of detail" (p. 177). However, before we can follow this advice, we must ask the question, "Accessible for whom?" Not all visual displays are equally effective for all audiences. Zwick et al. (2014) collected information about test users/consumers' interpretations of various visual representations of measurement error. They found that background knowledge was related to preferences for, and understanding of, the displays. Carswell and Ramzy (1997) found evidence that some interpretations of graphs varied by gender. Impara et al. (1991) found that teachers who had taken a measurement course as part of their training were better at correctly interpreting score reports. These results highlight the fact that there is not a one-size-fits-all approach and that the creators of these displays should actively work with test users/consumers to identify the formats and variables that most effectively convey the intended information to the population of interest.

For example, Figures 10 and 11 both illustrate changes in test scores over time. Figure 10 provides more detailed information than Figure 11 (i.e., additional ages and subjects; specific score values). This level of detail and sophistication may be appropriate for researchers or others with strong statistical backgrounds. However, the level of detail may make the display inaccessible to a nontechnical audience, for whom Figure 11 would be a better choice. Figures 12 and 13 both provide cross-state comparisons of scores. Figure 12 may be easier for nontechnical audiences to understand, however, it only allows for the comparison of one state (in this case, Nebraska) to all others. Figure 13 allows for the comparison of each state to every other state. However, the added complexity and unfamiliarity of the format result in the need for the inclusion of additional interpretive guidance.

In summary, there is no "best" display for all situations. These examples illustrate that the choice of the "best" graph and the need for interpretive instructions will depend on question(s) that the graph creator is endeavoring to answer. The choice of the most appropriate display is dependent on the interaction of display type, design choices, and audience considerations. Each of these factors influences the effectives of the display, and each therefore warrants careful consideration.

Choosing Indicators Uncertainty

There are many ways to show uncertainty beyond those that have been mentioned here. For an extensive list of the ways error bands and other measures of uncertainty can be integrated in to graphs, see Harris, 1999. Additional examples and a discussion of uncertainty in test-related graphs can be found in Wainer (2009, ch. 13). Figure 14 shows how error bars/bands can be applied to various graphical formats.

There is also an extensive range of design choices to consider when constructing error bars and other indicators of distributional information. Figure 15 shows some of these variations. These indicators may be used to illustrate the uncertainty around a single test score or a statistic (e.g., a group mean). Variations a–j are examples of error bands. Variations k–r are examples of ways to display distributional information. Variations a–c show the range of the bar only. Varia-

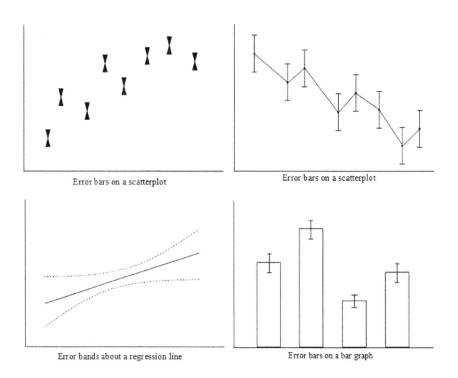

Error bars on a scatterplot

Error bars on a scatterplot

Error bands about a regression line

Error bars on a bar graph

FIGURE 14. Error bars/bands applied to various graph types (Harris, 1999)

tions d–f attempt to convey that the true scores are more likely in the center of the error bands, while variations g–i add emphasis to the midpoint. Options j and k show two sets of end makers. Cleveland and McGill (1984) suggest using this type of two-tiered error bars with 95% and 50% confidence intervals to indicate a "high probability range" and "a middle range for the sample-to-sample variation analogous to the box of a box graph" (p. 883).

The second row of Figure 15 (l–r) shows examples of indicators of distributional information. Most of these figures are variations of box-and-whisker plots (Tukey, 1977). Lane and Sándor (2009) argue that indicators of distributional information like these can be more appropriate than error bars in some cases because they provide more detailed information about the spread of data. There are multiple reasons for this. First, the significance of group differences may be ambiguous when using error bars. That is, when two separate error bars are used to indicate uncertainty around, for example, two different group means, each error bar indicates the uncertainty associated with that mean rather than the uncertainty associated with *the difference* between the two group means (which may be a more relevant piece of information, depending on the question the user hopes to answer). Second, these variations can provide more information than simple

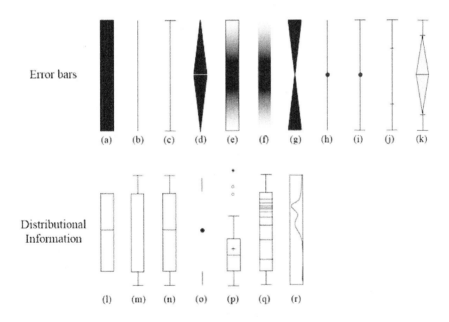

FIGURE 15. Examples of symbols to depict error bands and distributional information (Harris, 1999; Lane & Sándor, 2009; Tukey, 1977; Wainer, 2009; Zwick, Zapata-Rivera, & Hegarty, 2014)

error bars. These variations can show medians (l, n, o, p), means (p), minima and maxima (m–r), first and third quartiles (l–q), outliers (p), and more detailed distributional shapes (q and r). Tufte (2001), recommended design o, pointing out that it provides the same information as design n, but uses a much simpler representation. One downside of using distributional displays is that they may be viewed as more technical than simple error bars and therefore less appropriate for nontechnical audiences. The choice of which option to use will vary based on design preferences as well as the detail/information one desires to convey.

CONCLUSIONS AND RECOMMENDATIONS

It is important for test users/consumers to understand the level of uncertainty associated with test scores. Overconfidence in test scores can lead to misinterpretations or inappropriate uses of the results. This chapter discussed several ways in which measures of uncertainty can be integrated into visual displays used in the test development process. Multiple examples were provided in the areas of standard setting and score reporting.

The Standards make clear the need for reporting measures of uncertainty in ways that are understandable to test users/consumers. In order to meet this requirement, the following recommendations are offered:

1. Include indicators of uncertainty (e.g., error bands) directly on visual displays used in reports. Explanations of uncertainty buried in interpretive guides may be missed by test users/consumers. Whenever possible, visual displays should be constructed in such a way that the user/consumer is provided the necessary information for understanding either within, or in close proximity to, the display itself. Including these indicators in prominent locations decreases the likelihood of misinterpretation (Wainer, 2009).

2. Involve users/consumers in the construction of the visual displays. Research has shown that the effectiveness of a display type varies by audience. Goodman and Hambleton (2004) and Hambleton and Slater (1997) have also advocated for the piloting of score reports before operational use. Including stakeholders in a systematical evaluation will help to tailor the level and type of technical detail and aesthetic design to best fit the audience.

3. When there is variability in the preferences/needs of distinct groups of users/consumers, create customized versions of score reports for the different populations. This recommendation follows from the previous recommendation. In order to provide information to test users that is appropriate to their level of understanding, it may be necessary to produce tailored materials for different populations. Goodman and Hambleton (2004) and Hambleton and Slater (1997) also recommend the use of specialized reports for different audiences.

4. Echoing the recommendation of Foley and Buckendahl (2013), whenever possible, results from analyses (like those mentioned in Recommendation 2) should be shared with the professional community through journals and professional conference participation. Sharing this information (both effective and ineffective strategies) will allow those in the test development community to better serve test users/consumers.

REFERENCES

American Educational Research Association, American Psychological Association, and National Council on Measurement in Education (2014). Standards for educational and psychological testing. Washington, DC: American Educational Research Association.

Bertin, J. (1983). *Semiology of graphs*. (W. Berg, Trans.; H. Wainer, Technical Ed.). Madison: University of Wisconsin Press. (Original work published 1973)

Carswell, C. M., & Ramzy, C. (1997). Graphing small data sets: Should we bother? Behaviour & Information Technology, 16(2), 61–71.

Cizek, G. J. (Ed.). (2012). Setting performance standards: Foundations, methods, and innovations (2nd ed.). New York, NY: Routledge.

Cizek, G. J., & Bunch, M. B. (Eds.). (2007). Standard setting. Thousand Oakes, CA: Sage.

Cleveland, W. S. (1985). *The elements of graphing data.* Monterey, CA: Wadsworth Advanced Books and Software.

Cleveland, W. S., & McGill, R. (1984). Graphical perception: Theory, experimentation, and appliation to the development of graphical methods. Journal of the American Statistical Assication, 79, 531–554.

Cohen, A. S., & Wollack, J. A. (2006). Test administration, security, scoring, and reporting. In R. L. Brennan (Ed.), Educational measurement (4th ed., pp. 345–386). Westport, CT: Praeger.

Deng, N., & Yoo, H. (2009). Resources for reporting test score: A bibliography for the assessment community. Madison, WI: National Council on Measurement in Education.

Enders, C. K. (2010). Applied missing data analysis. New York, NY: Guilford.

Few, S. (2012). *Show me the numbers: Designing tables and graphs to enlighten* (2nd ed.). Burlingame, CA: Analytics.

Foley, B. P. (2014, April). *Evaluating an impact percentage smoothing vertically moderated standard setting design.* Paper presented at the annual meeting of the National Council on Measurement in Education, Philadelphia, PA.

Foley, B. P., & Buckendahl, C. W. (2013). Using visual displays to inform assessment design and development. In G. Schraw, M. McCrudden, & D. Robinson (Eds.). *Learning through visual displays* (pp. 417–445). Charlotte, NC: Information Age.

Goodman, D. P., & Hambleton, R. K. (2004). Student test score reports and interpretive guides: Review of current practices and suggestions for future research. Applied Measurement in Education, 17, 145–220.

Grigg, W., Lauko, M., & Brockway, D. (2006). The nation's report card: Science 2005 (NCES 2006-466). Washington, DC: U.S. Government Printing Office.

Haberman, S. J. (2008). When can subscores have value? Journal of Educational and Behavioral Statistics, 33(2), 204–229. doi:10.3102/1076998607302636.

Haberman, S. J., Sinharay, S., & Puhan, G. (2009). Reporting subscores for institutions. British Journal of Mathematical and Statistical Psychology, 62, 79–95.

Haertel, E. H. (2006). Reliability. In R. L. Brennan (Ed.), Educational measurement (4th ed., pp. 65–110). Westport, CT: Praeger.

Haladyna, T. M., & Kramer, G. A. (2004). The validity of subscores for a credentialing test. Evaluation and the Health Professions, 24(7), 349–368.

Hambleton, R. K., & Pitoniak, M. J. (2006). Setting performance standards. In R. L. Brennan (Ed.), Educational measurement (4th ed., pp. 433–470). Westport, CT: Praeger.

Hambleton, R. K., & Slater, S. C. (1997). Are NAEP executive summary reports understandable to policy makers and educators? (CSE Technical Report 430). Los Angeles, CA: Center for the Study of Evaluation.

Harris, R. L. (1999). Information graphics: A comprehensive illustrated reference. New York, NY: Oxford University Press.

Holland, P. W., & Dorans, N. J. (2006). Linking and equating. In R. L. Brennan (Ed.), Educational measurement (4th ed., pp. 187–220). Westport, CT: Praeger.

Impara, J. C., Divine, K. P., Bruce, F. A., Liverman, M. R., & Gay, A. (1991). Does interpretive test score information help teachers? Educational Measurement: Issues and Practice, 10(4), 16–18.

Institute for Credentialing Excellence. (2007). National Commission for Certifying Agencies standards for the accreditation of certification programs. Washington, DC: Author.

Kane, M. T. (2013). Validating the interpretations and uses of test scores. Journal of Educational Measurement, 50, 1–73.

Kolen, M. J., & Brennan, R. L. (2014). Test equating, scaling, and linking: Methods and practices (3nd ed.). New York, NY: Springer.

Lane, D. M., & Sándor, A. (2009). Designing better graphs by including distributional information and integrating words, numbers, and images. Psychological Methods, 14(3), 39–257.

Mayer, R. E. (2013). Fostering learning with visual displays. In G. Schraw, M. McCrudden, & D. Robinson (Eds.). Learning through visual displays (pp. 47-73). Charlotte, NC: Information Age.

Mazzeo, J., Lazer, S., & Zieky, M. J. (2006). Monitoring educational progress with group-score assessments. In R. L. Brennan (Ed.), Educational measurement (4th ed., pp. 681–699). Westport, CT: Praeger.

Moore, D. S. (2000). Statistics: Concepts and controversies (5th ed.). New York, NY: Freeman.

National Assessment of Educational Progress, National Center for Education Statistics, National Assessment Governing Board, Institute of Education Sciences, & U.S. Department of Education, Institute of Education Sciences, National Center for Education Statistics (n.d.). About the nation's report card. Retrieved from http://nationsreportcard.gov/about.aspx

National Center for Education Statistics (NCES). (1996a). NAEP 1994 reading report card for the nation and states. Washington, DC: Institute of Education Sciences, U.S. Department of Education.

National Center for Education Statistics (NCES). (1996b). NAEP 1994 trends in academic progress. Washington, DC: Institute of Education Sciences, U.S. Department of Education.

National Center for Education Statistics (NCES). (2010). *The nation's report card: Grade 12 reading and mathematics national and pilot state results* (NCES 2011-455). Washington, DC: Institute of Education Sciences, U.S. Department of Education.

National Center for Education Statistics (NCES). (2013). *The nation's report card: A first look: 2013 Mathematics and Reading* (NCES 2014-451). Washington, DC: Institute of Education Sciences, U.S. Department of Education.

Pastor, D. A., & Finney, S. J. (2013). Using visual displays to enhance understanding of quantitative research. In G. Schraw, M. McCrudden, & D. Robinson (Eds.), *Learning through visual displays* (pp. 387–415). Charlotte, NC: Information Age.

Playfair, W. (2005). The commercial and political atlas. In H. Wainer & I. Spence (Eds.), *The commercial and political atlas and statistical breviary* (pp. i–97). New York, NY: Cambridge University Press. (Original work published 1801)

Ryan, J. M. (2006). Practices, issues, and trends in student test score reporting. In S. M. Downing & T. M. Haladyna (Eds.), Handbook of test development (pp. 677–710). Mahwah, NJ: Erlbaum.

Scheaffer, R. L., Mendenhall, W., Ott, R. L., & Gerow, K. G. (2011). Elementary survey sampling (7th ed.). Independence, KY: Cengage Learning.

Sinharay, S. (2010). When can subscores be expected to have added value? Results from operational and simulated data (ETS RR-10-16). Princeton, NJ: Educational Testing Service.

Sinharay, S., Haberman, S., & Puhan, G. (2007). Subscores based on classical test theory: To report or not to report. Educational Measurement: Issues and Practice, 26(4), 21–28.

Thorndike, R. M., & Thorndike-Christ, T. M. (2011). Measurement and evaluation in psychology and education (8th ed.). Boston, MA: Prentice Hall.

Tufte, E. R. (2001). *The visual display of quantitative information* (2nd ed.). Cheshire, CT: Graphics.

Tukey, J. W. (1977). Exploratory data analysis. Reading, MA: Addison-Wesley.

Tukey, J. W. (1986). Sunset salvo. The American Statistician, 40, 72–76.

U.S. Department of Education, Institute of Education Sciences, National Center for Education Statistics (2014). The nation's report card mathematics 2013 state snapshot report: Nebraska grade 4 public school (NCES 2014-465NE4). Retrieved from http://nces.ed.gov/nationsreportcard/subject/publications/stt2013/pdf/2014465NE4.pdf

Van den Heuvel, J. R., Zenisky, A., & Davis-Becker, S. (2014, April). *Applying lessons learned in educational score reporting to credentialing.* Paper presented at the annual meeting of the American Educational Research Association, Philadelphia, PA.

Wainer, H. (1996). Depicting error. *The American Statistician, 50*(2), 101–111.

Wainer, H. (1997). *Visual revelations.* Mahwah, NJ: Erlbaum.

Wainer, H. (2005). *Graphical discovery: A trout in the milk and other visual adventures.* Princeton, NJ: Princeton University Press.

Wainer, H. (2009). *Picturing the uncertain world.* Princeton, NJ: Princeton University Press.

Wong, D. M. (2010). *The Wall Street Journal guide to information graphics: The dos and don'ts of presenting data, facts, and figures.* New York, NY: Norton.

Ysseldyke, J., & Nelson, J. R. (2002). Reporting results of student performance on large-scale assessments. In G. Tindal & T. M. Haladyna (Eds.), Large-scale assessment programs for all students: Validity, technical adequacy, and implementation (pp. 467–480). Mahwah, NJ: Erlbaum.

Zieky, M. J., Perie, M., & Livingston, S. A. (2008). Cutscores: A manual for setting standards of performance on educational and occupational tests. Princeton, NJ: Educational Testing Service.

Zwick, R., Zapata-Rivera, D., & Hegarty, M. (2014). Comparing graphical and verbal representations of measurement error in test score reports. *Educational Assessment, 19*, 116–138.

CHAPTER 11

VISUAL DISPLAYS FOR REPORTING TEST DATA

Making Sense of Test Performance

April L. Zenisky

ABSTRACT

Reporting assessment results is an essential part of the assessment-development process. Through results-reporting efforts, data about performance in a specific domain of interest is communicated to stakeholders, and this message must be crafted in light of test purpose and other details about nature of the test and the knowledge and skills assessed. Assessment results are typically thought of as numerical scores, but in fact current reporting practices encompass a far wider range of results, given the kinds of data involved and the different uses for test results that prevail. To this end, reporting efforts increasingly look to incorporate strategies for reporting that synthesize different data points to communicate a fuller picture of assessment information, and data visualization fulfills a critically important role in reporting practices. The present chapter provides an overview of results-reporting practices in light of test purpose and data elements (such as scores, performance levels, and projections) and also discusses data-visualization practices in two emerging areas for reporting (online communications and growth modeling). The chapter then concludes with a

Use of Visual Displays in Research and Testing: Coding, Interpreting, and Reporting Data,
pages 299–332.

synthesis of best practices from the psychometric reporting literature with respect to the use of data visualizations to communicate assessment data within and across user groups.

INTRODUCTION

While tests and test scores have been around for decades upon decades, the idea that score reports could be much more than just a name and a number on the printed page is a perspective that has been considerably slower to gain widespread traction among agencies charged with disseminating test results. This is, however, changing in many assessment contexts, as more and more tests are associated with high-stakes decisions and in many cases test-takers themselves (as well as other stakeholders) seek to mine the data for greater feedback on performance for the purpose of improving future performance. This shift in reporting focus for educational tests in the United States has been largely motivated by K–12 educational reform efforts such as No Child Left Behind (NCLB, 2002), but this transformation for reporting practices more generally is a phenomenon that is occurring regardless of borders and in contexts well beyond elementary and secondary education.

Visual displays have a critical role in this evolution of the reporting of test results, both for individuals and for groups. For test results to have meaning to stakeholders, those stakeholders must be able to put them in their proper context given the test purpose and use, and to make appropriate inferences about those results. Test score reports primarily fulfill an informational function, and while there are many ways to communicate quantitative data, well-crafted data displays can help bring out patterns or otherwise illustrate key points relative to a test's purpose and use.

The discussion of how to display results information in the context of score reporting begins with careful reflection of the test and report purpose and the kind of data to be communicated, and so this chapter begins with a brief review of what results reporting entails and the kinds of information that are often reported. It should be noted that in the present context, *displays* should be understood as graphical representations (such as charts or tables) to communicate a wide range of results data and other assessment information that may be numerical or categorical in nature. From there, the focus turns to the display strategies used in three main categories of results reporting: *summative, comparative,* and *feedback* data elements. In each of those areas, the aim is to reflect on displays used operationally and to draw out best practices for the communication of results given a variety of testing contexts. The chapter concludes with consideration of two particularly emerging areas for advances in reporting visualizations (online reporting and growth reporting), as well as a brief synthesis of guidance from the psychometric literature regarding the implementation and use of data displays.

In the present context, the practice of results reporting is based on the nature of the data being reported. The (typically) first consideration of results reporting is concerned with broad characterizations of performance for the total test or for highest-level subdomains. Such macrolevel characterizations are *summative* in nature and operate to communicate overall performance, knowledge, or skills relative to a construct or content area of interest. Summative results[1] (either in the form of scores and/or performance classifications) often seem to be prioritized among agencies and users alike because they offer a global, at-a-glance perspective that answers the primary questions of what the examinees knows and how they performed. Consequently, displays of summative data generally occupy prime real estate in the structure and format of report documents.

The next area of interest is the idea of *comparative* results. Though criterion-referenced tests and test interpretations have come to predominate in educational assessment (beginning with the work of Glaser (1963) and others, including Popham and Husek (1969) and continuing today), many agencies retain and promote normative elements in results reporting as a strategy for contextualizing performance. Typically, implementation of comparative results for individuals reports the score for an individual set against the backdrop of the average score for students in geographical groups such as school, district, and state, but there are other strategies for this in use as well, as well as a number of display approaches to communicating this information, which will be detailed later in this chapter.

The third major element of results reporting that typically has a presence in report document can be termed *feedback* results, in the sense that the data shared in this context aims to target examinees and other stakeholders to fine-grained details of performance, typically aimed at identifying specific areas for remediation, improvement, and/or advancement. Such results, which in some contexts are referenced as *diagnostic* reporting, involve a wide range of performance data, from subscores to item-level results.

A comment about the terminology used in this chapter: in some ways, the term "score report" itself can be a bit misleading, as the common (and perhaps, most persistent) connotation of a score report is as a record of an individual's performance, most often printed on an 8.5" by 11" piece of paper. However, the practice of results reporting at present is often quite different. The reporting of assessment results today is as likely to be for groups as it is for individuals, and the dissemination of results across intended audiences and user groups is increasingly digital rather than paper-based. For this reason, the term *results reporting* is used throughout this chapter to reference reporting efforts and materials/documents, to get away from the one-size-sits-all mentality implied by "a score report."

---

[1] Note that the term *summative* is used here to describe the level of data reporting that is focused on strategies for illustrating overall performance on a test and should not be construed as results reporting specific to some test purposes but not others; this is to say, summative data can be an element of reporting efforts for both summative and formative assessments.

RESULTS REPORTING: AN OVERVIEW

The 2014 edition of the *Standards for Educational and Psychological Testing* (American Educational Research Association, American Psychological Association, and National Council on Measurement in Education, 2014) positions reporting as a key responsibility for test development agencies in the context of supporting appropriate inferences specific to various audiences for reports. The focus of the reporting-related Standards is to provide test users with relevant and audience-specific information about what scores represent and which interpretations of scores are valid in a given testing context. While the Standards do not address the use of specific report elements (such as displays, but also tables, text, and numerical representations of data) as mechanisms for communication of test information, displays can and do present testing agencies with a clear opportunity for the effective presentation of results.

Stepping back for a moment, however, what *is* results reporting? As an activity that occurs part and parcel in the progression of test development, reporting encompasses the process by which data about human knowledge and skill (as measured by an instrument of some kind) is conveyed to intended users. This may involve performance details specific to individuals, but also operates for groups of test-takers as well. This is particularly relevant for the reporting that takes place in educational assessment, where groups can be based on geography (class, school, district, state, country), demographics (e.g., gender, race/ethnicity, socioeconomic status), or other relevant person attributes (such as students with individualized education plans [IEPs] or English learners). Of course, this distinction between individual and group-level reporting is a critically important one for report design and development, because the fundamental nature of the data available for inclusion in a report changes when the reporting context shifts from one to many, accompanied by a change in permissible interpretations.

In the case of individualized results, the intended audience is typically the examinee or that examinee's family: the data to be included on the report is specific to that individual and in most applications is protected by federal privacy statutes (Family Educational Rights and Privacy Act [FERPA], 1974). A sample of a typical student-level report is provided in Figures 1 and 2.

The fictional results displayed for Jane Marie Doe in Figures 1 and 2 on a state assessment are provided for three content areas (Language Arts, Mathematics, and Science), and the data elements in Figure 1 are typical of a fairly basic summative reporting effort, as described previously, focusing on scale scores, proficiency classifications, and a score range. The report itself is sectioned to draw attention first to the personal details for the student whose scores are being reported, and the bottom half of Figure 1 then provides the summary of performance for the three content areas. In this case, the information of interest is both proficiency levels and scale scores. The proficiency levels and the range of scores for each are listed on the left side of the graph, and then a simple column graph is used to visually represent those results, for both the specific score attained and the profi-

STATE Individual Student Report Spring 2016

Student: Doe, Jane Marie
STATE ID number: 12345678
Date of Birth: 5/17/2007
Grade: 3
Sex: Female

County: Hartford
District: Spring Valley
School: Meadow Elementary School
Local District/School ID number: 987654

Test Administrator: Smith, Sandy
Test Booklet number: 2016-123456

This report shows your child's results the Spring 2016 STATE TEST test administration in Language Arts, Mathematics and Science.

The STATE TEST measures your child's performance on selected benchmarks in Language Arts, Mathematics and Science as defined by the *Curriculum Content Standards*. Scores on this test are one indication of your child's achievement in relation to these content standards.

Your child's STATE TEST proficiency levels and scores

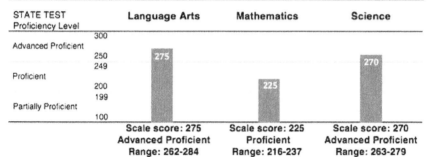

	Scale score: 275	Scale score: 225	Scale score: 270
	Advanced Proficient	Proficient	Advanced Proficient
	Range: 262-284	Range: 216-237	Range: 263-279

The STATE TEST score shows achievement on the date tested. If these same tests were taken again, it is likely that your child would score in the scale score ranges provided.

More about STATE TEST
Questions about your performance on the STATE TEST can be directed to your child's teacher. For more information about state assessments, including sample test questions, writing tasks, and proficiency level descriptions, consult the STATE Department of Education Website:
http://www.STATE.gov/education/assessment/

FIGURE 1. Page 1 of a fictional student-level score report

ciency level into which each content area score falls). At a glance, it is apparent that "Jane" has reached a high level of proficiency in Language Arts and Science, while her Mathematics performance is a bit lower, falling in the "Proficient" level.

The second page of the report (Figure 2) shows one approach to feedback reporting, providing further details about performance in each of the three content areas. The student's scale score in each area is reiterated, and a performance-level description is included to explain what skills and knowledge are typical at the

Jane's Language Arts Literacy Results

Jane scored a **275** in Language Arts Literacy and her performance is in the **Advanced Proficient** level.

Overall, students performing at the *Advanced Proficient* level in Writing establish and sustain a single focus, organize and connect ideas with effective transitions, and elaborate with vivid supporting details. The student at this level varies sentence structures, chooses precise words to convey meaning and message, and consistently uses the conventions of written language. S/he may take compositional risks.

Students performing at *Advanced Proficient* in Reading clearly and consistently demonstrate the ability to synthesize, analyze, and extend the meaning of the text. In addition, the Advanced Proficient reader interacts with the text and makes meaningful connections in order to generate and extend ideas in written responses.

What are your child's strengths and weaknesses in Language Arts Literacy?

Total Writing

Expository Task

Speculative Task

The Writing cluster consists of two writing prompts. The *Expository Task* requires students to compose an essay that explains a topic, and in the *Speculative Task* students use a brief scenario as a springboard for writing a story.

Total Reading

Working with Text

Analyzing Text

The Reading cluster targets two skill areas. *Working with Text* is comprised of items that focus on interpretive strategies. *Analyzing Text* includes evaluative strategies. Reading passages are *Narrative* or *Informational*.

Jane's Mathematics Results

Jane scored a **225** in Mathematics and her performance is in the **Proficient** level.

Students performing at the Proficient level in Mathematics demonstrate recall, recognition and application of facts and informational concepts. Proficient students perform routine procedures such as computing a sum, difference or product, and can use a specified procedure with accuracy. Proficient students understand and apply concepts of geometry and measurement. Proficient students demonstrate an understanding of how quantities are related to one another and how algebra can be used to concisely represent and analyze those relationships. Proficient students understand and apply the concepts and methods of data analysis, probability, and discrete mathematics. Proficient students use various forms of representation to illustrate steps to a solution and effectively communicate a variety of reasoning methods to solve multi-step problems.

What are your child's strengths and weaknesses in Mathematics?

Total Mathematics

Number & Numerical Operations

Geometry & Measurement

Patterns & Algebra

Data Analysis, Probability, & Discrete Mathematics

There are four clusters of skills and knowledge in the Mathematics test: *Number & Numerical Operations, Geometry & Measurement, Patterns & Algebra,* and *Data Analysis, Probability, & Discrete Mathematics*.

Jane's Science Results

Jane scored a **270** in Science and her performance is in the **Advanced Proficient** level.

Students performing at the Advanced Proficient level in Science can support scientific conclusions with valid contextual and visual data and make predictions based on the interactions of living things. This student is able to use interpretive skills to analyze visual and textual data in order to solve problems dealing with the application of force and energy. The advanced proficient student understands the difference between types of energy waves and can recognize and apply experimental principles and empirical data. The advanced proficient student can recognize the nature of the tides' relationship to Earth, Sun, and moon; interpret topographical maps; and identify the steps in the process of weathering and erosion.

What are your child's strengths and weaknesses in Science?

Total Science

Life Science

Physical Science

Earth Science

Science consists of three clusters: *Life, Physical,* and *Earth* sciences.

FIGURE 2. Page 2 of a fictional student-level score report.

performance-classification level attained by the student. Finally, for each content area, a graphical representation of subdomain performance is included. It is critically important to separate out considerations for the display of subscore information from the underlying data that is to be reported, as the inclusion of subscores will require a statistical mechanism for calculating such performance to be carried out in a statistically defensible way (see Sinharay, Puhan, & Haberman, 2011, for an introduction to the technical considerations that impact subscore computation). In terms of subscore display relative to Figure 2, the visual element here is used to characterize subdomain performance in the language of the performance levels and make that information readily apparent without presenting numerical scores.

The reporting elements shown in Figures 1 and 2 are but a single exemplar implementation of summative and feedback-reporting approaches. To expand on the contents of Figures 1 and 2, reporting documents for individuals may include a variety of data elements, such as a test history listing prior years' performance (where available/relevant), as well as a section that focuses on the present assessment's overall test score and subscores (where computed and provided). Proficiency classifications typically vary considerably across reporting contexts, as the number of proficiency categories may range from just two (pass or fail, which is common in certification and licensure testing) to three, four, or more. The National Assessment of Educational Progress (NAEP), used as a yardstick for measuring educational change in the United States among schoolchildren, has three defined proficiency categories (*Basic*, *Proficient*, and *Advanced*), and also reports results for the below *Basic* group. Reports can include normative results in the form of comparisons of interest (in K–12 testing in the United States, oftentimes a single student's performance is compared to the class, the district and the state; while results for classes, schools, and grades may be held against each other in aggregate as well). Some individual reports will include additional feedback information such as growth projections, results for individual test questions, and breakdowns of performance by item type.

Turning to group-level results, the main division among these reports concerns their purpose: some group reports are intended for within-school use and are essentially listings of individual performances (Figure 3) produced for use at a class or school level, while other group reports are true aggregations of scores or performance classifications (Figure 4) for clusters of individuals (which again could be based on geography, demographics, or other grouping variables). The true aggregations can be used for class results, but are often used by school building administrators at the grade or school level to find local patterns, or rolled up to district or state for use by other administrators to communicate broader trends of performance to audiences of educators or to the public at-large.

Figure 3 shows a sample roster-style report for the New Jersey Assessment of Skills and Knowledge (New Jersey Department of Education, 2012). In this specific example, the table with results contains student identifiers (name, testing system ID, student ID, and date of birth) followed by flags indicating other characteristics such a gender and presence of individualized education plan (IEP) or 504 plan, and then results, in the form of overall scale scores and points earned in each of several subdomain areas. This information is formatted as a table and is heavy on text, but structures assessment results for a group of individuals in a sequence to facilitate lookup of individual performance but *not* aggregation across the group. Again, the sample report shown in Figure 4 is but a typical example of

TEST DATE: SPRING 2012
REPORT PRINTED: 7/19/2012

New Jersey Assessment of Skills and Knowledge
Student Roster - Language Arts Literacy
Grade 6

COUNTY: 88 ANY COUNTY
DISTRICT: 7777 ANY DISTRICT
SCHOOL: 666 ANOTHER SCHOOL

STUDENTS PROCESSED: 35

POINTS EARNED BY CLUSTER [1]

STUDENT NAME NJ ASK ID NUMBER / SID	DOB	SEX	LEP	SE	504	ACCOM	OUT OF DIST	OUT OF RES	SPEC FORM	SCALE SCORE	WRITING 18.0 [2] 9.0	PERSUASIVE TASK 12.0 6.5	EXPLANATORY TASK 6.0 3.1	READING 52.0 28.5	WORKING WITH TEXT 28.0 13.0	ANALYZING TEXT 20.0 15.5	TOTAL 70.0 38.0
HILL, FRANCISCO 6191039480 / 0000012001	04/01/00	M								215	9.0	6.0	3.0	36.0	17.0	19.0	45.0
MITCHELL, HIRAN 6191039522 / 0000012007	10/02/00	M	3							215	11.0	8.0	3.0	34.0	16.0	18.0	45.0
AGWUEGBO, ERIC G 6190891097 / 0000012389	03/18/00	M								213	10.0	6.0	4.0	34.0	14.0	20.0	44.0
AMADI, RUSTY 6190891162 / 0000012476	02/10/00	M								213	10.0	6.0	4.0	34.0	14.0	20.0	44.0
BERRY, DANEL 8190607170 / 0000012040	04/05/00	M								210	10.0	6.0	4.0	33.0	14.0	19.0	43.0
MURAD, LUIS 6191039514 / 0000012005	06/13/00	M								210	9.0	6.0	3.0	34.0	16.0	16.0	43.0
BROOME, WILLIAM 6191039421 / 0000011993	06/21/00	M		14		AB				208	11.0	8.0	3.0	31.0	14.0	17.0	42.0
KRAYEM, TIEANDRA L 6190115992 / 0000012046	06/04/00	F	F1							208	8.0	4.0	4.0	34.0	18.0	16.0	42.0
ALHARAZIM, S LENY 6190891154 / 0000012475	11/06/00	F	1							196	9.0	6.0	3.0	28.0	12.0	15.0	37.0
GARDNER, JODY 6190057897 / 0000012047	08/18/00	F								194	10.0	6.0	4.0	26.0	13.0	13.0	36.0

[1] The numbers in this row are the number of possible raw score points for students who were scored on the full set of regular items.

[2] The numbers in this row are the statewide raw score means for students whose scale score is 200 and who were scored on the full set of regular items.

[3] A letter code appears for writing tasks that could not be scored for one of the following reasons:
FR = Fragment, NE = Not English, NR = No Response, OT = Off Topic.

88-7777-666
Page 2 of 5

FIGURE 3. Roster-style report of group performance (New Jersey Department of Education, 2012; Retrieved from http://www.state.nj.us/education/assessment/ms/5-8/ref/SIM12.pdf)

CLASS SCORE REPORT

What Is My Class's Average Mathematics Score?

Mathematics Achievement Results

CLASS AVERAGE SCORE

Your class's average score is 407. This is similar to the performance of the third-graders in your school, higher than that of third-graders in your district and lower than that of third-graders statewide.

Your Class's Average Score: 407

Limited	Basic	Proficient	Accelerated	Advanced
		District Average Score: 404	State Average Score: 420	
		School Average Score: 410		

FIGURE 4. Aggregation of performance for a class group (Ohio Department of Education, n.d.; retrieved from http://ohiokids.air.org/pdfs/OHSp06_4C_W_mu.pdf)

a roster-style report, and such documents can include other data (such as performance classifications) or be structured and/or represented differently. These types of reports could also include prior year results (when matching is available) and other test information, such as norm-referenced tests).

The exemplar report in Figure 4 is (purposefully) a rather simple display and functions as one data element among many on a report intended for teacher use. This is an aggregation of individual results, used to characterize a group of individual examinees on the basis of some defining grouping variable (here, membership in a specific teacher's class; other aggregations could include smaller groups within a class or based on other characteristics of interest, such as sex, race/ethnicity, lunch status, etc.). The data element is introduced by the question "What is My Class's Average Mathematics Score?" and the bar graph has a ticker to show where the average score for the class falls among the five labeled sections of the bar (corresponding to the five performance levels in use for this test). Also illustrated here are the comparison performances for the school, the district, and the state. It should be noted that this display is predicated on an interest in the reporting of central tendency—the mean score—for a group, and there are of course limitations of that statistic, but this display communicates that overall data point clearly and effectively.

Branching outward from the display shown in Figure 4, displays that show performance for aggregate reports for groups typically focus on either the average scale scores for groups, breakdown of performance level classifications, or illustrate performance by subdomain or item type. NAEP is an especially notable leader in the group-reporting realm, as the reporting of NAEP is entirely focused on groups, and much of NAEP's reporting efforts are targeted at audiences concerned with assessment and policy. A sample state-level report of performance-level results for Massachusetts relative to the nation is provided below in Figure 5.

This particular display in Figure 5 appears as one component among several others on the Massachusetts State Report Card for 2013 (U.S. Department of Education, Institute of Education Sciences, National Center for Education Statistics, 2014), and illustrates the proportion of students in each of the four NAEP achievement levels in Massachusetts for 2009 as compared to 2013, and the results for the nation in 2013 are also provided for additional context and comparison. Note too that the three separate bars shown in this display are recentered so as to facilitate the particular inferences about proportions of students in two composite achievement levels: the lower level encompasses those students who were classified as Below *Basic* or at *Basic* and the higher level is composed of those students who were classified as *Proficient* or *Advanced*. This display shows that while Massachusetts has a higher proportion of students in the upper two achievement levels relative to the results for public school students nationally, fewer Massachusetts students were in those upper categories in 2013 as compared to 2009. The design elements of this display serve to focus users on those two composite achievement levels, but users can also draw on the data presented to make inferences about the

Achievement-Level Percentages and Average Score Results

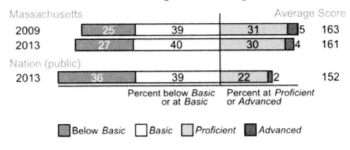

NOTE: Detail may not sum to totals because of rounding.

FIGURE 5.   State-level results (U.S. Department of Education, Institute of Education Sciences, National Center for Education Statistics, The Nation's Report Card: Mathematics 2013 State Snapshot Reports for Grade 12 - Massachusetts; Retrieved from http://nces.ed.gov/nationsreportcard/subject/publications/stt2013/pdf/2014082MA12.pdf)

individual achievement levels as well as within-state trends over time (and recall, this display is within a publication that is Massachusetts specific).

SUMMATIVE RESULTS REPORTING: STRATEGIES FOR SHOWING SCORES

As noted previously, summative results reporting (in the sense of both overall test scores and performance classifications) has historically figured prominently on report documents. This is to be expected, as the overall test score and performance indicators such as proficiency levels have been and continue to be central to the interpretation and use interests of a wide range of stakeholders.

The exemplar of an overall performance display for an individual previously shown in the lower portion of Figure 1 is typical of state approaches to reporting overall results. As noted earlier, that particular display shows results for three distinct content areas. Inclusion of elements such as (a) the score scale (including demarcations between proficiency levels), (b) a graphical representation of scores attained, and (c) textual reinforcement of the observed scale score, (d) the proficiency level attained, and (e) the score range based on the standard error of measurement are all relatively common to many individual reports for students. A slight variation on the reporting of individual results in an educational context is provided in Figure 6.

The display in Figure 6 shows results for a single content area, with short descriptors of the knowledge and skills expected at each proficiency level and comparisons to the school, district, and state. The display again links the individual's

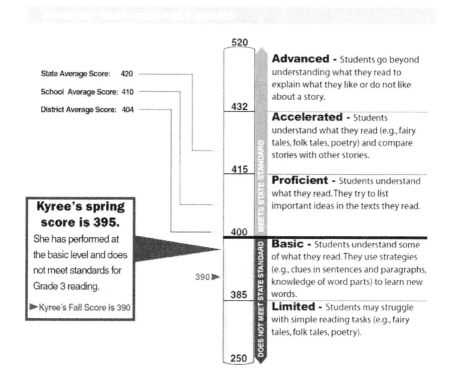

FIGURE 6. Sample of summative results for an individual (Ohio Department of Education, n. d.; Retrieved from https://education.ohio.gov/getattachment/Topics/Testing/Achievement-Tests/OAA_2012_FamilyGuide_DRAFT_7-5-12-6.pdf.aspx)

performance against reference groups of interest (the school, state, and district), but also highlights when a student has met or not met the state standards for Reading by drawing user attention to the cut score of 400 and in effect illustrating a pass-fail line that splits the five achievement levels. Here, students in the *Basic* and *Limited* categories have not met the state standard, while *Proficient, Accelerated*, and *Advanced* students have.

It is however necessary to look well outside of the realm of K–12 testing in the United States to find significant variation from those basic elements for reporting for individuals, though that may well be a function of the more or less consistent reporting interests and needs of families in the educational testing context. Figure 7 represents a substantial departure in the conceptualization of a display for individual results by prominently incorporating a speedometer motif for an assessment of language proficiency. The set of four column graphs to the right correspond to subdomain scores.

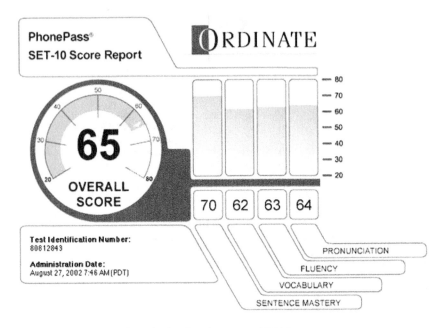

FIGURE 7.   Display of results for the PhonePass SET-10 assessment

The score scale in the overall score section is visually clear in showing where the score obtained falls relative to the score scale. The use of the vertical bars on the right-hand portion of this display also provide a visually clean overview of performance in each of the four subdomain areas.

Turning to group reporting of overall results, the nature of the data available to be communicated may be much broader, and consequently the range of possible displays much larger. Group-level summative reports fulfill several different roles in terms of communication, focusing either on scores or on proportions of individuals in reporting groups, and either at a single point in time or as part of trend reporting. The NAEP achievement-level results shown in Figure 5 offer one example of group-level reporting showing changes in proportions for proficiency groups over a period of two test administrations encompassing 4 years. Figure 8 is also a graphic pulled from NAEP reporting, showing trend lines for student groups based on race/ethnicity starting with the 1990 administration. Some key elements to point out here include the use of dotted lines to denote administrations where accommodations were not permitted (prior to 1996), the addition of the reporting category of "Two or more races" in 2000, and the connection of scale score results to NAEP Achievement levels on the right side of the chart. This display, among many others, is online at http://www.nationsreportcard.gov/reading_math_2013/#/gains-by-group, and when users click on the individual trend lines as suggested, the average scale scores for each data point are displayed, and

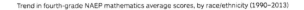

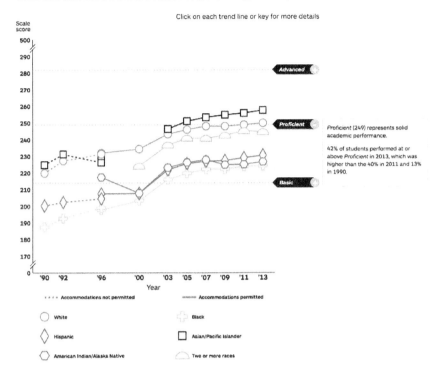

FIGURE 8.   NAEP scale score trend results for students by race/ethnicity (U.S. Department of Education, Institute of Education Sciences, National Center for Education Statistics, National Assessment of Educational Progress (NAEP), 2013 Mathematics and Reading Assessments; Retrieved from http://www.nationsreportcard.gov/reading_math_2013/#/gains-by-group

these results are marked with a "*" to denote significant differences relative to the comparison year of 2013 (which itself is customizable by users).

The primary intent in the selection of the displays shown here (Figures 6 through 8) is to refocus the conversation about displays in the context of results reporting in order to reiterate the importance of the choices agencies make about the data to be shown and their purpose(s) for reporting. For example, Figure 8 is a trend display. It includes a great deal of relevant information, such as the scale scores and the achievement levels and an administration policy change, but most importantly, it illustrates a main pattern of increasing achievement *in the presence of persistent gaps*. To carry on with the NAEP example, NAEP is primarily an assessment with a policy purpose, and consequently, results reporting in NAEP should primarily fulfill policy aims, and the display choices should likewise be purposeful and relevant to the overall reporting purpose.

COMPARATIVE RESULTS REPORTING: COMMUNICATING CONNECTIONS

The next area of interest for displays in results reporting is the idea of display strategies for comparative data. For individual-level results, an example of a strategy for facilitating comparisons between the performance of an individual relative to reference groups of interest is present in Figure 6: in that sample report, the users can relatively quickly obtain an impression of the individual's standing

Percentage comparison between states and the nation for public school students at or above *Proficient* in fourth-grade NAEP mathematics: 2013

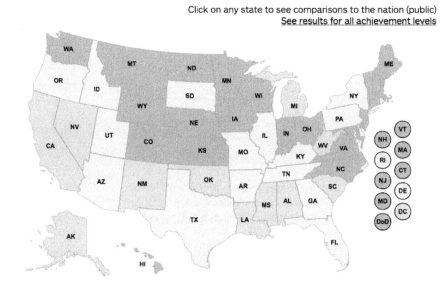

Click on any state to see comparisons to the nation (public)
See results for all achievement levels

NOTE: DoD = Department of Defense Education Activity (DoDEA).

| Higher percentage than the nation (public) | Percentage not significantly different from the nation (public) | Lower percentage than the nation (public) |

FIGURE 9.   NAEP state map comparison (U.S. Department of Education, Institute of Education Sciences, National Center for Education Statistics, National Assessment of Educational Progress (NAEP), 2013 Mathematics and Reading Assessments; Retrieved from http://www.nationsreportcard.gov/reading_math_2013/#/state-performance)

relative to significant comparison groups, and such inferences are subject to the standard cautions for norm-referenced test interpretations more generally. A parallel norm-referenced comparison is provided in Figure 4 for the performance of a class grouping as compared to school, district, and state averages.

There are, however, some innovations in displays and display strategies in the area of comparative results reporting. The clickable state maps used by NAEP in recent years constitute one such example. The map in Figure 9 is designed to facilitate between-state comparisons on NAEP's 4th-grade mathematics test using the 2013 results. Here, the states are color-coded to show how the percentage of students at or above *Proficient* in each state compares to the national percentage. This tool is also clickable, allowing users to change the reference group (from national public) as desired.

The use of maps as a visual mechanism for illustrating performance can be quite effective: in the NAEP example, the display itself is can be manipulated so that the user can select the reference group to be any state of interest, but even in static reporting contexts, the contrast of higher- and lower-achieving jurisdictions can be powerful in facilitating interpretations about comparisons (Zenisky & Hambleton, 2007).

Another display to illustrate comparisons of performance is shown in Figure 10. The bar chart is color-coded by achievement levels, where the achievement level results for the district of Hartford is compared to the overall Connecticut state data, and the results are broken down for English language learners (ELLs) and non-ELLs for the district and the state. Online users of these data can click on

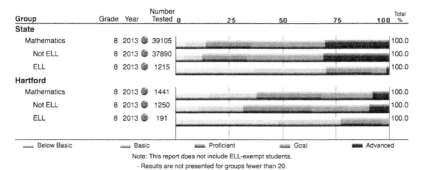

FIGURE 10.   Connecticut Mastery Test results (http://solutions1.emetric.net/CMT-Public/CMTCode/ChartSelections.aspx)

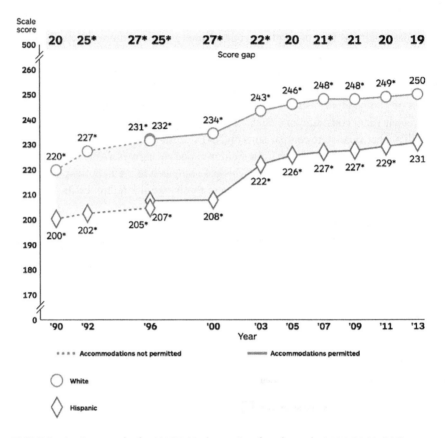

FIGURE 11. Gap results for NAEP Mathematics, fourth grade 1990-2013 (U.S. Department of Education, Institute of Education Sciences, National Center for Education Statistics, National Assessment of Educational Progress (NAEP), 2013 Mathematics and Reading Assessments; Retrieved from www.nationsreportcard. gov/reading_math_2013/#/state-performance)

the pie chart icons shown to see pop-up pie charts of these data (with percentages displayed) as well.

This display is comparable to the NAEP display of performance levels shown in Figure 5, where again, the focus is on a visual representation of performance levels, to facilitate part-whole comparisons (Hartford to the state, and ELL/non-ELL to overall performance).

Any discussion of comparative results, focusing largely on group comparisons must include some reference to reporting of score gaps. Figure 11 shows a line-graph approach used in NAEP to report performance over time for Hispanic and White examinees. The magnitude of the score gap between the two groups is il-

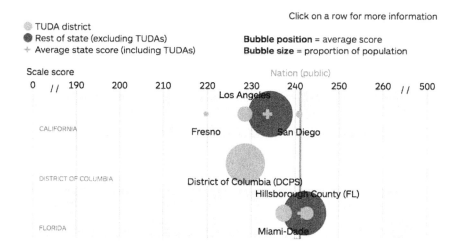

FIGURE 12. Results comparing NAEP Trial Urban Districts to Home States (partial sample); Retrieved from http://www.nationsreportcard.gov/reading_math_tuda_2013/#/tuda-comparison

lustrated visually with the line but is also reported directly by placing the values for the size of the group score differences at each time point along the top of the graph, in bold-type font (with significance denoted with a "*"). In this example, the line graph makes it possible for the viewer to clearly see that pattern over a specific time frame. Such a display enables the viewer to efficiently identify and understand the trend between the two groups over time, particularly as it affects the size of the gap.

Finally, in the area of comparative reporting, one additional, particularly innovative, display found in the reporting materials for NAEP's Trial Urban District Assessment (TUDA) is designed to foster inferences about the urban districts relative to each district's home state. In Figure 12, the display technique of "bubbles" is used to illustrate comparisons: as noted in the legend near the top of the figure, bubble size has meaning as proportion of population, position tells average score, and the plus sign denotes the average score for the state excluding the TUDA district(s) for the state. For example, the California results in Figure 12 show that San Diego is a small district relative to the whole of California (and is smaller than Los Angeles Unified School District), but the performance of San Diego is higher on average than Fresno, Los Angeles, or the state.

This bubble display uses a range of visual elements to communicate information in a meaningful way. In inferential statistics, sample size is critically important to attaching meaning to results, and here, bubble size is intended to convey that information. Likewise, positioning matters as a way to illustrate score given the presentation of the score scale along the top of the display. Though only a portion of this display is included here, the listing of participant states and TUDA districts represents an especially novel strategy for comparative reporting that significantly reduces the use of numbers and instead relies on graphic elements to communicate highly complex data about student performance within and across units of analysis (here, states and urban districts).

FEEDBACK RESULTS REPORTING:
FACILITATING THE FINER-GRAINED FINDINGS

The final area of interest in discussing broad groupings of results concerns feedback reporting. Feedback can take many forms in results reporting, but most typically is motivated by an interest in greater specificity of results, below the level of overall scores or even high-level subdomains. This is most often included for the purpose of helping examinees improve performance in the future. In recent years, the movement to include feedback-related data elements on reports has largely come about as a result of examinee and stakeholder requests, because as tests have acquired increasingly high-stakes uses, the intended users of the data have sought to mine the data for guidance about next steps and/or strategies-targeted improvement. Broadly speaking, displays used for feedback reporting span a relatively wide range of charts and tables. The statistical data represented on those displays is most readily conceptualized as a score (raw or scaled) obtained relative to an overall score available in each of a subareas of interest (which for example, could be defined as content, cognitive levels, or item type), although other approaches to feedback reporting are also in use, as described below.

To begin, some feedback-reporting elements are focused on items and item types. In Massachusetts, the individual student report for the Massachusetts Comprehensive Assessment System (MCAS) displays individual student responses to all individual items (and a selection of items are released annually, though this is not typical of high-stakes educational assessments). The Massachusetts report is online at http://www.doe.mass.edu/mcas/2013/pgguide/g3-8-10English.pdf. The individual candidate report for the Massachusetts Test of Educator Licensure (MTEL) describes subarea performance in two ways. The first strategy shown in Figure 13 describes the proportion of multiple choice items the candidate answered correctly, and the second strategy offers a characterization of the quality of the candidate's open-response answers (Figure 13).

The relatively simple tabular display in Figure 13 offers a straightforward break-down of examinee performance relative to several dimensions of interest (subareas and item types). Of course, this information is primarily useful for the failing candidates, to aid in preparation for future retests by focusing examinees on elements of where their performance might have been more deficient, that underlie the overall score or performance designation. The practice of feedback reporting at the item type or even item level is also seen in some educational test results that report efforts at the group level, where the proportion of selected and

Subarea/Section Name	Range of Number of Items in Subarea	Description of Your Subarea Performance			
		For Multiple-Choice Items You Answered Correctly:			
		Most or all items	Many of the items	Some of the items	Few or no items
Foundations of Reading Development	31 or more	✓			
Development of Reading Comprehension	21 to 30			✓	
Reading Assessment and Instruction	11 to 20			✓	
		For Open-Response Items Your Responses Were:			
		Thorough	Adequate	Limited	Weak, Blank/ Unscorable
Integration of Knowledge and Understanding	2		✓		

FIGURE 13.   Item type breakdown for the Massachusetts Test of Educator Licensure (MTEL) (Evaluation Systems, Pearson; Retrieved from http://www.mtel.nesinc.com/PDFs/MTEL_Score_Report_Explanation_Web.pdf)

constructed-response items answered correctly by the group is provided (often to the user group of educators).

Feedback data on score reports can also be structured as text, where observed test results from individual examinees (what they answered right and wrong) is used to develop brief points that summarize areas of relative strength and weakness that are displayed on their reports. Research done by Hambleton, Sireci, and Huff (2008) on the SAT used item response modeling, scale anchoring, and item mapping (methods described by Beaton & Allen, 1992 and Zwick, Senturk, Wang, & Loomis, 2001) to characterize the meaning of different score intervals on the SAT score scale. This strategy was implemented in the SAT Skills Insight online tool at http://sat.collegeboard.org/practice/sat-skills-insight, in which sample questions keyed to various score intervals are provided for the SAT Reading, Mathematics, and Writing sections. These types of approaches (where quantitative data about items is mapped to levels of performance or to specific points on the score scale) is a viewed by agencies and users alike as a way to connect performance to more helpful statements about what examinees know and can do.

There are, of course many other ways to provide feedback data to individuals. Some certification and licensure companies have incorporated feedback reporting in their reporting documents; the American Institute of Certified Public Accountants (AICPA) has developed a strategy of reporting subdomain performance for individuals using a reference group composed of candidates just above the passing cut score. A candidate's performance on each subdomain is compared to the performance of that reference group and characterized as weaker, comparable, or stronger. The information, as depicted in Figure 14, is aimed at candidates who are near passing so that they may strategically target their study efforts given how their own performance aligns to just-passing candidates

As in Figure 13, this subdomain performance reporting strategy is a table-style display with information present in certain cells to suggest broad areas of strengths and weakness in a candidate's skills (as noted above, framed relative to

Your performance Compared to Passing Candidates*
by Content Area

Content Area (% of multiple choice questions)	Weaker	Comparable	Stronger
Ethics & Responsibilities (15-19%)		Comparable	
Business Law (17-21%)		Comparable	
Federal Tax (11-15%)	Weaker		
Property Transactions (12-16%)	Weaker		
Individual Taxation (13-19%)			Stronger
Entity Taxation (18-24%)	Weaker		

FIGURE 14.   Example of subdomain reporting on the Uniform CPA Exam (American Institutes of Certified Public Accountants; Retrieved from http://www.aicpa.org/BecomeACPA/CPAExam/PsychometricsandScoring/CandidatePerformanceReport/DownloadableDocuments/Sample_CandidatePerformanceReport.pdf)

the specified reference group). A challenge for this approach is the choice of reference group, but this again connects to purpose; in credentialing, the emphasis is so much on the pass-fail line, and so the reference group is purposefully constructed to reflect the performance of passing candidates *whose scores are quite near the cut score*. For failing candidates, that reference group is likely to be most informative, because it focuses failing examinees on areas that they need to work on to improve so that they too can become just like the just-passing candidates. At the end of the day, in certification and licensure, a just-passing candidate and a top-scoring candidate have both demonstrated the required competency.

The subdomain approach to feedback reporting has been an especial area of psychometric activity in recent years across testing contexts and settings (Haberman, 2008; Haberman, Sinharay, & Puhan, 2009; Lyrén, 2009; Monaghan, 2006). Where there is interest in more detail about performance, the idea of subscores is in the conversation because they are perceived as more specific (and therefore informative for identifying areas for improvement) than the overall score. However, the main challenge for subscore reporting is the fundamental psychometric problem of low reliability (described in Ling, 2012), and ultimately, utility. In many testing applications (outside of diagnostic testing), there are often too few items that measure a specific subdomain or topic area to compute subscores that are reliable for the intended use of guidance for next steps. Returning to the 2014 *Standards for Educational and Psychological Testing* (2014) cited earlier in this chapter, there are standards that address the cautions that agencies must consider in the reporting of subscores, including Standard 2.3 (which concerns the expectation that estimates of precision should be reported) and Standard 6.10 (that agencies must provide guidance about appropriate interpretations, which includes reference to reliability and intended uses). It is for these reasons that agencies have adopted more of the types of subdomain or subscore reporting strategies such as that shown previously in Figure 14, where the subscore reporting is not in terms of scores but rather using categorical approaches to characterize performance comparisons with respect to relevant reference groups.

THE ROAD AHEAD IN VISUALIZATIONS FOR REPORTING TEST RESULTS

Though an incredible amount of advancement has occurred in recent years with regard to the processes for developing and evaluating reports (Goodman & Hambleton, 2004; Zenisky & Hambleton, 2012, Zapata-Rivera, 2011), there remains great opportunity in the area of reporting for research into effective displays and communication strategies. In particular, while the considerable body of work on data visualization by Tufte, Cleveland, and Wainer have brought much-needed attention to the topic for the betterment of many score reporting efforts, the mechanisms for dissemination and the results themselves are evolving, and the way that users interact with displays of test results is changing. Results are also taking on higher and higher stakes, and the need for users to understand complex test data is growing in importance. Thus, visualizations clearly have a key role in results reporting. In the remainder of this chapter, the focus is on two areas of particular challenge (and opportunity) for data visualization in the reporting realm.

Online Reporting

How people are accessing, reviewing, and engaging with test results has changed immensely in recent years, with the increasing use and prevalence of digital delivery for report dissemination. Across reporting contexts, display choices have typically been subject to reasonable statistical and validity considerations but constrained further by printing limitations. The expense of color printing and the realities of paper size and page borders have long served as the basis for fairly constant boundaries for report structure and appearance, and as a consequence engendered a relatively formulaic approach to the design and layout of reporting documents. But, as reporting systems have been implemented online in recent years, the nature and format of opportunities to display data has expanded considerably. This is the case particularly in terms of implementing displays that are user-generated or possess clickable elements that can be manipulated or otherwise link to additional contextual information.

To this end, one reporting system that serves as a leader in the area of digital dissemination in terms of empowering users in the creation and use of data displays is the Data Explorer software that is implemented for public use as the NAEP Data Explorer (NDE; http://nces.ed.gov/nationsreportcard/naepdata/) and in four international assessment offshoots (the PISA International Data Explorer, the PIRLS International Data Explorer, the TIMSS International Data Explor-

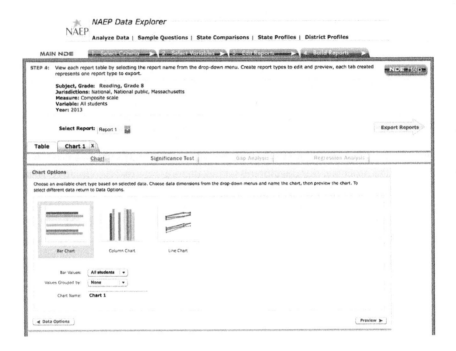

FIGURE 15. Customizability of displays within the NAEP Data Explorer software (U.S. Department of Education, Institute of Education Sciences, National Center for Education Statistics; Retrieved from http://nces.ed.gov/nationsreportcard/naepdata/)

er, and the U.S. PIAAC International Data Explorer, all accessible from http://nces.ed.gov/surveys/international/ide/). Broadly speaking, these online data tools are structured so as to function as menu-driven data analysis software websites, where users can submit queries to obtain descriptive results and also carry out significance tests, gap analyses, and regression analyses as well. What is especially remarkable about the Data Explorer software is the level of customizability present for users not only in terms of analysis capabilities but also for supporting and even promoting the visualization of data: as shown in Figure 15, in using the NDE to investigate results for Grade 8 Reading, users have the option to create bar charts, column charts, and line charts, customize the values represented by the bars, columns, or lines, and to select how values are grouped.

The charts themselves are further editable, in that, for example, users can choose colors or insert patterns on bars or other elements. Depending on the data of interest, the tool also has options for users to generate color-coded maps to illustrate comparative performance and to create doughnut graphs.[2]

---

[2] A tutorial on the creation of charts within the NDE is available at http://nces.ed.gov/nationsreportcard/ndehelp/tutorial/lesson7.asp.

Customizability is an increasingly expected element of reporting results in educational assessments, in part through the emergence of tools such as these. Many U.S. states offer tools inspired by the NDE and its international counterparts, which themselves are typically constructed and programmed to display results in accordance with accepted statistical conventions, taking into account the statistical properties of various scores, score scales, and other types of results, such as performance categories. The presence of high levels of customizability in results reporting, particularly in visualizations, is at once both promising and concerning. Tools such as these offer flexibility and opportunity over the static reporting systems of old, but they also allow for greater potential for misinterpretation and overinterpretation of results on the part of users, because control of the data and its display shifts from the testing agency to the user. With choice comes responsibility, and so reporting systems must be designed to ensure that the analyses and displays generated adhere to professional standards of statistical quality, validity, and reliability.

Growth Percentiles/Projectiles

Another important area of results reporting that is finding its way into many educational reporting efforts is the reporting of growth. There are numerous strategies and methods that have been developed and deployed operationally to compute indices of growth at both the individual and group (classroom) level. O'Malley, Murphy, McClarty, Murphy, and McBride (2011), in their overview of student growth models, characterized approaches to student growth as three general types:

- *Growth to Proficiency models*: Student performance is compared to a yearly growth target in order to reach a defined "proficiency" within a set number of years.
- *Value/Transition Tables*: Growth is considered relative to change in performance category assignment over years (e.g., movement from "Needs Improvement" to "Proficient").
- *Projection models*: Student performance is predicted using past and current student performance and the performance of prior cohorts in the target grades.

The mathematical and statistical underpinnings of these methods are beyond the scope of the present chapter but are available in considerable detail elsewhere, including Betebenner (2009), Castellano and Ho (2013), O'Malley, McClarty, Magda, and Burling (2011), and Auty (2008). In any case, while numerous approaches to communication of these results have emerged in reporting efforts, no systematic study of these displays for communication of these results has yet been undertaken (Zenisky & Hambleton, 2014).

At the outset of reporting results for measures of student growth, there are several key considerations that impact how visualizations of growth could be implemented. Chief among these considerations is model choice, because the nature of the statistical information to be communicated is a driving factor in what information about growth can and should be shared on a score report for families, educators, and/or educational administrators. Related to this is an accounting of the statistical assumptions of each model, which likewise define what is and is not possible from a reporting standpoint. Next, reporting for growth model results will vary considerably based on their appropriateness/relevance for individual reports and group reports, and the landscape of approaches (text, graphical displays, and/or tables) encompasses a range of strategies. The final consideration in reporting such results is the issue of score error for the growth model calculations. The standard error or measurement for scale scores sporadically appear on student score reports at present, and at present this pattern seems to be continuing in the context of reporting growth results. The standard error of measurement on reports is already problematic for users, and growth scores are even less reliable than test scores and so the need for error bands is even greater than with single scores.

The individual student growth display used in Georgia (Figure 16) is structured to show performance over two years' worth of data as well as next year's projection, and implements a bar chart strategy to illustrate that data. The horizontal arrow with the wording "TYPICAL GROWTH 56th Percentile" that connects the learner's Grade 3 and Grade 4 performance signifies the magnitude of growth achieved by the student in the current year. In this case, the student's growth between those grades is in the 56th percentile and therefore is characterized as *typical*.

ENGLISH/LANGUAGE ARTS

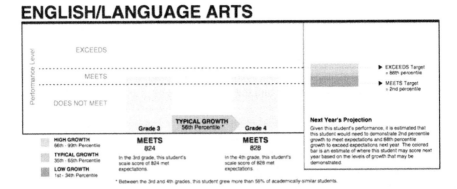

FIGURE 16. Georgia Individual Growth Report (Georgia Department of Education; Retrieved from http://www.gadoe.org/Curriculum-Instruction-and-Assessment/Assessment/Documents/GSGM_CRCT_SampleReport.pdf)

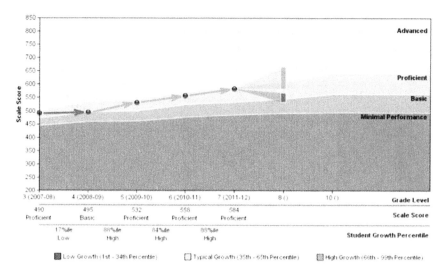

FIGURE 17. Wisconsin Individual Growth Report (Wisconsin Department of Public Instruction; Retrieved from http://oea.dpi.wi.gov/files/oea/pp/sgp-median-report-guide13.ppt)

The display in Figure 16 might well be viewed as particularly intense from a processing perspective, because it involves both a report of observed performance (on the left) as well as a projection of possible performance based on current observations, independent of any intervention (on the right-hand side of the display). It relays details about five types of results (scale scores, performance levels, percentiles of growth, levels of growth, and projection of performance relative to a target), using color, bar charts, and layout choice (where a user must look across the page from the past to the future) to convey all of that information.

The next figure (Figure 17) is another approach to displaying individual student growth, from the state of Wisconsin. There is a certain element of similarity to the displays shown in Figures 16 and 17 in terms of how growth for individuals is displayed. Key features employed include (a) the use of color, (b) the presence of arrows, (c) reporting of results relative to performance levels, (d) the display of multiple years, and (e) efforts to quantify the amount of growth.

The results in Figure 17 are predicated on five years' worth of observed data to project performance in year six (here, eighth grade). Note here that the graph itself positions the scale score range on one side (information that was not included in Figure 16), as well as the performance levels on the other side. Below the graph is shown what the students' grade level was in a given year, followed by the score and proficiency level attained, and then the student growth percentile results appear between years (effectively, between tests) expressed as both numerical percentiles and with labels to described the size of the growth observed given those

**Growth Scores and Ratings
for DEMO, TEACHER A.**
2012-2013

Name	Number of Student Scores	Unadjusted Mean Growth Percentile	Adjusted Mean Growth Percentile	Adjusted MGP Lower Limit	Adjusted MGP Upper Limit	Growth Rating	Growth Score
DEMO, TEACHER A.	80	52	52	46	57	Effective	13

Teacher Performance By Subject or Group

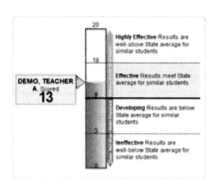

Group	Number of Student Scores	Unadjusted Mean Growth Percentile	Adjusted Mean Growth Percentile	Adjusted MGP Lower Limit	Adjusted MGP Upper Limit
All	80	52	52	46	57
Math	60	54	53	48	59
ELA	20	47	47	37	58
Students with Disabilities	3	.	.	.	.
ELL	3	.	.	.	.
Economically Disadvantaged	49	50	51	43	57
Low Achieving	3	.	.	.	.
High Achieving	7	.	.	.	.

FIGURE 18. Sample Growth Report for a Teacher (New York State Education Department; Retrieved from https://www.engageny.org/file/108051/download/4-8-teacher-brochure-13-14.pdf?token=c5b4j7zkhNlfnvqqB2t-ASTqz9Sgjl0wTgNQa-lfTOTo)

intervals. While the projection for eighth grade is shown as a range, no data is included to indicate the quality of the projection other than the range, and it may not be readily clear to a reader why the projections are what they are (such as, why the likelihood of "typical growth" might be lower for this student than "low growth").

Figure 18 below shifts the focus from results for an individual student to teacher evaluation reporting, for a single teacher. This example is from New York State. Here, the growth percentile results for a teacher's 80 students are aggregated to compute a mean student growth percentile (SGP) for a teacher, along with an upper and lower bound, and provide that teacher with a rating category (here, "Effective"). The report also includes a graphical display of that rating, and a breakdown of mean SGP results for specific student subgroups.

As with the two previous figures illustrating approaches to characterizing growth, the display in Figure 18 uses student test scores to make inferences about the magnitude of change in scores over time. The goal of Figure 18 is to communicate indicators of teacher effectiveness that are derived from collecting individual results and aggregating them, where the key outcome of interest is denoted by a value of "13" on a scale ranging from 0 to 20 and a label of "Effective." One potentially problematic element of the graphic in Figure 18 is the use of equal in-

FIGURE 19. Growth Modeling Results for School Districts (Colorado Department of Education; Accessible from http://www.cde.state.co.us/schoolview/colorado-growthmodel)

tervals on the column graph though the cut scores presented (3, 9, 18) indicate that the intervals are not equal. This disconnect of results and scale may lend itself to erroneous interpretations, especially in complex reporting scenarios such as this, and should be avoided in results reporting when possible.

The final display of interest in the area of growth reporting is a bubble graph display, used to account for district magnitude in facilitating comparisons. A bubble graph was shown previously in Figure 12 as an example of comparison reporting of mean scores in NAEP; here, the comparison of interest is the magnitude of growth exhibited at the level of districts. The quadrants on the graph represent dimensions of achievement and growth, and the graph itself can be adjusted by the user to modify which data points (here, districts) are displayed.

As with the NAEP TUDA results in Figure 12, bubble size in Figure 19 illustrates size of district, and bubble positioning along the x-axis is determined by the median SGP shown by students in a specified district. A district's placement along the y-axis is based on the percentage of students whose scores are in the upper performance levels on the assessment ("At or above Proficient"). At a glance, therefore, each bubble provides a considerable amount of performance data. One additional strategic element of this display to be noted are the text boxes of interpretive guidance in each of the four quadrants of the display, where for example districts that appear in the upper right of the graph exhibit higher achievement and higher growth, as compared to districts in the lower left quadrant, which have higher growth but lower percentages of students in those upper performance levels. This approach to reporting illustrates a choice to prioritize not only the growth results but also achievement, with the presence of the familiar reporting result of performance levels. For users of this type of graph, the combination signifies a particular way of thinking about assessment results, that there may well be more than one way to look at the data, and the ultimate goal is often not only high achievement but also improvement in the rate of change over time.

The reporting of growth results, as with other areas of results reporting, clearly encompasses a range of data and is aimed at various audiences, from students and families to educators and administrators. The data of interest are complex, and consequently, the visualizations produced can be intricate. As use of growth models and projections continue to increase, more systematic consideration of the display strategies must intensify through experimental studies and field-testing of the displays with intended users.

BEST PRACTICES FROM THE PSYCHOMETRIC LITERATURE

In reflecting on the various displays shown here (and generalizing to the innumerable charts, graphs, and tables used every day in results reporting across test settings and contexts), there are a few resources that offer broad guidance applicable across the range of results reporting described to this point in the chapter. A first priority in developing reports and report resources is validity, and Hattie (2009) put together some principles for report development that offer clear and concise guidance to report developers about how the reporting choices made affect validity (Table 1). A number of these principles specifically address how report development should proceed with respect to the use of quality visualizations. The principles most directly relating to visual displays of results reporting are marked with a "*" in Table 1 and briefly discussed below.

Chief among these is Hattie's Principle 3: "Readers of Reports need a guarantee of safe passage," which suggests that reports should be structured so that users focus first on the results of greatest importance and flow through the report from that point. The use of well-designed graphics is also viewed as a critical component of safe passage, in Hattie's conceptualization. Principle 6 likewise advocates for a minimization of numbers to maximize the amount of interpretations, and this can lead report developers to develop better pictures to tell the reporting story, beyond reliance on tables and raw numbers. The development and maintenance of a clear and consistent theme is the focus of Principle 7, which advocates for a series or sequence of reports where each one clearly accomplishes one task (in terms of communication of results), and uses graphics effectively to target that message. Principle 10 ("A Report should minimize scrolling, be uncluttered, and maximize the seen over the read") draws on a number of recommendations from Wainer (1997) and Tufte (1983, 1990) to make the following points about data visualizations in results reporting:

- Reports should be uncluttered;

TABLE 1. Hattie's (2009) Fifteen Principles to Promote Validity in Results Reporting

Number	Principle
1	The validity of Reports is a function of the Reader's correct and appropriate inferences and/or actions about the test takers performance based on the scores from the test.
2	That evidence is needed to demonstrate how Readers are interpreting reports.
3*	Readers of Reports need a guarantee of safe passage.
4	Readers of Reports need a guarantee of destination recovery.
5	Maximize interpretations and minimize the use of numbers.
6*	Minimize the amount of "numbers" and maximize the amount of interpretations.
7*	The answer is never more than 7 plus or minus two.
8	Each report needs to have a major theme.
9	Anchor the tool in the task domain.
10*	A Report should minimize scrolling, be uncluttered, and maximize the 'seen' over the 'read'.
11	A Report should be designed to address specific questions.
12	A Report should provide justification of the test for the specific applied purpose and for the utility of the test in the applied setting.
13	A Report should be timely to the decisions being made (formative, diagnostic, summative, and ascriptive).
14	Those receiving reports need information about the meaning and constraints of any report.
15*	Reports need to be conceived as actions not screens to print.

- Text should be used judiciously to support and improve interpretations;
- Bar charts facilitate comparisons;
- Data should be grouped in meaningful ways;
- Boxes or graphics can highlight main findings; and
- Color should be used purposefully.

Hattie's (2009) final principle (number 15) offers a clarion call for the use of quality graphics in advancing the notion that reports must be conceived of as actionable, not as something to print, orienting users to *do* something with the information contained in reports. From Hattie's perspective, visualizations have a critical role in making reports understood, and thereby the results reporting efforts have value and promote the valid use of assessment data.

Further guidance about the use of displays in reports comes from a review of reports from 11 states, three commercial test providers, and two Canadian provinces carried out by Goodman and Hambleton (2004). While the Goodman and Hambleton paper contains a wealth of guidance for numerous aspects of report development, structure, and design, it is also particularly instructive in terms of its findings for displays. The authors were firm in their belief that clear graphic displays were critical in the production of useful reports, in that such graphics can draw users to major findings quickly and effectively (a point that echoes Hattie's Principle 3; 2009). They also suggested that agencies should take care not to create displays that were too complex or busy: they found that the most useful displays are those that fulfilled a very specific role within the larger report document (where a particular graphic is used to communicate a distinct point about individual or group performance, aligned to Hattie's Principle 7). This idea of specificity driving the creation of a graphic is aided by the conceptualization of displays as specific report elements; for example, on an individual student report, the reporting of summative scores is a report element, and the display used for that data element should be first and foremost concerned with effective communication of those results.

The work done by Wainer, Hambleton, and Meara (1999) to evaluate some redesigns of NAEP graphics stands out as one of the few empirical studies completed in this area, and there too are found some recommendations for the development of effective displays. One such recommendation advances the idea that displays should be "seen" and not "read", per Hattie's Principle 10 (2009). A clear purpose (Principle 7) and avoidance of clutter (Principle 10) are also prominent findings in the Wainer et al. (1999) research. These ideas of minimizing clutter, highlighting results, and simple and clear graphs are further endorsed by Ryan (2006).

Finally, a recent paper by Hullman, Rhodes, Rodriguez, and Shah (2011) comes at the issue of quality visualizations in test results reporting from the perspective of graph comprehensions and data interpretation. The first point made by these authors concerns graph comprehension as a function of format: the choice of graph type must be directly linked to the nature of the data to be presented. For example, achievement gap results over time seems especially well suited to a line graph, as shown in Figures 8 and 11 previously. Some important concerns about the use of graphics in general were mentioned, however, including the potential for overinterpretation, a deficit in prior knowledge of graph literacy, and/or oversimplified or incorrect interpretations. Notably, where the information to be displayed is more reliable, Hullman et al. (2011) suggest that those data should be presented visually, while less reliable information might be better off in numerical or qualitative formats. Furthermore, to circle back to Hattie's (2009) point that reports should be actionable, Hullman et al. (2011) also recommend that displays should be created so as to support and promote the active engagement of users, both in terms of being tailored to the needs of specific users and with respect to requiring users to carry out some inferences and invest some thought in them (beyond simple visual processes).

Table 2 is provides a synthesis of the key considerations for the use of visual elements in the domain of reporting assessment results. This guidance operates at a highly general level, above specific reporting aims and data elements, to provide

TABLE 2.   A Synthesis of Guidance for Display Development Processes

Conceptual Considerations	• Determine the key inference or message of interest for the intended user(s)/ audience(s) of the report • Think about the data to be represented and what display strategies are appropriate for the data in terms of data type, reliability, and the unit of reporting (individual or group) • Frame questions about the data and reporting efforts in ways that will invest and engage users
Document Structure	• Use techniques of design and layout to format the report to call attention to the most important result(s) relative to the report purpose
Display Selection	• Identify display types appropriate for accomplishing the specific reporting purpose(s) • Consider ways to make key results more readily 'seen' • Convey numerical results using graphics whenever possible • Use graphics for results that are highly reliable; use tables and text for less reliable information
Developing Displays	• Focus on the key result in each display and avoid reporting too many different data elements • Minimize the use of numbers to convey trends or other main ideas • Be purposeful with data elements such as the use of color or shading, size, and position, as all of these can be used to convey information • Label displays with relevant data elements (scale score ranges, cutscores) • Ensure that displays are consistent with the data of interest in terms of how scale intervals are represented
Review and Revision	• Try out displays with intended users by means of focus groups or one-on-one data collection techniques to identify potentially problematic elements of displays before operational use

broad assistance in conceptualizing and developing purposeful visualizations for reporting test results.

The information presented in Table 2 is organized around five key areas: *Conceptual Considerations, Document Structure, Display Selection, Developing Displays*, and *Review and Revision*. These principles reflect the literature and best practices for developing reports reviewed throughout this chapter and also align with the broader report development steps advanced by Zenisky and Hambleton (2012).

CONCLUSIONS

Be it the display of interest a line graph, a bar chart, a bubble graph, a color-coded map, a honeycomb, a pictograph, or something else entirely, data visualizations have an essential role in aiding the interpretability of test results. The literature advocates for the main results to feature prominently in reporting resources, and well-designed graphics—such as those included here—certainly offer a wealth of opportunities to help to focus intended users on key results, given all relevant data considerations and reporting purposes. By drawing users to specific interpretations, such visualizations help results move from the abstract to accessible, and thereby actionable. The promise (and perhaps, peril!) of reporting practices now lies in the emerging world of data dashboards and other online reporting tools, where control of reporting shifts from the testing agency or governing body to the user. The customizability of displays available in online reporting offers users the chance to engage with data at a high level and obtain results with a high degree of relevance, but such tools must be carefully considered and developed in light of the principles referenced here.

To that end, a final key point to be made in the development of graphics for reporting results is the idea that the creation of such graphics (and the online tools by which such graphics are generated) must be viewed as both iterative and collaborative. The work of formulating these visualizations should of course be informed by the principles for best practices referenced above, but the ultimate judges of a display's utility are the users. Much like the research by Wainer et al. (1999) that helped to identify a number of potential improvements to NAEP displays by sharing them with a population of policymakers, report development across contexts and settings benefits from review by intended audiences and incorporation of their feedback. These types of tryouts of displays can be on small or large scale and can be more or less formal, but the utility of nonpsychometric, nontesting agency eyes on displays is high and is a critical component of the report-development process advanced by Zenisky and Hambleton (2012). The displays in use across summative, comparative, and feedback reporting are increasingly creative and informative for a range of reporting needs and purposes, as evidenced by Figures 1 through 19 here, and reporting practices using these visualizations can only benefit from continued research and effort on the part of agencies to ensure the use of quality displays in results reporting.

REFERENCES

American Educational Research Association, American Psychological Association, and National Council on Measurement in Education. (2014). *Standards for Educational and Psychological Testing*. Washington, DC: American Educational Research Association.

Auty, W. (2008). Implementer's guide to growth models. *Council of Chief State School Officers.* Retrieved from http://www.ccsso.org/Documents/2008/Implementers_Guide_to_Growth_2008.pdf

Beaton, A. E., & Allen, N. L. (1992). Interpreting scales through scale anchoring. *Journal of Educational Statistics, 17*(2), 191–204.

Betebenner, D. (2009). Norm- and criterion-referenced student growth. *Educational Measurement: Issues and Practice, 28*(4), 42–51.

Castellano, K. E., & Ho, A. D. (2013). *A practitioner's guide to growth models*. Washington, DC: Council of Chief State School Officers.

Family Educational Rights and Privacy Act of 1974, 20 U.S.C. § 1232g (1974).

Glaser, R. (1963). Instructional technology and the measurement of learning outcomes. *American Psychologist, 18*, 519–521.

Goodman, D. P., & Hambleton, R. K. (2004). Student test score reports and interpretive guides: Review of current practices and suggestions for future research. *Applied Measurement in Education, 17*(2), 145–220.

Haberman, S. J. (2008). When can subscores have value? *Journal of Educational and Behavioral Statistics, 33*(2), 204–229.

Haberman, S. J., Sinharay, S., & Puhan, G. (2009). Reporting subscores for institutions. *British Journal of Mathematical and Statistical Psychology, 62*(1), 79–95.

Hambleton, R. K., Sireci, S., & Huff, K. (2008). *Development and validation of enhanced SAT score scales using item mapping and performance category descriptions* (Final Report). Amherst: University of Massachusetts, Center for Educational Assessment.

Hattie, J. (2009, April). *Visibly learning from reports: The validity of score reports.* Paper presented at the meeting of the National Council on Measurement in Education, San Diego, CA.

Hullman, J., Rhodes, R., Rodriguez, F., & Shah, P. (2011, November). *Research on graph comprehension and data interpretation: Implications for score reporting* (ETS RR-11-45). Paper presented at the ETS Score Reporting conference, Princeton, NJ.

Ling, G. (2012). *Why the Major Field Test in Business does not report subscores: Reliability and construct validity evidence* (ETS RR-12-11). Princeton, NJ: Educational Testing Service.

Lyrén, P.-E. (2009). Reporting subscores from college admission tests. *Practical Assessment, Research, and Evaluation, 14*(4), 1–10.

Monaghan, W. (2006, July). *The facts about subscores* (ETS R&D Connections No. 4). Princeton, NJ: Educational Testing Service. Retrieved from http://www.ets.org/Media/Research/pdf/RD_Connections4.pdf

New Jersey Department of Education. (2012). *2012 Score Interpretation manual grades 3-8.* Trenton, NJ: Author. Retrieved from http://www.state.nj.us/education/assessment/ms/5-8/ref/SIM12.pdf

No Child Left Behind (NCLB) Act of 2001, Pub. L. No. 107-110, § 115, Stat. 1425 (2002).

O'Malley, K. J., McClarty, K. L., Magda, T., & Burling, K. (2011). *Making sense of the metrics: Student growth, value-added models, and teacher effectiveness* (Research Bulletin #19). Iowa City, IA: Pearson. Retrieved from http://www.pearsonassessments.com/hai/images/tmrs/bulletin-19-makingsenseofmetrics.pdf

O'Malley, K. J., Murphy, S., McClarty, K. L., Murphy, D., & McBride, Y. (2011). *Overview of student growth models.* (Test, Measurement, & Research Services White Paper). Iowa City, IA: Pearson. Retrieved from http://www.pearsonassessments.com/hai/Images/tmrs/Student_Growth_WP_083111_FINAL.pdf

Popham, W. J., & Husek, T. R. (1969). Implications of criterion-referenced measurement. *Journal of Educational Measurement, 6*, 1–9.

Ryan, J. M. (2006). Practices, issues, and trends in student test score reporting. In S. M. Downing & T. M. Haladyna (Eds.), *Handbook of test development.* Mahwah, NJ: Erlbaum.

Sinharay, S., Puhan, G., & Haberman, S. J. (2011). An NCME instructional module on subscores. *Journal of Educational Measurement, 30*(3), 29–40.

Tufte, E. R. (1983). *The visual display of quantitative information.* Cheshire, CT: Graphics.

Tufte, E. R. (1990). *Envisioning information.* Cheshire, CT: Graphics.

U.S. Department of Education, Institute of Education Sciences, National Center for Education Statistics. (2014). *The Nation's Report Card: Mathematics 2013 State Snapshot Report.* Washington, DC: Author. Retrieved from http://nces.ed.gov/nationsreport-card/subject/publications/stt2013/pdf/2014082MA12.pdf

Wainer, H. (1997). *Visual revelations: Graphical tales of fate and deception from Napoleon Bonaparte to Ross Perot.* New York, NY: Copernicus.

Wainer, H., Hambleton, R. K., & Meara, K. (1999). Alternative displays for communicating NAEP results: A redesign and validity study. *Journal of Educational Measurement, 36*(4), 301–335.

Zapata-Rivera, D. (2011, November). *Designing and evaluating score reports for particular audiences* (ETS RR-11-45). Paper presented at the ETS Score Reporting conference, Princeton, NJ.

Zenisky, A. L., & Hambleton, R. K. (2007). *Navigating 'The Nation's Report Card" on the World Wide Web: Site user behavior and impressions.* Technical report for the Comprehensive Evaluation of NAEP. [Also Center for Educational Assessment Report No. 625. Amherst, MA: University of Massachusetts, Center for Educational Assessment.]

Zenisky, A. L., & Hambleton, R. K. (2012). Developing test score reports that work: The process and best practices for effective communication. *Educational Measurement: Issues and Practice, 31*(2), 21–26.

Zenisky, A. L., & Hambleton, R. K. (2014, April). *Making growth score reporting more meaningful to users: Some thoughts to guide research and practice.* Paper presented at the annual meeting of the National Council on Measurement in Education, Philadelphia, PA.

Zwick, R., Senturk, D., Wang, J., & Loomis, S. C. (2001). An investigation of alternative methods for item mapping in the National Assessment of Educational Progress. *Educational Measurement: Issues and Practice, 20*(2), 15–25.

BIOGRAPHIES

EDITOR BIOS

Chad W. Buckendahl, PhD, is a Senior Psychometrician and Director of Education, Licensure, and Professional Certification Services with Alpine Testing Solutions. He provides psychometric and testing policy consultation and leads validation and research projects for a range of testing programs. Dr. Buckendahl's research interests are applied psychometrics, including alignment, legal/policy issues, standard setting, test evaluation, and validity. He was a co-principal investigator for the *Evaluation of the National Assessment of Educational Progress* (2009), a chapter co-author for *Setting Performance Standards: Foundations, Methods, and Innovations* (2nd ed., 2012), *Assessment of Higher Order Thinking Skills* (2011), *Handbook of Test Development* (2006), and *Defending Standardized Testing* (2006), and co-editor and chapter co-author for *High Stakes Testing in Education: Science and Practice in K–12 Settings* (2011). Dr. Buckendahl has also served on committees for membership, outreach, and program for the National Council on Measurement in Education (NCME) and as an associate editor for *Applied Measurement in Education* (AME). He currently serves as a psycho-

Use of Visual Displays in Research and Testing: Coding, Interpreting, and Reporting Data, pages 333–339.

metric reviewer for the National Commission for Certifying Agencies (NCCA) and editor of the *Journal of Applied Testing Technology* (JATT).

Matthew T. McCrudden is an Associate Professor of Educational Psychology, Victoria University of Wellington in New Zealand. He has a PhD in learning and technology and an MA in cognition, learning, and development. He teaches courses in educational psychology, learning and motivation, and research methods. He has published numerous articles and books in the area of human learning. His research interests include how characteristics of tasks (e.g., prereading instructions), learners (e.g., prior knowledge/beliefs), and instructional materials (e.g., visual displays) are related to cognition and learning. Currently, he serves an associate editor for *Contemporary Educational Psychology* and is on several other editorial boards.

Gregory Schraw is a Professor of Educational Psychology and Director of the Center for Research, Evaluation and Assessment at the University of Nevada, Las Vegas. Dr. Schraw holds a PhD in cognition and learning and an MS in applied statistics. He has published widely in the areas of human learning (e.g., metacognition, the design and use of visual displays to improve learning, situational interest, the role of text relevance, college student cheating), teacher beliefs (e.g., the intersection of epistemological and ontological beliefs, measurement of beliefs), and applied use of testing, measurement, research for improving classroom learning (e.g., the assessment of higher order thinking skills, measuring metacognition, the validity of student evaluations of teaching, improving evidence-based practice). He currently serves as an associate editor of the *Journal of Educational Psychology* and is on six other editorial review boards.

AUTHOR BIOS

John W. Creswell is Professor of Educational Psychology at the University of Nebraska-Lincoln. He has authored numerous articles on mixed methods research, qualitative methodology, general research design, and 25 books (including new editions). His newest book, *A Concise Introduction to Mixed Methods Research* was published in April 2014. For 5 years, Dr. Creswell served as a co-director at the Office of Qualitative and Mixed Methods Research at the University of Nebraska-Lincoln. He was the founding co-editor for the *Journal of Mixed Methods Research*. Dr. Creswell was a Senior Fulbright Scholar to South Africa in 2008 and to Thailand in 2012. In 2011, he served as a co-leader of a national working group at NIH developing "best practices" for mixed methods research in the health sciences. Dr. Creswell was a Visiting Professor at Harvard's School of Public Health in 2013 and received an honorary doctorate from the University of Pretoria, South Africa, in 2014. He is the President of the Mixed Methods International Research Association for 2014–2015. He serves as the Director of the College of Education and Human Sciences Mixed Methods Academy at the University of Nebraska-Lincoln.

Sara J. Finney has a dual appointment at James Madison University as Professor in the Department of Graduate Psychology and as an Assessment Specialist in the Center for Assessment and Research Studies. In addition to teaching multivariate statistics and structural equation modeling for the assessment and measurement PhD program, she is coordinator of the quantitative psychology concentration within the psychological sciences MA program. She is the recipient of several teaching, mentoring, and research awards. Much of her research involves the application of structural equation modeling to better understand the functioning of self-report instruments and issues associated with examinee motivation. Her research has appeared in such journals as *Educational and Psychological Measurement, Contemporary Educational Psychology*, and *International Journal of Testing*.

Florian C. Feucht is an Associate Professor of Educational Psychology at the University of Toledo, Ohio. Dr. Feucht holds a PhD in educational psychology (USA) and a PhD in Education Sciences (Germany). In his scholarship, he focuses on personal epistemology in the classroom context and news media literacy of high school students. Dr. Feucht is also specialized in the use of technology to support large-scale data collections and analyses in qualitative research. Dr. Feucht conducted a variety of classroom and cross-cultural research studies around the world and successfully publishes his empirical and conceptual work in peer-reviewed journals and book chapters.

Brett P. Foley, PhD, is a psychometrician with Alpine Testing Solutions. He has worked with many types of testing programs, including credentialing, educational, and information technology certification. Additionally, he has provided general educational measurement and related policy consultation and has led validation research in alignment and standard setting. Dr. Foley received his PhD in quantitative, qualitative, and psychometric methods from the Department of Educational Psychology at the University of Nebraska-Lincoln. He is the current Website Content Editor for the National Council on Measurement in Education and is a past president of the Northern Rocky Mountain Educational Research Association. His research interests include standard setting, policy considerations in testing, and using visual displays to inform the test development process.

Tim Guetterman is an applied research methodologist in the University of Nebraska-Lincoln's College of Education and Human Sciences Mixed Methods Academy. His professional interests, teaching, and research writings are in research methodology, namely mixed methods and general research design, particularly as applied to evaluation and assessment. His professional experience is in the field of evaluation with a focus on education and healthcare programs. Current projects focus on mixed methods integration strategies, the use of assessment findings, and the skills needed to conduct mixed methods research.

Antonio P. Gutierrez is an Assistant Professor of Educational Research at Georgia Southern University (GSU). Prior to this, he served as the Grant Writer and Coordinator for the Center for Mathematics, Science, and Engineering Education at the University of Nevada, Las Vegas (UNLV), and currently serves as an Affiliate Faculty in the Interdisciplinary STEM Institute at GSU. Dr. Gutierrez received a PhD in educational psychology, with emphases in cognition and learning, research methods, evaluation, and statistics from UNLV. His research interests are in the areas of higher order thinking processes, most notably, metacognition, problem solving and reasoning, errors in human judgment and decision making, epistemological beliefs in scientific reasoning, memory and attention, and engagement (i.e., utility value beliefs, interest, academic emotions, and relevance of instruction). Dr. Gutierrez's current research focuses on (a) enhancing comprehension monitoring in adolescents and adult learners through improving calibration, (b) improving the theory and measurement of calibration, (c) the effects of video game design and metacognitive strategy training on calibration and confidence of performance judgments, and (d) studying the role of visual display design on learning outcomes.

Udo Kuckartz is a Professor of research methodology at the Philipps University, Marburg, Germany, and the director of MAGMA (Marburg Research Group on Methods & Evaluation). He teaches social research methods, statistics, and quantitative methods as well as qualitative methods. Since the end of the 1980s, he has been a specialist in computer-assisted qualitative data analysis software and developed the software MAXQDA (formerly WINMAX) in 1989. He has published 18 books and nearly 200 articles, mostly in the German language. In 2014, Sage published his book *Qualitative Text Analysis. A Guide to Methods, Practice & Using Software*. His research interests include environmental attitudes and behavior, awareness of global climate change, and environmental communication.

David M. Lane is an Associate Professor in psychology, statistics, and management at Rice University. He holds an MA in child study from Tufts University and a PhD in psychology from Tulane University. Dr. Lane's research focus is human factors/human computer interaction and has an interest in the display of data and in numeracy. In addition to teaching a graduate course in statistics, he is the Director of Graduate Studies in psychology. Dr. Lane has published nearly 100 articles in journals including *Psychological Methods*, *Psychological Review*, *Amercan Psychologist*, *Human-Computer Interaction*, and *Journal of Experimental Psychology: Human Perception and Performance*. He is the project lead on the project Online Statistics Education: An Interactive Multimedia Course of Study.

Gwen C. Marchand is a Lincy Assistant Professor of Education in the Department of Educational Psychology and Higher Education at the University of Nevada, Las Vegas. Dr. Marchand's research focuses on personal and contextual aspects of student motivation and engagement, particularly with students in urban settings. She teaches courses in program evaluation, research methods, motivation, and multilevel statistical modeling. Dr. Marchand was awarded an APA Division 15 Early Career Award and a Lincy Institute Research Fellowship for her work with alternative education students.

Lori Olafson is a Professor in the Department of Educational Psychology and Higher Education at the University of Las Vegas, Nevada, where she also serves as the executive director for the Office of Research Integrity. Dr. Olafson holds a PhD in language education from the University of Calgary (Alberta). In her scholarship, she focuses on personal epistemology and moral reasoning in a variety of contexts.

Dena A. Pastor has a dual appointment at James Madison University as a Professor in the Department of Graduate Psychology and as an Assessment Specialist in the Center for Assessment and Research Studies. She teaches courses in hierarchical linear modeling, categorical data analysis, and data management. Her research applies statistical and psychometric techniques to the modeling and measurement of college student learning and development. Her publications have appeared in *Contemporary Educational Psychology*, *Applied Psychological Measurement*, and *Applied Measurement in Education*.

Vicki L. Plano Clark (PhD, University of Nebraska-Lincoln) is an Assistant Professor in the Quantitative and Mixed Methods Research Methodologies concentration of Educational Studies at the University of Cincinnati. As a methodologist specializing in mixed methods research, Dr. Plano Clark studies and applies research that integrates quantitative and qualitative approaches. Her scholarship focuses on delineating useful designs for conducting mixed methods research, examining procedural issues associated with these designs, and examining larger questions about the contexts for the adoption and use of mixed methods. She currently serves as an ASSOCIATE Editor for the *Journal of Mixed Methods Research* and recently became a founding co-editor of the new *Mixed Methods Research Series* with Sage Publications.

Khahlia Sanders (MA, University of Cincinnati) is a doctoral student in educational studies at the University of Cincinnati. Khahlia's research interests include arts-informed, transformative, and mixed method research methodologies, teacher professional development, Black feminism(s), and culturally responsive pedagogy. Prior to doctoral studies, Khahlia was a program manager and Director of Training and Learning for Public Allies Cincinnati, an AmeriCorp program focused on leadership development and asset-based community development. She has also taught math and science in Cincinnati's charter school system. As she continues her graduate school journey, she looks forward to a creative, innovative, and productive career in academia and advancing data visualization within mixed methods research.

Andreas Stefik is an Assistant Professor at the University of Nevada, Las Vegas. He completed his PhD in computer science at Washington State University in 2008 and also holds a bachelor's degree in music. Stefik's research focuses on computer programming languages and development environments, with an emphasis on how competing language designs impact people in practice. He won the 2011 Java Innovation Award for his work on the National Science Foundation funded Sodbeans programming environment and is the inventor of the Quorum Programming Language.

Joseph Stevens received his PhD in psychology and quantitative methods from the University of Arizona. He is currently a Professor in the Department of Educational Methodology, Policy, and Leadership, College of Education, University of Oregon. He was formerly professor of education at the University of New Mexico. He also worked at the Psychological Corporation and as a measurement statistician at Educational Testing Service. He teaches graduate courses in statistics and research methods, including Advanced Research Design, Hierarchical Linear Modeling, and Structural Equation Modeling. His interests are in individual differences, including exceptional children, school effects and accountability, measurement, validity, research design, and longitudinal modeling.

April L. Zenisky is Senior Research Fellow and Director of Computer-Based Testing Initiatives in the Center for Educational Assessment (CEA) at the University of Massachusetts, Amherst, where her primary responsibilities at the CEA involve project management and operational psychometrics for computer-based tests for adult basic education programs in Massachusetts. Her main research interests include results reporting, technology-based item types, and computerized test design, and her work has appeared in numerous peer-reviewed journals such as *Applied Measurement in Education*, *Educational Measurement: Issues and Practice*, and *Journal of Applied Testing Technology*. She has also authored or co-authored a number of book chapters, and at present she is also the Associate Editor of the *International Journal of Testing*.

Keith Zvoch is an Associate Professor in the Department of Educational Methodology, Policy and Leadership at the University of Oregon. Dr. Zvoch teaches advanced research design and multivariate statistics courses. His research interests include the measurement and evaluation of school performance and the study of early childhood literacy interventions. Dr. Zvoch is currently the co-principal investigator on a federally funded grant entitled, *Identifying Mediating and Moderating Mechanisms to Address Outcomes Associated with Poverty for Adolescents with Disabilities: Secondary Analysis of Data from the National Longitudinal Transition Study-2.* Dr. Zvoch has published extensively in education, evaluation, and child development journals.

CPSIA information can be obtained at www.ICGtesting.com
Printed in the USA
BVOW06s1423211215

430724BV00002B/2/P